GCSE Edexcel

Combined Science

A wise woman once said, "There's no combustion without oxygen, and no Edexcel GCSE Combined Science exam success without practice." Truly profound.

Well as luck would have it, this super CGP book is simply bursting with realistic exam-style questions for every topic. All the core practicals are covered too and there are plenty of targeted analysis questions to test those tricky AO3 skills.

We've also included sections of mixed questions for Biology, Chemistry and Physics, just like in the real exams. You'll find complete answers to every question at the back. Enjoy!

Exam Practice Workbook
Higher Level

Contents

✓ Use the tick boxes to check off the topics you've completed.

Section 11 — States of Matter and Mixtures

Section 12 — Chemical Changes

Section 13 — Extracting Metals and Equilibria

Section 14 — Groups in the Periodic Table

Section 15 — Rates of Reaction and Energy Changes

Section 16 — Fuels and Earth Science

Section 17 — Motion and Forces

Section 18 — Conservation of Energy

Section 19 — Waves and the Electromagnetic Spectrum

Section 20 — Radioactivity

Section 21 — Forces and Energy

You can find some useful information about What to Expect in the Exams and other exam tips at cgpbooks.co.uk/GCSEComb-EdexH/Exams

Published by CGP

Editors: Ellen Burton, Andy Hurst, Paul Jordin, Jake McGuffie, Sarah Pattison, Charlotte Sheridan, Sarah Williams.

Contributors: Ian H. Davis, Mark Edwards, Barbara Mascetti, Bethan Parry, Alison Popperwell, Christopher Workman.

With thanks to Jan Greenway for the copyright research.

ISBN: 978 1 78908 998 1

Percentile growth chart on page 18 reproduced with kind permission of the RCPCH/Harlow Printing.

Data in Figure 1 on page 49 source: Health Survey for England 2018. Licensed under the Open Government Licence v3.0 http://www.nationalarchives.gov.uk/doc/open-government-licence/version/3/

Figure 2 on page 49 contains information from NHS Digital. Licensed under the current version of the Open Government Licence. https://www.nationalarchives.gov.uk/doc/open-government-licence/version/3/

Page 89 contains public sector information published by the Health and Safety Executive and licensed under the Open Government Licence. http://www.nationalarchives.gov.uk/doc/open-government-licence/version/3/

Graph on page 172 contains public sector information licensed under the Open Government Licence v3.0. http://www.nationalarchives.gov.uk/doc/open-government-licence/version/3/

Data used to construct the graph on page 172: Satellite sea level observations - NASA's Goddard Space Flight Center.

Data for the global temperature anomaly and CO_2 concentration in the table on page 173: NOAA National Centers for Environmental information, Climate at a Glance: Global Time Series, published October 2022, retrieved on October 31, 2022 from https://www.ncdc.noaa.gov/cag/.

Definition of health on page 286 reproduced from the WHO website, The Constitution of the World Health Organization. https://www.who.int/about/governance/constitution. Accessed: 3rd October 2022.

Clipart from Corel®
Illustrations by: Sandy Gardner Artist, email sandy@sandygardner.co.uk
Printed by Elanders Ltd, Newcastle upon Tyne

Based on the classic CGP style created by Richard Parsons.

How to Use This Book

- Hold the book <u>upright</u>, approximately <u>50 cm</u> from your face, ensuring that the text looks like <u>this</u>, not ̄s̄īɥ̄ʇ̄. Alternatively, place the book on a <u>horizontal</u> surface (e.g. a table or desk) and sit adjacent to the book, at a distance which doesn't make the text too small to read.

- In case of emergency, press the two halves of the book together <u>firmly</u> in order to close.

- Before attempting to use this book, familiarise yourself with the following <u>safety information</u>:

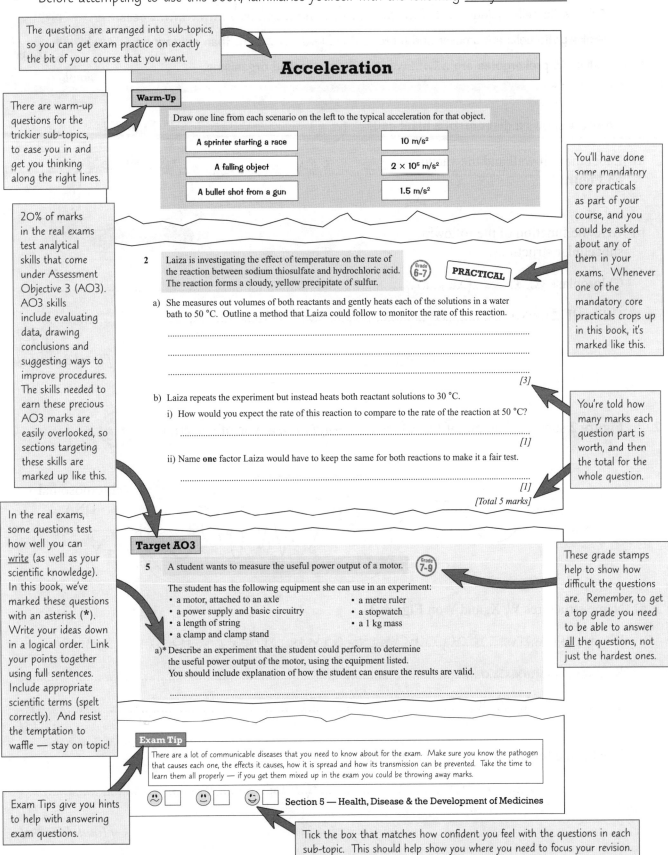

The questions are arranged into sub-topics, so you can get exam practice on exactly the bit of your course that you want.

Acceleration

Warm-Up

There are warm-up questions for the trickier sub-topics, to ease you in and get you thinking along the right lines.

Draw one line from each scenario on the left to the typical acceleration for that object.

A sprinter starting a race	10 m/s²
A falling object	2 × 10⁶ m/s²
A bullet shot from a gun	1.5 m/s²

You'll have done some mandatory core practicals as part of your course, and you could be asked about any of them in your exams. Whenever one of the mandatory core practicals crops up in this book, it's marked like this.

20% of marks in the real exams test analytical skills that come under Assessment Objective 3 (AO3). AO3 skills include evaluating data, drawing conclusions and suggesting ways to improve procedures. The skills needed to earn these precious AO3 marks are easily overlooked, so sections targeting these skills are marked up like this.

2   Laiza is investigating the effect of temperature on the rate of the reaction between sodium thiosulfate and hydrochloric acid. The reaction forms a cloudy, yellow precipitate of sulfur.   (Grade 6-7)   **PRACTICAL**

a) She measures out volumes of both reactants and gently heats each of the solutions in a water bath to 50 °C. Outline a method that Laiza could follow to monitor the rate of this reaction.

....

....

....
[3]

b) Laiza repeats the experiment but instead heats both reactant solutions to 30 °C.

i) How would you expect the rate of this reaction to compare to the rate of the reaction at 50 °C?

....
[1]

ii) Name **one** factor Laiza would have to keep the same for both reactions to make it a fair test.

....
[1]

[Total 5 marks]

You're told how many marks each question part is worth, and then the total for the whole question.

In the real exams, some questions test how well you can <u>write</u> (as well as your scientific knowledge). In this book, we've marked these questions with an asterisk (*). Write your ideas down in a logical order. Link your points together using full sentences. Include appropriate scientific terms (spelt correctly). And resist the temptation to waffle — stay on topic!

Target AO3

5   A student wants to measure the useful power output of a motor.   (Grade 7-9)

The student has the following equipment she can use in an experiment:
- a motor, attached to an axle
- a power supply and basic circuitry
- a length of string
- a clamp and clamp stand
- a metre ruler
- a stopwatch
- a 1 kg mass

a)* Describe an experiment that the student could perform to determine the useful power output of the motor, using the equipment listed. You should include explanation of how the student can ensure the results are valid.

....

These grade stamps help to show how difficult the questions are. Remember, to get a top grade you need to be able to answer <u>all</u> the questions, not just the hardest ones.

Exam Tip

There are a lot of communicable diseases that you need to know about for the exam. Make sure you know the pathogen that causes each one, the effects it causes, how it is spread and how its transmission can be prevented. Take the time to learn them all properly — if you get them mixed up in the exam you could be throwing away marks.

Exam Tips give you hints to help with answering exam questions.

☹ ☐   😐 ☐   🙂 ☐   Section 5 — Health, Disease & the Development of Medicines

Tick the box that matches how confident you feel with the questions in each sub-topic. This should help show you where you need to focus your revision.

Section 1 — Key Concepts in Biology

Cells

Use the words on the right to correctly fill in the gaps in the passage.
You don't have to use every word, but each word can only be used once.

single
complex
multi
plant
animal
bacterial
simple

Eukaryotic cells include ....Animal............. and .....plant................. cells.

Prokaryotic cells are smaller and more ....simple.............. than eukaryotic

cells. All prokaryotes are ...single.................-celled organisms.

1 **Figure 1** shows a diagram of a plant cell. Grade 4-6

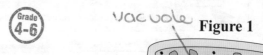

Figure 1

a) Label the cell wall and the vacuole
on **Figure 1**.

[1]

b) Give the function of the following
subcellular structures:

Chloroplast ...where..photosynthesis..occurs...

Cell wall ..Supports....the..cell..and..strengthens..it...............................

[2]

[Total 3 marks]

2 **Figure 2** shows a diagram of *Pseudomonas aeruginosa*, a type of bacterium. Grade 4-6

Figure 2

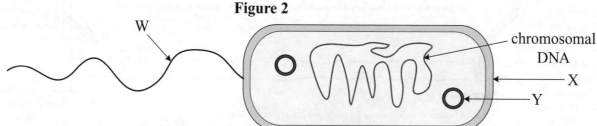

chromosomal
DNA
X
Y

a) Name structures W, X, and Y on **Figure 2**.

W ..Flagellum..-.long.hair.like.structure,..rotates..to..move..bacterium

X ..Cell..membrane...

Y ..Plasmid..dna..

[3]

b) What is the function of the chromosomal DNA?

...Controls..cells..activities..and..replication...

[1]

[Total 4 marks]

3 Proteins are synthesised within cells. This is done when information from genes is used to join together a sequence of amino acids. The second half of the process is called translation.

Grade 4-6

a) Name **one** subcellular structure where genes are found within:

i) eukaryotic cells.

...Cell membrane........Nucleus.. [1]

ii) prokaryotic cells.

....Flagellum...Chromosomal DNA., plasmid DNA........................ [1]

b) Name the subcellular structure involved in the translation of genetic material in protein synthesis.

.........ribosome.. [1]

c) Once proteins have been synthesised, they may need to leave the cell.
Name the subcellular structure that controls which substances leave the cell.

.........Cell membrane.. [1]

[Total 4 marks]

4 **Figure 3** and **4** are diagrams of two different types of specialised cell.
One is a muscle cell and the other is a skin cell. They are not drawn to scale.

Grade 7-9

Figure 4

Figure 3

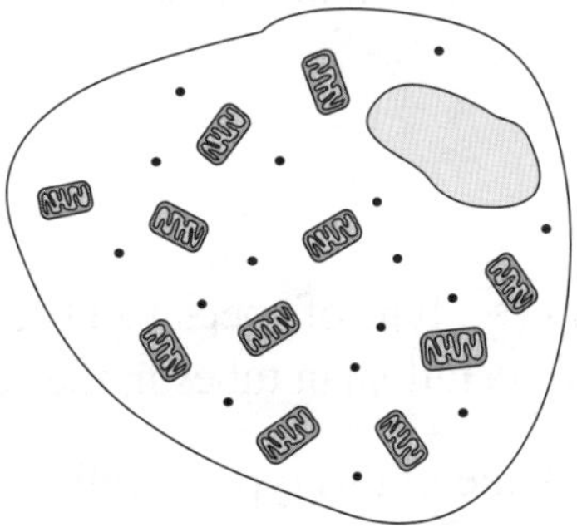

Which cell, **Figure 3** or **Figure 4**, is more likely to be a muscle cell? Explain your answer.

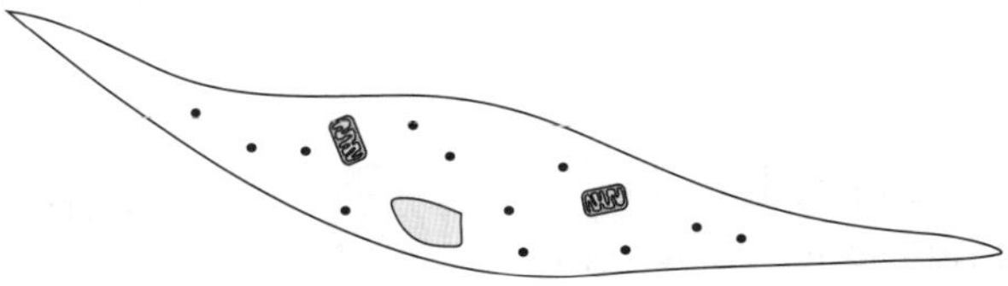

....figure four is more likely to be a muscle cell since it....
contains more mitochondria. Muscle cells need a lot of....
energy in order to contract. So they need mitochondria....
which is the site of respiration, the process which....
transfers energy to the cell.

[Total 4 marks]

Exam Tip

Make sure you really know the difference between the structures of plant and animal cells (both eukaryotes) and bacterial cells (prokaryotes). Learn all the subcellular structures each one contains and the function of each of those parts — then you should be well-prepared for whatever cell-based questions the examiners throw at you.

Section 1 — Key Concepts in Biology

Specialised Cells

1 An egg cell is fertilised when the nucleus of an egg cell and the nucleus of a sperm cell fuse together. Both egg cells and sperm cells are haploid. *Grade 4-6*

a) Elephant body cells contain 56 chromosomes.
How many chromosomes will an elephant egg cell contain?

....

[1]

b) Describe the role of a sperm's acrosome in fertilisation.

....

....

[2]

c) i) Explain why the membrane of an egg cell changes its structure immediately after fertilisation.

....

....

....

[2]

ii) Explain how the cytoplasm of an egg cell is adapted to its function.

....

....

[1]

[Total 6 marks]

2 **Figure 1** shows a type of specialised cell which can be found in the lining of the fallopian tubes in the female reproductive system. *Grade 6-7*

Figure 1

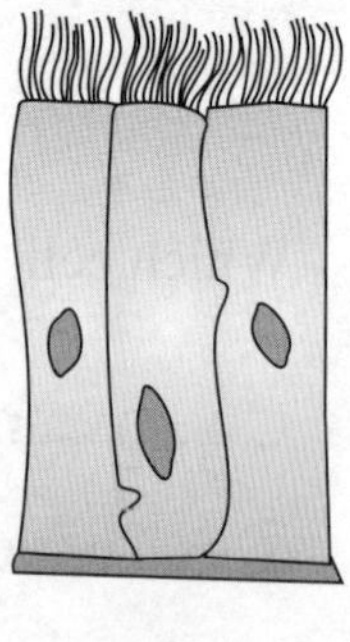

a) What is the name of this type of cell?

....

[1]

b) When an egg cell is ready to be fertilised, it moves through the fallopian tubes towards the uterus. Explain how the cells shown in **Figure 1** might be involved in this process.

....

....

....

....

[2]

[Total 3 marks]

Microscopy

1 A student wants to use a light microscope to view a sample of onion cells.
Figure 1 shows a diagram of the light microscope that she plans to use.

Grade
4-6

Figure 1

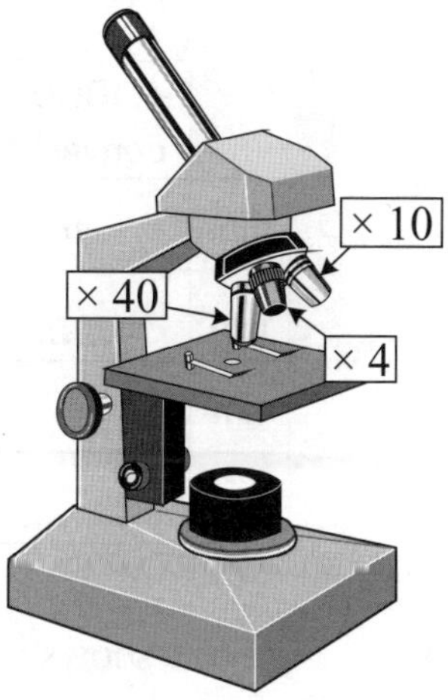

a) i) The three different objective lenses are labelled in **Figure 1** with
their magnification. Which lens should the student select first when
viewing her cells?

....
[1]

ii) After she has selected the objective lens, she looks down the
eyepiece and uses the adjustment knobs. Describe the purpose of
the adjustment knobs.

....

....

....
[1]

iii) The student wants to see the cells at a greater magnification.
Describe the steps that she should take.

....

....

....
[2]

b) After she has viewed the cells, she wants to produce a scientific drawing of them.
Her teacher has advised her to use smooth lines to draw the structures she can see.
Give **two** other ways in which she can ensure she produces an accurate and useful drawing.

1. ....

2. ....
[2]

c) The student compares the image that she can see with an image of onion cells viewed with an
electron microscope. Suggest how the two images would differ. Explain your answer.

....

....

....

....
[3]
[Total 9 marks]

More Microscopy

1 Fill in the table below to show how the units in the left-hand column are converted into different units and expressed in standard form.

	÷ 1000 will convert to:	× 1000 will convert to:	in standard form, original unit will be:
mm	m	μm	× 10⁻³ m
μm	....	....	.... m
nm	....	....	.... m
pm	....		.... m

2 Write words in the boxes to correctly complete the following magnification formulae:

total magnification =

[............................] magnification ×

[............................] magnification

magnification = image size / [............................]

1 **Figure 1** shows an image of a sample of epithelial cells viewed using a light microscope. An eyepiece lens with a magnification of × 10 and an objective lens with a magnification of × 100 were used to view the cells.

Figure 1

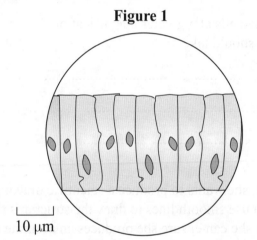

10 μm

a) i) Calculate the total magnification used to view the cells.

total magnification = ...
[1]

ii) Estimate the average height of the cells.

average height of the cells = ... μm
[1]

b) A student examines another cell type at the same magnification and finds its average height to be 8 μm. This can be expressed in standard form as

☐ A 8 × 10⁻⁶ m   ☐ B 0.8 × 10⁻⁶ m   ☐ C 8 × 10⁻¹² m   ☐ D 0.8 × 10⁻¹² m
[1]

[Total 3 marks]

2 A student observed blood cells under a microscope. A scale drawing of one of the cells is shown in **Figure 2**.

Figure 2

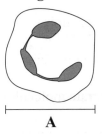

A

a) **A** is the cell width. The real width of **A** is 0.012 mm.
Calculate the magnification of the image.

magnification = ...

[2]

b) The cell is then viewed with a magnification of × **400**.
Calculate the new width of the image in mm.

width of image = ... mm

[2]

[Total 4 marks]

3 A plant cell is magnified 1000 times under a light microscope. The length of the image of the plant cell is 10 mm.

a) Calculate the actual length of the plant cell in μm.

actual length of plant cell = ... μm

[3]

b) An electron microscope is used to look inside the cell in more detail.
A virus particle is noticed that measures 4×10^{-5} mm in width.
Calculate the width of the virus in nm.

.... nm

[3]

[Total 6 marks]

Section 1 — Key Concepts in Biology

Enzymes

1 Enzymes are biological catalysts. (Grade 4-6)

a) State how a catalyst affects the rate of a reaction.

....

[1]

b) Name the part of an enzyme where substrate molecules bind.

....

[1]

c) Enzymes have a 'high specificity' for their substrate. Describe what this means.

....

....

[1]

[Total 3 marks]

2 The concentration of substrate molecules affects the rate of an enzyme-controlled reaction. (Grade 6-7)

a) Which of the graphs below (**A**, **B**, **C** or **D**) correctly shows how the rate of an enzyme-controlled reaction is affected by substrate concentration?

☐ **A**

Rate of reaction / Substrate concentration

☐ **C**

Rate of reaction / Substrate concentration

☐ **B**

Rate of reaction / Substrate concentration

☐ **D**

Rate of reaction / Substrate concentration

[1]

b) Explain why increasing the substrate concentration fails to affect the rate of an enzyme-controlled reaction after a certain point.

....

....

....

[2]

[Total 3 marks]

3   Temperature affects the rate of enzyme activity. Enzyme A has an optimum temperature of 38 °C. **Figure 1** shows enzyme A before and after being exposed to a temperature of 60 °C.

Figure 1

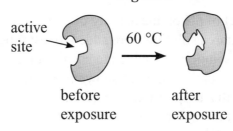

Enzyme A's activity will be different at 38 °C and 60 °C. Explain why.

....

....

....

....

[Total 3 marks]

4   A scientist investigated the effect of pH on the activity of an enzyme by calculating the rate of reaction for several pH values. His results are shown in **Figure 2**.

Figure 2

pH	3.6	3.8	4.0	4.4	4.8	5.0	5.2
Rate (cm³ s⁻¹)	2.0	5.0	8.0	11.0	8.0	4.0	1.0

a) i) Use the grid in **Figure 3** to draw a graph using the values in **Figure 2**. Include a curve of best fit.

[2]

ii) Determine the optimum pH for this enzyme.

....

[1]

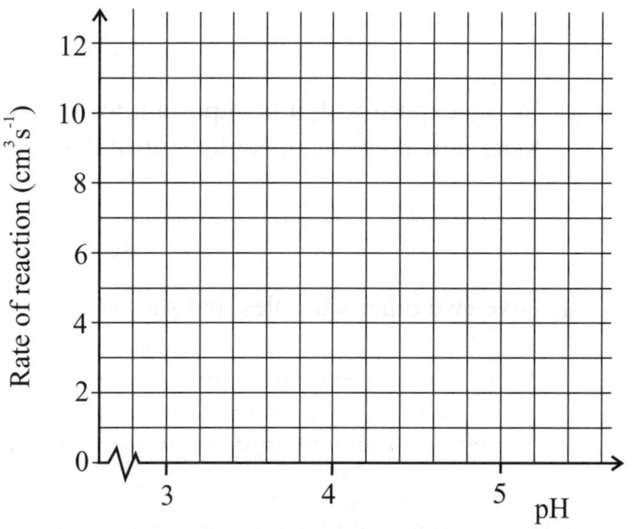

b) Describe and explain the effect on enzyme activity of increasing the pH above the optimum level.

....

....

....

....

[3]

[Total 6 marks]

Figure 3

More on Enzymes

1 The enzyme amylase is involved in the breakdown of starch into simple sugars.

A student investigated the effect of pH on the activity of amylase in starch solution. Amylase and starch solution were added to test tubes X, Y and Z. A different buffer solution was added to each test tube. Each buffer solution had a different pH value, as shown in **Figure 1**. Spotting tiles were prepared with a drop of iodine solution in each well. Iodine solution is a browny-orange colour but it turns blue-black in the presence of starch.

Figure 1

Test tube	pH
X	4
Y	6
Z	11

Every 30 seconds a drop of the solution from each of the test tubes was added to a separate well on a spotting tile. The resulting colour of the solution in the well was recorded as shown in **Figure 2**.

Figure 2

Time (s)	30	60	90	120	150
Tube X	Blue-black	Blue-black	Blue-black	Browny-orange	Browny-orange
Tube Y	Blue-black	Browny-orange	Browny-orange	Browny-orange	Browny-orange
Tube Z	Blue-black	Blue-black	Blue-black	Blue-black	Blue-black

a) State the pH at which the rate of reaction was greatest. Explain your answer.

....

....

....

[2]

b) Suggest an explanation for the results in tube **Z**.

....

....

[1]

c) i) In any experiment, it is important to control the variables that are not being tested. State how the student could control the temperature in the test tubes.

....

[1]

ii) Give **two** other variables that should be controlled in this experiment.

1. ....

2. ....

[2]

d) The student repeated her experiment at pH 7 and got the same results as she got for her experiment at pH 6. Describe how she could improve her experiment to find whether the reaction is greatest at pH 6 or 7.

....

....

[1]

[Total 7 marks]

Enzymes in Breakdown and Synthesis

1   **Figure 1** shows how different molecules are broken down by enzymes.

Figure 1

carbohydrate ⟶ **A** ⟶ simple sugars   **B** ⟶ protease ⟶ **C**

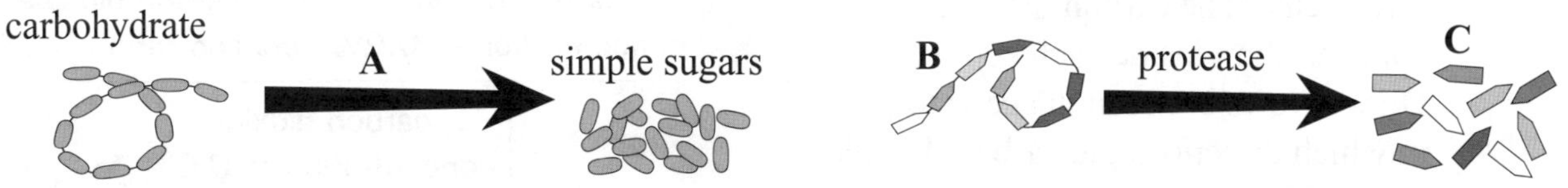

a) Name the molecules labelled A-C in **Figure 1**.

A ....

B ....

C ....

[3]

b) Explain why the breakdown of large molecules into smaller components is necessary for organisms.

....

....

....

[2]

[Total 5 marks]

2   Orlistat is a drug that is used to help lower obesity rates.
It works by preventing lipase from working in the digestive system.

Explain why patients taking Orlistat may have oily faeces.

....

....

....

....

....

[Total 3 marks]

Exam Tip

Examiners tend to like asking questions about enzymes — that's because they can make you draw together lots of your knowledge in a single question. For example, you might get asked how temperature affects the breakdown of lipids — you'd need to know that lipases are enzymes which breakdown lipids and how temperature affects enzyme activity.

Section 1 — Key Concepts in Biology

Diffusion, Osmosis and Active Transport

The diagram on the right shows three cells. The carbon dioxide concentration inside each cell is shown. Draw arrows between the cells to show in which directions the carbon dioxide will diffuse.

| carbon dioxide concentration = 0.2% | carbon dioxide concentration = 1.5% |

carbon dioxide concentration = 3.0% ← cell

1 The cell membrane is important in controlling what substances can enter or leave a cell. **Grade 4-6**

a) Describe the process of diffusion.

....

....

[2]

b) Which of these types of molecule is too large to diffuse through a cell membrane? Tick **one** box.

☐ **A** protein

☐ **B** oxygen

☐ **C** glucose

☐ **D** water

[1]

[Total 3 marks]

2 Osmosis is a form of diffusion. **Grade 4-6**

a) In which **one** of these scenarios is osmosis occurring?

☐ **A** Water is moving from the mouth down into the stomach.

☐ **B** Sugar is being taken up into the blood from the gut.

☐ **C** A plant is absorbing water from the soil.

☐ **D** Oxygen is entering the blood from the lungs.

[1]

b) Give the definition of osmosis.

....

....

....

[3]

[Total 4 marks]

3 Diffusion, osmosis and active transport all involve the movement of molecules. *(Grade 6-7)*

Figure 1

partially permeable membrane

water molecules

sucrose molecules

oxygen molecules

Draw arrows in the boxes underneath **Figure 1** to illustrate the direction of the net movement of the following:

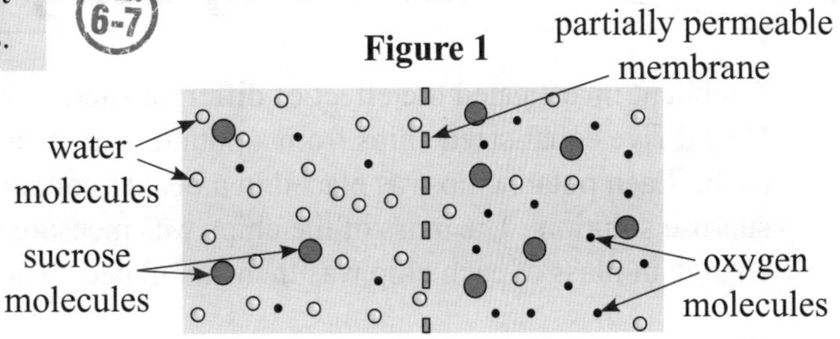

a) sucrose molecules moving by active transport:

[1]

b) water molecules moving by osmosis:

[1]

c) oxygen molecules moving by diffusion:

[1]

[Total 3 marks]

4 Amino acids are absorbed in the gut by active transport. **Figure 2** shows a diagram of amino acids being absorbed into the bloodstream across the epithelial cells of the gut. *(Grade 6-7)*

Figure 2

A

epithelial cell

BLOODSTREAM

GUT

amino acids

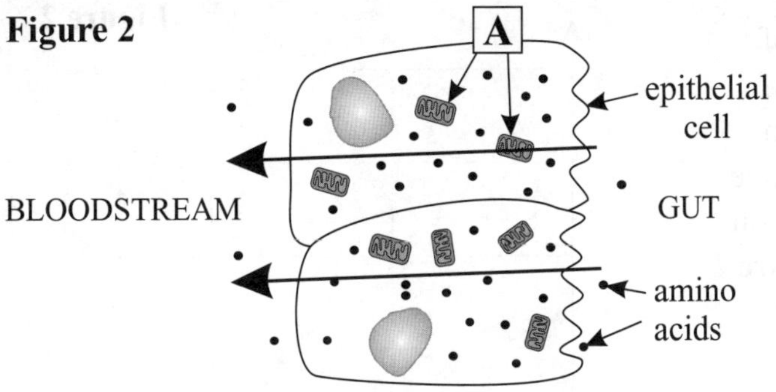

a) Using **Figure 2**, explain why active transport is necessary for the absorption of amino acids into the bloodstream.

....

....

....

....

[3]

b) Explain why the subcellular structures labelled **A** on **Figure 2** are needed in this process.

....

....

....

[2]

[Total 5 marks]

PRACTICAL

Investigating Osmosis

1 A student investigated the effect of different sucrose solutions on pieces of potato. He cut five equal-sized chips from a potato, and measured and recorded the mass of each. Each potato chip was placed in a beaker containing a different concentration of sucrose solution. The mass of the chips was measured after one hour, and the percentage change in mass of each chip was then calculated. The results are shown in **Figure 1**.

a) The mass of the potato chip in Beaker 5 was 10.0 g before the experiment and 9.3 g afterwards. Calculate the percentage change in mass of the potato chip in Beaker 5.

Figure 1

	Beaker				
	1	2	3	4	5
Concentration of sucrose solution (M)	0.1	0.3	0.5	0.7	0.9
% change in mass of potato chip	9	2	−3	−6	....

Change in mass = ... %

[1]

b) Explain what caused the increase in mass of the potato chips in Beakers 1 and 2.

....

....

[2]

c) Draw a graph of concentration of sucrose solution against percentage change in mass on the grid in **Figure 2**. Include a curve of best fit.

Figure 2

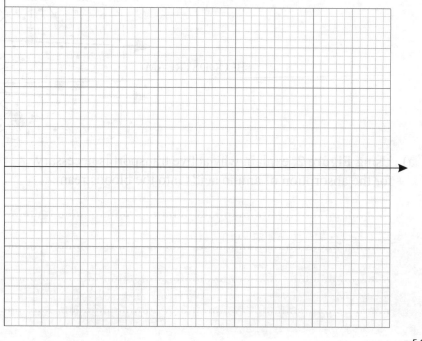

[4]

d) The student wanted to find a concentration of sucrose that would not cause the mass of the potato chip to change. Describe how the student could do this using the graph of the results.

....

....

[1]

[Total 8 marks]

Target AO3

2   A student is investigating osmosis. She takes three beakers and puts a different concentration of sucrose solution into each one. Then she places a length of Visking tubing (a partially permeable membrane) containing 0.5 M sucrose solution into each beaker. She places a glass capillary tube in the Visking tubing so that the end dips into the sucrose solution. A diagram of her experiment is shown in **Figure 3**.

Figure 3

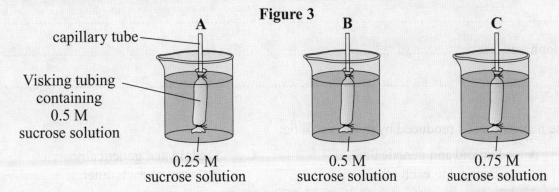

capillary tube

Visking tubing containing 0.5 M sucrose solution

A   B   C

0.25 M sucrose solution   0.5 M sucrose solution   0.75 M sucrose solution

The student records the level of the sucrose solution in each beaker and each capillary tube at the start of the experiment. She plans to record the level of the solution in each beaker every 30 minutes for 8 hours.

a)   Give **two** variables that the student should keep constant in this experiment.

   ....

   ....

   [2]

b)   Predict what will happen to the level of the solution in Beaker B after 1 hour. Explain your answer.

   ....

   ....

   ....

   [2]

c)   Describe and explain what you would expect to happen to the level of solution in Beaker C over the course of 8 hours.

   ....

   ....

   ....

   ....

   ....

   [4]

   [Total 8 marks]

Exam Tip

If you get a question in the exam where you need to explain the effects of osmosis, make sure you word your answer really carefully. For example. remember to write about the movement of <u>water</u> molecules (not just molecules) and talk about <u>water</u> concentration (not just 'the concentration') — these details will show the examiners you really know your stuff.

Section 2 — Cells and Control

Mitosis

1 Damaged skin tissue can be repaired by mitosis. *Grade 6-7*

a) Describe what happens in each of these stages of mitosis:

Prophase ....

....

Telophase ....

....

[4]

b) The new skin cells produced by mitosis will be:

☐ **A** Diploid and genetically identical to each other.

☐ **C** Diploid and genetically different to each other.

☐ **B** Haploid and genetically identical to each other.

☐ **D** Haploid and genetically different to each other.

[1]

c) Other than tissue repair, give **one** reason why an organism's cells divide by mitosis.

....

[1]

[Total 6 marks]

2 Mitosis is part of the cell cycle. *Grade 6-7*

a) Before mitosis occurs, a cell goes through interphase. Describe what happens to the cell's DNA during interphase and explain why this process is necessary.

....

....

[2]

b) **Figure 1** shows a cell undergoing mitosis.

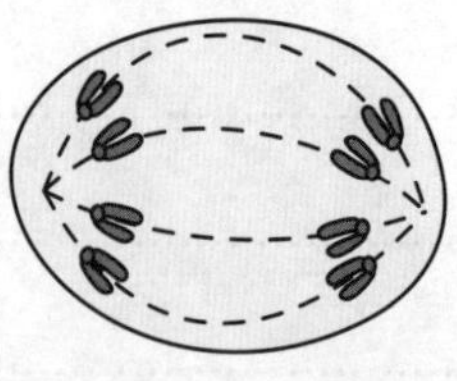

i) Name the stage of mitosis that the cell is going through.

....

[1]

ii) Describe what is happening during this stage.

Figure 1

....

....

[2]

c) The cell cycle is not complete until cytokinesis has occurred.
Describe what happens during cytokinesis.

....

[1]

[Total 6 marks]

Cell Division and Growth

1   **Figure 1** shows a flowering plant. Grade 4-6

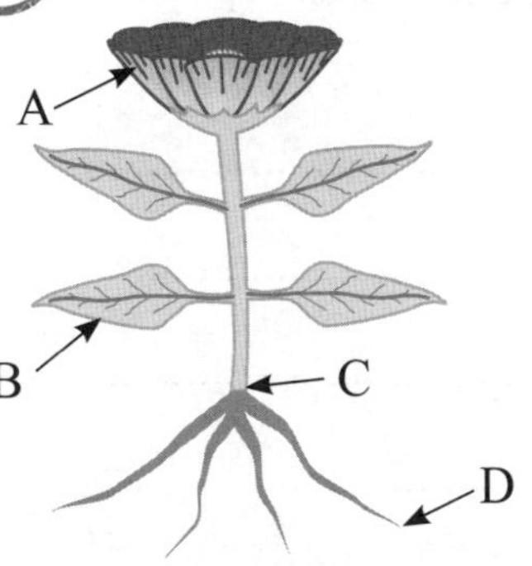

Figure 1

a)   Which label (**A-D**) shows a site where growth usually occurs by cell division?

☐ **A**   ☐ **B**   ☐ **C**   ☐ **D**

[1]

b)   Name the main process by which plants grow in height.

....

[1]

[Total 2 marks]

2   Animals start life as embryos, which grow and develop. Grade 6-7

a)   State the purpose of cell differentiation in an animal embryo.

....

[1]

b)   Describe **two** differences between the growth of animals and the growth of plants.

1.   ....

....

2.   ....

....

[2]

[Total 3 marks]

3   A tumour can occur in any organ in the body. Not all tumours are cancerous. Grade 6-7

a)   Explain how a tumour forms.

....

....

....

[3]

b)   Describe the point at which a tumour is classed as a cancer.

....

[1]

[Total 4 marks]

4 Percentile charts are used to record and monitor a child's growth.

a) A child's mass was recorded regularly and plotted on the percentile chart shown in **Figure 2**. The crosses represent the child's mass.

i) Explain what the line labelled '25th' on the chart represents.

....

....

....

....

[2]

Figure 2

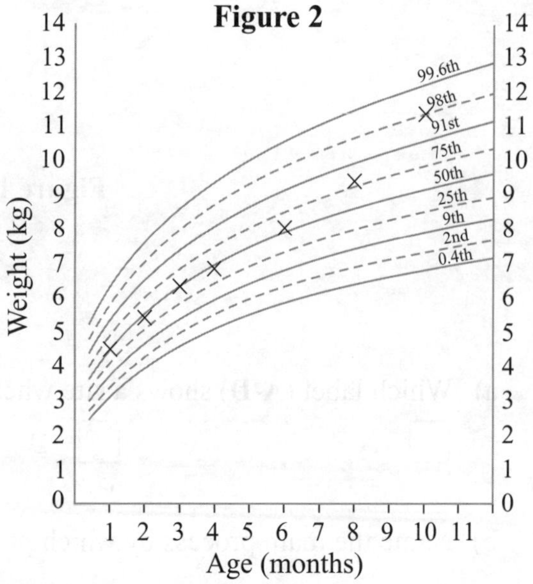

ii) Describe the growth trend shown on the chart and suggest why a doctor might be concerned about the child's growth.

....

....

....

....

....

[3]

b) Give **two** other measurements that could be plotted on a percentile chart to monitor growth.

1. ....   2. ....

[2]

[Total 7 marks]

5 **Figure 3** shows the mass of an animal plotted against its age in weeks.

a) Calculate the rate of growth between 0 and 60 weeks. Give your answer to 2 significant figures.

Figure 3

rate of growth = ... kg week^{-1}

[2]

b) The animal reaches full growth at 300 weeks. Comment on the amount of cell differentiation you'd expect to be occurring at the point marked **X** on the graph. Explain your answer.

....

....

....

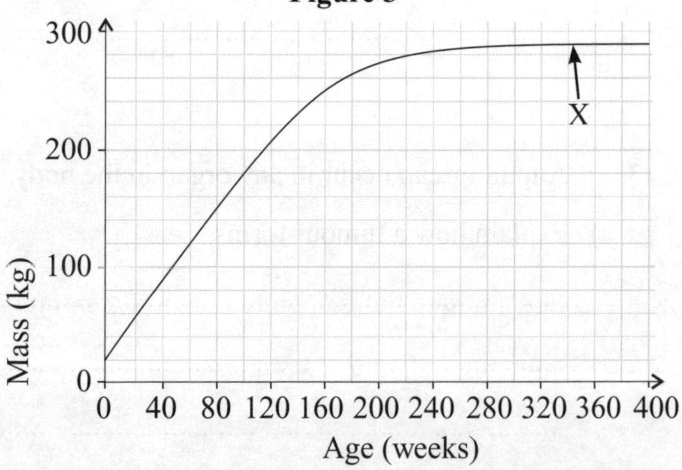

[2]

[Total 4 marks]

Section 2 — Cells and Control

Stem Cells

Circle the correct words shown in bold to complete the passage below.

Stem cells are able to **differentiate** / **mutate** to become **specialised** / **unspecialised** cells.

Stem cells found in **adults** / **early human embryos** can produce any type of cell at all.

In plants, stem cells are found in areas of the plant that are **growing** / **photosynthesising**.

Plant stem cells can produce **only a small number of cell types** / **any cell type**.

1   Scientists can use stem cells to grow new cells, which they can then use to test new drugs on.   (Grade 4-6)

  a) Stem cells are

    ☐ **A** gametes   ☐ **B** specialised   ☐ **C** undifferentiated   ☐ **D** differentiated

[1]

  b) i) Explain **one** reason why scientists may prefer to use embryonic stem cells for research rather
        than adult stem cells.

        ....

        ....

[2]

     ii) Suggest **one** reason why people are against research involving embryonic stem cells.

        ....

[1]

  c) Scientists can also use plant stem cells in drug research.
     Name the plant tissue that produces stem cells.

        ....

[1]

[Total 5 marks]

2   Scientists are researching whether it's possible to use embryonic
    stem cells to produce insulin-secreting cells, which could potentially   (Grade 7-9)
    be implanted in a patient in order to cure them of type 1 diabetes.

    Explain **two** potential risks of using stem cells to cure type 1 diabetes.

    ....

    ....

    ....

    ....

    ....

[Total 4 marks]

Section 2 — Cells and Control

The Nervous System

Use the words below to complete the following sentences about the nervous system. Each word can only be used once.

motor   sensory   receptors   effectors

The body has lots of sensory .... , which detect environmental stimuli.

When this happens, nervous impulses are sent along .... neurones

to the central nervous system. From the central nervous system, impulses are sent

along .... neurones to .... which produce a response.

1   Motor neurone disease occurs when motor neurones stop working as they should.   **Grade 7-9**

a) **Figure 1** shows a motor neurone.

Figure 1

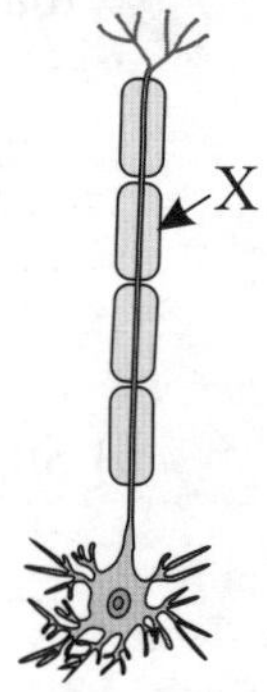

i) Add an arrow to **Figure 1** to show the direction a nervous impulse
would travel along the neurone.

[1]

X

ii) Name the part labelled **X** and describe its function.

....

....
[2]

iii) Describe **two** structural differences between a motor neurone and a sensory neurone.

1. ....

....

2. ....

....
[2]

b) Explain why a person with motor neurone disease may have difficulty swallowing.

....

....
[2]

c) A motor neurone is 58 cm long. An impulse travels along it at 110 m s^{-1}.
Calculate how long it would take the impulse to travel the length of the neurone
in milliseconds. Give your answer to 3 significant figures.

.... ms
[3]
[Total 10 marks]

Target AO3

2   Two students are investigating the sensitivity of the skin
    on different areas of the body using the method below.

1. Blindfold the person to be tested.
2. Tape two toothpicks onto a ruler so that they are 50 mm apart.
3. Lightly press the two toothpicks onto the person's arm.
4. Ask whether the person can feel one or two toothpicks.
5. If they can feel two toothpicks, move the toothpicks 5 mm closer together and
    repeat steps 3 and 4. Keep doing this until they can only feel one toothpick.

The students repeated the experiment for different areas of the body, and repeated it three times
per area. Each time, they recorded the distance between the toothpicks at which the person could
only feel one toothpick. Their results are shown in **Figure 2**.

Figure 2

Area of the body	Forearm			Palm			Back of hand		
Repeat	1	2	3	1	2	3	1	2	3
Distance between toothpicks (mm)	30	30	45	5	5	5	25	20	15

a) The students calculated the mean distance between toothpicks for each area of the body.
    Explain why the students repeated their readings and calculated a mean for each area.

    ....

    ....

    [1]

b) Calculate the uncertainty in the students' results for the back of the hand.

    .... mm

    [2]

c) Suggest how the accuracy of this experiment could be improved.

    ....

    ....

    [1]

d) The students think that the third repeat reading for the forearm is an anomalous result.
    Suggest how the students could confirm that the result is anomalous.

    ....

    ....

    [1]

e) The students conclude from their results that the palm is the most sensitive part of the body.
    Explain why this is **not** a valid conclusion.

    ....

    ....

    [2]

    [Total 7 marks]

Section 2 — Cells and Control

Synapses and Reflexes

1 Humans have many different reflexes. *(Grade 4-6)*

a) Reflexes are

☐ **A** slow and under conscious control   ☐ **C** rapid and automatic

☐ **B** rapid and under conscious control   ☐ **D** slow and automatic

[1]

b) **Figure 1** shows a diagram of a reflex arc.

Figure 1

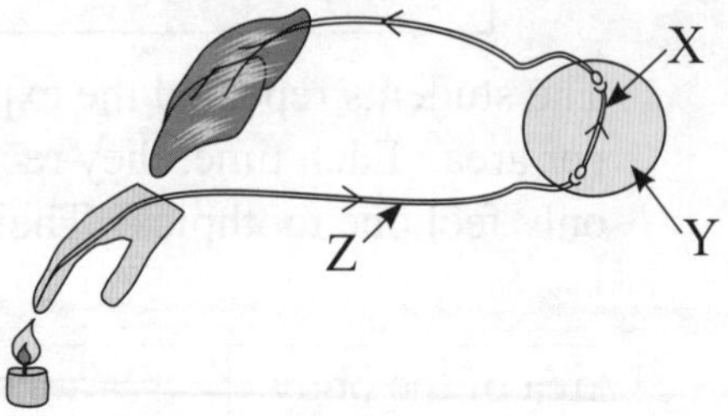

i) Name the structure labelled **X**.

....

[1]

ii) Name **two** parts of the body that the part of the diagram labelled **Y** could represent.

1. ....   2. ....

[2]

iii) Name the structure labelled **Z** and describe its function.

....

....

[2]

iv) State the purpose of the reflex arc shown in **Figure 1**.

....

[1]

[Total 7 marks]

2 Some stimuli are interpreted by the brain as being painful. When receptors detect these stimuli, impulses are passed to the spinal cord and then to the brain. Opioid drugs can relieve pain, partly because they prevent the release of neurotransmitters from certain sensory neurones.

With reference to synapses, explain how opioids can relieve pain. *(Grade 7-9)*

....

....

....

....

[Total 3 marks]

Exam Tip

The pathway that nervous impulses take in a reflex arc is always the same — receptor, sensory neurone, relay neurone (in the spinal cord or an unconscious part of the brain), motor neurone, effector. Learn this pathway (and understand that synapses connect neurones) then you'll be able to tackle any question on reflexes, even if it's a reflex you've not learnt.

Sexual Reproduction and Meiosis

1 Gametes are produced by meiosis. Human gametes are egg and sperm cells. *(Grade 4-6)*

a) Gametes contain...

☐ **A** ...twice as many chromosomes as other body cells.

☐ **B** ...a quarter of the number of chromosomes in other body cells.

☐ **C** ...three times as many chromosomes as other body cells.

☐ **D** ...half the number of chromosomes in other body cells.

[1]

b) Meiosis results in the production of...

☐ **A** ...two genetically identical daughter cells.

☐ **B** ...four genetically identical daughter cells.

☐ **C** ...two genetically different daughter cells.

☐ **D** ...four genetically different daughter cells.

[1]

c) State the name given to the cell formed from two gametes at fertilisation.

....

[1]

[Total 3 marks]

2 **Figure 1** shows a diploid cell about to undergo meiosis. *(Grade 6-7)*

Figure 1   **Figure 2**

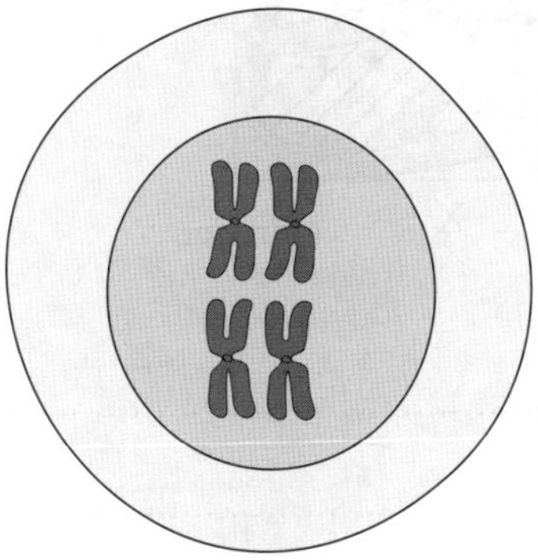

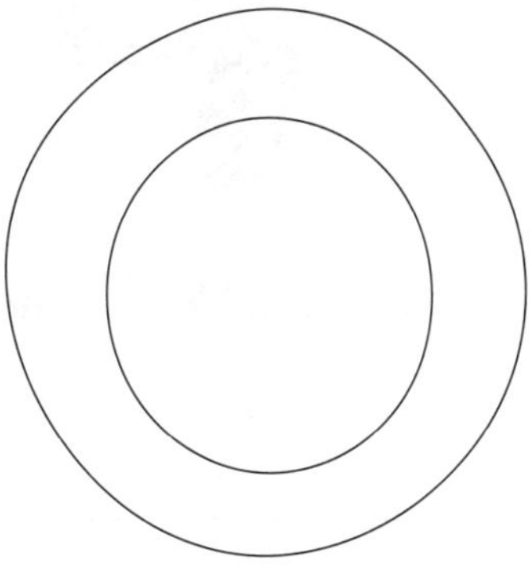

a) Complete **Figure 2** to show the number of chromosomes in a haploid gamete of this organism.

[2]

b) Explain why haploid gametes are necessary for sexual reproduction.

....

....

....

[2]

[Total 4 marks]

DNA

1 Scientists have studied the human genome. **Grade 4-6**

a) What is a genome?

☐ **A** All of an organism's DNA.　　☐ **C** All of an organism's genes.

☐ **B** All of an organism's proteins.　☐ **D** All of an organism's DNA and proteins.

[1]

b) The human genome contains over 20 000 genes.
Explain what is meant by the term 'gene'.

....

....
[1]

c) Describe how DNA is stored in the nucleus of eukaryotic cells.

....

....
[2]

[Total 4 marks]

2 **Figure 1** shows a section of a DNA double helix. **Grade 4-6**

Figure 1

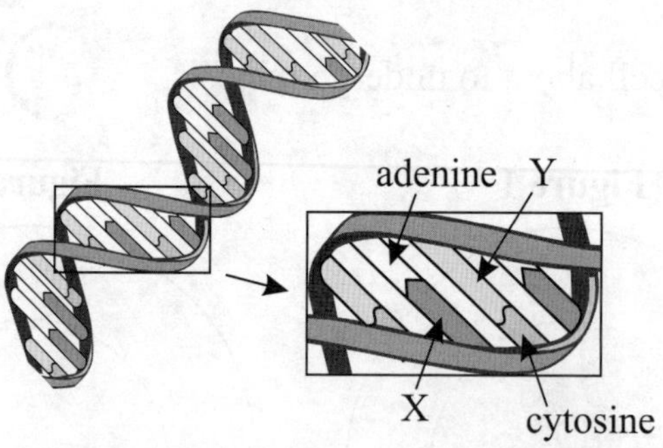

a) Name the bases labelled **X** and **Y** on **Figure 1**.

X: ....

Y: ....
[2]

b) What is meant by the term 'double helix'?

....
[1]

c) DNA is a polymer. Explain what this means.

....

....
[1]

[Total 4 marks]

3   A student is extracting DNA from an apple. He begins by breaking up the apple using a food blender. He then adds an 'extraction solution' to the fruit pulp.   *(Grade 6-7)*

a) Apart from water, state **two** components of the 'extraction solution'.

1. ....   2. ....

[2]

b) The student filters the mixture into a boiling tube.
Explain what the student needs to do next to obtain a DNA precipitate.

....

....

....

[2]

[Total 4 marks]

4   When a DNA molecule denatures, the bonds between bases on opposite DNA strands break and the two strands separate. **Figure 2** shows how the percentage of denatured DNA in a sample changes as the sample is heated.   *(Grade 7-9)*

Figure 2

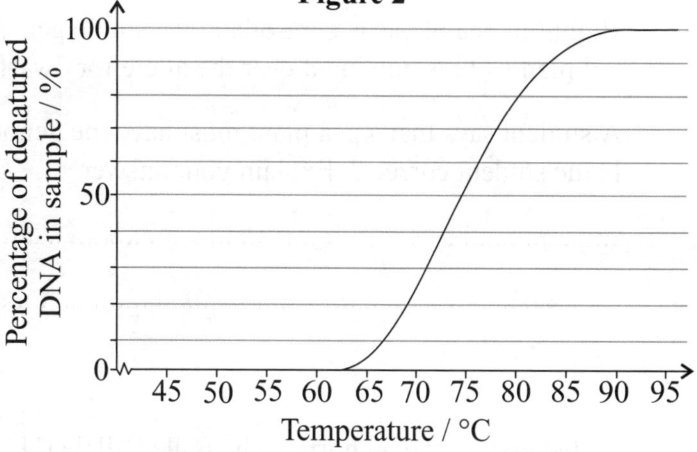

a) Name the bonds that break when a DNA molecule denatures.

....

[1]

b) Give **two** observations that could be made from the data in **Figure 2**.

1. ....

....

2. ....

....

[2]

c) The DNA sample above contains 8.14×10^4 base pairs.
Calculate how many base pairs have separated at 70 °C.
Give your answer in standard form to 3 significant figures.

.... base pairs

[2]

[Total 5 marks]

Section 3 — Genetics

Genetic Diagrams

Warm-Up

Draw lines to match the words on the left to the correct definition on the right.

genotype — Having two alleles the same for a particular gene.

phenotype — The combination of alleles an organism has.

allele — The characteristics an organism has.

heterozygous — Having two different alleles for a particular gene.

homozygous — A version of a gene.

1 Height in pea plants is controlled by a single gene. The allele for tall plants (T) is dominant over the allele for dwarf plants (t). *(Grade 4-6)*

A student says that a pea plant must have the genotype TT to be tall. Is the student correct? Explain your answer.

....

....

[Total 2 marks]

2 Polled cattle have no horns. The polled allele (N) is dominant over the allele for horns (n). A farmer wants to breed a herd of polled cattle. *(Grade 6-7)*

a) The farmer breeds a polled bull with a horned cow. Both the bull and the cow are homozygous for their trait.

Complete the Punnett square on the right to show the genotypes of the offspring.

....	....
....	....
....	....

[1]

b) The farmer later breeds a heterozygous polled bull with several heterozygous polled cows. Give the likely ratio of polled cattle : horned cattle in the calves. Draw a genetic diagram to explain your answer.

ratio of polled calves : horned calves ....

[2]

[Total 3 marks]

3 **Figure 1** shows a tabby cat. Tabby cats have a distinctive banding pattern on their fur. The banding is controlled by a single gene. The allele for banding (B) is dominant over the allele for solid colour fur (b).

Figure 1

a) State the **two** possible genotypes for the cat shown in **Figure 1**.

1. .... 2. ....

[2]

b) A heterozygous tabby cat breeds with a cat with solid-colour fur.

i) Draw a genetic diagram to show the probability of one of the offspring being a tabby.

probability of one of the offspring being a tabby: ....

[2]

ii) The heterozygous tabby and the cat with solid-colour fur have 6 kittens. State how many of these kittens are likely to be tabby.

....

[1]

[Total 5 marks]

4 Hair length in Syrian hamsters is controlled by a single gene. The allele for short hair (H) is dominant over the allele for long hair (h).

Grade 7-9

Explain how a breeder could determine the genotype of a short-haired hamster.

....

....

....

....

....

....

[Total 4 marks]

Exam Tip

You've really got to learn all the scientific words related to this topic (dominant, recessive, homozygous, etc.). Not only could you be asked to define them in the exam, it's assumed you'll know what the terms mean when they're used in questions. It's hard to get the right answer if you don't know what the question's asking you, so get learning that vocab.

Section 3 — Genetics

More Genetic Diagrams

1   **Figure 1** shows how the biological sex of offspring is determined.

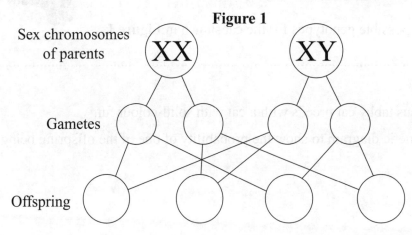

Figure 1

Sex chromosomes of parents

Gametes

Offspring

a)   Complete **Figure 1** to show the sex chromosomes of the gametes and the offspring.

[1]

b)   Give the ratio of male to female offspring. ....

[1]

[Total 2 marks]

2   PKU is a genetic disorder caused by a recessive allele (h). **Figure 2** shows a family pedigree for a family in which one of the children has PKU.

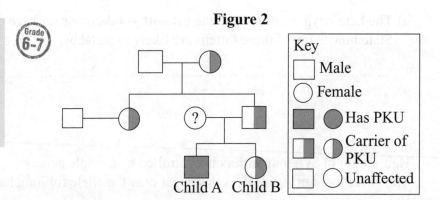

Figure 2

Key

☐ Male

◯ Female

■ ● Has PKU

◨ ◐ Carrier of PKU

☐ ◯ Unaffected

Child A   Child B

a)   i)   State the genotype of child A. ....

[1]

    ii) State the **two** possible genotypes of Child A's mother.

      1. ....   2. ....

[2]

b)   Two carriers of PKU have a child. Complete the Punnett square to show the percentage probability that they will have a child who does **not** have the disorder.

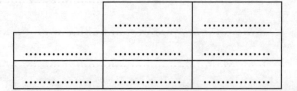

probability of having a child who does not have the disorder: ....%

[2]

[Total 5 marks]

Variation

1 Mutations can have different effects on the phenotype of an organism. (Grade 4-6)

a) Explain what is meant by the term 'phenotype'.

....
[1]

b) Which **one** of the following statements is true?

☐ **A** A single mutation usually has a large effect on an organism's phenotype.

☐ **B** Most mutations affect an organism's phenotype, but only slightly.

☐ **C** Most mutations have no effect on an organism's phenotype.

☐ **D** A single mutation never has any effect on an organism's phenotype.
[1]

[Total 2 marks]

2 An experiment was carried out into the causes of variation in plant height. Three different controlled environments (A, B and C) were set up. Five plants of the same species were grown from seed in each environment. The heights of all the plants were measured after six weeks and are shown in **Figure 1**. (Grade 6-7)

Figure 1

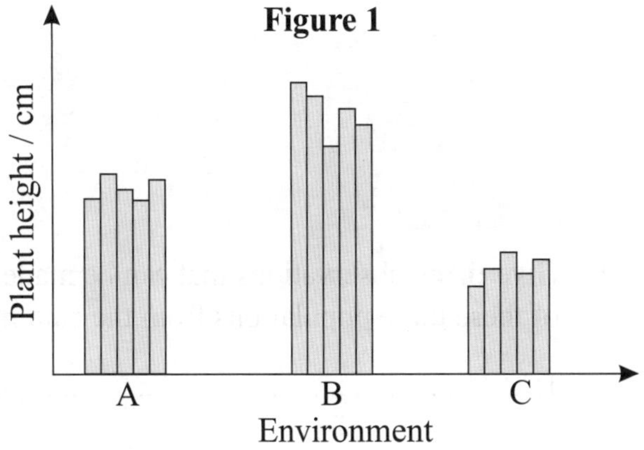

a) Some variation in plants is genetic and can be caused by mutations. Give **one** other cause of genetic variation within a plant species.

....
[1]

b) Some variation in plants can be caused by the environment. What name is given to a characteristic caused by environmental variation?

☐ **A** an assisted characteristic   ☐ **C** an additional characteristic

☐ **B** an acquired characteristic   ☐ **D** an advanced characteristic
[1]

c) Using the information in **Figure 1**, explain whether variation in plant height in this species is caused by genes, the environment or both.

....

....

....

....
[4]

[Total 6 marks]

Section 3 — Genetics

3   The heterozygosity index (H) can be used to measure the genetic variation in a population. H always has a value between 0 and 1. The closer the value to 1, the more alleles there are in the population. **Figure 2** shows the value of H for three different populations of the same species in two different years. The populations reproduce via sexual reproduction.

Figure 2

	Population 1	Population 2	Population 3
Value of H in 2005	0.42	0.41	0.48
Value of H in 2015	0.43	0.40	0.52

a) Calculate the difference in the mean value of H for the three populations, between 2005 and 2015.

Difference in mean value: ....

[3]

b) Give **three** observations that can be made about the genetic variation of these three populations from the data in **Figure 2**.

1. ....

....

2. ....

....

3. ....

....

[3]

c) Would you expect the population of an organism that only reproduces via asexual reproduction to have a higher or lower value of H than the populations shown in **Figure 2**? Explain your answer.

....

....

....

....

[2]

[Total 8 marks]

The Human Genome Project

1   Scientists hope to be able to use knowledge gained from the Human Genome Project to improve the treatment of disease.   *Grade 6-7*

a) Outline the aim of the Human Genome Project.

....

....

[1]

b) Describe **one** way in which knowledge gained from the Human Genome Project and related research could help scientists to develop new and better medicines.

....

....

[1]

c) Explain **one** way in which the Human Genome Project has affected the testing or treatment of inherited disorders.

....

....

....

....

[2]

[Total 4 marks]

2   Some genetic variants have been discovered that are associated with an increased risk of developing late onset Alzheimer's disease. However, there are currently no medically approved genetic tests for these variants.   *Grade 6-7*

a) Explain **one** possible benefit of testing a person for genetic variants that are associated with an increased risk of developing Alzheimer's disease later in life.

....

....

....

[2]

b) Give **two** possible drawbacks of testing a person for these genetic variants.

1. ....

....

2. ....

....

[2]

[Total 4 marks]

Section 3 — Genetics

Natural Selection and Evidence for Evolution

Fill in the blanks in the paragraph below using some of the words on the right.

predation
beneficial
survival
competition
offspring
used to
adapted to
stronger

Natural selection describes how .... alleles become more common in a population. Selection pressures such as .... and .... mean that not all organisms will survive and reproduce. Individuals with alleles that make them better .... their environment are more likely to survive and pass on their alleles to their ....

1   Organisms can only adapt to their environment if there is genetic variation in the population.   Grade 4-6

a)   Individuals in a population show genetic variation because of differences in their:

☐ **A** selection pressures   ☐ **C** cells

☐ **B** alleles   ☐ **D** adaptations

[1]

b)   How do new alleles arise in a population of organisms?

....

[1]

[Total 2 marks]

2   Bacteria can quickly evolve resistance to a particular antibiotic.   Grade 6-7

a)   Suggest **one** reason why bacteria can evolve quickly.

....

[1]

b)   Explain how a bacterium could become less affected by a particular antibiotic.

....

[1]

c) i)   State the selection pressure involved when bacteria develop resistance to an antibiotic.

....

[1]

ii) Explain how antibiotic resistance becomes more common in a population over time.

....

....

....

[3]

[Total 6 marks]

3 Warfarin is an anti-blood-clotting drug. It can be used as a poison to kill rats. Some rat populations have evolved to become resistant to Warfarin.

Grade 7-9

a) Explain **one** benefit to the rats of developing resistance to Warfarin.

....

....

[2]

b) **Figure 1** shows how the percentage of Warfarin-resistant rats in a population changed after the introduction of Warfarin as a rat poison. Explain how this data provides evidence for evolution.

....

....

....

....

....

....

....

....

[4]

Figure 1

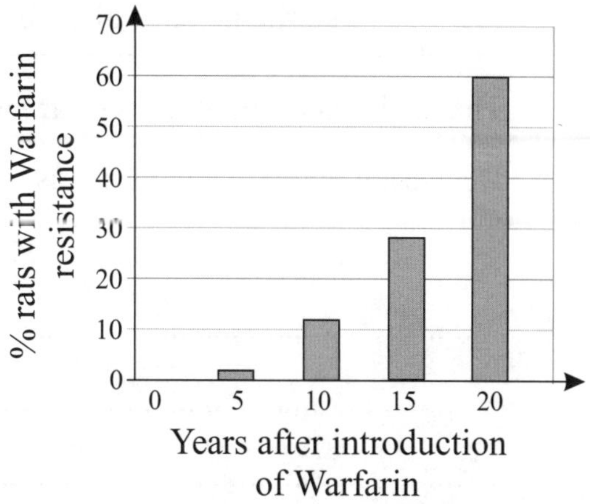

(Bar chart: y-axis "% rats with Warfarin resistance" from 0 to 70; x-axis "Years after introduction of Warfarin" with values 0, 5, 10, 15, 20. Bars at approximately 2 (year 5), 12 (year 10), 28 (year 15), 60 (year 20).)

[Total 6 marks]

4* A population of finches on an island mainly eat seeds. The finches vary in the size of their beaks. Larger beaks are better for breaking apart larger seeds, whereas smaller beaks are better for picking up and eating smaller seeds. A storm kills off many of the plants that produce larger seeds.

Grade 7-9

Describe how evolution by natural selection may lead to a change in the beak size in the population of finches, following the storm.

....

....

....

....

....

....

....

....

[Total 6 marks]

Exam Tip

Natural selection is a big favourite with examiners, so make sure you learn it well. If you get asked about natural selection in a context you haven't heard of before, don't panic — the process always involves the same steps in the same order. You just need to apply what you know to the information you're given in the question.

Target AO3

5   A scientist has samples of two strains of the same species of bacterium, strain A
     and strain B. This species of bacterium is usually killed by the antibiotic ampicillin,
     but the scientist believes that strain B may have become resistant to ampicillin.

The scientist has the following materials and equipment:

> - ampicillin solution
> - samples of bacterial strain A and strain B, growing in nutrient broth solution
> - sterile small glass bottles, with lids
> - sterile nutrient broth solution (suitable for growing this species of bacterium)
> - sterile pipettes of different sizes

The sterile nutrient broth is clear, but turns cloudy when bacteria grow in it.

a)* Devise a method that the scientist could use to test his hypothesis using this equipment.

....

....

....

....

....

....

....

....

....

....

....

....

....

[6]

b)   Suggest **one** reason why it is important that the scientist makes sure that all of the material
     from the experiment is disposed of safely when it is over.

....

....

[1]

[Total 7 marks]

Exam Tip

You could be asked to write a method for an experiment in your exams. If you are, don't worry. Just think carefully
through what you'd need to do if you were actually doing the experiment, and write it all down in a sensible order.
Remember to include details of what you would do to make it a fair test — otherwise your results wouldn't be valid.

Fossil Evidence for Human Evolution

Show the age of the fossils on the right by putting the correct name into each of the boxes on the timeline below.

'Lucy'   'Ardi'

'Turkana Boy'

....

.... million years ago

....

....

1   'Turkana Boy' is a fossil of the species *Homo erectus*.

a) 'Turkana Boy' was discovered by the scientist:

☐ **A** Carl Woese

☐ **B** Charles Darwin

☐ **C** Alfred Russel Wallace

☐ **D** Richard Leakey

[1]

b) Give **two** features of the 'Turkana Boy' skeleton, which suggest that his species was more human-like than the species of 'Ardi' or 'Lucy'.

1. ....

2. ....

[2]

[Total 3 marks]

2   Human ancestors began using stone tools around 2.6 million years ago.
Being able to date stone tools allows scientists to see how they developed over time.

Figure 1

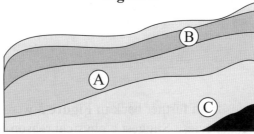

a) i) **Figure 1** shows the distribution of three stone tools (A-C) across the layers of rock at a fossil site. Put the stone tools in most likely order of age, from oldest to youngest.

....

[1]

Section 4 — Natural Selection and Genetic Modification

ii) Apart from studying the layers of rock that the tools are found in, give **two** methods that a scientist could use to date the stone tools at this fossil site.

1. ....

2. ....

[2]

b) Explain how stone tools provide evidence for the evolution of the brain in human ancestors.

....

....

....

[2]

[Total 5 marks]

3   An anthropologist is comparing a number of skeletons of human ancestors. He estimates their brain sizes using their skull remains. His results are shown in **Figure 2**. **Figure 3** shows a timeline for the evolutionary history of some human ancestor species.

Grade 6-7

Figure 2

Specimen	1	2	3
Brain size (cm^3)	950	325	457

Figure 3

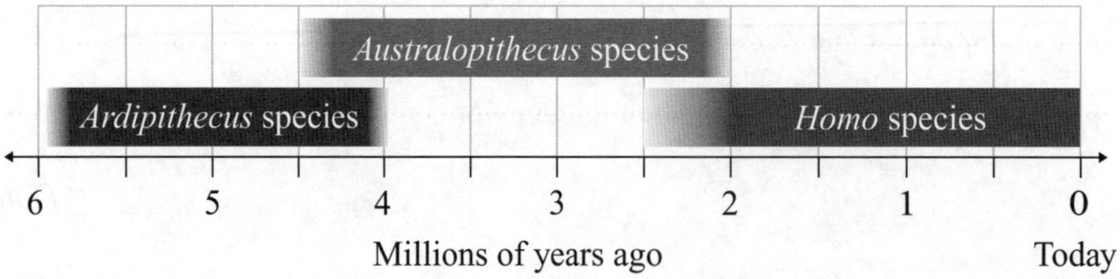

a) Use **Figures 2** and **3** to determine which specimen (1, 2 or 3) is:

i) a *Homo* species ....

ii) an *Australopithecus* species ....

iii) an *Ardipithecus* species ....

[2]

b) Evidence suggests that species from further back in **Figure 3** were generally shorter in height than the more recent species. Suggest a physical reason for this.

....

[1]

[Total 3 marks]

Section 4 — Natural Selection and Genetic Modification

4 Hominids are humans and their ancestors. Fossil hominids provide evidence for the evolutionary relationship between humans and apes.

Figure 4 shows the bone structure of a chimpanzee foot. Chimpanzees are apes. It also shows the foot bones of two incomplete fossil hominids and the bone structure of a human foot. Fossil A is older than fossil B.

Figure 4

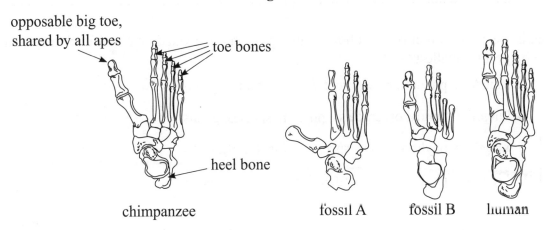

a) i) Using **Figure 4**, give **one** feature shared by **fossil A** and the chimpanzee, which is not found in humans.

....

[1]

ii) Suggest an explanation for why this feature is not found in humans.

....

....

[2]

b) How do the hominid fossils in **Figure 4** provide evidence for a shared common ancestor between humans and chimpanzees?

....

....

[1]

c) **Fossil B** belongs to the same species as the fossil 'Lucy'.
Other than differences in the foot structure, describe **one** difference you would expect to find between fossil B's skeleton and a chimpanzee's skeleton.

....

....

[1]

[Total 5 marks]

Exam Tip

Make sure you know how features in our hominid ancestors changed over the course of evolutionary history.
As hominids evolved to be more like humans and less like apes, legs became longer, arms became shorter and brains increased in size. Feet also become more adapted to walking than climbing trees.

Section 4 — Natural Selection and Genetic Modification

Classification

1 Classification involves arranging living organisms into groups. In one system of classification, organisms are first arranged into five groups called kingdoms. *Grade 4-6*

a) Write down the five kingdoms in this classification system.

....
[1]

b) What is the correct order of the following groups in the five kingdom classification system, from biggest to smallest?

☐ **A** kingdom, phylum, class, order, family, species, genus

☐ **B** kingdom, family, order, class, phylum, species, genus

☐ **C** kingdom, phylum, genus, species, class, family, order

☐ **D** kingdom, phylum, class, order, family, genus, species

[1]

[Total 2 marks]

2 Nowadays, the three domain classification system is widely used to classify organisms. One of the domains is Eukarya. *Grade 4-6*

a) Fungi are part of the Eukarya domain.
State **three** other types of organism in the Eukarya domain.

....
[1]

b) Name the other **two** domains in the three domain system.

....
[2]

[Total 3 marks]

3 Changes in technology and chemical analyses led to the development of the three domain classification system in 1977. *Grade 6-7*

a) Explain how DNA sequencing techniques can be used to determine relationships between organisms.

....

....

....
[2]

b) Explain how genetic analysis led to the prokaryote kingdom being split into two domains.

....

....

....
[2]

[Total 4 marks]

Selective Breeding

1 Selective breeding can be used to produce organisms with characteristics that are useful to humans.

Grade 4-6

   a) Suggest **two** uses of selective breeding in agriculture.

     1. ....

     2. ....

[2]

   b) Suggest **one** use of selective breeding in medical research.

     ....

[1]

[Total 3 marks]

2 A farmer discovers that some of his dairy cows produce a little more milk per day than the rest of his herd.

Grade 7-9

   a) Explain the steps that the farmer could take to breed a herd of cows with high milk yields from his existing herd.

     ....

     ....

     ....

     ....

     ....

[3]

   b) Weaver Syndrome is a genetic defect found in dairy cows. After successfully breeding cows with high milk yields, the farmer notices that more of his cows have Weaver Syndrome than in his previous herd. Suggest a reason for this.

     ....

     ....

     ....

[2]

   c) Explain why the emergence of an infectious disease, such as bovine tuberculosis, may be more of an issue for the farmer's new herd than for his previous herd.

     ....

     ....

     ....

     ....

[3]

[Total 8 marks]

Genetic Engineering

Warm-Up

Draw lines to connect each word or phrase on the
left with the statement describing it on the right.

restriction enzyme	a type of vector
plasmid	cuts DNA open
ligase	an organism with DNA from a different species
GM organism	sticks DNA ends together
vector	transfers DNA into a cell

1   Genetic engineering involves modifying the genome of one
organism by introducing a gene from another organism.

Grade 6-7

a) i) Outline how a desired gene would be isolated from an organism.

....

....

[1]

ii) Explain how a vector can be used to insert the gene into a bacterial cell.

....

....

....

....

[3]

b) Which of these is an example of a vector used in genetic engineering?

☐ **A** a hybridoma

☐ **B** a virus

☐ **C** a glucose molecule

☐ **D** a protein

[1]

c) Explain **one** advantage of being able to insert the gene for a desired protein into a bacterial cell.

....

....

[2]

[Total 7 marks]

2 Genetically modified corn plants are grown in many parts of the world due to their pest resistance.

Grade 6-7

a) Apart from pest resistance, give another example of a beneficial characteristic that could be introduced into a crop by genetic modification.

....

[1]

b) Give **two** reasons why some people may have concerns about the use of genetically modified crops in agriculture.

1. ....

....

2. ....

....

[2]

[Total 3 marks]

3* A scientist discovers that she is able to genetically modify hens to produce particular proteins in the whites of their eggs.

Grade 7-9

Discuss the potential advantages of the scientist's findings in medicine and other areas, and also the concerns that some people may have over genetically engineering animals.

....

....

....

....

....

....

....

....

....

....

....

[Total 6 marks]

Exam Tip

Make sure you know plenty of arguments both for and against genetic engineering — they're the sort of thing examiners love to ask about. And don't forget the basic principles of using vectors and enzymes to genetically modify an organism — the techniques may vary a little depending on whether it's an animal/plant etc., but the basic idea is still the same.

Section 4 — Natural Selection and Genetic Modification

Health and Disease

Write the type of pathogen that causes each of the diseases below, using the words on the right. You may use a word more than once, or not at all.

Chalara ash dieback	....	protist
Tuberculosis	....	virus
Malaria	....	fungus
Cholera	....	bacterium

1   The World Health Organisation (WHO) monitors the health of people worldwide and coordinates research into communicable and non-communicable diseases.   Grade 4-6

a) Give the WHO's definition of health.

    ....

    ....

                                                                                                                        [2]

b) Describe the difference between a communicable and a non-communicable disease.

    ....

    ....

                                                                                                                        [1]

                                                                                                        [Total 3 marks]

2   Tuberculosis is caused by a pathogen.   Grade 4-6

a) Describe how the pathogen that causes tuberculosis is spread between individuals.

    ....

    ....

                                                                                                                        [1]

b) Give **one** effect of tuberculosis on the human body.

    ....

                                                                                                                        [1]

c) Describe **one** way in which the spread of the pathogen that causes tuberculosis may be reduced.

    ....

    ....

                                                                                                                        [1]

                                                                                                        [Total 3 marks]

3 Chalara ash dieback disease was originally noticed in ash trees in Poland in the 1990s. In 2012, a case of ash dieback was diagnosed in Britain, and it is now very widespread.

(Grade 6-7)

a) Give **two** symptoms of chalara ash dieback disease.

....

[2]

b) Suggest **one** way in which the disease may have been transmitted from Poland to Britain.

....

[1]

c) Describe **one** precaution that could be taken to limit any further spread of the disease.

....

....

[1]

[Total 4 marks]

4* Malaria is caused by a microorganism called *Plasmodium*. *Plasmodium* can only cause malaria if it is able to complete its growth cycle, which can only happen if temperatures are high enough. In many countries affected by malaria, climate change is leading to an increase in temperature at higher altitudes, where malaria was not previously present.

(Grade 7-9)

Explain why it may be advisable for people in high altitude areas of countries affected by malaria to learn how to use mosquito nets.

....

....

....

....

....

....

....

....

....

....

....

....

[Total 6 marks]

Exam Tip

There are a lot of communicable diseases that you need to know about for the exam. Make sure you know the pathogen that causes each one, the effects it causes, how it is spread and how its transmission can be prevented. Take the time to learn them all properly — if you get them mixed up in the exam you could be throwing away marks.

   Section 5 — Health, Disease & the Development of Medicines

STIs

1 *Chlamydia* is a disease which may result in infertility. **Grade 4-6**

    a) Name the type of pathogen that causes *Chlamydia*.

    ....

                                             [1]

    b) State how *Chlamydia* is most commonly transmitted between individuals.

    ....

                                             [1]

    c) i) The National Chlamydia Screening Programme was set up to reduce the
          spread of *Chlamydia* in the UK. Explain **one** reason why screening individuals
          without symptoms could help to reduce the spread of the disease.

        ....

        ....

        ....

                                        [2]

      ii) Give **one** additional method for preventing the spread of *Chlamydia*.

        ....

                                          [1]

                                  [Total 5 marks]

2 HIV is a virus that eventually leads to AIDS in the people it infects. **Grade 6-7**

    a) Explain why a person with AIDS may become seriously ill due to infection by another pathogen.

    ....

    ....

    ....

                                             [2]

    b) Suggest an explanation as to why, in order to protect themselves from HIV,
       drug users should not share needles.

    ....

    ....

    ....

                                             [2]

                                  [Total 4 marks]

Fighting Disease

1 The body has many features which it can use to protect itself against pathogens. (Grade 4-6)

  a) Give **one** example of a physical barrier against pathogens in humans.

  ....

  [1]

  b) What is the name of the enzyme present in tears which kills bacteria on the surface of the eye?

  ☐ **A** carbohydrase   ☐ **B** protease   ☐ **C** amylase   ☐ **D** lysozyme

  [1]

  c) Name the chemical which kills most pathogens that reach the stomach.

  ....

  [1]

  [Total 3 marks]

2 B-lymphocytes are a type of white blood cell involved in the specific immune response. (Grade 6-7)

  a) State what is meant by the term 'specific immune response'.

  ....

  [1]

  b) Explain how B-lymphocytes help the body to fight against invading pathogens.

  ....

  ....

  ....

  ....

  [4]

  [Total 5 marks]

3 Primary cilia dyskinesia (PCD) is a disease in which cilia don't work properly.
Suggest an explanation as to why people with PCD are likely to get frequent lung infections. (Grade 7-9)

  ....

  ....

  ....

  ....

  ....

  [Total 3 marks]

Memory Lymphocytes and Immunisation

1 Antibodies are important proteins in the immune response to a pathogen. **Figure 1** shows how the concentration of a particular antibody in the blood of a person changes over time.

Grade 6-7

a) At which point on the graph (**A**, **B**, **C** or **D**) are memory lymphocytes first produced?

☐ **A**

☐ **B**

☐ **C**

☐ **D**

[1]

Figure 1

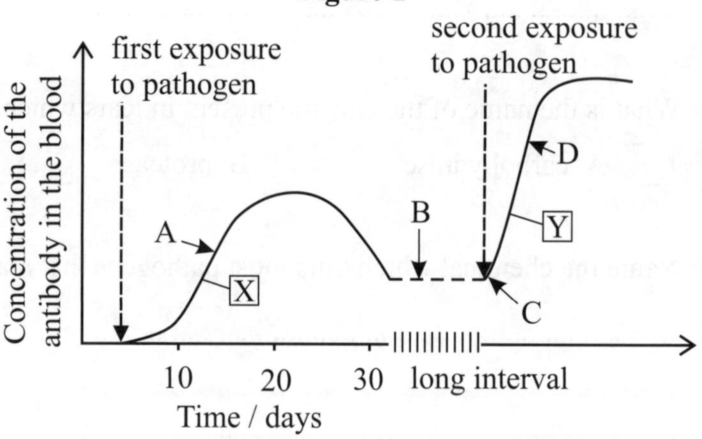

Concentration of the antibody in the blood

first exposure to pathogen

second exposure to pathogen

A

X

B

C

D

Y

10   20   30   long interval

Time / days

b) Explain why the curve on **Figure 1** labelled **Y** is steeper than the curve labelled **X**.

....

....

....

....

....

[3]

[Total 4 marks]

2 In 1988 the World Health Organisation began a global immunisation programme to try to eradicate polio.

Grade 7-9

a) Before being used in immunisation, the virus which causes polio is first treated with a chemical called formaldehyde. Suggest a reason for this.

....

[1]

b) Explain why a person who has been immunised against polio would be less likely to develop the disease if the virus entered their body.

....

....

....

....

....

[3]

[Total 4 marks]

Section 5 — Health, Disease & the Development of Medicines

Antibiotics and Other Medicines

1 New drugs have to undergo pre-clinical and clinical testing before they can be used. *(Grade 4-6)*

  a) i) Preclinical testing is carried out on:

☐ **A** healthy human volunteers   ☐ **C** patients in a hospital

☐ **B** human cells, tissues and dead animals   ☐ **D** human cells, tissues and live animals

[1]

   ii) Give **one** thing which is investigated during the pre-clinical testing of drugs.

....

[1]

  b) Suggest why very low doses of the drug are given at the start of clinical trials.

....

[1]

  c) Placebos and double-blind methods are often used in clinical trials.

   i) Explain why placebos are used.

....

....

[1]

   ii) Explain why double-blind trials are used.

....

....

[1]

[Total 5 marks]

2 Antibiotics are used to cure many different diseases. *(Grade 6-7)*

  a) Explain why antibiotics can be used to treat bacterial pathogens in humans.

....

....

[2]

  b) Antibiotics are not effective against viruses.
     Suggest an explanation as to why it is difficult to develop drugs that target viral pathogens.

....

....

....

[2]

[Total 4 marks]

    Section 5 — Health, Disease & the Development of Medicines

Non-Communicable Diseases

1   Non-communicable diseases are not spread by pathogens, instead they are associated with risk factors.   *(Grade 4-6)*

    a)   Describe what is meant by a 'risk factor' for a disease.

      ....

      ....

      [1]

    b)   Describe how drinking too much alcohol can cause liver disease.

      ....

      ....

      [2]

    c)   Give **one** disease which is associated with smoking.

      ....

      [1]

      [Total 4 marks]

2*   Being overweight or obese in childhood is an important risk factor for developing obesity as an adult. One of the aims of the UK government's Better Health campaign is to tackle childhood obesity.   *(Grade 7-9)*

    Explain which lifestyle factors Better Health is likely to tackle and the economical reasons why the government may have developed this campaign.

      ....

      ....

      ....

      ....

      ....

      ....

      ....

      ....

      ....

      [Total 6 marks]

Exam Tip

Think carefully about 6 mark questions like the one on this page. Don't just start scribbling everything you know about the topic. Stop and think first — work out what the question is wanting you to write about, and then make sure you write enough points to bag yourself as many marks as possible. Good job you've got some practice on this page...

Target AO3

3   Figures **1** and **2** show the prevalence of adult obesity in England and the number of people diagnosed with diabetes in England, respectively, between 2012 and 2018.

Figure 1

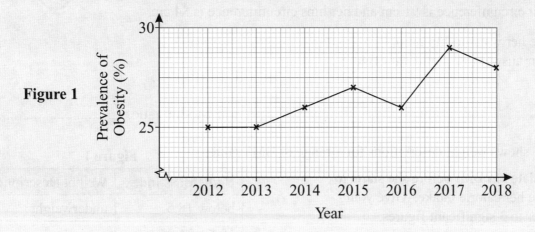

Figure 2

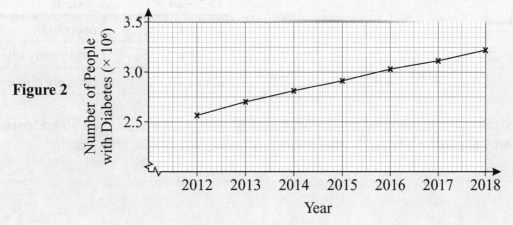

a) Describe the trend shown in **Figure 2**.

....

....

[1]

b) A student says: "the increasing rate of obesity has caused the rate of diabetes to increase". Evaluate the student's statement using the data shown in **Figures 1** and **2**.

....

....

....

....

....

....

....

....

[4]

[Total 5 marks]

     Section 5 — Health, Disease & the Development of Medicines

Measures of Obesity

1 A woman decides to lose weight by reducing her calorie intake. She is 170 cm tall and before she starts to reduce her calorie intake she has a mass of 73.5 kg. Her waist circumference is 91 cm and her hips circumference is 84 cm.

a) Calculate her waist-to-hip ratio.
Give your answer to 2 significant figures.

waist-to-hip ratio = ...
[1]

b) **Figure 1** shows weight descriptions for a range of BMI values.

Figure 1

i) Calculate her BMI before she starts to reduce her calorie intake. Give your answer to 3 significant figures.

Body Mass Index	Weight Description
below 18.5	underweight
18.5 - 24.9	normal
25 - 29.9	overweight
30 - 40	moderately obese
above 40	severely obese

BMI = ...kg m^{-2}
[3]

ii) After six months of her reduced calorie intake her BMI is calculated as 19. Using **Figure 1**, explain why her doctor advised her to consider increasing her calorie intake again.

....
[1]

[Total 5 marks]

2 Patients at a health centre had their BMI and waist-to-hip ratios calculated as part of a survey. The results of five of the patients are shown in **Figure 2**. A waist-to-hip ratio over 1 in men and over 0.85 in women indicates obesity.

a) Using **Figure 2**, explain which patient (**A-E**) is most at risk of developing cardiovascular disease.

Figure 2

Patient	Sex	BMI	Waist-to-hip ratio
A	Female	19.2	0.9
B	Male	26.1	0.9
C	Female	30.3	1.2
D	Female	30.5	0.7
E	Male	30.6	1.0

....
....
....
[2]

b) **Patient D** is a fitness instructor. Explain why her BMI may be misleading when assessing her risk of developing obesity-related disorders.

....
....
....
[2]

[Total 4 marks]

Section 5 — Health, Disease & the Development of Medicines

Treatments for Cardiovascular Disease

Warm-Up

Use the correct words to fill in the gaps in the passage. Not all of them will be used.

asthma   cystic fibrosis   arteries

heart   lungs   respiration rate   veins   strokes   blood pressure

Cardiovascular disease is a term used to describe diseases of the blood vessels and

.... A high level of cholesterol in the blood and a high

.... can lead to cardiovascular disease by causing fatty

deposits to build up in .... This restricts blood flow,

which can lead to problems such as ....

1. Doctors were assessing the heart of a patient who had recently suffered from a heart attack. They noticed that one of the main arteries supplying the heart muscle was narrowed.

Grade 6-7

a) Give **two** pieces of lifestyle advice the doctors are likely to give to the patient.

1. ....

2. ....

[2]

b) The doctors tell the patient he could have a surgical procedure to reduce the chance of having another heart attack.

   i) Explain how a surgical procedure could improve the patient's condition.

   ....

   ....

   [2]

   ii) If the patient decides to go ahead with surgery, give **two** risks he should be made aware of.

   1. ....

   2. ....

   [2]

c) Give **two** examples of medication that the patient could take to improve his condition. Explain what each medication does.

   1. ....

   ....

   2. ....

   ....

   [4]

   [Total 10 marks]

   Section 5 — Health, Disease & the Development of Medicines

Section 6 — Plant Structures and Their Functions

Photosynthesis

Complete the following passage using words on the right. You do not need to use all the words.

Photosynthesis is carried out by organisms such as green plants

and .... It uses energy transferred by

.... to produce ....

This energy is absorbed by subcellular structures called

....

mitochondria

glucose   algae

fungi   chloroplasts

minerals

fructose

light

1   Photosynthesis is a chemical reaction, which allows
photosynthetic organisms to generate their own food source.   Grade 4-6

a)   Complete the word equation for photosynthesis.

.... + ... → .... + ...

[1]

b)   Photosynthesis is an endothermic reaction. This means that:

☐   **A**   energy is taken in during the reaction.

☐   **B**   energy is transferred to the surroundings during the reaction.

☐   **C**   energy is made during the reaction.

☐   **D**   energy is broken down during the reaction.

[1]

[Total 2 marks]

2   The sugar produced in photosynthesis can be broken
down to transfer energy as part of respiration in a plant.   Grade 6-7

a)   Give **one** other way in which a plant uses the sugar produced by photosynthesis.

....

[1]

b)   Explain why photosynthesis is important for the majority of life on Earth.

....

....

....

....

[3]

[Total 4 marks]

3 *Myriophyllum* is an aquatic plant. A student decided to investigate the effect of light intensity on the rate of photosynthesis in *Myriophyllum*.

The student set up a conical flask containing a solution of sodium hydrogencarbonate next to a lamp. She then took five *Myriophyllum* plants and placed them in the conical flask. Finally, she sealed and attached a gas syringe to the test tube and measured the amount of gas collected from the flask in two hours. She repeated this for four more flasks at different distances from the lamp. Her results are shown in **Figure 1**.

Figure 1

Conical flask	Distance away from light (cm)	Gas collected (cm³)	Rate of gas production (cm³ h⁻¹)
1	0	7.8	3.9
2	10	5.0	2.5
3	20	6.0	3.0
4	30	3.4	1.7
5	40	1.2	X

a) Name the gas collected in the gas syringe.

....

[1]

b) Calculate the rate of gas production in **Conical flask 5**.

X = ... cm³ h⁻¹

[1]

c) i) Using the results in **Figure 1**, describe and explain the effect of the distance from the lamp on the rate of gas production in *Myriophyllum*.

....

....

....

....

[3]

ii) Suggest **one** way in which you could increase your confidence in the answer you gave to part c) i).

....

[1]

d) Explain why it is important that the test tubes are all next to the same lamp.

....

....

[2]

[Total 8 marks]

Section 6 — Plant Structures and Their Functions

Limiting Factors in Photosynthesis

1 The distance of a plant from a light source affects the plant's rate of photosynthesis. Grade 6-7

a) Name the mathematical law that governs the relationship
between light intensity and distance from a light source.

....

[1]

b) A plant is 40 cm away from a light source. The plant is moved so that it is 20 cm away from the
same light source. Describe how the intensity of light reaching the plant will change.

....

[1]

c) Describe how carbon dioxide concentration also affects the rate of photosynthesis.

....

....

[2]

[Total 4 marks]

2 **Figure 1** shows how temperature affects
the rate of photosynthesis in a green plant. Grade 6-7

Figure 1

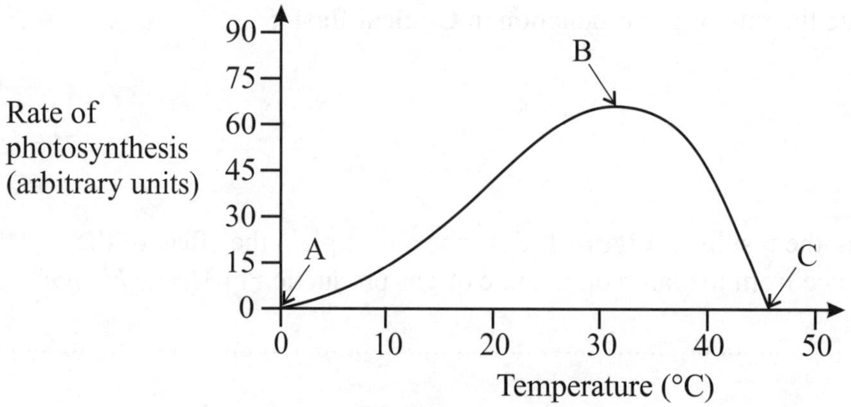

Rate of
photosynthesis
(arbitrary units)

a) Describe and explain the shape of the curve in **Figure 1** between points **A** and **B**.

....

....

....

[2]

b) Describe and explain the shape of the curve between points **B** and **C**.

....

....

....

....

[3]

[Total 5 marks]

Transport in Plants

The diagrams below show two different types of vessel involved in the transport of substances in plants. Label them using the words on the right.

A. ....

B. ....

C. ....

D. Cell wall strengthened by

....

E. ....

F. ....

xylem tube

dead cells

living cells

end wall with pores

phloem tube

lignin

1 Xylem and phloem tubes are important vessels, which run the length of a plant. *(Grade 4-6)*

a) i) Name **one** molecule transported via the phloem.

....
[1]

ii) Name **two** molecules transported via the xylem.

1. .... 2. ....
[2]

b) Transport via the phloem:

☐ **A** requires energy.   ☐ **C** only occurs in the leaves.

☐ **B** is called transpiration.   ☐ **D** only moves substances upwards from the roots.
[1]
[Total 4 marks]

2 *Pythium aphanidermatum* is a pathogen that can infect the roots of a plant, leading to the destruction of many of the root hair cells. *(Grade 7-9)*

a) Explain how *Pythium* infection may disrupt the transpiration stream.

....

....

....
[2]

b) Why might plants infected with *Pythium* show signs of nutrient deficiency?

....

....

....
[2]
[Total 4 marks]

Stomata and Transpiration

1 Stomata are mostly found on the lower surface of leaves. Grade 4-6

a) State the main function of the stomata.

....

[1]

b) Name the cells which control the size of the stomata.

....

[1]

c) Explain how the stomata can affect the movement of water up the plant by transpiration.

....

....

....

....

[3]

[Total 5 marks]

2 A group of students were investigating the effect of air flow on the rate of transpiration. They set up their apparatus as shown in **Figure 1**. Grade 6-7

Figure 1

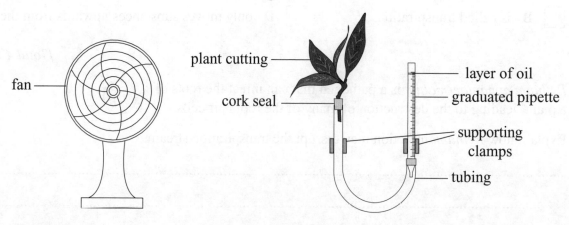

a) The tubing and graduated pipette were filled with water.
Suggest why a layer of oil was added to the surface of the water in the pipette.

....

[1]

The students recorded the change in the volume of water in the pipette over 30 minutes, in normal conditions. They repeated this five times. They then carried out these steps with the fan turned on to simulate windy conditions. **Figure 2** on the next page shows their results.

Section 6 — Plant Structures and Their Functions

Figure 2

	Repeat	1	2	3	4	5	Mean
Water uptake in 30 minutes (cm³)	Still Air	1.2	1.2	1.0	0.8	1.1	1.1
	Moving Air	2.0	1.8	2.3	1.9	1.7	1.9

b) Draw a bar chart to show the mean water uptake for still air and moving air.

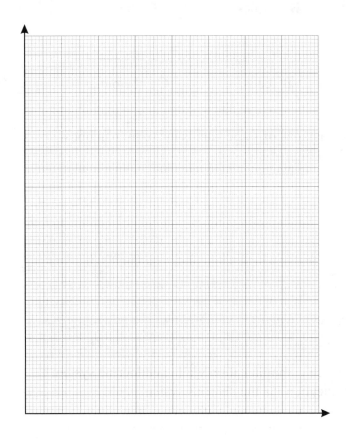

[2]

c) Describe the relationship between air flow around the plant and transpiration rate.

....

[1]

d) Explain the effect of air flow on the rate of transpiration.

....

....

....

[2]

e) Assuming that the mean rate of water uptake is equal to the mean rate of transpiration, calculate the rate of transpiration for the plant in moving air. Give your answer in cm³ hour⁻¹.

.... cm³ hour⁻¹

[2]

[Total 8 marks]

Section 6 — Plant Structures and Their Functions

Hormones

1   The endocrine system is a collection of glands in the body that secrete hormones.   `Grade 4-6`

a) Endocrine glands secrete hormones directly into

☐ **A** cells   ☐ **B** tissues   ☐ **C** blood   ☐ **D** organs

[1]

b) Hormones are

☐ **A** tissues   ☐ **B** cells   ☐ **C** chemicals   ☐ **D** enzymes

[1]

c) **Figure 1** shows the positions of some glands in the human body. Name glands A to E in **Figure 1**.

Figure 1

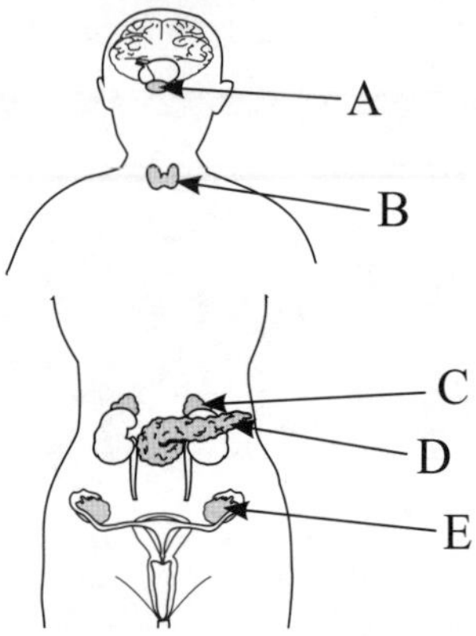

A ....

B ....

C ....

D ....

E ....

[5]

d) State **two** ways in which communication via the endocrine system differs from communication via the nervous system.

1. ....

2. ....

[2]

[Total 9 marks]

2   Males produce a greater amount of testosterone than females. One of the consequences of this, is that males' bones are more dense than females' bones.   `Grade 6-7`

a) Based on the information above, name **one** of testosterone's target organs.

....

[1]

b) A possible treatment for prostate cancer is to have the testes removed.
    Explain why men who have had their testes removed are more at risk of developing brittle bones.

....

....

....

[2]

[Total 3 marks]

Adrenaline and Thyroxine

The graph below shows the change in the level of a hormone controlled by a negative feedback response over time.
Use the words on the right to fill in the labels on the graph.

normal   increase in   stimulated
inhibited   decrease in

.... level of hormone detected

release of hormone ....

.... level of hormone

.... level of hormone detected

Blood hormone level

Time

release of hormone ....

---

1 The hormone adrenaline is produced in times of fear or stress. *(Grade 4-6)*

a) Name the glands that release adrenaline.

....

[1]

b) Give **one** effect that adrenaline has on the body.

....

[1]

c) Name the response that adrenaline prepares the body for.

....

[1]

[Total 3 marks]

---

2 Thyroxine is a hormone. *(Grade 6-7)*

a) State **one** role of thyroxine in the body.

....

[1]

b) Explain how the body prevents the level of thyroxine in the blood from getting too high.

....

....

....

....

[3]

[Total 4 marks]

      Section 7 — Animal Coordination, Control and Homeostasis

The Menstrual Cycle

1 Oestrogen is a hormone involved in the menstrual cycle. **(Grade 4-6)**

a) Name the gland that releases oestrogen.

....

[1]

b) Name the hormone that stimulates oestrogen production.

....

[1]

c) Describe how oestrogen effects the uterus lining.

....

[1]

[Total 3 marks]

2 **Figure 1** shows how levels of four different hormones change during the menstrual cycle. **(Grade 6-7)**

Figure 1

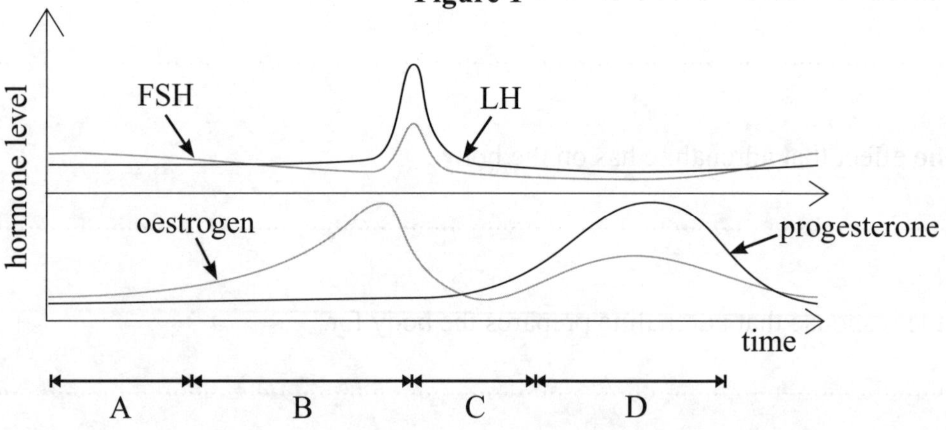

a) During which time period marked on **Figure 1** does menstruation occur?

☐ **A**   ☐ **B**   ☐ **C**   ☐ **D**

[1]

b) Add an arrow (↑) to the *x*-axis on **Figure 1**, to show the time at which ovulation occurs.

[1]

c) Before ovulation can occur, a follicle must mature. Name the hormone that causes this.

....

[1]

d) Explain how the uterus lining is maintained in the days after ovulation.

....

....

....

[3]

[Total 6 marks]

Section 7 — Animal Coordination, Control and Homeostasis

Controlling Fertility

1 Many people choose barrier methods of contraception to prevent pregnancy. [Grade 4-6]

a) Give **one** example of a barrier method of contraception.

....

[1]

b) Describe how barrier methods of contraception work.

....

[1]

c) Give **two** advantages of barrier methods of contraception over hormonal methods of contraception.

1. ....

2. ....

[2]

[Total 4 marks]

2 Polycystic ovarian syndrome (PCOS) is a common cause of infertility in women. Women with the disorder don't ovulate regularly. [Grade 6-7]

a) Explain why a woman with PCOS may find it hard to get pregnant.

....

....

....

[1]

b) Explain how clomifene therapy could help a woman with PCOS become pregnant.

....

....

....

[3]

c) If clomifene therapy doesn't help the woman to become pregnant, multiple eggs could be collected from the woman's ovaries and then fertilised using the man's sperm. One or two of the resulting embryos could then be transferred to the woman's uterus.

i) State the name given to this process.

....

[1]

ii) Explain why hormones are given to the woman at the beginning of this process.

....

[1]

[Total 6 marks]

Section 7 — Animal Coordination, Control and Homeostasis

3 Some methods of hormonal contraception use oestrogen to help prevent pregnancy. **(Grade 6-7)**

a) Explain how oestrogen in hormonal contraceptives helps to prevent pregnancy.

....

....

[2]

b) Many people prefer to use hormonal methods of contraception rather than barrier methods.
Give **two** advantages of hormonal methods of contraception over barrier methods of contraception.

1. ....

2. ....

[2]

[Total 4 marks]

4 The mini pill is a method of oral contraception. It contains progesterone and needs to be taken around the same time every day. **(Grade 6-7)**

a) Many women who take the mini pill don't ovulate.

i) Explain how taking the mini pill may prevent ovulation.

....

....

....

[3]

ii) It's not only the effect on ovulation that makes the mini pill an effective contraceptive.
Explain **one** other way in which the mini pill can prevent pregnancy.

....

....

[2]

b) Although the mini pill is an effective method of contraceptive, a couple may still be advised to
use a condom during intercourse. Suggest why.

....

[1]

c) The contraceptive implant is a small tube, which is inserted beneath the skin of the arm and
continuously releases progesterone. It is effective for three years. Suggest **one** reason why a
woman may choose to have a contraceptive implant rather than using the mini pill.

....

[1]

[Total 7 marks]

Exam Tip

Knowing the roles of the hormones that control the menstrual cycle is really important when it comes to understanding
how these hormones are used to control fertility. So make sure you've got it all sorted out in your head.

Section 7 — Animal Coordination, Control and Homeostasis

Homeostasis — Control of Blood Glucose

1 Homeostasis involves the regulation of blood glucose concentration. *Grade 4-6*

a) Explain what is meant by the term 'homeostasis'.

....

[1]

b) Name the gland in the body that monitors and controls blood glucose concentration.

....

[1]

[Total 2 marks]

2 In an experiment, the blood glucose concentration of a person was recorded at regular intervals in a 90 minute time period. Fifteen minutes into the experiment, a glucose drink was given. **Figure 1** shows the results of the experiment. *Grade 7-9*

Figure 1

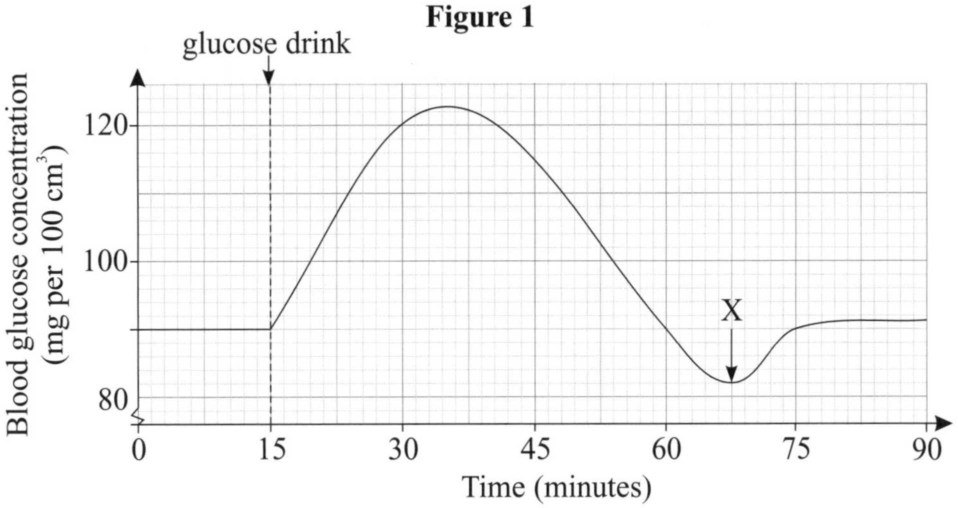

glucose drink

Blood glucose concentration (mg per 100 cm³)

120

100

80

0   15   30   45   60   75   90

Time (minutes)

X

a) Explain what is happening to the blood glucose concentration between 15 and 60 minutes.

....

....

....

[3]

b) i) Name the hormone being released by the pancreas at point **X** on the graph.

....

[1]

ii) Explain how the hormone released at point **X** affects the blood glucose concentration.

....

....

....

[3]

[Total 7 marks]

     Section 7 — Animal Coordination, Control and Homeostasis

Diabetes

1   A patient visits her health centre because she is concerned
she is at risk of developing type 2 diabetes.   **Grade 6-7**

   a)   i)   Firstly, a nurse measures the patient's mass and height. Explain why he does this.

....

....

               [2]

     ii) Next the nurse uses his tape measure to take **two** other measurements of the patient's body.
Suggest which two measurements he takes. Explain your answer.

....

....

....

               [3]

   b)   Give **two** treatments that the patient's doctor might recommend if
the patient was later diagnosed with type 2 diabetes.

     1. ....

     2. ....

               [2]

   c)   Describe the underlying causes of type 2 diabetes.

....

....

               [2]

               [Total 9 marks]

2   In rare cases, type 1 diabetes may be treated with a pancreas transplant.   **Grade 7-9**

   a)   i)   Explain why a pancreas transplant could be used to treat a person with type 1 diabetes.

....

....

               [2]

     ii) Suggest **one** reason why a pancreas transplant is rarely used to treat type 1 diabetes.

....

....

               [1]

   b)   State the main form of treatment for type 1 diabetes.

....

               [1]

               [Total 5 marks]

Exchange of Materials

Warm-Up

Complete the calculations below to work out the
surface area and volume of the shape on the right.

Surface area: (8 mm × .... mm) × 2
+ (8 mm × .... mm) × 4
= .... mm²

Volume: .... mm × .... mm × .... mm
= .... mm³

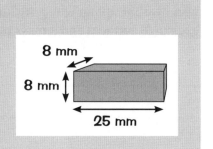

8 mm
8 mm
25 mm

1   In order to survive, mammals, like all organisms,
must exchange substances with their environment.

a) Give **two** substances that a mammal must transport into its body in order to survive.

....

[2]

b) Give **two** substances that a mammal must get rid of in order to survive.

....

[2]

[Total 4 marks]

2   A student was investigating the effect of size on the uptake of substances by diffusion.
He cut different sized cubes of agar containing universal indicator and placed them
in beakers of acid. He timed how long it took for the acid to diffuse through to the
centre of each cube (and so change the colour of the agar).

Figure 1 shows the relationship between the surface area and volume of the agar cubes.

Figure 1

Cube size (cm)	Surface area (cm²)	Volume (cm³)	Simple ratio
2 × 2 × 2	24	8	3:1
3 × 3 × 3	**X**	**Y**	2:1
5 × 5 × 5	150	125	**Z** : 1

a) Calculate the values of X, Y and Z in **Figure 1**.

X = ... cm²

Y = ... cm³

Z = ...

[3]

b) Explain which cube would take the longest to change colour.

....

....

[1]

[Total 4 marks]

Specialised Exchange Surfaces — the Alveoli

1 Sticklebacks are a type of freshwater fish. They have specialised exchange surfaces, called gills, and a mass transport system powered by a heart. Explain why a stickleback needs both specialised exchange surfaces and a mass transport system in order to survive.

Grade **6-7**

....

....

....

....

....

....

[Total 4 marks]

2 **Figure 1** shows an alveolus in the lungs. Grade **6-7**

Figure 1

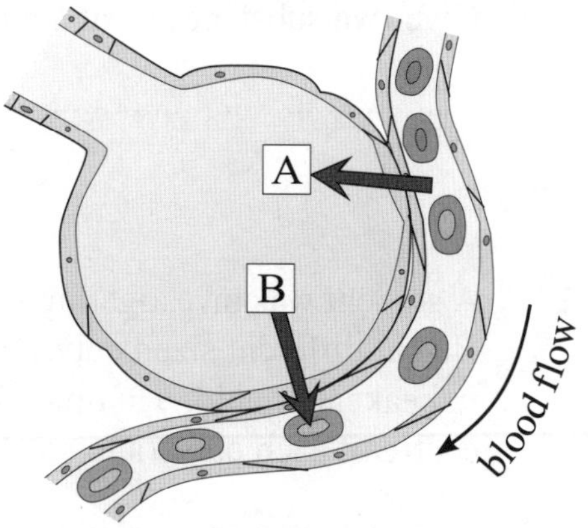

a) Name the gases A and B.

A ....

B ....

[2]

b) Gases A and B move down their concentration gradients by diffusion. Explain how the blood flow at an alveolus ensures there is a high rate of diffusion for both gases following the inhalation of air.

A

B

blood flow

....

....

....

....

[3]

c) Other than a good blood supply, explain **two** ways in which alveoli in the lungs are adapted for gas exchange.

1. ....

....

2. ....

....

[4]

[Total 9 marks]

Section 8 — Exchange and Transport in Animals

Circulatory System — Blood

1 The blood is composed of different components, each of which has a different function. (Grade 4-6)

a) Which of the following are types of white blood cell?

☐ **A** phagoctytes and lysozymes ☐ **C** phagoctytes and erythrocytes

☐ **B** phagoctytes and lymphocytes ☐ **D** erythrocytes and lymphocytes

[1]

b) Name the component of the blood that produces antibodies.

....

[1]

c) Describe the structure and function of blood plasma.

....

....

[2]

[Total 4 marks]

2 The components of blood can be separated by spinning them at high speed. **Figure 1** shows a tube of blood that has been separated in this way. (Grade 6-7)

Figure 1

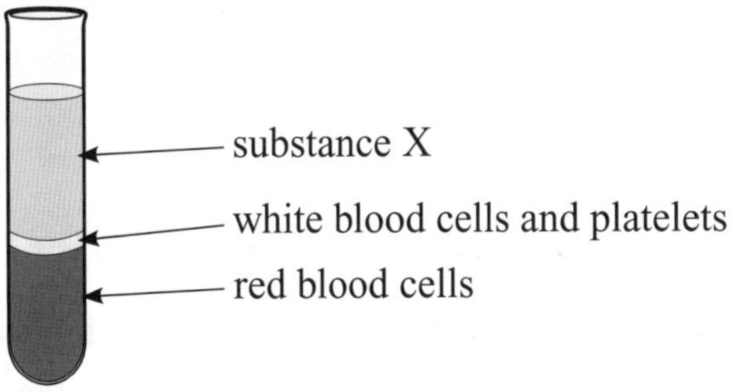

— substance X

— white blood cells and platelets

— red blood cells

a) Identify the substance labelled X in **Figure 1**.

....

[1]

b) Red blood cells have a biconcave shape. Explain how this allows them to fulfil their function.

....

....

[2]

c) A scientist analysing the blood sample found that it had a lower than normal concentration of platelets. Explain one problem the patient may experience due to this.

....

....

....

[2]

[Total 5 marks]

Circulatory System — Blood Vessels

Label each of the following diagrams to indicate whether they represent a capillary, artery or vein.

Diagrams not to scale.

A. ....   B. ....   C. ....

1   Blood vessels can be identified by their structure or location in the body.   **Grade 4-6**

a) i) Name the type of blood vessel that has valves.

   ....

   [1]

   ii) Describe the purpose of valves in a blood vessel.

   ....

   [1]

b) Name the type of blood vessel that joins up to form veins.

   ....

   [1]

   [Total 3 marks]

2   Different types of blood vessel perform different functions.   **Grade 6-7**

a) Veins and arteries both have a layer of smooth muscle within their walls. Which of these types of blood vessel has a thicker layer of muscle? Explain your answer with reference to their functions.

   ....

   ....

   ....

   ....

   [4]

b) Capillaries are very narrow. Explain how this allows them to fulfil their function.

   ....

   ....

   [2]

   [Total 6 marks]

Target AO3

3 An investigation was carried out into the elasticity of arteries and veins.

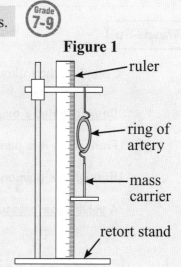

Figure 1

The experiment was set up as shown in **Figure 1**.
The method used was as follows:

1. Cut a ring of tissue from an artery and attach it to the hook.
2. Attach a mass carrier to the bottom of the ring.
3. Measure the length of the ring with the mass carrier attached.
4. Add a 10 g mass to the mass carrier.
5. Measure the length of the ring with the mass attached,
    and then again with the mass removed.
6. Repeat steps 4 and 5 with a 20 g mass, 30 g mass, etc.
7. Repeat the experiment using a ring of vein of the same width.

The percentage change between the original length of the ring with
just the mass carrier attached and its length after each mass was removed
was calculated for each mass. The results are plotted in **Figure 2**.

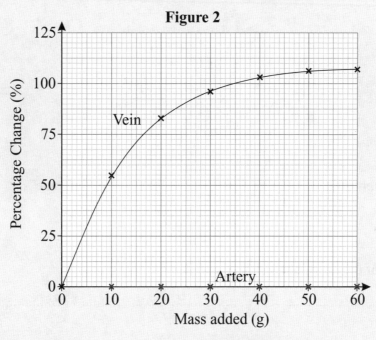

a) Describe what the graph shows for each type of blood vessel.

....

....

....

....

....

....

[4]

b) Suggest **one** safety precaution that should be carried out for this experiment.

....

[1]

[Total 5 marks]

Section 8 — Exchange and Transport in Animals

Circulatory System — Heart

Complete the following passage by circling the correct underlined words or phrases.

Deoxygenated / oxygenated blood enters the right atrium through the vena cava / aorta.

From there it is pumped into the right ventricle / pulmonary vein. Then it is pumped up

through the pulmonary vein / artery towards the lungs / rest of the body.

A valve / low pressure prevents the blood from flowing back into the right atrium.

1   The heart pumps blood around the body. **Figure 1** shows a diagram of the heart.

Figure 1

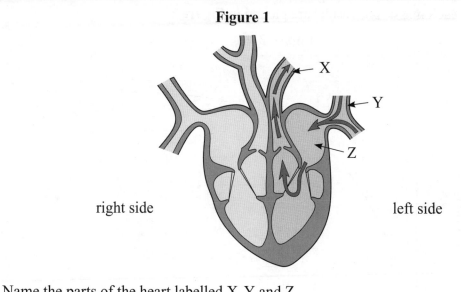

right side   left side

a)   Name the parts of the heart labelled X, Y and Z.

X: ....   Y: ....   Z: ....
[3]

b)   Draw arrows on **Figure 1** to show the direction of blood flow through the right side of the heart.
[1]
[Total 4 marks]

2   The walls of the chambers of the heart are adapted for their functions.

Explain how and why the walls of the ventricles differ in thickness.

....

....

....

....

....
[Total 3 marks]

3 A scientist was investigating the effect of height on cardiac output in athletes. He predicted that taller athletes would have a greater cardiac output than shorter athletes, as taller athletes are likely to have larger hearts. Before he measured their heights, the scientist measured the stroke volume and resting heart rate of each athlete, and calculated their cardiac output. His results for two of the athletes are shown in **Figure 2**.

Grade
7-9

Figure 2

Athlete	1	2
Heart rate (bpm)	57	Y
Stroke volume (cm³)	84	65
Cardiac output (cm³ min⁻¹)	X	4095

a) Explain what is meant by the term 'stroke volume'.

....

....

[1]

b) Calculate the cardiac output for Athlete **1**.

Cardiac output = ... cm³ min⁻¹
[2]

c) Calculate the heart rate for Athlete **2**.

Heart rate = ... bpm
[2]

d) Suggest an explanation as to why the scientist predicted that a larger heart would result in a greater cardiac output.

....

....

....

....

....

[3]

e) The scientist asks the athletes to cycle for 10 minutes to increase their heart rate. Explain how exercise will affect the athletes' cardiac output.

....

[1]

[Total 9 marks]

Exam Tip

The structure of the heart and the way blood flows through it can be pretty tricky to get your head around. In the exam you might find it helpful to sketch a quick diagram of the heart and the way blood flows through it to help you answer questions on it. Make sure you really know how to calculate heart rate, stroke volume and cardiac output too.

Respiration

1   Respiration is an exothermic reaction. It can occur either aerobically or anaerobically.   **Grade 6-7**

   a) What does it mean if a reaction is exothermic?

   ☐ **A** It releases energy to the environment.

   ☐ **B** It produces carbon dioxide.

   ☐ **C** It takes in energy from the environment.

   ☐ **D** It is used in metabolism.

   [1]

   b) Explain why respiration reactions are essential for the life of an organism.

   ....

   ....

   [2]

   c) i) Name a substance that is broken down in both aerobic and anaerobic respiration.

   ....

   [1]

   ii) Name a substance that is broken down in aerobic respiration but not in anaerobic respiration.

   ....

   [1]

   iii) Name the products of aerobic respiration.

   ....

   [2]

   d) Give **one** reason why it may be more beneficial for the body to use aerobic respiration to transfer energy most of the time, rather than using anaerobic respiration.

   ....

   ....

   [1]

   e) Give **one** example of a situation in which a person may begin to respire anaerobically.

   ....

   [1]

   f) Describe how the products of anaerobic respiration differ between plants and animals.

   ....

   ....

   ....

   [3]

   [Total 12 marks]

2 The air that a person inhales has a different composition from the air that they exhale. **Figure 1** shows the percentages of different gases in the inhaled air and in the exhaled air.

a) Explain the difference in the values for the percentage of oxygen in inhaled and exhaled air.

Figure 1

	Inhaled air (%)	Exhaled air (%)
Nitrogen	78	78
Oxygen	21	16
Carbon dioxide		
Other gases	0.9	0.9

....

....

....

....

[1]

b) Explain how the percentage of carbon dioxide would differ between inhaled and exhaled air.

....

....

[2]

[Total 3 marks]

3 A scientist was measuring the effects of exercise on respiration. He asked a male volunteer to jog for 10 minutes on a treadmill. The speed of the treadmill was increased over the course of the 10 minutes, so that he was gradually working harder, until at the end he felt unable to do any more exercise. **Figure 2** shows the oxygen consumption (the amount of oxygen used by the body per minute) of the man during the exercise.

Figure 2

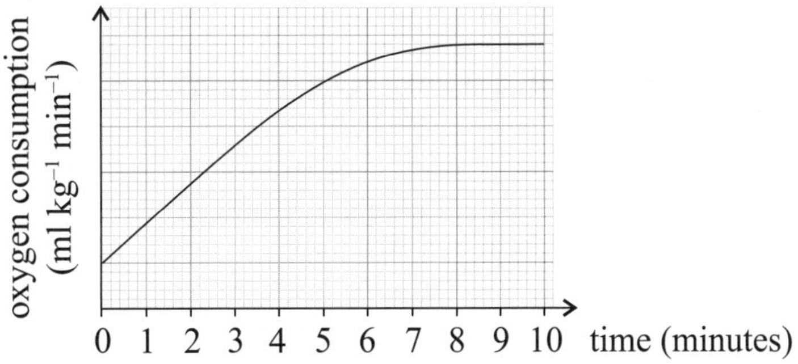

a) Describe how oxygen consumption changed during the exercise.

....

....

[2]

b) In the final two minutes of the exercise, the man was respiring anaerobically. Explain how the scientist may know this by looking at the graph in **Figure 2**.

....

....

....

....

[2]

[Total 4 marks]

Section 8 — Exchange and Transport in Animals

Investigating Respiration

1   An experiment was set up using two sealed beakers, each with a carbon dioxide monitor attached. The set up is shown in **Figure 1**.

Figure 1

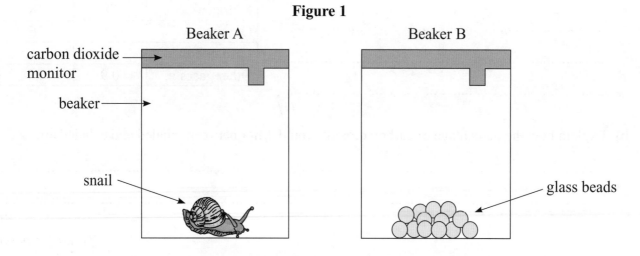

The percentage (%) of carbon dioxide in the air in both beakers was measured at the start of the experiment and again after 2 hours. The results are shown in **Figure 2**.

Figure 2

Time	% carbon dioxide in the air	
(hours)	Beaker A	Beaker B
0	0.04	0.04
2	0.10	0.04

a) Suggest **one** ethical consideration that must be taken into account during this experiment.

....

[1]

b) Explain the purpose of the glass beads in Beaker B.

....

....

[2]

c) Explain the results for Beaker A.

....

....

[1]

d) Explain how the level of oxygen in Beaker A would have changed during the experiment.

....

....

[2]

[Total 6 marks]

Target AO3

2   A student is investigating respiration in germinating peas. She predicts that germinating peas will respire, and so will release energy as heat.

The student sets up her experiment as shown in **Figure 3**.

Figure 3

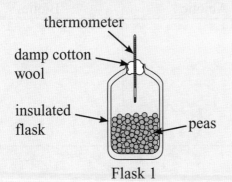

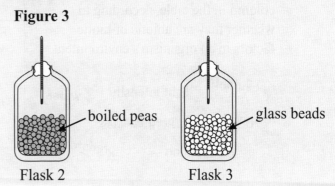

The student records the temperature of each flask at the beginning of the experiment (day 0), then every day for three days.

Figure 4 shows her results.

Figure 4

Day	Temperature (°C)		
	Flask 1	Flask 2	Flask 3
Day 0	20	20	20
Day 1	23	20	20
Day 2	25	21	20
Day 3	28	22	20

a)   Give **two** variables that the student needed to control to make the experiment a fair test.

....

....

[2]

b)   The student's results could have been affected by random error.
Suggest **one** way that the student could reduce the effect of any random error on her results.

....

....

[1]

c)   Flasks 2 and 3 are control experiments. Explain why the student included both of these controls.

....

....

....

[2]

d)   The student hypothesises that the temperature of flask 2 increased slightly over the course of the experiment due to the presence of respiring microorganisms on the surface of the peas.
Suggest how the student could modify her method in order to test this hypothesis.

....

....

[1]

[Total 6 marks]

Section 8 — Exchange and Transport in Animals

Ecosystems & Interactions Between Organisms

Warm-Up

Put the words below into the correct column in the table, according to whether they are abiotic or biotic factors in an organism's environment.

Abiotic	Biotic

pollutants   light intensity   water

temperature   prey species

competition   predators

1   There are different levels of organisation within a habitat.   (Grade 4-6)

a) A community is

☐ **A** all the organisms of one species living in a habitat.

☐ **B** all the organisms of different species living in a habitat.

☐ **C** all the organisms of one population living in a habitat.

☐ **D** all of the abiotic and biotic factors in an habitat.

[1]

b) Explain what is meant by the term 'ecosystem'.

....

[1]

[Total 2 marks]

2   Grasses make their own food by photosynthesis. In grassland communities, the grass leaves provide insects with shelter, a place to breed and a source of food. Visiting birds feed on insects.   (Grade 6-7)

a) Explain what you would expect to happen to the birds visiting the grassland if a new insect predator entered the ecosystem.

....

....

[2]

b) The number of birds visiting the grassland decreases. What would you eventually expect to happen to the number of grass plants? Explain your answer.

....

....

....

[3]

[Total 5 marks]

3 A cuckoo is a type of bird that lays its eggs in the nest of another bird. When the cuckoo egg hatches, the cuckoo chick kills some of the offspring of the host and the host bird raises the cuckoo chick as if it was its own.

Grade 6-7

a) Name the type of interaction between a cuckoo chick and its host. Explain your answer.

....

....

[2]

b) Ants often live in the hollow thorns on a certain species of tree. The ants living in the trees feed on the trees' nectar. When herbivores try to graze on the trees, the ants bite them. Some ant species have also been shown to protect the trees from harmful bacteria.

Which of the following statements best describes the relationship between the ants and the trees?

☐ **A** The ants are parasites because they depend entirely on the trees to survive.

☐ **B** The relationship is mutualistic because both the ants and the trees benefit from it.

☐ **C** The relationship is parasitic because the host is harmed and doesn't benefit from it.

☐ **D** The relationship is mutualistic because the trees depend on the ants to survive.

[1]

[Total 3 marks]

4 Prickly acacia is a tree species native to Africa, and parts of Asia. It was introduced to Australia many years ago. It has invaded large areas of land in the warmer parts of the country. The trees grow best in areas with a high average temperature and where there is plenty of water, such as along rivers or on flood plains where there is seasonal flooding.

Grade 6-7

a) Australia experienced particularly high rainfall in the 1950s and 1970s. Explain how the prickly acacia population in Australia may have changed during these periods.

....

....

[2]

b) Global temperature is thought to be increasing. What may happen to the distribution of prickly acacia in Australia over the next few decades? Explain your answer.

....

....

....

[2]

c) When prickly acacia invade an area it can negatively impact the populations of various grasses in that area. Explain why this might be the case.

....

....

[2]

[Total 6 marks]

Section 9 — Ecosystems and Material Cycles

Investigating Ecosystems

1   A group of students used a quadrat with an area of 0.5 m² to investigate the
number of buttercups growing in a field. They counted the number of buttercups
in the quadrat in ten randomly selected places. **Figure 1** shows their results.

Figure 1

Quadrat Number	Number of buttercups
1	15
2	13
3	16
4	23
5	26
6	23
7	13
8	12
9	16
10	13

a) i) Explain why it is important that the quadrats were randomly placed in the field.

    ....
    [1]

    ii) Describe a method that could have been used to randomly place the quadrats.

    ....
    [1]

b) What is the modal number of buttercups in a quadrat in **Figure 1**?

    .... buttercups
    [1]

c) What is the median number of buttercups in **Figure 1**?

    .... buttercups
    [1]

d) Calculate the mean number of buttercups per 0.5 m² quadrat.

    .... buttercups per 0.5 m²
    [1]

e) The total area of the field was 1750 m².
    Estimate the number of buttercups in the whole of the field.

    .... buttercups
    [2]

    [Total 7 marks]

PRACTICAL

2 A belt transect was carried out from the edge of a small pond, across a grassy field and into a woodland. The distributions of four species of plant were recorded along the transect, along with the soil moisture and light levels. **Figure 2** shows the results.

Grade 6-7

Figure 2

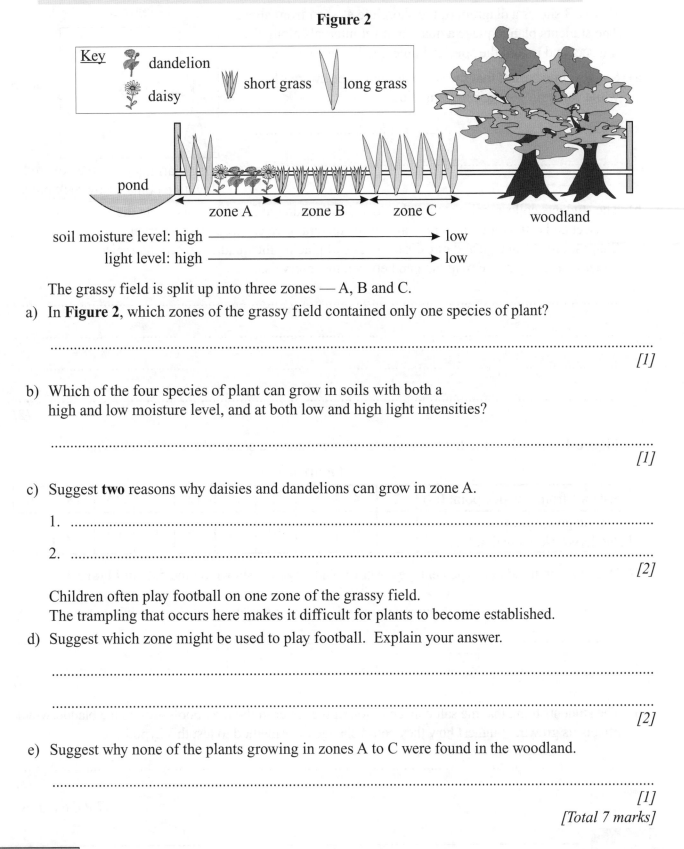

The grassy field is split up into three zones — A, B and C.

a) In **Figure 2**, which zones of the grassy field contained only one species of plant?

....

[1]

b) Which of the four species of plant can grow in soils with both a high and low moisture level, and at both low and high light intensities?

....

[1]

c) Suggest **two** reasons why daisies and dandelions can grow in zone A.

1. ....

2. ....

[2]

Children often play football on one zone of the grassy field.
The trampling that occurs here makes it difficult for plants to become established.

d) Suggest which zone might be used to play football. Explain your answer.

....

....

[2]

e) Suggest why none of the plants growing in zones A to C were found in the woodland.

....

[1]

[Total 7 marks]

Exam Tip

Be careful with any calculations you're asked to make — the maths on the previous page isn't hard, but you need to make sure you don't mix up the mean, mode and median.

Section 9 — Ecosystems and Material Cycles

3   A group of students are using a transect to investigate the distribution of organisms across a rocky shore.

Grade 6-7

PRACTICAL

Figure 3 shows a diagram of the shoreline as seen from above. The students plan to place a quadrat at set intervals along the transect and record the species in the quadrat at each point.

Figure 3

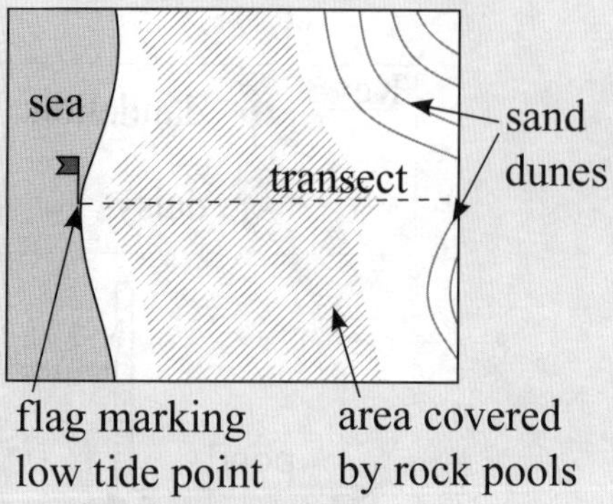

sea

transect

sand dunes

flag marking low tide point

area covered by rock pools

a) Suggest **one** hazard that the students should be aware of while carrying out their investigation.

....

....
[1]

b) The students collect their data by placing a 1 m² quadrat at 2 m intervals along the transect and estimating the percentage of the quadrat area covered by each organism. Suggest **one** advantage and **one** disadvantage of placing the quadrat at 2 m intervals rather than every metre, with no gap between the intervals.

....

....

....

....
[2]

Figure 4 shows the data that the students collected about a seaweed called bladderwrack.

Figure 4

Distance from low tide point (m)	2	4	6	8	10	12	14	16	18	20
Percentage cover of bladderwrack in quadrat (%)	0	0	2	10	15	25	40	65	80	75

c) Describe the trend in the percentage cover of bladderwrack shown by the data in **Figure 4**.

....

....

....
[2]

d) The students think that the salt concentration of the water in the rock pools around the bladderwrack affects its growth. Suggest how they could change their method to test this hypothesis.

....
[1]

[Total 6 marks]

Exam Tip

If you have time at the end of the exam, have a quick peep back at your answers to make sure that everything you've written is clear and that you've fully answered each question. For example, if you were asked to give advantages and disadvantages for a particular topic, make sure you've written an answer that actually covers both of them.

Human Impacts on Biodiversity

1 Possums are a type of marsupial mammal native to Australia. In the 1800s they were introduced by humans into New Zealand for the fur trade.

Grade **6-7**

Suggest **two** reasons why possums may have negatively affected species native to New Zealand.

1. ....

....

2. ....

....

[Total 2 marks]

2 Human interactions with ecosystems can change the abiotic conditions, reducing biodiversity.

a)* Explain how the application of fertilisers on farmland may reduce the biodiversity of nearby water sources.

Grade **7-9**

....

....

....

....

....

....

....

....

....

[6]

b) Fish can be farmed in nets in the ocean. However, this method of fish farming can cause similar problems to excess fertilisers in surrounding waters. Suggest an explanation for this.

....

....

[2]

c) Explain **two** other potential impacts of open water fish farms on the biodiversity of their surrounding environment.

1. ....

....

2. ....

....

[2]

[Total 10 marks]

Section 9 — Ecosystems and Material Cycles

Conservation and Biodiversity

1 Conservation efforts often aim to protect a single endangered species, e.g. the panda.

Grade 6-7

a) Explain **one** reason why efforts to protect one species may help to protect many others as well.

....

....

....

[2]

b) Suggest **one** reason why the protection of a species may benefit the economy of a country.

....

....

[1]

[Total 3 marks]

2* Human activity has reduced the forest cover in Ethiopia significantly. Land that used to be covered by trees is now more exposed to rainfall in the rainy season, leading to increased soil loss through erosion, and heat from the Sun during the dry season, leading to drought. Reforestation programmes employ local people to plant trees over large areas of land.

Grade 7-9

Discuss why reforestation may be beneficial for Ethiopia. Include details about the potential benefits for biodiversity, local farmers and Ethiopian society.

....

....

....

....

....

....

....

....

....

....

....

[Total 6 marks]

Section 9 — Ecosystems and Material Cycles

The Carbon Cycle

1   **Figure 1** shows an unfinished diagram of the carbon cycle.

Figure 1

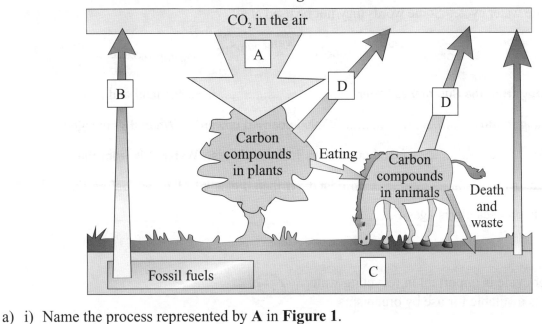

a) i) Name the process represented by **A** in **Figure 1**.

....

[1]

ii) Describe the importance of process **A** for an ecosystem.

....

....

[1]

b) Name the process represented by **B** in **Figure 1**.

....

[1]

c) Process **C** in **Figure 1** is decay. Describe the importance of decay in the carbon cycle.

....

....

[2]

d) Give **one** biotic and **one** abiotic component of the ecosystem represented in **Figure 1**.

Biotic: ....

Abiotic: ....

[2]

[Total 7 marks]

Exam Tip

In the exam you could be tested on any part of the carbon cycle, so make sure you know the whole of it and not just bits of it. Try sketching the whole cycle out and make sure you can link each bit together. Don't have your arrows going the wrong way round, and make sure you understand why the carbon is moving around, e.g. because of respiration. Sorted.

Section 9 — Ecosystems and Material Cycles

The Water Cycle

Choose from the words below to complete the sentences
about the water cycle. Some words may not be used at all.

precipitation   evaporate   warms   cools   water vapour   carbon dioxide   condense

Energy from the Sun makes water .... from the land and sea,

turning it into .... This is carried upwards. When it gets higher

up it .... and condenses to form clouds. Water falls from the

clouds as .... onto land. It then drains into the sea, before the

whole process starts again.

1 The water cycle is important in recycling water
so that it is available for use by organisms.

Grade
4-6

a) Potable water is:

☐ **A** sea water.

☐ **B** drinking water.

☐ **C** contaminated water.

☐ **D** evaporated water.

[1]

b) Explain why sea water is not suitable for drinking by humans.

....

[1]

[Total 2 marks]

2 Somalia is a country on the eastern coast of Africa.
In 2011, a lack of rainfall in Somalia led to a severe drought.

Grade
7-9

Describe and explain **one** method of desalination which may
have been used in Somalia to provide water suitable for drinking.

....

....

....

....

....

....

[Total 4 marks]

☹ ☐   ☺ ☐   ☺ ☐

The Nitrogen Cycle

1   Nitrogen makes up roughly 78% of the gases in the atmosphere. Carbon dioxide makes up only 0.04%. Plants need to absorb both gases in order to survive and grow.

Grade 4-6

a) Give **one** reason why plants need nitrogen in order to grow.

....

[1]

b) Plants absorb carbon dioxide from the air. Which of the following sentences (**A-D**) describes why plants must rely on microorganisms in order to absorb nitrogen?

☐   **A**   The nitrogen in the atmosphere is too dense.

☐   **B**   The nitrogen in the atmosphere is too unreactive.

☐   **C**   Plants only need nitrogen in their roots.

☐   **D**   The nitrogen in the atmosphere is too far away from the plants' leaves.

[1]

[Total 2 marks]

2   **Figure 1** shows a simplified diagram of the nitrogen cycle.

Grade 4-6

Figure 1

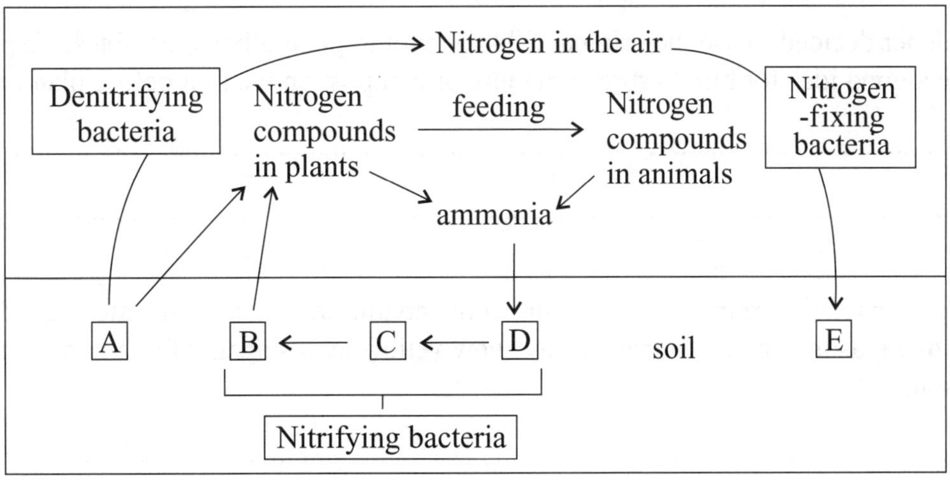

a) All of the letters on **Figure 1** represent a type of mineral ion.
List **all** of the letters on **Figure 1** which represent:

i) nitrites

....

ii) ammonium ions

....

iii) nitrates

....

[5]

Section 9 — Ecosystems and Material Cycles

b) Lightning can cause a reaction between nitrogen and oxygen in the air to produce nitrates. What type of reaction is this?

☐ **A** nitrification ☐ **B** denitrification ☐ **C** decomposition ☐ **D** nitrogen fixation

[1]

c) Describe the role of decomposers in the nitrogen cycle.

....

....

[2]

[Total 8 marks]

3 Yellow leaves are a common symptom of nitrogen deficiency in plants. A gardener noticed that some of his cabbages were showing yellow leaves. He then decided to replant his cabbages in a plot in which he had previously grown pea plants. Peas are a type of legume. After replanting, the cabbages' growth improved and their leaves became less yellow.

Grade
7-9

a) Explain why the cabbages' leaves became less yellow after replanting.

....

....

....

....

[3]

b) The gardener decided to use the original cabbage plot to plant other vegetables. Explain why it might be a good idea for him to spread manure or compost on the plot before planting anything.

....

....

[1]

c) Denitrifying bacteria are most active in anaerobic conditions, such as in waterlogged soils. Explain **one** reason why the cabbages may show yellow leaves again after a particularly wet season.

....

....

....

....

[3]

[Total 7 marks]

Exam Tip

The nitrogen cycle is a bit more complicated than either the water cycle or the carbon cycle, and a lot of the names for the different processes sound really quite similar. Before you do anything else, make sure you get the differences between nitrification, nitrogen fixation, decomposition and denitrification sorted in your head. Drawing out the cycle always helps.

Section 9 — Ecosystems and Material Cycles

Chemical Equations

1 Hydrogen gas is used as a reactant in the Haber Process. It can be made using the following reaction.

$$CH_4 + H_2O \rightarrow CO + 3H_2$$

Which of the following word equations correctly describes this reaction? Tick **one** box.

☐ **A** methane + water → carbon dioxide + hydrogen

☐ **B** ethane + water → carbon dioxide + hydrogen

☐ **C** methane + water → carbon monoxide + hydrogen

☐ **D** methane + water → carbon + oxygen + hydrogen

[Total 1 mark]

2 Calcium carbonate chips were reacted with nitric acid at room temperature. The products of the reaction were water, a gas and a salt solution.

Complete the reaction equation by adding state symbols to describe the reaction.

$$CaCO_3(\ldots\ldots) + 2HNO_3(\ldots\ldots) \rightarrow Ca(NO_3)_2(\ldots\ldots) + H_2O(\ldots\ldots) + CO_2(\ldots\ldots)$$

[Total 2 marks]

3 Sodium metal can react with oxygen molecules in the air to form sodium oxide (Na_2O).

Write a balanced equation for this reaction.

....

[Total 2 marks]

4 In a chemical reaction, sulfuric acid and aluminium metal react to form hydrogen gas and a salt solution of aluminium sulfate.

Ben has written this equation for the reaction:

$$Al_{(s)} + H_2SO_{4\,(aq)} \rightarrow Al_2(SO_4)_{3\,(aq)} + H_{2\,(g)}$$

a) Explain what is meant by the symbol '(aq)' in the chemical equation.

....

[1]

b) Ben's equation is not balanced. Write a balanced chemical equation for this reaction.

....

[1]

[Total 2 marks]

5 Nitric acid can be made using ammonia.

   a) The first stage in the manufacture of nitric acid is to oxidise ammonia, NH_3, to nitrogen(II) oxide, NO. Balance the equation for the reaction.

$$......... NH_3 + ... O_2 \rightarrow .... NO + ... H_2O$$

[1]

   b) The reaction below shows the final stage in the manufacture of nitric acid. The equation is not balanced correctly. Explain how you can tell.

$$2NO_2 + O_2 + H_2O \rightarrow 2HNO_3$$

....

....

[1]

[Total 2 marks]

6 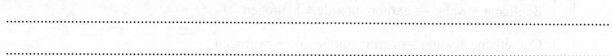 Silver chloride, AgCl, can be made by reacting silver nitrate, $AgNO_3$, and sodium chloride, NaCl, together in a precipitation reaction.

$$AgNO_{3\,(aq)} + NaCl_{(aq)} \rightarrow AgCl_{(s)} + NaNO_{3\,(aq)}$$

   a) How can you tell from the reaction equation that this is a precipitation reaction?

....

[1]

   b) Write a balanced ionic equation for the reaction above.

....

[2]

[Total 3 marks]

7 Balance the following symbol equation to show how sulfur reacts with nitric acid.

$$S + HNO_3 \rightarrow H_2SO_4 + NO_2 + H_2O$$

....

[Total 1 mark]

8 Zinc reacts with tin sulfate solution in a redox reaction. The full reaction equation is shown below.

$$Zn_{(s)} + SnSO_{4\,(aq)} \rightarrow ZnSO_{4\,(aq)} + Sn_{(s)}$$

Write the ionic equation for the reaction above.

....

[Total 2 marks]

Hazards and Risk

1 Eric is carrying out an experiment using some hazardous chemicals. One of the chemicals is stored in a flask, marked with the label shown in **Figure 1**.

Grade 4-6

Figure 1

a) Which of the following hazards are associated with the contents of the flask? Tick **one** box.

- [ ] **A** oxidising
- [ ] **C** harmful
- [ ] **B** corrosive
- [ ] **D** highly flammable

[1]

b) Suggest **one** safety precaution that Eric should take when using the chemical from the flask.

....

[1]

[Total 2 marks]

2 A lab technician is cleaning up a lab after an experiment. The experiment involved using chemicals from flasks marked with the label shown in **Figure 2**.

Grade 6-7

With reference to **Figure 2**, explain why the technician needs to be careful when disposing of the chemicals.

Figure 2

....

....

[Total 2 marks]

3* A student is planning an experiment to assess how the rate of a certain reaction changes with concentration. The reaction involves her using chemicals that are marked as harmful and corrosive. It also produces a gas.

Grade 7-9

Construct a risk assessment to outline the hazards associated with the experiment and the safety precautions that the student should take to reduce them.

....

....

....

....

....

....

....

[Total 6 marks]

The History of the Atom

Warm-Up

Draw **one** line from each atomic model to the correct description of that model.

Atomic Model	Description

Plum pudding model

A positively charged 'ball' with negatively charged electrons in it.

A small, positively charged nucleus surrounded by a 'cloud' of negative electrons.

Bohr's model

Electrons in fixed orbits surrounding a small, positively charged nucleus.

Rutherford's nuclear model

Solid spheres with a different sphere for each element.

1   Models of the atom have changed over time. **Grade 4-6**

Which of the following statements is the best description of what scientists thought an atom was like before the electron was discovered? Tick **one** box.

☐ **A** Tiny solid spheres that can't be divided.   ☐ **C** Flat geometric shapes.

☐ **B** Formless 'clouds' of matter.   ☐ **D** Discrete packets of energy.

[Total 1 mark]

2   In 1911, Rutherford, Geiger and Marsden carried out the gold foil experiment. They fired positively charged alpha particles at gold foil. They predicted that most of the particles would pass straight through the foil and a few might be deflected slightly. **Grade 6-7**

a)   Describe what actually happened to the alpha particles during the gold foil experiment and explain why it happened.

....

....

....

....

[4]

b)   Name the scientist who adapted Rutherford's nuclear model by suggesting that electrons orbit the nucleus at specific distances.

....

[1]

[Total 5 marks]

The Atom

1   **Figure 1** shows the structure of a certain atom.   (Grade 4-6)

   a) Name the region where most of the
       mass of the atom is concentrated.

       .... *[1]*

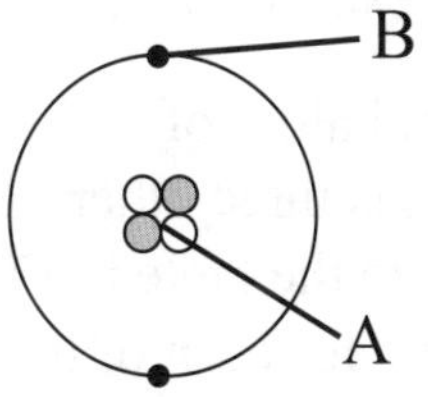

Figure 1

   b) What is the name of particle **B**?

       ....

       [1]

   c) State the **two** subatomic particles which are present in region **A**.

       ....

       [1]

   d) Use the relative charges of the subatomic particles to
       explain why an atom has no overall charge.

       ....

       ....

       ....

       ....

       [3]

   e) The atom shown in **Figure 1** has an atomic number of 2.
       What is the name of the element that the atom in **Figure 1** makes up? Tick **one** box.

       ☐ **A** hydrogen   ☐ **B** lithium   ☐ **C** helium   ☐ **D** beryllium

       [1]

       [Total 7 marks]

2   A potassium atom can be represented by the nuclear symbol $^{39}_{19}K$.   (Grade 4-6)

   a) What is the mass number of $^{39}_{19}K$?

       ....

       [1]

   b) What is the atomic number of $^{39}_{19}K$?

       ....

       [1]

   c) How many protons, neutrons and electrons does an atom of $^{39}_{19}K$ have?

       protons: ....   neutrons: ....   electrons: ....

       [3]

       [Total 5 marks]

Isotopes and Relative Atomic Mass

1 This question is about isotopes.

a) A neutral atom of sulfur, ^{32}S, has 16 electrons.
Sulfur has three other naturally occurring isotopes, with mass numbers 33, 34 and 36.
Complete the table in **Figure 1**, giving the number of protons, neutrons and
electrons for each of the naturally occurring isotopes of sulfur.

Isotope	Number of Protons	Number of Neutrons	Number of Electrons
^{32}S	....	....	16
^{33}S	....	....	....
^{34}S	....	....	....
^{36}S	....	....	....

Figure 1

[3]

b) Atom **X** has a mass number of 51 and an atomic number of 23.
Atom **Y** has a mass number of 51 and an atomic number of 22.
Atom **Z** has a mass number of 52 and an atomic number of 23.

Identify which pair of atoms are isotopes and explain why.

....

....

....

[3]

[Total 6 marks]

2 **Figure 2** shows some information about three isotopes of silicon.

Name	Atomic Number	Mass Number	Abundance (%)
Silicon-28	14	28	92.2
Silicon-29	14	29	4.70
Silicon-30	14	30	3.10

Figure 2

a) How many neutrons does an atom of silicon-29 contain?

neutrons = ...
[1]

b) Work out the relative atomic mass of silicon.

relative atomic mass = ...
[2]

[Total 3 marks]

3 Bromine has two main isotopes: Br-79 and Br-81. (Grade 6-7)

a) Give the definition of the term **isotopes**.

....

....

[1]

b) Bromine has an atomic number of 35. Calculate the number of neutrons in both isotopes.

Br-79 : .... neutrons

Br-81 : .... neutrons

[1]

c) The relative isotopic abundances of bromine-79 and bromine-81 are 12.67 and 12.32 respectively. Calculate the relative atomic mass of bromine. Give your answer to 2 significant figures.

relative atomic mass = ...

[2]

[Total 4 marks]

4 The relative atomic mass of every element can be found in the periodic table. (Grade 6-7)

a) Give the definition of the **relative atomic mass** of an element.

....

....

[2]

b) Explain why some elements have relative atomic masses that are not whole numbers.

....

....

[1]

[Total 3 marks]

5 Gallium can exist as two stable isotopes: Ga-69 and Ga-71. (Grade 7-9)

Give than 60.1% of gallium atoms are Ga-69 atoms, and the rest are Ga-71 atoms, calculate the relative atomic mass of gallium.

relative atomic mass = ...

[Total 3 marks]

Exam Tip

Don't let isotopes confuse you. Just because they've got different numbers of neutrons, a pair of isotopes will still have the same number of protons, so they're still the same element. Those relative atomic mass calculations aren't too bad either. Remember — if your isotopic abundances are given as percentages, then they should always add up to 100%.

Section 10 — Key Concepts in Chemistry

The Periodic Table

1 Chemical elements are arranged in the periodic table. (Grade 4-6)

a) How are the elements ordered in the modern periodic table?

....

[1]

b) Why do elements in groups have similar chemical properties? Tick **one** box.

[ ] **A** They have the same number of shells of electrons.

[ ] **B** They have the same number of outer shell electrons.

[ ] **C** They all have at least one full inner shell of electrons.

[ ] **D** The atoms of the elements are similar in size.

[1]

[Total 2 marks]

2 Mendeleev created an early version of the periodic table, in which he arranged the elements according to their atomic masses and their properties. Mendeleev left some gaps in his table. (Grade 6-7)

a) Explain why Mendeleev left gaps in his table.

....

....

[1]

b) Mendeleev used his table to predict the properties of undiscovered elements that would fit in the gaps he left. One of these was an element in Group 4, which Mendeleev called **eka-silicon**. **Figure 1** shows some properties of the Group 4 elements silicon and tin, plus some predictions about the properties of eka-silicon.

	Silicon (Si)	Eka-silicon (Ek)	Tin (Sn)
Atomic Mass	28	72	119
Density in g/cm^3	2.3	?	7.3
Appearance	grey/silver non-metal	grey metal	grey metal
Formula of oxide	SiO_2	EkO_2	SnO_2
Formula of chloride	$SiCl_4$	?	$SnCl_4$
Reaction with acid	None	?	Slow

Figure 1

Use the information in **Figure 1** to predict the following properties of eka-silicon:

i) Density: ....

ii) Formula of chloride: ....

iii) Reaction with acid: ....

[3]

[Total 4 marks]

Section 10 — Key Concepts in Chemistry

Electronic Configurations

1   The atomic number of neon is 10.   (Grade 6-7)

How many electrons does neon have in its **outer shell**?

☐ **A** 2   ☐ **C** 8

☐ **B** 6   ☐ **D** 10

[Total 1 mark]

2   The atomic number of sulfur is 16.   (Grade 6-7)

a) Write down the electronic structure of sulfur.

....

[1]

b) Draw a diagram to show how the electrons are arranged in a single sulfur atom.

[1]

[Total 2 marks]

3   Magnesium is found in group 2 and period 3 of the periodic table.   (Grade 6-7)

a) Explain how you could use this information to **deduce** the electronic structure of magnesium.

....

....

....

....

....

[3]

b) Give the electronic structure of magnesium.

....

[1]

[Total 4 marks]

Section 10 — Key Concepts in Chemistry

Ions

The formulas of the ion formed by four mystery elements are shown below. Draw lines to match each of the ions to the correct description of the element that it was formed from.

A^+	A non-metal from Group 6
D^-	A metal from Group 2
X^{2+}	A metal from Group 1
Z^{2-}	A non-metal from Group 7

1 Ions can have either a positive or a negative charge. *Grade 6-7*

a) Describe what happens to an atom when it turns into a negative ion.

....

[1]

b) Magnesium is in Group 2 of the periodic table.

i) Predict what charge a magnesium ion will have.

....

[1]

ii) Magnesium has the atomic number 12.
Calculate the number of electrons found in one magnesium ion.

number of electrons = ...

[1]

[Total 3 marks]

2 Potassium can react with oxygen to form the ionic compound potassium oxide. *Grade 7-9*

a) Which of following shows the correct formula for potassium oxide?

☐ **A** KO ☐ **B** KO_2 ☐ **C** K_2O ☐ **D** K_2O_2

[1]

b) The most common isotope of oxygen has an atomic number of 8 and a mass number of 16.
How many protons, neutrons and electrons would an oxide ion have?

protons = ...
electrons = ...
neutrons = ...

[3]

[Total 4 marks]

Ionic Bonding

1   Ionic bonding is one of the three types of chemical bonds found in compounds.   Grade 4-6

a)   In which of the following compounds are the particles held together by ionic bonds?
Put a tick in the box next to the compound that you think is ionic.

☐ calcium chloride   ☐ carbon dioxide

☐ nitrogen monoxide   ☐ phosphorus trichloride

[1]

b)   **Figure 1** shows the formation of the ionic compound lithium chloride from its elements, but it is incomplete. Complete **Figure 1** by drawing an arrow to show the transfer of the electron, adding the charges of the ions and completing the chloride ion to show the electrons in its outer shell.

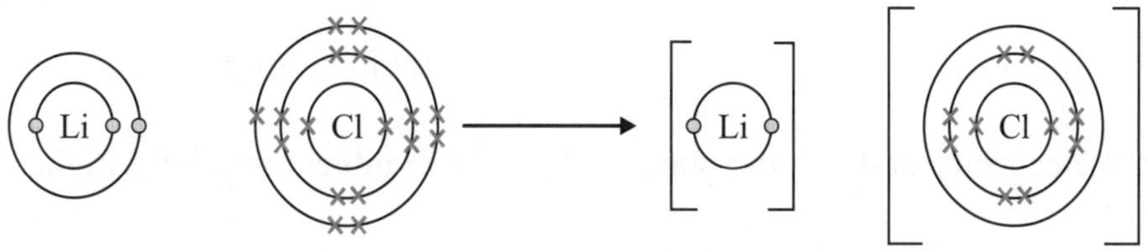

Figure 1

[3]

c)   Name the force that holds the ions together in an ionic bond.

....

[1]

d)   Suggest how you can tell from a dot and cross diagram that the
particles in a compound are held together by ionic bonds.

....

....

[1]

[Total 6 marks]

2   Calcium fluoride, CaF_2, is an ionic compound.   Grade 6-7

Draw a dot and cross diagram to show the bonding in calcium fluoride.
You should include the charges on the ions in your diagram.

[Total 4 marks]

 ☐   ☐   ☐

Section 10 — Key Concepts in Chemistry

Ionic Compounds

Circle the correct words or phrases below so that the statement is correct.

In an ionic compound, the particles are held together by <u>weak</u>/<u>strong</u> forces of attraction.

These forces act <u>in all directions</u>/<u>in one particular direction</u> which results in the particles

bonding together to form <u>giant lattices</u>/<u>small molecules</u>.

1   This question is about the structure and properties of ionic compounds.   (Grade 4-6)

   a) Which of the following properties is **not** typical for an ionic compound?
      Tick **one** box.

   ☐ **A** high boiling point   ☐ **C** high melting point

   ☐ **B** conduct electricity in the liquid state   ☐ **D** conduct electricity in the solid state

[1]

   b) Name the type of structure that ionic compounds have.

   ....

[1]

[Total 2 marks]

2   Sodium chloride is an ionic compound.   (Grade 6-7)

   a) Describe the structure of a crystal of sodium chloride. You should state:
      • What particles are present in the crystal.
      • How these particles are arranged.
      • What holds the particles together.

   ....

   ....

   ....

   ....

   ....

[4]

   b) Explain why sodium chloride has a high melting point.

   ....

   ....

[2]

[Total 6 marks]

3 Potassium bromide has a lattice structure that is similar to sodium chloride.

a) Complete **Figure 1** below to show the position and charge of the ions in potassium bromide. Write a symbol in each blank circle to show whether it is a potassium ion or a bromide ion.

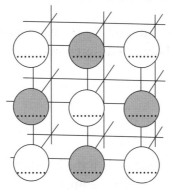

Figure 1

[3]

b) Give **one advantage** and **one disadvantage** of using the type of diagram above to represent the structure of an ionic compound.

Advantage: ....

Disadvantage: ....

[2]

c) State whether potassium bromide is likely to be **soluble** or **insoluble** in water.

....

[1]

[Total 6 marks]

4 **Figure 2** shows some data about the ionic compound lithium chloride. For each of the properties shown, explain how the structure of lithium chloride causes this property.

Boiling point / °C	Electrical conductivity of solid	Electrical conductivity of solution
1382	Low	High

Figure 2

Boiling point ....

....

....

Electrical conductivity of solid ....

....

Electrical conductivity of solution ....

....

[Total 6 marks]

Exam Tip

Don't panic if you're asked about an ionic compound that you haven't met before. Think about what you do know about ionic compounds, and read the question carefully to make sure you've picked up on any extra information given.

Section 10 — Key Concepts in Chemistry

Covalent Bonding

1 This question is about the forces in simple molecular substances. **Grade 4-6**

a) Compare the strength of the bonds that hold the atoms in a molecule together with the forces that exist between different molecules.

....

....

[2]

b) When a simple molecular substance melts, is it the bonds between atoms or the forces between molecules that are broken?

....

[1]

[Total 3 marks]

2 Silicon has the electronic structure 2.8.4. **Grade 6-7**

Use this information to predict how many covalent bonds one atom of silicon will form in a simple molecule. Explain your answer.

....

....

....

[Total 2 marks]

3 Nitrogen has the electronic structure 2.5. Chlorine has the electronic structure 2.8.7. Nitrogen trichloride, NCl_3, is a covalent compound. In each molecule of NCl_3, one nitrogen atom is covalently bonded to three chlorine atoms. **Grade 6-7**

a) Draw a dot and cross diagram to show the bonding in **one molecule** of nitrogen trichloride. You only need to include the outer shell electrons of each atom.

[3]

b) Predict, with reasoning, whether nitrogen trichloride can conduct electricity.

....

....

[1]

[Total 4 marks]

4 Hashim says: "Covalent bonds are very strong, so you need a lot of energy to separate the atoms in a covalent compound. This means simple molecular substances must have high melting and boiling points."

Grade 6-7

Is Hashim correct? Explain your answer.

....

....

....

....

....

....

[Total 3 marks]

5 Methane and poly(ethene) are both substances that are made up of molecules whose atoms are joined together by covalent bonds.

Grade 7-9

a) Briefly describe how the carbon and hydrogen atoms in methane, CH_4, bond to gain stable electronic structures.

....

....

....

....

[4]

b) What type of molecule is poly(ethene)?

....

[1]

c) At room temperature and pressure, methane is a gas, while poly(ethene) is a solid. Suggest why poly(ethene) has a higher boiling point than methane.

....

....

....

....

[4]

[Total 9 marks]

Exam Tip

If you answered these questions correctly, then that's a pretty good sign that you know all about simple molecules and covalent bonding. But don't forget, that's only part of the story — you need to be able to compare simple molecular substances with all the other types of structure covered in this topic, such as ionic structures and giant covalent structures.

Section 10 — Key Concepts in Chemistry

Giant Covalent Structures and Fullerenes

1 The diagrams below show two different types of carbon structure.

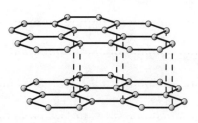

Figure 1   **Figure 2**

a) Name the two carbon structures shown.

   i) **Figure 1**: ....

   [1]

   ii) **Figure 2**: ....

   [1]

b) Both of the structures shown are able to conduct electricity.
   Explain why this is possible.

   ....

   ....

   ....

   [2]

c) Which of the two forms of carbon shown would you expect to have a **higher** melting point?
   Explain your answer.

   ....

   ....

   ....

   ....

   [3]

d) Name **one** other type of carbon structure, and draw a diagram below to show its bonding.

   Structure: ....

   [2]

   [Total 9 marks]

Metallic Bonding

1 This question is about how the structure and bonding of metals affects their properties.

a) Draw a labelled diagram to show how the metal ions and
the electrons that take part in bonding are arranged in a metal.

[3]

b) Explain how the metal ions are held together in this arrangement.

....

....
[2]

c) i) State whether metals generally have high or low boiling points. Explain your answer.

....

....
[2]

ii) A student has samples of two solids, marked **A** and **B**. One is copper, a metallic element, and
the other is iodine, a non-metal element. Solid **A** has a melting point of 1085 °C and solid **B**
has a melting point of 114 °C. Suggest which of the solids is iodine and explain your answer.

....

....
[1]

d) Explain why metals are good conductors of electricity.

....

....
[2]

e) Explain how the structure of metals means they are able to be bent and shaped.

....

....

....
[2]

[Total 12 marks]

Exam Tip

Metals have some really nifty properties, and being able to explain all the properties of metals requires you to be really
familiar with metallic bonding. Remember, it's because of those layers of positive metal ions and that sea of electrons that
metals behave the way they do. Make sure you're able to explain the bonding in metals and link it to their properties.

Section 10 — Key Concepts in Chemistry

Conservation of Mass

1 A student mixes 3.0 g of silver nitrate solution and 15.8 g of sodium chloride solution together in a flask and seals it with a bung. The following precipitation reaction occurs:

$$AgNO_{3\,(aq)} + NaCl_{(aq)} \rightarrow AgCl_{(s)} + NaNO_{3\,(aq)}$$

Predict the total mass of the contents of the flask after the reaction. Explain your answer.

....

....

....

[Total 2 marks]

2 A student is investigating a reaction between zinc and hydrochloric acid. The reaction produces hydrogen gas and a solution of zinc chloride. The student's experimental set-up is shown in **Figure 1**.

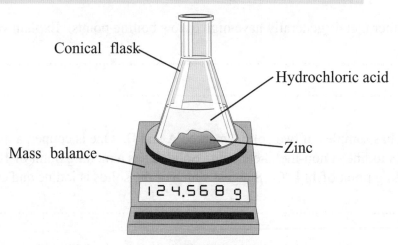

Figure 1

a) How would you expect the mass of the conical flask and its contents to change over the course of the reaction? Explain your answer.

....

....

....

[2]

b) The student repeats the reaction, but this time attaches a gas syringe to the top of the flask. How would you expect the mass of the apparatus and its contents to change over the course of the reaction? Explain your answer.

....

....

....

....

[2]

[Total 4 marks]

Relative Masses and Chemical Formulas

Warm-Up

Match up the following formulas with the correct relative formula mass of the substance.

F_2 38

C_2H_6 40

CaO   30

NaOH   56

1 The compound butane-1,4-diamine has the molecular formula $C_4H_{12}N_2$. Which of the following is the empirical formula of butane-1,4-diamine? *(Grade 4-6)*

☐ **A** C_2H_5N ☐ **B** $C_2H_6N_2$ ☐ **C** CH_3N ☐ **D** C_2H_6N

[Total 1 mark]

2 Decaborane is a compound with the molecular formula $B_{10}H_{14}$. *(Grade 4-6)*

What is the empirical formula of decaborane?

empirical formula = ...

[Total 1 mark]

3 **Figure 1** shows the displayed formula of the compound dithionic acid. *(Grade 4-6)*

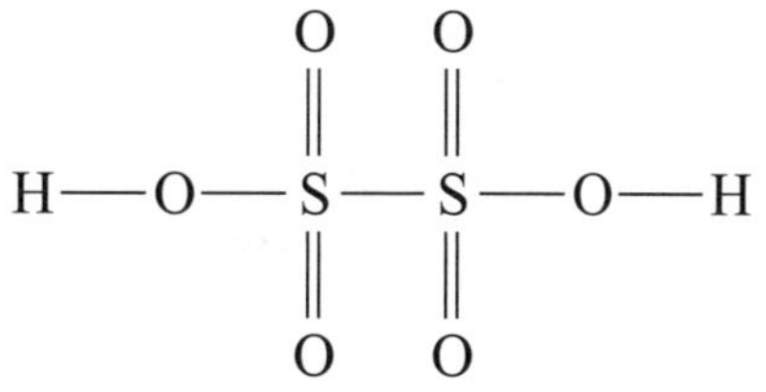

$$H-O-S(=O)(=O)-S(=O)(=O)-O-H$$

Figure 1

a) What is the molecular formula of this compound?
Give your answer in the form $H_aS_bO_c$, where a, b and c are whole numbers.

....

[1]

b) What is the empirical formula of this compound?

empirical formula = ...

[1]

[Total 2 marks]

Section 10 — Key Concepts in Chemistry

4 The formula of the compound barium nitrate is $Ba(NO_3)_2$. (Grade 6-7)

Find the relative formula mass of barium nitrate.

relative formula mass = ...

[2]

5 Oct-1-ene is a compound with the molecular formula C_8H_{16}. (Grade 6-7)
Emmy says the empirical formula of oct-1-ene is C_2H_4.

Is Emmy correct? Explain your answer.

....

....

....

[Total 1 mark]

6 An oxide of an element, X, has the formula X_2O_3. (Grade 7-9)
The relative formula mass of X_2O_3 is 160.

Calculate the relative atomic mass of element X.

relative atomic mass = ...

[Total 3 marks]

7 Compound Q has the empirical formula C_2HF. (Grade 7-9)
The relative formula mass of compound Q is 132.

What is the molecular formula of compound Q?

molecular formula = ...

[Total 3 marks]

Section 10 — Key Concepts in Chemistry

Moles and Concentration

1 What is the approximate number of atoms in 1 mole of carbon atoms? *(Grade 4-6)*

☐ **A** 7.23×10^{23} atoms

☐ **C** 6.02×10^{-23} atoms

☐ **B** 7.23×10^{24} atoms

☐ **D** 6.02×10^{23} atoms

[Total 1 mark]

2 A student makes a saline solution by dissolving 36 g of sodium chloride in 0.40 dm³ of water. What is the concentration of the solution? *(Grade 4-6)*

☐ **A** 90 g dm⁻³   ☐ **B** 14.4 g dm⁻³   ☐ **C** 14 400 g dm⁻³   ☐ **D** 0.090 g dm⁻³

[Total 1 mark]

3 A pharmacist is synthesising aspirin, $C_9H_8O_4$, as part of a drugs trial. After the experiment, the pharmacist calculates that she has made 12.4 moles of aspirin. What mass of aspirin has the pharmacist made? *(Grade 4-6)*

The relative atomic mass, A_r, of C = 12, of H = 1 and of O = 16.

$C \times 9 = 12 \times 9 = 108$
$H \times 8 = 1 \times 8 = 8$ $= 180$
$O \times 4 = 16 \times 4 = 64$

mass = ...180.. g

[Total 2 marks]

4 How many atoms are there in 7 moles of ammonia, NH_3? Give your answer to 3 significant figures. *(Grade 6-7)*

.... atoms

[Total 2 marks]

5 A student makes up a volume of a standard solution of copper sulfate with a concentration of 75.0 g dm⁻³. He does this by dissolving powdered copper sulfate in 220 cm³ of water. *(Grade 6-7)*

Calculate the mass of copper sulfate that was used to make the solution.

mass = ... g

[Total 1 mark]

Section 10 — Key Concepts in Chemistry

6 A student dissolves 56 g of potassium chloride in 400 cm³ of water. *(Grade 6-7)*

a) Calculate the concentration of the resultant potassium chloride solution in g dm⁻³.

concentration = ... g dm⁻³

[1]

b) The student wants to make a solution with the same concentration using only 300 cm³ of water. Use your answer from part a) to calculate the mass of potassium chloride that the student will need to add to this volume of water to create a solution with the same concentration.

mass = ... g

[1]

[Total 2 marks]

7 A lab technician is making up some solutions for students to use in some of their classes. *(Grade 7-9)*

a) The technician makes a standard solution of sodium hydroxide for a titration experiment. She makes 600 cm³ of the solution at a concentration of 52 g dm⁻³.

Calculate the number of moles of sodium hydroxide used to make the solution.
Relative formula mass, M_r, of NaOH = 40

number of moles = ...

[2]

b) i) The technician also makes a standard solution of sodium carbonate. The solution has a concentration of 80.0 g dm⁻³ and was made by adding 36.0 g of sodium carbonate to a volume of water. Calculate the volume of water, in cm³, that she used to make the solution.

volume of water = ... cm³

[2]

ii) For a separate experiment, the technician needs a sodium carbonate solution with a concentration of 40.0 g dm⁻³.
What can she do to her 80.0 g dm⁻³ solution to make it this concentration?

....

[1]

[Total 5 marks]

Section 10 — Key Concepts in Chemistry

8 A sample of an unknown element contains 1.204×10^{25} atoms. **Grade 7-9**

a) How many moles of atoms of the element are in the sample?

number of moles = ...

[1]

b) Given that the atoms have a mean mass of 9.3×10^{-23} g, what is the identity of the element?

....

[2]

[Total 3 marks]

9 A student is investigating an unidentified acid, which is made up of oxygen, sulfur and hydrogen atoms. **Grade 7-9**

a) Given that 3.5 moles of the acid has a mass of 343 g, what is the relative formula mass of the acid?

relative formula mass = ...

[1]

b) The percentage mass of the acid made up of oxygen atoms is 65%.
To the nearest whole number, how many moles of oxygen atoms are in one mole of the acid?

number of moles = ...

[2]

c) In one mole of the acid, there is one mole of sulfur atoms.
Deduce the chemical formula of the acid.

chemical formula = ...

[3]

[Total 6 marks]

Section 10 — Key Concepts in Chemistry

Calculating Empirical Formulas

1 An oxide of lead contains 2.07 g of lead and 0.16 g of oxygen. What is the empirical formula of the lead oxide?

$A_r(Pb) = 207$, $A_r(O) = 16$

empirical formula = ...

[Total 2 marks]

2 53.66 g of an oxide of copper contains 10.8 g of oxygen by mass. Calculate the empirical formula of the copper oxide.

$A_r(Cu) = 63.5$, $A_r(O) = 16$

empirical formula = ...

[Total 3 marks]

3 83% of the mass of a certain hydrocarbon is made up of carbon atoms. Calculate the empirical formula of the hydrocarbon.

$A_r(C) = 12$, $A_r(H) = 1$

empirical formula = ...

[Total 3 marks]

4 A student carried out an experiment to calculate the empirical formula of an oxide of iron. She burnt 3.808 g of iron until it had all reacted. She found that the weight of the product was 5.440 g.

a) Suggest a piece of equipment that the student could use to carry out the reaction in.

....

[1]

b) Calculate the empirical formula of the iron oxide formed during the experiment.
$A_r(Fe) = 56$, $A_r(O) = 16$

empirical formula = ...

[3]

[Total 4 marks]

Section 10 — Key Concepts in Chemistry

Limiting Reactants

1 James is investigating the reactivity of some metals. As part of his investigation, he places a piece of magnesium metal in a flask containing an excess of hydrochloric acid and monitors the reaction. The reaction produces hydrogen gas and a metal salt solution. *Grade 4-6*

a) Which of the reactants is the limiting reactant?

....

[1]

b) James repeats the experiment but changes the starting quantities of magnesium and acid. He lets the reaction proceed to completion, and notes that once the reaction has finished, the reaction vessel contains a small amount of grey metal and a clear solution.

In this second experiment, what is the limiting reactant? Explain your answer.

....

....

....

[2]

[Total 3 marks]

2 An industrial process converts the alkene ethene into ethanol, according to the reaction below. *Grade 6-7*

$$C_2H_4 + H_2O \rightarrow CH_3CH_2OH$$

What mass of ethanol can be made from 53 g of ethene, given that water is in excess?

mass = ... g

[Total 2 marks]

112

3 The following equation shows the complete combustion of ethane in air.

$$2C_2H_6 + 7O_2 \rightarrow 4CO_2 + 6H_2O$$

a) In a complete combustion reaction, some ethane reacted with exactly 128 g of oxygen. Calculate the mass of water produced. Give your answer to three significant figures.

mass = ... g

[3]

b) A company burns ethane to generate power for an industrial process.

As part of a carbon-reducing scheme, the company can only produce a maximum 4.4 tonnes of carbon dioxide per day (where 1 tonne = 1 000 000 g). What is the maximum mass, in tonnes, of ethane that the company can burn each day so as not to exceed the limit of carbon dioxide?

mass = ... tonnes

[3]

[Total 6 marks]

4 Urea, $(NH_2)_2CO$, is a compound that can be synthesised industrially using the following reaction.

$$2NH_3 + CO_2 \rightarrow (NH_2)_2CO + H_2O$$

a) A company makes 120.6 tonnes of urea each day (where 1 tonne = 1 000 000 g). What mass of carbon dioxide, in tonnes, is required to make this mass of urea?

mass = ... tonnes

[3]

b) Usually the reaction happens in an excess of ammonia. However, a leak in a pipe means the mass of ammonia entering the reaction chamber on one day is reduced to 59.5 tonnes.

What is the decrease, in tonnes, in the amount of urea produced on this day?

decrease in mass = ... tonnes

[4]

[Total 7 marks]

Balancing Equations Using Masses

1 Viola reacts 200 g of a metal, **X**, with oxygen. The result of the reaction is 280 g of a single product, which is an oxide of metal **X**.

a) What mass of oxygen was used in the reaction?

mass = ... g
[1]

b) Given that Viola's reaction produced 5 moles of X oxide,
write a balanced symbol equation for the reaction of **X** with oxygen.
$A_r(X) = 40$, $A_r(O) = 16$

....
[4]
[Total 5 marks]

2 1.0 g of warm sodium was added to a gas jar containing 1.0 g of chlorine gas (Cl_2). They reacted to form sodium chloride. The equation for the reaction is $2Na + Cl_2 \rightarrow 2NaCl$. Determine which reactant was the **limiting reactant** in this reaction.

$A_r(Na) = 23$, $M_r(Cl_2) = 71$

....
[Total 3 marks]

3 A scientist gently heats tin and iodine together. They react to form a single product, which is a metal halide. Given that 3.57 g of tin reacts exactly with 15.24 g of iodine, write a balanced equation for this reaction.

$A_r(Sn) = 119$, $M_r(I_2) = 254$, $M_r(\text{metal halide}) = 627$

....
[Total 5 marks]

Section 10 — Key Concepts in Chemistry

States of Matter

Identify which of the following statements is **false**. Tick **one** box.

Particles in liquids are free to move past each other but tend to stick together. ☐

Particles of a substance in the liquid state have more energy than particles of the same substance in the solid state. ☐

There is hardly any force of attraction between particles in gases. ☐

Particles in liquids are held in fixed positions by strong forces. ☐

1   Substances can exist in three states of matter: solid, liquid or gas. (Grade 4-6)

a)   In which of these three states of matter are the forces of attraction between the particles **strongest**?

....

[1]

b)   Name the state of matter illustrated in **Figure 1**.

Figure 1

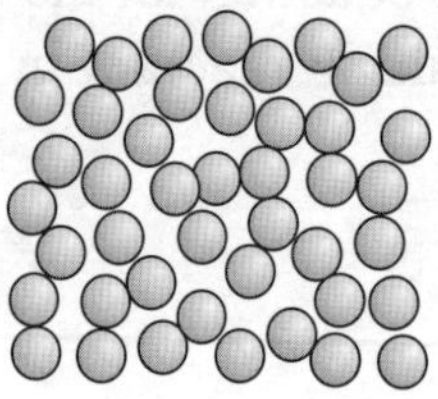

....

[1]

[Total 2 marks]

2   A student has a sample of a solid substance. She heats it gradually until it turns into a liquid. (Grade 6-7)

Describe the differences between the particles in the substance when it is in the liquid state and when it is in the solid state. Give your answer in terms of the movement of the particles and the amount of energy that they have.

....

....

....

....

....

[Total 3 marks]

Changes of State

1 The equations below show four processes that use water as a starting material.

    A: $H_2O_{(l)} \rightarrow H_2O_{(s)}$ **B**: $2H_2O_{(l)} + 2Na_{(s)} \rightarrow 2NaOH_{(aq)} + H_{2(g)}$

    C: $H_2O_{(l)} \rightarrow + H_2O_{(g)}$ **D**: $2H_2O_{(l)} \rightarrow 2H_{2(g)} + O_{2(g)}$

a) State which equation shows evaporation.

....

[1]

b) State which **two** equations show chemical changes and explain your answer.

....

....

[2]

[Total 3 marks]

2 **Figure 1** shows some properties of four elements.

Figure 1

Name	Melting point / °C	Boiling point / °C	Appearance		
			solid	liquid	gas
fluorine	−220	−188	colourless	bright yellow	pale yellow
mercury	−39	357	silvery metallic	silvery metallic	n/a
bromine	−7	59	red-brown	red-brown	orange
rubidium	39	688	silvery-white metallic	silvery-white metallic	n/a

During an experiment, samples of each of these four elements were placed in separate test tubes. All four test tubes were then gradually cooled together, from 25 °C to −200 °C.

Describe what you would expect to observe during the experiment as it progressed.
In your answer you should describe what you think will happen to each sample.

....

....

....

....

....

....

....

[Total 4 marks]

Section 11 — States of Matter and Mixtures

Purity

1 Misty-Marie is doing a chemistry experiment.
The instructions say she needs to use pure water.
Stanley offers her a bottle labelled '100% Pure Spring Water'.

Grade 4-6

Suggest why Stanley's water is unlikely to be suitable for Misty-Marie's experiment.

....

....

....

....

[Total 2 marks]

2 Copper can be made extremely pure. The melting points of two samples
of copper were measured. Sample **A** had a melting point of 1085 °C
and sample **B** melted over the range 900 – 940 °C.

Grade 4-6

Suggest which of the samples, **A** or **B**, was the **most pure**. Explain your answer.

....

....

....

[Total 2 marks]

3 A scientist is comparing samples of two substances.
One sample is a pure compound, but the other is a mixture.
Both substances are solids at room temperature.

Grade 4-6

a) The scientist decides to work out which is the pure compound by heating both
samples and recording their melting points. Explain how she will be able to tell
which is the pure compound, even if she does not know its melting point.

....

....

....

[2]

b) Suggest what apparatus the scientist could use to
measure the melting points of the substances in the lab.

....

[1]

[Total 3 marks]

Separating Mixtures

1   **Figure 1** shows a set of equipment you could use for separating a mixture in the lab.

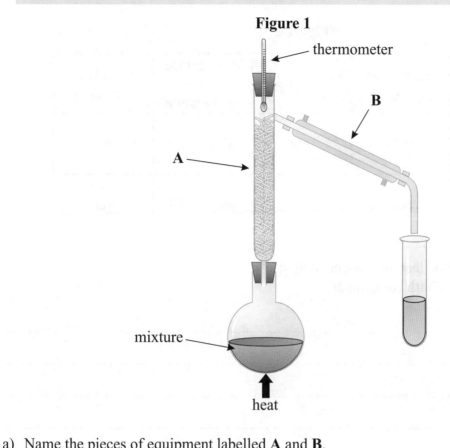

Figure 1

a) Name the pieces of equipment labelled **A** and **B**.

   i) **A**: ....

   [1]

   ii) **B**: ....

   [1]

b) i) What is the name of the separation method this equipment would be used for?

   ....

   [1]

   ii) Describe what type of mixture you would use this method to separate.

   ....

   ....

   [2]

   iii) Reuben is using this method to separate a mixture.
        His mixture contains a substance that is flammable.
        Suggest a suitable piece of equipment that he could use to heat the mixture.

   ....

   [1]

   [Total 6 marks]

2* A student wants to separate the components of a mixture.
The mixture is a white powder composed of barium sulfate and potassium iodide.
Figure 2 shows some information about the two compounds in the mixture.

Figure 2

Name	Melting point / °C	Boiling point / °C	Appearance at room temperature	Soluble in water?
barium sulfate	1580	1600	white solid	no
potassium iodide	681	1330	white solid	yes

Describe a detailed method that the student could use
to obtain pure samples of **both** compounds.

....

....

....

....

....

....

....

....

....

....

....

....

....

....

....

....

[Total 6 marks]

Section 11 — States of Matter and Mixtures

3 Sodium chloride dissolves in water, but not in ethanol.
Sodium chloride has a melting point of 801 °C and a boiling point of 1413 °C.
Ethanol has a melting point of –114 °C and a boiling point of 78 °C.

a) Suggest a purification method which would separate a mixture of sodium chloride and ethanol, but **not** a mixture of sodium chloride and water. Explain your answer.

....

....

....

....

[3]

b) Suggest a purification method which would separate a mixture of sodium chloride and water and would **also** separate a mixture of sodium chloride and ethanol. Explain your answer.

....

....

....

[2]

[Total 5 marks]

4 **Figure 3** lists the boiling points of three compounds.

Figure 3

Name	Formula	Boiling point / °C
cyclopentane	C_5H_{10}	49
cyclohexane	C_6H_{12}	81
ethyl ethanoate	$C_4H_8O_2$	77

Suggest why a mixture of cyclohexane and ethyl ethanoate might be more difficult to separate than a mixture of cyclohexane and cyclopentane.

....

....

....

....

....

[Total 2 marks]

Exam Tip

You might find some of these separation techniques cropping up in questions about other practicals — you often need to use one of them at the end of an experiment to separate out a pure sample of the product from the reaction mixture.

Section 11 — States of Matter and Mixtures

Target AO3

5   A student was given a solution containing water, ethanol and the salts bismuth iodide and potassium chloride. Bismuth iodide is soluble in ethanol and potassium chloride is soluble in water. The boiling point of ethanol is 78 °C and both salts have melting points above 400 °C.

Here is the method the student plans to use to produce pure samples of the two salts:

> 1. Using distillation apparatus, heat the mixture to 120 °C to separate the ethanol from the solution.
> 2. Pour the remaining mixture through a filter to remove the solid bismuth iodide.
> 3. Pour the filtrate into an evaporating dish.
> 4. Gently heat the filtrate until dry potassium chloride crystals are left.

a)   Evaluate whether the student's method will work.
     Explain your answer.

     ....

     ....

     ....
                                                                                                                          [1]

b)   Explain how the method should be changed to produce separate samples of each salt.

     ....

     ....
                                                                                                                          [2]

c)   The student suggests using a Bunsen burner to heat the mixture in step 1.
     Suggest a risk of this if the mixture contains a large amount of ethanol.

     ....
                                                                                                                          [1]

d)   Potassium hydrogencarbonate is another water-soluble salt.
     The student planned to produce potassium hydrogencarbonate crystals by heating a sample of potassium hydrogencarbonate solution in an evaporating dish until no more liquid remains.
     However, potassium hydrogencarbonate decomposes on heating.
     Describe a method that the student could use to ensure they make pure, dry crystals.

     ....

     ....

     ....
                                                                                                                          [2]

                                                                                                        [Total 6 marks]

Exam Tip

You might be given a method in the exam with lots of different steps — the examiner could introduce errors for you to spot in any of them. Read and think about each part of the method carefully to spot any potential problems.

Section 11 — States of Matter and Mixtures

Chromatography

1   Olivia analysed an unknown mixture of liquids using paper chromatography. The solvent she used was ethanol. The chromatogram she produced is shown in **Figure 1**.

Figure 1

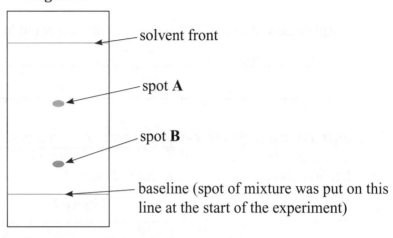

a) Name the mobile phase in Olivia's experiment

....

[1]

b) What does this chromatogram tell you about the number of components in the mixture? Explain your answer.

....

....

[2]

c) Calculate the R_f value of spot **B**. Use a ruler to help you.

$$R_f = \frac{\text{distance travelled by solute}}{\text{distance travelled by solvent}}$$

R_f = ...

[3]

d) Olivia is given a list of five chemicals. She is told that her mixture is made up of a combination of some of the chemicals on the list. Explain how Olivia could use pure samples of the chemicals on the list to identify the components of the mixture using paper chromatography.

....

....

....

....

[2]

[Total 8 marks]

Section 11 — States of Matter and Mixtures

2 Lamar wants to analyse the composition of a sample of ink.
The ink is made up of a number of dyes dissolved in a solvent.

a) The boiling point of the solvent is lower than the boiling point of any of the dyes.

i) Suggest a method Lamar could use to separate the mixture of dyes from the solvent.

....

[1]

ii) Explain how this method can provide data that could help Lamar to identify the solvent.

....

....

[1]

b) Lamar uses paper chromatography to analyse the mixtures of dyes in the ink.
He compares the mixture with five different water soluble dyes, A to E.
After 30 minutes, the chromatogram in **Figure 2** was obtained.

Figure 2

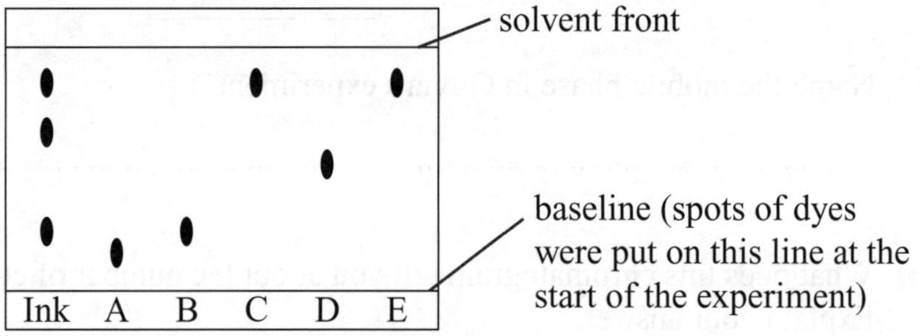

solvent front

baseline (spots of dyes were put on this line at the start of the experiment)

Ink   A   B   C   D   E

Outline the procedure for setting up and running this experiment.

....

....

....

....

....

....

[5]

c) Explain the results shown on Lamar's chromatogram.

....

....

....

....

....

....

[4]

[Total 11 marks]

Target AO3

3   A student set up a chromatography experiment to investigate a sample of ink which contained a mixture of several different compounds.

a)   The chromatogram from the student's experiment is shown in **Figure 3**.

Figure 3

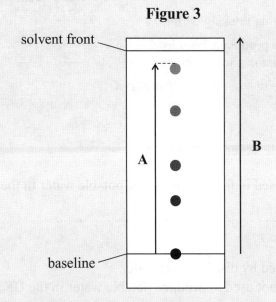

What **two** conclusions could the student make about the compounds in the ink?
Explain your answers.

....

....

....

....

[4]

b)   The student used distances **A** and **B** to calculate the R_f value for one of the compounds.
Explain the **two** mistakes that the student has made and what they should have done instead.

....

....

....

....

[4]

[Total 8 marks]

Exam Tip

If you're asked to suggest possible conclusions about an experiment, be careful that you don't assume something that isn't mentioned. You'll only get marks for conclusions that can be worked out from the information you're given.

       Section 11 — States of Matter and Mixtures

Water Treatment

1 This question is about potable water. **Grade 4-6**

a) Name **one** source of water used in the production of potable water in the UK.

....

[1]

b) Potable water can be produced by distilling sea water.
Explain why this method is not used to produce potable water in the UK.

....

....

[2]

[Total 3 marks]

2 A purification plant uses multiple steps to purify water. **Grade 6-7**

a) When the water arrives at a water purification plant, it is passed through wire meshes and gravel beds to remove large solid impurities. Give the name of this step.

....

[1]

b) Some water purification plants use aluminium sulfate to carry out a sedimentation step.
How does the aluminium sulfate contribute to the purification process?

....

....

[1]

c) The purification process ends with chlorination.
Describe what happens to the water during this process and state why it is carried out.

....

....

[2]

[Total 4 marks]

Acids and Bases

Warm-Up

Circle the statements below that are **true**.

As H^+ concentration increases, pH decreases.

Acids contain lots of OH^- ions.

Neutral substances have a pH of 8.

Alkalis turn Universal indicator blue/purple.

Acids have pHs of less than 7.

Alkalis are soluble bases.

1 This question is about acids and bases.
Figure 1 shows the pH values of some everyday substances.

Grade 4-6

Figure 1

Substance	pH
Beer	4
Bicarbonate of soda	9
Milk	7

a) Write the name of the substance in **Figure 1** that is an acid.

....

[1]

b) What colour would you expect to see if phenolphthalein was added to bicarbonate of soda solution?

....

[1]

c) Which ion is produced by an acid in aqueous solution? Tick **one** box.

☐ **A** Cl^-

☐ **B** H^+

☐ **C** OH^-

☐ **D** OH^+

[1]

[Total 3 marks]

2 Which of the following equations shows a neutralisation reaction? Tick **one** box.

Grade 4-6

☐ **A** $HNO_3 + LiOH \rightarrow LiNO_3 + H_2O$

☐ **B** $Mg + H_2O \rightarrow MgO + H_2$

☐ **C** $Na_2O + H_2O \rightarrow 2NaOH$

☐ **D** $C_4H_{10} + 6\frac{1}{2}O_2 \rightarrow 4CO_2 + 5H_2O$

[Total 1 mark]

3 Acids and bases react together in neutralisation reactions. (Grade 4-6)

a) Write the general word equation for a neutralisation reaction between an acid and a base.

....

[1]

b) In terms of hydrogen ions and hydroxide ions, write an ionic equation
for a neutralisation reaction in aqueous solution.

....

[1]

[Total 2 marks]

4 Kevin has samples of three different alkaline solutions. Solution **A** has a pH of 11, solution **B** has a pH of 13 and solution **C** has a pH of 8. State which of Kevin's solutions has the **lowest** concentration of hydroxide ions and explain your answer. (Grade 6-7)

....

....

....

[Total 2 marks]

5 Haifa is investigating the properties of a sample of dilute hydrochloric acid, HCl. (Grade 6-7)   **PRACTICAL**

a) She puts 100 cm³ of the acid into a flask.
Suggest a piece of apparatus that Haifa could use to accurately measure out 100 cm³ of the acid.

....

[1]

b) Haifa adds a measured mass of powdered calcium hydroxide to the flask. It reacts completely.
She takes a sample of the resultant solution and tests its pH using universal indicator paper.

i) Suggest what colour the universal indicator paper will turn
when Haifa adds a spot of the solution. Explain your answer.

....

....

[3]

ii) Haifa repeats the same procedure several times. After she adds the fifth lot of calcium hydroxide, she sees a small amount of unreacted solid left at the bottom of the flask.
Suggest what colour the universal indicator paper will turn at this point. Explain your answer.

....

....

[3]

[Total 7 marks]

Section 12 — Chemical Changes

Strong and Weak Acids

1   Tamal has two beakers, each containing a sample of a different acid.
The acid in beaker X is **stronger** than the acid in beaker Y.
The acid in beaker Y is **more concentrated** than the acid in beaker X.

Which row of the table in **Figure 1** could describe the contents of the two beakers? Tick **one** box.

Figure 1

	Beaker X	Beaker Y
☐ **A**	0.002 mol/dm³ HCl	4.0 mol/dm³ CH₃COOH
☐ **B**	4.0 mol/dm³ HCl	0.002 mol/dm³ CH₃COOH
☐ **C**	0.002 mol/dm³ CH₃COOH	4.0 mol/dm³ HCl
☐ **D**	4.0 mol/dm³ CH₃COOH	0.002 mol/dm³ HCl

[Total 1 mark]

2   Methanoic acid, HCOOH, is a **weak acid**.

a) Explain what is meant by the term 'weak acid'.

....

....
[1]

b) Write a chemical equation to show how methanoic acid acts as a weak acid.

....
[2]

[Total 3 marks]

3   Jackie is carrying out an experiment to measure how
the pH of a strong acid is affected by its concentration.

a) Jackie takes a sample of an acidic solution, A, made by dissolving a solid acid in deionised water.
He wants to make his sample of the acid more concentrated.
Which of the following things could he do? Tick **one** box.

☐   **A** Add a more dilute solution of the acid to the sample.

☐   **B** Add more water to the sample.

☐   **C** Add more solution the same as A to the sample.

☐   **D** Dissolve more solid acid in the sample.

[1]

b) At a certain dilution, the hydrogen ion concentration is 0.001 mol/dm³ and the acid has a pH of 3.
Jackie increases the concentration of hydrogen ions in the sample to 0.1 mol/dm³.
What is the new pH of the acid?

....
[1]

[Total 2 marks]

Section 12 — Chemical Changes

Reactions of Acids

1 June reacts a metal and an acid together in a flask. Which of the following describes the products of this reaction? Tick **one** box.

Grade 4-6

- [ ] **A** A salt and water.
- [ ] **B** A salt and carbon dioxide gas.
- [ ] **C** A salt, water and carbon dioxide gas.
- [ ] **D** A salt and hydrogen gas.

[Total 1 mark]

2 Complete **Figure 1** to show the chemical formulas of the salts created in the reactions involving the following acids.

Grade 6-7

Figure 1

	Hydrochloric acid (HCl)	Nitric acid (HNO_3)	Sulfuric acid (H_2SO_4)
Zinc metal (Zn)	$ZnCl_2$	....	$ZnSO_4$
Calcium carbonate ($CaCO_3$)	$CaCl_2$	$Ca(NO_3)_2$	....
Sodium hydroxide (NaOH)	NaCl	$NaNO_3$	....
Potassium carbonate (K_2CO_3)	....	KNO_3	K_2SO_4

[Total 4 marks]

3 Pauline mixes zinc carbonate, $ZnCO_3$, with hydrochloric acid, HCl, and notes that the mixture starts to bubble as a gas is given off.

Grade 6-7

a) Give the name of the gas that is responsible for the bubbles in the reaction. Describe a test you could perform to identify this gas.

....

....

[3]

b) Write a balanced chemical equation for the reaction between hydrochloric acid and zinc carbonate.

....

[2]

c) What is the name of the salt produced by the reaction?

....

[1]

[Total 6 marks]

Making Insoluble Salts

1 Insoluble salts can be made by precipitation reactions.
Which of the following equations describes a precipitation reaction? Tick **one** box.

Grade 4-6

- [ ] **A** $CuO_{(s)} + 2HCl_{(aq)} \rightarrow CuCl_{2(aq)} + H_2O_{(l)}$
- [ ] **B** $HCl_{(aq)} + NaOH_{(aq)} \rightarrow NaCl_{(aq)} + H_2O_{(l)}$
- [ ] **C** $2HNO_{3(aq)} + ZnCO_{3(s)} \rightarrow Zn(NO_3)_{2(aq)} + H_2O_{(l)} + CO_{2(g)}$
- [ ] **D** $Pb(NO_3)_{2(aq)} + 2NaCl_{(aq)} \rightarrow PbCl_{2(s)} + 2NaNO_{3(aq)}$

[Total 1 mark]

2 Jerry is making a sample of silver chloride, an insoluble salt, by mixing two salt solutions.

Grade 6-7

a) Suggest two salt solutions that Jerry could mix to make silver chloride.

....

....

[1]

b) Once Jerry has made the salt, he pours the whole
solid and salt solution into a filter funnel, as shown in **Figure 1**.

Figure 1

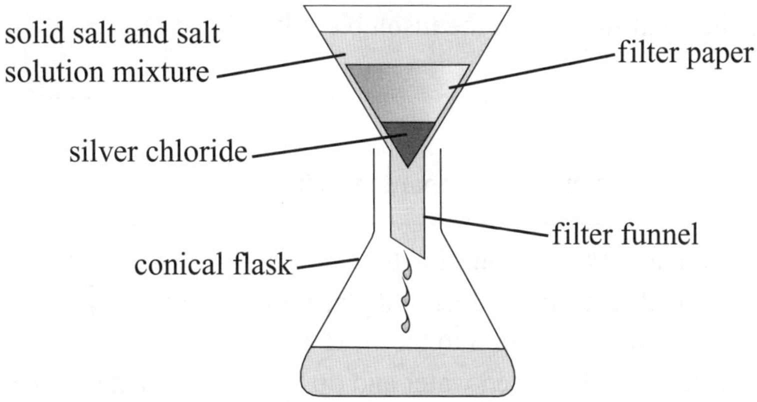

What has Jerry done wrong? Explain how this could affect
the mass of solid salt that he collects from the solution.

....

....

....

[2]

c) After Jerry has isolated the salt, he washes it with deionised water.
Explain why he uses deionised water as opposed to tap water.

....

....

[1]

[Total 4 marks]

3 The students in a chemistry class are investigating the properties of calcium salts. (Grade 6-7)

a) They plan to carry out reactions to make calcium nitrate, $Ca(NO_3)_2$, and calcium sulfate, $CaSO_4$.
Before they start, four students predict whether the salts will be soluble or insoluble.
Which prediction is correct? Tick **one** box.

☐ **A** Ashley: "Both calcium salts will be insoluble."

☐ **B** Benni: "Both reactions will make soluble calcium salts."

☐ **C** Chen: "We'll get an insoluble precipitate of calcium sulfate,
but calcium nitrate is soluble in water."

☐ **D** Dermot: "Calcium sulfate dissolves in water, but calcium nitrate doesn't,
so only calcium nitrate will form as a precipitate."

[1]

b) In a third reaction, the students want to produce the insoluble salt calcium carbonate, $CaCO_3$.
Suggest two soluble salts they could react together to make a precipitate of calcium carbonate.

....

....

[2]

[Total 3 marks]

4 Davina reacts aqueous iron(III) nitrate solution, $Fe(NO_3)_3$, with aqueous
sodium hydroxide solution, NaOH, to make an insoluble salt containing iron. (Grade 6-7)

a) Write down the chemical formula of the insoluble salt.

....

[1]

b) Davina used the following method to prepare the salt:

1. Mix the sodium hydroxide solution with the iron(III) nitrate solution in a beaker and stir.
2. Line a filter funnel with filter paper and place it in a conical flask.
   Pour the contents of the beaker into the filter paper.
3. Rinse the beaker with deionised water and tip this into the filter paper.
4. Rinse the contents of the filter paper with deionised water.

i) Explain why Davina rinsed the beaker and added the rinsings to the filter paper.

....

[1]

ii) After completing step 4, Davina wants to dry the solid product. Suggest how she could do this.

....

[1]

iii) Given that Davina used an excess of iron(III) nitrate solution, state which **three** ions
will be present in the solution that is left in the conical flask at the end of the experiment.

....

[2]

[Total 5 marks]

Making Soluble Salts

Nina is making the soluble salt zinc chloride by reacting zinc with hydrochloric acid.
She wants to prepare a pure, dry sample of solid zinc chloride.
The equipment Nina has available is listed below.
Circle the pieces of equipment below that you would expect Nina to use.

pipette

filter funnel

desiccator

fume cupboard

thermometer

water bath

methyl orange indicator

oonical flask

safety glasses

burette

condenser

fractionating column

filter paper

1   The following steps are parts of a method you could use to produce
a pure, dry sample of the soluble salt magnesium sulfate, MgSO$_4$,
from solid magnesium hydroxide and sulfuric acid.

1   Slowly heat the solution to evaporate off some of the water.

2   Filter the solid off and dry it in a desiccator.

3   Filter out the excess solid using a filter funnel and filter paper.

4   Add magnesium hydroxide to a flask containing warm sulfuric acid.
Continue adding the magnesium hydroxide until no more reacts
(at this point, the excess solid will just sink to the bottom of the flask).

5   Leave the solution to crystallise.

a) Which is the correct order that these steps should be carried out in? Tick **one** box.

☐   **A** 4, 1, 3, 2, 5

☐   **B** 1, 4, 2, 5, 2

☐   **C** 4, 3, 1, 5, 2

☐   **D** 3, 1, 2, 5, 4

[1]

b) Write a balanced symbol equation, including state symbols, that describes the
reaction between magnesium hydroxide, Mg(OH)$_2$, and sulfuric acid, H$_2$SO$_4$.

....

[3]

[Total 4 marks]

Section 12 — Chemical Changes

132

2 Andy is making a sample of potassium sulfate by reacting potassium hydroxide, KOH, and sulfuric acid, H_2SO_4, together.

(Grade 6-7)

a) Potassium sulfate is a soluble salt. Explain what is meant by the term soluble in this context.

....

[1]

b) Write a balanced chemical equation for this reaction.

....

[2]

c) Andy uses a titration method to add a potassium hydroxide solution to the acid until he reaches the end point, which is shown by a change in colour of an indicator in the solution. He then crystallises the solution to obtain the salt. Will this produce a pure sample of the salt? Explain your answer.

....

....

[1]

[Total 4 marks]

3 Copper sulfate is a soluble salt that can be made by the reaction between sulfuric acid, H_2SO_4, and copper oxide, CuO.

(Grade 7-9) **PRACTICAL**

a) Write a balanced chemical equation for the reaction between sulfuric acid and copper oxide.

....

[2]

b)* Outline how you could prepare a pure, dry sample of copper sulfate in the lab from sulfuric acid and copper oxide.

....

....

....

....

....

....

....

....

....

[6]

[Total 8 marks]

Section 12 — Chemical Changes

Electrolysis

1 As part of an industrial process, a sample of potassium chloride, KCl, was electrolysed. *(Grade 4-6)*

a) Before the potassium chloride is electrolysed, it either has to be molten or dissolved in solution. Explain why this is necessary.

....

....

[2]

b) During the electrolysis of molten potassium chloride, potassium ions are reduced to potassium metal. At which electrode would you expect this reaction to occur?

....

[1]

[Total 3 marks]

2 Electrolysis is carried out on a solution of copper chloride, $CuCl_2$, using inert electrodes. *(Grade 6-7)*

a) Which of the following ions is **not** present in the solution? Tick **one** box.

☐ **A** H^+ ☐ **B** H_2O^- ☐ **C** Cl^- ☐ **D** Cu^{2+}

[1]

b) What would you expect to see happen at:

i) the anode? ....

ii) the cathode? ....

[2]

[Total 3 marks]

3 A solution of sodium chloride, NaCl, is electrolysed using platinum electrodes. *(Grade 6-7)*

a) Platinum electrodes are an example of inert electrodes.
Explain what is meant by the term 'inert' when referring to electrodes.

....

[1]

b) The sodium chloride solution contains dissolved sodium chloride and water only. List the ions that are present in solution during the electrolysis of sodium chloride solution using inert electrodes.

....

[2]

c) Write balanced half equations to show the reactions that occur at:

i) the anode ....

ii) the cathode ....

[4]

[Total 7 marks]

134

4 The half-equation for the reaction at the cathode during an electrolysis experiment is $Pb^{2+} + 2e^- \rightarrow Pb$. The half-equation for the reaction at the anode is $2I^- \rightarrow I_2 + 2e^-$.

Grade 6-7

a) Give the definition of the term **electrolyte**.

....

[2]

b) Give the chemical formula of the electrolyte in this experiment,
given that it's a molten ionic compound.

....

[1]

[Total 3 marks]

5* A student is investigating the electrolysis of sodium chloride solution using inert electrodes. Describe how you would set up an electrochemical cell to carry out this investigation and predict what you would observe happening at each electrode as the reaction progressed.

Grade 6-7

....

....

....

....

....

....

....

....

....

[Total 6 marks]

6 When sodium sulfate solution is electrolysed using inert electrodes, sodium is not discharged at the cathode.

Grade 7-9

a) Explain why sodium **is not** discharged at the cathode and state what product **is** discharged instead.

....

....

[3]

b) State which **two** products are discharged at the anode.

....

[2]

c) Suggest an alternative electrolysis experiment that could be
carried out that **would** produce sodium metal at the cathode.

....

[2]

[Total 7 marks]

7   Marco is investigating the electrolysis of copper sulfate. He sets up two cells as shown in **Figure 1**. In cell A, Marco uses platinum electrodes. In cell B, he uses pure copper electrodes. The cells are identical in all other respects.

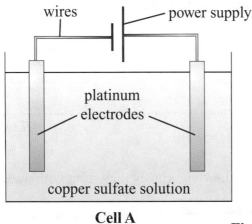
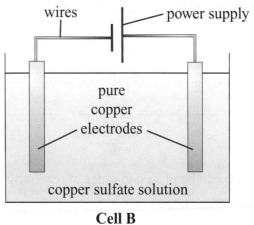

Figure 1

a) Both cells are turned on and left for 1 hour. Given that the masses of the two cells were the same at the start of the electrolysis, how would you expect them to compare after 1 hour? Explain your answer. Use appropriate half equations to justify your conclusion.

....

....

....

....

....

....

[6]

b) A similar cell to cell B can be used to purify copper. Give **one** similarity and **one** difference between the cell used to purify copper in industry and cell B.

....

....

[2]

[Total 8 marks]

8   Write half-equations to show what reactions occur at the cathode and the anode when acidified water is electrolysed.

Cathode: ....

Anode: ....

[Total 4 marks]

Exam Tip

It's important to remember that when you electrolyse aqueous solutions (rather than molten salts) what products are made will depend on the reactivity of all the ions present in the solution. Make sure you've learnt which ions will be discharged from which solutions. And get plenty of practice at writing half-equations too — they're really important...

Section 12 — Chemical Changes

Reactivity Series and Reactivity of Metals

1 The reaction that occurs when a metal is burnt in oxygen can be described as an oxidation reaction. Explain why, using ideas about the transfer of oxygen. **Grade 4-6**

....

....

....

[Total 2 marks]

2 Metals can be placed in order of reactivity based on how vigorously they react with water. **Grade 4-6**

a) Write a word equation for the reaction of sodium with water.

....

[1]

b) Explain, using ideas about oxidation, why iron reacts
much more slowly with cold water than sodium does.

....

....

[1]

[Total 2 marks]

3 Some metals can react with water. **Grade 6-7**

a) i) Complete the symbol equation below for the reaction of calcium and water.
Include state symbols.

$$Ca_{(s)} + 2H_2O_{(l)} \rightarrow \text{.........................} + \text{.........................}$$

[2]

ii) Identify which element is oxidised. Explain your answer in terms of oxygen.

....

....

[2]

iii) Suggest a metal which will react more vigorously with water than calcium.
Explain your answer.

....

....

[2]

b) Put the metals sodium, zinc and potassium in order,
based on how vigorously you think they would react with water.

Most vigorous .... Least vigorous

[1]

[Total 7 marks]

4 Which of the statements below about metal reactivity is **incorrect**? Tick **one** box. Grade 6-7

☐ **A** The easier it is for a metal atom to form a positive ion, the less reactive it will be.

☐ **B** The more resistant a metal atom is to oxidation, the less reactive it will be.

☐ **C** In a reactivity series, you will find a reactive metal above a less reactive metal.

☐ **D** The more reactive a metal is, the faster its reaction with water will be.

[Total 1 mark]

5 Amal performed some experiments to investigate the reactivity of metals. Grade 6-7

a) First, Amal placed pieces of four different metals into dilute hydrochloric acid.
Figure 1 shows what the four experiments looked like after 1 minute.

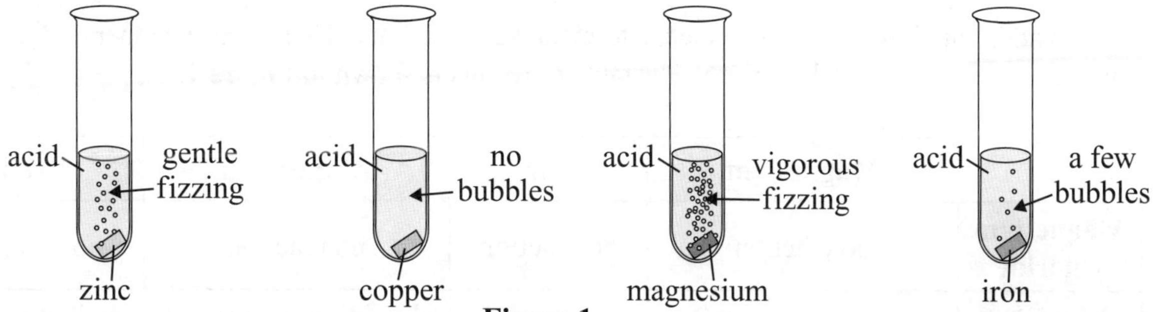

acid — gentle fizzing — zinc   acid — no bubbles — copper   acid — vigorous fizzing — magnesium   acid — a few bubbles — iron

Figure 1

Use **Figure 1** to put these metals in order of reactivity, starting with the **most reactive**.

....

[1]

b) Next, Amal was given samples of three mystery metals, marked **X**, **Y** and **Z**. She put small pieces of each of the metals in cold water. If there was no reaction with cold water, she tested the metal to see if it would react with steam. Her results are shown in **Figure 2**.

Metal	Any reaction with cold water?	Any reaction with steam?
X	Reacts vigorously. Hydrogen gas is produced.	
Y	no reaction	Reacts vigorously. Metal is coated with a white solid. Hydrogen gas is produced.
Z	no reaction	no reaction

Figure 2

i) Metal **Y** was zinc. It reacted with the steam to produce hydrogen gas and a white solid. Name the white solid that was produced by this reaction.

....

[1]

ii) One of the other metals Amal was given was sodium.
Suggest whether sodium was metal **X** or metal **Z**. Give a reason for your answer.

....

....

[1]

[Total 3 marks]

Section 13 — Extracting Metals and Equilibria

Displacement Reactions

1   A student carries out a displacement reaction by reacting magnesium with
    an aqueous solution of iron chloride to produce magnesium chloride and iron.

$$Mg_{(s)} + FeCl_{2(aq)} \rightarrow MgCl_{2(aq)} + Fe_{(s)}$$

Explain why this displacement reaction is an example of a redox reaction.

....

....

[Total 2 marks]

2   Shaun adds small pieces of some metals to metal salt solutions. He records whether
    or not any reaction has taken place. His table of results is shown in **Figure 1**.

	Magnesium	**Silver**	**Aluminium**	**Lead**
Magnesium chloride	no reaction	no reaction	no reaction	no reaction
Silver nitrate	magnesium nitrate and silver formed	no reaction	aluminium nitrate and silver formed	lead nitrate and silver formed
Aluminium chloride	magnesium chloride and aluminium formed	no reaction	no reaction	no reaction
Lead nitrate	magnesium nitrate and lead formed	no reaction	aluminium nitrate and lead formed	no reaction

Figure 1

a) Shaun says "My results show that lead is more reactive than silver."
    Do you agree? Explain your answer.

....

....

[1]

b) Construct a balanced symbol equation for the reaction between magnesium
    and aluminium chloride, $AlCl_3$.

....

[2]

c) Nickel is above lead in the reactivity series. Nickel is a shiny grey metal and nickel nitrate
    is green in solution. Lead is a dull grey metal and lead nitrate is colourless in solution.
    Suggest what Shaun would observe if he added nickel to lead nitrate solution.

....

....

....

[2]

[Total 5 marks]

Extracting Metals Using Carbon

1   The method used to extract metals from their ores can be determined using the reactivity series. Part of the reactivity series is shown in **Figure 1**.

Potassium	K	Most Reactive
Calcium	Ca	
Aluminium	Al	
Carbon	C	
Zinc	Zn	
Tin	Sn	
Copper	Cu	Least Reactive

Figure 1

a) Give the definition of a metal ore.

....

....

[1]

b) Suggest how copper is extracted from its ore in industry.

....

....

[1]

c) State **one** other metal from **Figure 1** that can be extracted in the same way as copper.

....

[1]

[Total 3 marks]

2   Iron is extracted from its ore, iron oxide (Fe_2O_3), in a blast furnace using carbon.

a) Write a balanced equation for this reaction.

....

[2]

b) A certain batch of iron ore that contains impurities of zinc oxide and calcium oxide is reacted in a blast furnace. After the reaction is complete, any metal produced by the reaction was removed. Any unreacted ore was left in the reaction vessel.

The iron metal product was tested for purity and was found to contain traces of another metal. Suggest an identity for the other metal. Explain why it is present.

....

....

....

....

[3]

[Total 5 marks]

Section 13 — Extracting Metals and Equilibria

Other Methods of Extracting Metals

1 Aluminium is a metal that is widely used in construction. It can be extracted from its ore, aluminium oxide.

Grade 4-6

a) What is the name given to the technique used to extract aluminium from its ore?

....

[1]

b) As part of the extraction process, aluminium oxide is mixed in cryolite. What is the purpose of mixing the aluminium oxide with cryolite?

....

[1]

c) Pure aluminium is more expensive to buy than many metals which are extracted from their ores by reduction with carbon. Explain how the extraction process contributes to the higher cost of pure aluminium.

....

....

....

[2]

[Total 4 marks]

2 The increasing demand and the limited supply of metal-rich ores means that scientists are now developing new ways to extract metal from low-grade ores.

Grade 6-7

a) Describe how phytoextraction is used to extract some metals from their ores.

....

....

....

....

....

[4]

b) Give **one** advantage and **one** disadvantage of using phytoextraction to extract metals from their ores.

....

....

....

[2]

c) Name one other biological method of extracting metals from low-grade ores.

....

[1]

[Total 7 marks]

Section 13 — Extracting Metals and Equilibria

Recycling

1 This question is on recycling. (Grade 6-7)

a) An alternative to recycling is disposing of waste into landfill.
Give **one** disadvantage associated with using landfill to dispose of waste.

....

[1]

b) Avoiding using landfill is one environmental advantage of recycling. Give **two** other
environmental reasons why recycling is considered more sustainable than making new materials.

....

....

[2]

c) Give **two** economic benefits of recycling.

....

....

[2]

[Total 5 marks]

2 Rachel is sorting some rubbish that has accumulated around her house. (Grade 6-7)

a) Rachel has three pieces of rubbish made from three different materials, **A**, **B** and **C**.
Some data about the materials is shown in **Figure 1**.

Material	Availability of resource	Energy to recycle	Energy to extract
A	Abundant	High	Low
B	Limited	Low	High
C	Limited	Medium	High

Figure 1

From the data given, which material in **Figure 1** is the **best** to recycle? Explain your answer.

....

....

....

....

[2]

b) Rachel is able to recycle plastic bottles at her local recycling centre.
Given that many parts of the manufacturing process involve using fractions of crude oil,
explain why it is important to recycle plastics.

....

....

[1]

[Total 3 marks]

Section 13 — Extracting Metals and Equilibria

Life Cycle Assessments

A company is developing a new product. Identify the factors that they should consider when producing a life cycle assessment. Tick **two** boxes.

Colour of the product ☐   Demand for the product ☐

Recyclability of the product ☐   Attractiveness of the product ☐

Source of raw materials ☐   Profitability of the product ☐

1   A furniture company is designing a new range of chairs for children.
They need to decide whether the chairs will be made out of polypropene or timber.   *Grade 6-7*

a) The company carries out a life cycle assessment of both possible products.
Describe the purpose of a life cycle assessment.

....

....

[1]

b) Some data about the two materials are shown in **Figure 1**.

Material	Source	Relative Energy Cost to Make/Extract	Cost
Timber	Trees	1	Medium
Poly(propene)	Crude oil	15	Low

Figure 1

Use the data in **Figure 1** to explain which material would be the **best** choice to make the chairs from, in terms of sustainability. Explain your answer.

....

....

....

....

....

[3]

c) Suggest **two** factors, other than those given in **Figure 1**, that the company should consider in their life cycle assessment when deciding whether to make the chairs from timber or polypropene.

....

....

[2]

[Total 6 marks]

2 A garden tool company is considering the environmental costs of producing a rake. **Grade 6-7**

a) The rake contains components made from iron.
Suggest **two** environmental problems associated with extracting iron from its ore.

....

....

[2]

b) The rake contains parts that cannot be recycled, so the company thinks
that it is likely to be disposed of in landfill at the end of its life span.
Give **one** disadvantage of disposing of waste using landfill.

....

[1]

c) The rake is sold in plastic packaging.
Suggest a sustainable way that consumers could dispose of the packaging.

....

[1]

[Total 4 marks]

3 A toy company is carrying out a life cycle assessment of four prototype toys. **Grade 7-9**
Figure 2 displays some of the data from their assessments.

Toy	CO_2 emissions (kg)	Solvent use (dm³)	Energy consumption (MJ)
A	16.2	3981	267.84
B	14.8	2672	212.26
C	14.9	3876	159.82
D	12.4	2112	174.56

Figure 2

Using the data in the table, evaluate the relative environmental impact of producing each toy.

....

....

....

....

....

....

....

[Total 4 marks]

Exam Tip

You may be given data and asked to figure out which product has the biggest or smallest environmental impact.
It's likely that there won't be an obvious answer at first glance — some products may have really low CO_2 emissions
but may pollute lots of water. You'll have to look at all the factors and decide which product is the best or worst overall.

Section 13 — Extracting Metals and Equilibria

Target AO3

4   **Figure 3** contains life cycle assessment data for two types of soft drink container.

Figure 3

	Glass Bottles	**Aluminium Cans**
Raw Materials	Sand, soda ash and limestone	Aluminium ore
Manufacturing	• Have to be produced at very high temperatures • Their production releases greenhouse gases	• Require large amounts of electricity to extract aluminium from the ore • Their production releases greenhouse gases
Usage	Can be refilled and reused	Usually only used once
Disposal	Widely recycled and used to produce new glass	Can be continually recycled as a source of aluminium

a)   Use information from **Figure 3** to suggest **one** way in which glass bottles are
     more environmentally friendly than aluminium cans.

     ....

     [1]

b)   Aluminium cans can also be produced from recycled aluminium cans.
     Evaluate whether the life cycle assessment for aluminium cans produced from recycled cans
     would be more positive or negative than the life cycle assessment for aluminium cans in **Figure 3**.

     ....

     ....

     ....

     [2]

c)   Certain glass objects cannot be recycled with the glass bottles.
     Explain why this negatively affects the life cycle assessment of the glass bottles.

     ....

     ....

     [2]

d)   Suggest another useful comparison that could be added to the disposal section of these LCAs.

     ....

     ....

     [1]

     [Total 6 marks]

Exam Tip

An important skill in the exam is to consider potential impacts that haven't been given as part of the
life cycle assessment. Companies may produce assessments that make their products look great when they are actually
environmentally damaging. This is why it's important to consider all the information you can before answering.

Section 13 — Extracting Metals and Equilibria

Dynamic Equilibrium

Complete the paragraph below by circling the correct option from the choices.

The Haber Process is <u>an irreversible / a reversible</u> reaction that forms <u>ammonia / sulfuric acid</u> from hydrogen and nitrogen. The nitrogen used in the process is extracted from <u>the air / crude oil</u> and the hydrogen is extracted from <u>the air / natural gas</u>.

The conditions used for the Haber Process are a temperature of <u>200 °C / 450 °C</u>, a pressure of <u>250 atm / 200 atm</u> and in the presence of an <u>iron / aluminium</u> catalyst.

1 Dynamic equilibrium can only be achieved in reversible reactions. (Grade 4-6)

a) Compare the rates of the forwards and backwards reactions at dynamic equilibrium. State how this affects the concentrations of reactants and products present at dynamic equilibrium.

....

....

[2]

b) Dynamic equilibrium can only be reached in a closed system. Explain what is meant by a 'closed system'.

....

....

[1]

c) During a certain reversible reaction, the equilibrium lies to the left. How should the concentration of the reactants be altered in order to increase the rate of product formation?

....

[1]

[Total 4 marks]

2 An aqueous solution of blue copper(II) ions can react with chloride ions to form a yellow copper compound. The ionic equation for this reaction is: $Cu^{2+} + 4Cl^- \rightleftharpoons [CuCl_4]^{2-}$ (Grade 6-7)

a) What does the symbol '$\rightleftharpoons$' mean in this reaction?

....

[1]

b) A solution containing copper(II) ions is mixed with a solution containing chloride ions in a flask. The solution quickly turns green. When observed for a few minutes no further change in colour can be seen. Explain these observations.

....

....

....

[2]

[Total 3 marks]

Section 13 — Extracting Metals and Equilibria

Le Chatelier's Principle

1 The equilibrium position of a reaction is dependent on the conditions that the reaction is carried out under.

Grade 4-6

a) What does Le Chatelier's Principle say about the effect of changing the conditions of a reversible reaction at equilibrium?

....

[1]

b) State **two** conditions you could change in order to alter the position of equilibrium of a reaction that happens in solution.

....

....

[2]

[Total 3 marks]

2 Methanol can be manufactured industrially from a gas mixture of carbon monoxide and hydrogen in the following reaction: $CO_{(g)} + 2H_{2(g)} \rightleftharpoons CH_3OH_{(g)}$. This occurs over a Cu-ZnO-Al_2O_3 catalyst, under conditions of 250 °C and 50 –100 atm. The forward reaction is exothermic.

Grade 6-7

a) Under a certain set of conditions, the equilibrium lies to the right. Describe what this means, in terms of the concentration of products and reactants.

....

....

[1]

b) Identify which of the following statements is **false**. Tick **one** box.

☐ **A** A decrease in the concentration of CO shifts the position of equilibrium to the left.

☐ **B** Increasing the concentration of H_2 shifts the position of equilibrium to the right.

☐ **C** Increasing the temperature to 470 °C shifts the position of equilibrium to the left.

☐ **D** The Cu-ZnO-Al_2O_3 catalyst shifts the position of equilibrium to the right.

[1]

c) Amara says, to increase the yield of the reaction, they should decrease the pressure of the reaction. Russell disagrees. Which student do you agree with? Explain your answer.

....

....

....

....

[2]

[Total 4 marks]

3 A mixture of iodine monochloride (ICl) and chlorine is sealed in a gas syringe. The gases react in a reversible reaction to form iodine trichloride (ICl_3) and eventually reach an equilibrium. The equation for the reaction is: $ICl_{(g)} + Cl_{2(g)} \rightleftharpoons ICl_{3(s)}$. 〔Grade 7-9〕

a) Given that the forward reaction is exothermic, explain how the relative quantities of ICl and ICl_3 would change if the mixture was heated, and all other conditions remained the same.

....

....

....
[2]

b) Explain how the relative quantities of ICl and ICl_3 would change if the plunger were pushed into the syringe, and the temperature remained constant.

....

....

....
[3]

[Total 5 marks]

4 Dinitrogen tetroxide (N_2O_4) is a colourless gas. It decomposes in a reversible reaction to form the brown gas, nitrogen dioxide (NO_2). The reaction equation is: $N_2O_{4(g)} \rightleftharpoons 2NO_{2(g)}$. 〔Grade 7-9〕

a) When a sample of N_2O_4 is left to decompose in a sealed tube, a pale brown colour can be seen. If this mixture is heated, the colour becomes a darker brown. Explain this observation and predict whether the forward reaction is exothermic or endothermic.

....

....

....
[3]

b) Explain how you would expect the colour of the equilibrium mixture to change if the pressure of the mixture is decreased, and all other conditions are kept the same.

....

....

....

....
[3]

[Total 6 marks]

Exam Tip

Working out what happens to the position of an equilibrium when you change the conditions can be a bit of a brain twister. Just remember that for any change that's made, the reaction will try to do the opposite. So if you increase the temperature the endothermic reaction will speed up, if you increase the pressure the equilibrium will move to the side where there are fewer moles of gas, and if you increase the concentration of a reactant you'll get more products.

Section 13 — Extracting Metals and Equilibria

Target AO3

5   A scientist investigated the gas phase reaction between sulfur dioxide and oxygen.
The equation for this reversible reaction is: $2SO_{2(g)} + O_{2\,(g)} \rightleftharpoons 2SO_{3\,(g)}$.
Figure 1 shows how the concentration of sulfur dioxide and sulfur trioxide change with time.

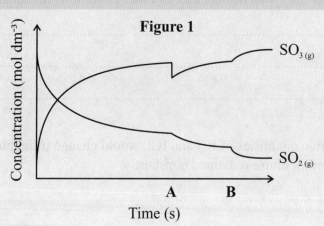

Figure 1

a)   Suggest what happened to cause the change in concentration of SO_3 at time **A** and shortly after.

....

....

[2]

b)   Increasing the temperature of the reaction causes the amount of SO_3 produced
by the reaction to decrease. Use this information to determine whether the
forward reaction is endothermic or exothermic, and justify your answer.

....

....

....

[2]

c)   State whether the pressure was decreased or increased at time **B**. Explain your answer.

....

....

....

[2]

d)   In a separate reaction, SO_3 is added to a container,
which is then sealed to form a closed system.
Sketch a graph of the concentrations of sulfur
dioxide and sulfur trioxide versus time for the
reaction, $2SO_{3\,(g)} \rightleftharpoons 2SO_{2\,(g)} + O_{2\,(g)}$, assuming the
reaction takes place at a constant low pressure.

[2]

[Total 8 marks]

Exam Tip

As well as asking you to draw graphs, the examiner may ask you to interpret and explain what a graph tells you about
a reaction. Make sure you understand how the key changes in the graph relate to the reaction in the question.

Group 1 — Alkali Metals

1 The alkali metals are found in Group 1 of the periodic table. [Grade 4-6]

a) Which of the following statements is the **best** description of the alkali metals? Tick **one** box.

- [ ] **A** Soft metals with relatively high melting points.
- [ ] **B** Soft metals with relatively low melting points.
- [ ] **C** Hard metals with relatively high melting points.
- [ ] **D** Hard metals with relatively low melting points.

[1]

b) The alkali metals readily react to form ionic compounds.
Explain why their ions usually have a charge of +1.

....

....

[2]

[Total 3 marks]

2 A teacher is demonstrating the reactions between water and some alkali metals to her class. In one reaction, she adds a small piece of potassium to cold water. [Grade 6-7]

a) Name the **two** products of this reaction.

....

[2]

b) Describe what you would expect to see if a small piece of potassium was added to cold water.

....

....

....

....

[2]

c) It is **not** safe to carry out the reaction between rubidium and water in the laboratory.
Explain why this is the case, using ideas about the electronic configurations of Group 1 metals.

....

....

....

....

....

[3]

[Total 7 marks]

Group 7 — Halogens

1   Amelia is testing gases. (Grade 4-6)

Figure 1 shows a gas being tested.

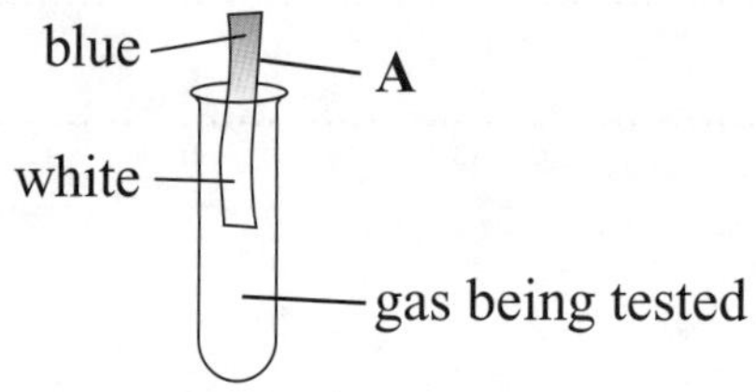

blue — A

white

gas being tested

Figure 1

a) Identify the item labelled **A** in **Figure 1**.

....

[1]

b) Suggest which gas was present in the test tube.

....

[1]

[Total 2 marks]

2   The halogens can react with alkali metals to form metal halide salts. (Grade 4-6)

a) Name the metal halide salt that will be formed when the following pairs of elements react.

i) Bromine and sodium.

....

[1]

ii) Iodine and potassium.

....

[1]

b) When chlorine gas reacts with lithium, the salt lithium chloride, LiCl, is formed.
   Write the balanced symbol equation for this reaction.

....

[2]

[Total 4 marks]

3 A chemist is carrying out some reactions involving halogens. Grade 6-7

a) i) In his first experiment he reacts hydrogen gas with chlorine gas.
Write a balanced chemical equation for this reaction.

....

[2]

ii) The chemist dissolves the product of this reaction in water and adds universal indicator.
What colour will the solution turn? Explain your answer.

....

....

[2]

b) The chemist carries out another reaction at room temperature and pressure, using a different
gaseous halogen. Determine which of the halogens he must be using. Explain your answer.

....

....

[2]

c) Describe the appearance of bromine at room temperature.

....

[2]

[Total 8 marks]

4 The reactivity of halogens is dependent on their electronic configuration. Grade 7-9

a) Describe the electronic configuration of the halogens and how it changes down Group 7.

....

....

....

[2]

b) Sodium reacts violently with fluorine, at room temperature, to form sodium fluoride.
Predict how astatine might react with sodium at room temperature. Explain your answer.

....

....

....

....

....

[3]

[Total 5 marks]

Exam Tip

One of the most important things to learn about Group 7 elements is the trend you find in reactivity as you go down or up the group. And you need to be able to explain this trend using the electronic structure of the halogens. Smashing.

Section 14 — Groups in the Periodic Table

Halogen Displacement Reactions

1 Josie investigated the reactions that occur when chlorine, bromine or iodine are added to different sodium halide solutions. **Figure 1** shows her results.

	Sodium chloride solution ($NaCl_{(aq)}$, colourless)	Sodium bromide solution ($NaBr_{(aq)}$, colourless)	Sodium iodide solution ($NaI_{(aq)}$, colourless)
Add chlorine water ($Cl_{2\,(aq)}$, colourless)	no reaction	solution turns orange	....
Add bromine water ($Br_{2\,(aq)}$, orange)	no reaction	....	solution turns brown
Add iodine water ($I_{2\,(aq)}$, brown)	no reaction	no reaction	no reaction

Figure 1

a) Use your knowledge of the reactivity trend of the halogens to fill in the missing results in **Figure 1**.

[2]

b) Explain why there was no reaction when Josie added iodine water to sodium bromide solution.

....

....

[2]

c) i) Construct a balanced symbol equation for the reaction that happened when Josie added chlorine water to sodium bromide solution.

....

[2]

ii) Explain, in terms of electrons, why the reaction between chlorine water and sodium bromide solution can be described as a redox reaction.

....

....

....

[2]

d) Astatine is below iodine in Group 7. Predict whether chlorine water would react with sodium astatide solution. Explain your answer.

....

....

[2]

[Total 10 marks]

Section 14 — Groups in the Periodic Table

Group 0 — Noble Gases

1 Old-style filament light bulbs contain a thin metal filament. If these light bulbs were filled with air, oxygen would react with the filament causing it to burn away. To avoid this, the light bulbs are filled with argon.

Explain why argon is suitable for this use, including ideas about electronic structure.

....

....

....

....

[Total 3 marks]

2 The noble gases are inert gases that make up Group 0 of the periodic table.

Figure 1 shows some information about the first four noble gases.

Element	Symbol	Boiling point (°C)	Density (kg m^{-3})
Helium	He	−269	0.18
Neon	Ne	−246	0.90
Argon	Ar	−186	?
Krypton	Kr	−153	3.7

Figure 1

a) i) The element below krypton in Group 0 is xenon.
Use the information in **Figure 1** to predict what the boiling point of xenon will be.

boiling point = ... °C

[1]

ii) Use the information in **Figure 1** to predict the density of argon.

density = ... kg m^{-3}

[1]

b) Would you expect the boiling point of radon to be higher or lower than the boiling point of xenon? Explain your answer.

....

....

[1]

[Total 3 marks]

Exam Tip

Make sure you get lots of practice at questions like Q2, where you're given information about some of the elements in a group and asked to use it to predict something about another element in the group. They need careful thinking through.

Section 14 — Groups in the Periodic Table

Reaction Rate Experiments

1 A scientist reacts hydrochloric acid with marble chips to form calcium chloride, water and carbon dioxide gas.   **PRACTICAL**

a) He decides to measure the volume of carbon dioxide formed to work out the rate of the reaction. Outline a method the scientist could follow to monitor the volume of gas produced over the course of the reaction.

....

....

....

....

[3]

b) **Figure 1** shows a graph of his results. On **Figure 1**, sketch a curve that shows how the volume of gas produced would change over time if the experiment was carried out at a higher temperature.

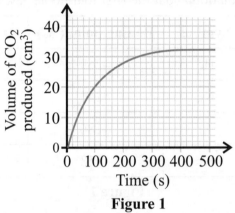

Figure 1

[2]

c) The scientist repeated the reaction using different quantities of reactants. Reaction **X** used 0.500 g of marble chips and an excess of 0.100 mol dm^{-3} hydrochloric acid. Using **Figure 2**, determine which of the following sets of conditions could have resulted in reaction **Y**. Tick **one** box.

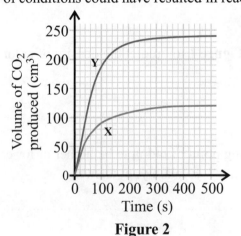

Figure 2

☐ **A** 0.250 g of marble chips and an excess of 0.100 mol dm^{-3} hydrochloric acid.

☐ **B** 1.00 g of marble chips and an excess of 0.100 mol dm^{-3} hydrochloric acid.

☐ **C** 0.250 g of marble chips and an excess of 0.200 mol dm^{-3} hydrochloric acid.

☐ **D** 1.00 g of marble chips and an excess of 0.200 mol dm^{-3} hydrochloric acid.

[1]

[Total 6 marks]

2 Laiza is investigating the effect of temperature on the rate of the reaction between sodium thiosulfate and hydrochloric acid. The reaction forms a cloudy, yellow precipitate of sulfur.

Grade 6-7 **PRACTICAL**

a) She measures out volumes of both reactants and gently heats each of the solutions in a water bath to 50 °C. Outline a method that Laiza could follow to monitor the rate of this reaction.

....

....

....
[3]

b) Laiza repeats the experiment but instead heats both reactant solutions to 30 °C.

i) How would you expect the rate of this reaction to compare to the rate of the reaction at 50 °C?

....
[1]

ii) Name **one** factor Laiza would have to keep the same for both reactions to make it a fair test.

....
[1]

[Total 5 marks]

3 Shabnam reacted magnesium ribbons with hydrochloric acid. As the reaction proceeded, hydrogen gas was produced.

Grade 6-7

Shabnam carried out two different reactions, **M** and **N**, using two different concentrations of acid in order to see how concentration affects the rate of reaction. All of the other variables were kept the same during both of the experiments. A graph of her results is shown in **Figure 3**.

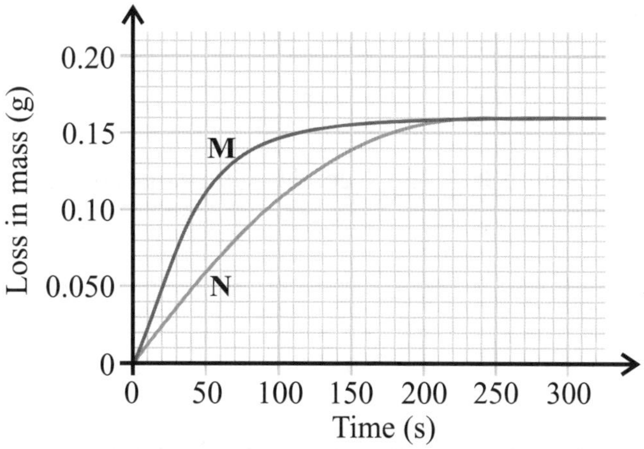

Figure 3

a) Which reaction, **M** or **N**, used a higher concentration of hydrochloric acid? Explain your answer.

....

....
[2]

b) Using the graph, calculate the rate of reaction **N** between 0 and 50 seconds.

rate = ... g s^{-1}
[2]

[Total 4 marks]

Section 15 — Rates of Reaction and Energy Changes

4   A student wanted to calculate the rate of reaction between nitric acid
     and zinc. He carried out two experiments under the same conditions,
     but in one he used zinc ribbons and in the other he used zinc powder.

The graph in **Figure 4** shows the rate of reaction for both experiments, labelled **Q** and **R**.

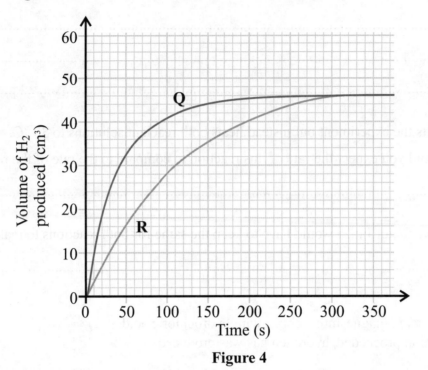

Figure 4

a) i) Calculate the rate of reaction **Q** at 50 seconds. Give your answer to 2 significant figures.

rate = ... cm^3 s^{-1}

[3]

ii) Calculate the rate of reaction **R** at 120 seconds. Give your answer to 2 significant figures.

rate = ... cm^3 s^{-1}

[3]

b) State which reaction, **Q** or **R**, used the powdered zinc. Explain your answer.

....

....

....

[3]

[Total 9 marks]

Exam Tip

Drawing a tangent at a specific point on a curve can be quite tricky. You need to make sure that it has the same
gradient as the curve at that specific point. Drawing a tangent too different from the correct gradient could make a big
difference to your final answer, so take your time and try moving your ruler around a bit first to find the best position.

Section 15 — Rates of Reaction and Energy Changes

Collision Theory

A student is investigating the reaction between nitric acid and calcium carbonate under three different conditions, **A**, **B** and **C**. All other variables are kept the same. Circle the condition that will result in the greatest rate of reaction.

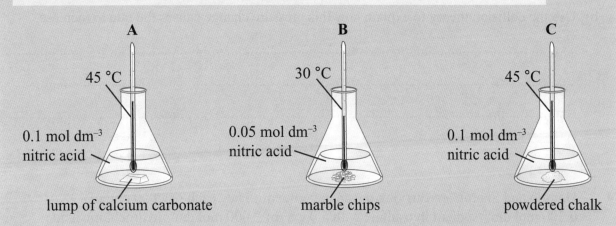

A

45 °C

0.1 mol dm^{-3} nitric acid

lump of calcium carbonate

B

30 °C

0.05 mol dm^{-3} nitric acid

marble chips

C

45 °C

0.1 mol dm^{-3} nitric acid

powdered chalk

---

1 This question is about the rate of a chemical reaction between two reactants, one of which is in solution, and one of which is a solid. Grade 4-6

a) Which of the following changes would **not** cause the rate of the chemical reaction to increase? Tick **one** box.

⬜ **A** Increasing the concentration of the solution.

⬜ **B** Heating the reaction mixture to a higher temperature.

⬜ **C** Using a larger volume of the solution, but keeping the concentration the same.

⬜ **D** Grinding the solid reactant so that it forms a fine powder.

[1]

b) What is the name given to the minimum amount of energy which particles must have if they are to react when they collide?

....

[1]

[Total 2 marks]

2 This question is about the rate of the reaction between magnesium and hydrochloric acid. The chemical equation for the reaction is: Grade 6-7

$$Mg_{(s)} + 2HCl_{(aq)} \rightarrow MgCl_{2(aq)} + H_{2(g)}$$

Using collision theory, explain why cutting the magnesium into smaller pieces affects the rate of this reaction.

....

....

....

[Total 2 marks]

Section 15 — Rates of Reaction and Energy Changes

3 The Sabatier reaction can be used industrially to make methane from carbon dioxide and hydrogen in the following reaction:

$$CO_{2(g)} + 4H_{2(g)} \rightarrow CH_{4(g)} + 2H_2O_{(g)}$$

Grade 6-7

a) How could the pressure be altered to **increase** the rate of the reaction?

....

[1]

b) Use the collision theory to explain how this pressure change causes the rate to increase.

....

....

....

[2]

[Total 3 marks]

4 Horatio and Sharon are carrying out an experiment. They each react 50 cm³ of 0.300 mol dm⁻³ sodium thiosulfate with 5.0 cm³ of 2.000 mol dm⁻³ hydrochloric acid.

Grade 6-7

a) Horatio carries out his reaction at room temperature. Sharon heats her reactants to 45 °C and carries out the reaction in a 45 °C water bath. Horatio thinks that his reaction will have taken place much more quickly than Sharon's reaction. Is Horatio correct? Explain your answer using collision theory.

....

....

....

....

....

[3]

b) i) Sharon repeats her experiment using different concentrations of hydrochloric acid. Which of the following concentrations of hydrochloric acid would result in the **slowest** rate of reaction? Tick **one** box.

☐ **A** 0.350 mol dm⁻³ hydrochloric acid

☐ **B** 1.250 mol dm⁻³ hydrochloric acid

☐ **C** 2.100 mol dm⁻³ hydrochloric acid

☐ **D** 0.550 mol dm⁻³ hydrochloric acid

[1]

ii) Explain your answer.

....

....

[2]

[Total 6 marks]

Section 15 — Rates of Reaction and Energy Changes

Catalysts

1 Enzymes are a type of catalyst. (Grade 4-6)

   a) Identify which of the following catalysts is an example of an enzyme. Tick **one** box.

     ☐ **A** Iron: a catalyst used in the Haber process.

     ☐ **B** Manganese(IV) oxide: a catalyst used in the decomposition of hydrogen peroxide.

     ☐ **C** RuBisCO: a catalyst used in photosynthesis.

     ☐ **D** Vanadium pentoxide: a catalyst used in the Contact process.

[1]

   b) Give **one** example of when enzymes are used as catalysts in industrial processes.

     ....

[1]

[Total 2 marks]

2 Zola is observing the decomposition of hydrogen peroxide.
The reaction is very slow. Meredith tells her to repeat the experiment (Grade 6-7)
with manganese(IV) oxide powder, and the rate of reaction increases.

   a) Zola determines that the manganese(IV) oxide must have acted as a catalyst.
Explain how a catalyst works to increase the rate of reaction.

     ....

     ....

     ....

[2]

   b) Why does Zola only need to use a small mass of
manganese(IV) oxide powder to catalyse the reaction?

     ....

[1]

   c) The reaction profiles for both the catalysed and the uncatalysed reactions are shown in **Figure 1**.
Identify what each of the labels, A–D, show.

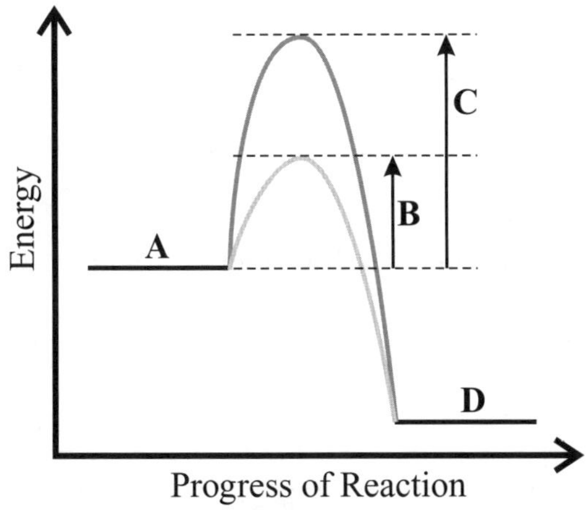

A: ....

B: ....

....

C: ....

....

D: ....

[4]

Figure 1

[Total 7 marks]

Section 15 — Rates of Reaction and Energy Changes

Endothermic and Exothermic Reactions

1 Which of the following energy changes describes an exothermic reaction? Tick **one** box.

	Energy of products	**Temperature of surroundings**
A	Greater than reactants	Increases
B	Less than reactants	Increases
C	Greater than reactants	Decreases
D	Less than reactants	Decreases

[Total 1 mark]

2 The thermal decomposition of calcium carbonate is an endothermic reaction.

Sketch and label a reaction profile for this reaction on the axes below. Label the activation energy.

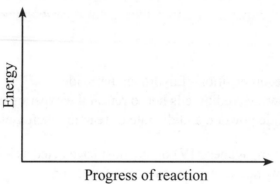

[Total 3 marks]

3 A company is looking for a reaction with a low activation energy to use in a hand warmer. The reaction profiles for the reactions being investigated are shown in **Figure 1**.

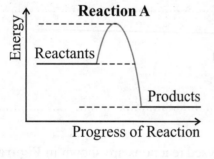 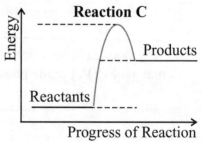

Figure 1

a) Define 'activation energy'.

....

....

[1]

b) Suggest which reaction would be **most suitable** for using in a hand warmer. Explain your answer.

....

....

....

[3]

[Total 4 marks]

Section 15 — Rates of Reaction and Energy Changes

Measuring Temperature Changes

1   A student is investigating the temperature change that occurs when he dissolves the same number of moles of two different salts, **A** and **B**, in water.

Grade 6-7

a) Suggest **three** essential pieces of apparatus needed for the investigation.

....

....

[3]

b)* Describe a method that the student could use to carry out his investigation. Include details of any variables that would need to be controlled.

....

....

....

....

....

....

....

....

....

[6]

c) The student's results are shown in **Figure 1**. Complete the table.

Salt	Initial temperature (°C)	End temperature (°C)	Temperature change (°C)
A	21.0	16.0	....
B	21.0	26.5	....

Figure 1

[2]

d) Which of the statements below about the student's experiment is correct? Tick **one** box.

   ☐ **A** Both salts dissolved exothermically.

   ☐ **B** Salt A dissolved exothermically, but salt B dissolved endothermically.

   ☐ **C** Salt A dissolved endothermically, but salt B dissolved exothermically.

   ☐ **D** Both salts dissolved endothermically.

[1]

[Total 12 marks]

 ☐   ☐   ☐

Bond Energies

Which of the following statements is true? Tick **one** box.

☐ A During exothermic reactions, the energy taken to break the bonds in the reactants is greater than the energy released by making the bonds in the products.

☐ B During endothermic reactions, the energy released by breaking bonds in the reactants is less than the energy taken to make the bonds in the products.

☐ C During exothermic reactions, the energy taken to break the bonds in the reactants is less than the energy released by making the bonds in the products.

☐ D During endothermic reactions, the energy taken to break the bonds in the reactants is less than the energy released by making the bonds in the products.

1 Look at **Figure 1**. It shows the bond energies of some bonds.

Bond	Bond energy (kJ mol^{-1})
C — H	413
C — O	358
H — O	463
C = C	614
C — C	347

Figure 1

a) Use **Figure 1** to work out the energy change of the following reaction between ethene and water.

$$\text{H}_2\text{C}=\text{CH}_2 \ + \ \text{H}_2\text{O} \rightarrow \text{H}-\text{CH}_2-\text{CH}_2-\text{O}-\text{H}$$

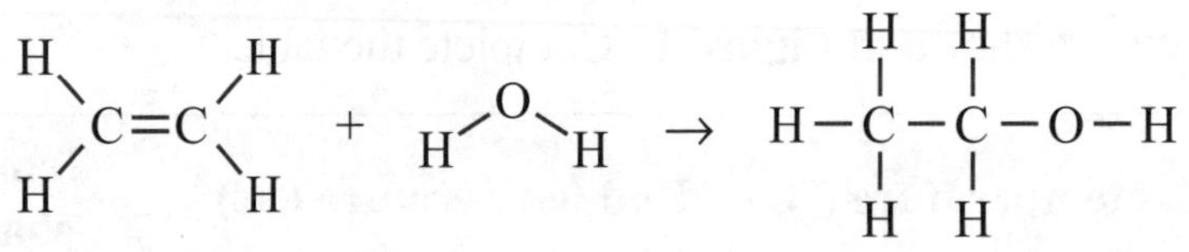

Energy change = ... kJ mol^{-1}

[3]

b) Using your answer to a), state whether the reaction between ethene and water is endothermic or exothermic. Explain your answer.

....

....

[2]

[Total 5 marks]

2 The energy change of the following reaction is −119 kJ mol⁻¹.

$$H-\underset{\underset{H}{|}}{\overset{\overset{H}{|}}{C}}-\underset{\underset{H}{|}}{\overset{\overset{H}{|}}{C}}-H \quad + \quad Cl-Cl \quad \rightarrow \quad H-\underset{\underset{H}{|}}{\overset{\overset{H}{|}}{C}}-\underset{\underset{H}{|}}{\overset{\overset{Cl}{|}}{C}}-H \quad + \quad H-Cl$$

a) Compare the energy released by forming bonds in the products
   in this reaction with the energy used to break bonds in the reactants.

   ....

   ....

   [1]

b) Use this information, as well as the data in **Figure 2**,
   to work out the approximate bond energy of an H—Cl bond.

Figure 2

Bond	Bond energy (kJ mol⁻¹)
C — H	413
C — C	347
C — Cl	339
Cl — Cl	239

Bond energy = ... kJ mol⁻¹
   [3]

c) Use your answer from b) to rank the bonds from **Figure 2**,
   and the H—Cl bond in order of strength, from weakest to strongest.

   ....

   [1]

   [Total 5 marks]

Exam Tip

In questions involving calculating energy changes from bond energies (or vice versa), it can be really useful to draw out the displayed formulas of the chemicals that you're dealing with (unless you're given them in the question of course). Displayed formulas show all of the atoms in a molecule and all the bonds between them, so doing this makes it much easier to see what bonds have broken and what new bonds have been made during a chemical reaction.

     Section 15 — Rates of Reaction and Energy Changes

Fractional Distillation and Hydrocarbons

Warm-Up

Draw a line to match each of the following fractions of crude oil with one of its main uses.

Bitumen	Fuel for aircraft
Diesel	Surfacing roads and roofs
Kerosene	Fuel for cars and trains.

1 Crude oil is a complex mixture of hydrocarbons. **Grade 4-6**

a) What is a hydrocarbon?

....

[2]

b) To which homologous series do most of the hydrocarbons in crude oil belong? Tick **one** box.

☐ **A** alkenes

☐ **B** alkanes

☐ **C** alcohols

☐ **D** carboxylic acids

[1]

c) Crude oil is a finite resource. What does this mean?

....

[1]

[Total 4 marks]

2 The hydrocarbons in crude oil belong to several different homologous series. Compounds in a homologous series all share the same general formula. Give **three** other characteristics of the compounds in a homologous series. **Grade 6-7**

....

....

....

....

....

[Total 3 marks]

3   Propane, C_3H_8, is a hydrocarbon present in the gas fraction of crude oil.   (Grade 6-7)

a) Propane can be used as a fuel by burning it in oxygen.

   i) Why do hydrocarbons make good fuels?

....

[1]

   ii) Write a balanced symbol equation for the complete combustion of propane.

....

[2]

b) Propane is a very small hydrocarbon molecule. Which of the following statements about propane is **true**? Tick **one** box.

☐ **A** It has a low boiling point and is hard to ignite.

☐ **B** It has a high boiling point and is easy to ignite.

☐ **C** It has a low boiling point and is easy to ignite.

☐ **D** It has a high boiling point and is hard to ignite.

[1]

[Total 4 marks]

4   Kerosene, diesel oil and fuel oil are all fractions of crude oil that can be used as fuels. The average chain length of the hydrocarbons in kerosene is shorter than those in diesel oil. The average chain length of the hydrocarbons in diesel oil is shorter than those in fuel oil.   (Grade 6-7)

a) State which of the three fractions named above has the highest boiling point. Explain your answer with reference to the information above.

....

....

[2]

b) Compare the viscosity of kerosene and fuel oil. Explain your answer with reference to the information above.

....

....

[2]

c) Compare the ease of ignition of kerosene and diesel oil. Explain your answer with reference to the information above.

....

....

[2]

[Total 6 marks]

Section 16 — Fuels and Earth Science

5 Crude oil can be separated using the process of fractional distillation. The length of the hydrocarbon chains is fundamental to this process.

Figure 1 shows the boiling points of two molecules that are present in two of the fractions produced by the fractional distillation of crude oil.

Hydrocarbon	Chemical formula	Boiling point (°C)
Heptane	C_7H_{16}	98
Triacontane	$C_{30}H_{62}$	450

Figure 1

a) Triacontane is present in the fuel oil fraction. Give **two** uses of fuel oil.

....

....

[2]

b) i) Which of these two hydrocarbons would you expect to be collected **further down** the fractionating column?

....

[1]

ii) Explain your answer, with reference to the intermolecular forces present between the hydrocarbon molecules.

....

....

....

....

....

....

....

....

[5]

c) A scientist tests the viscosity of heptane, triacontane and a third alkane, alkane **X**. She finds that alkane **X** is more viscous than both heptane and triacontane. Suggest which fraction of crude oil alkane **X** is likely to have been taken from.

....

[1]

[Total 9 marks]

Exam Tip

Remember that if you're given one physical property of a hydrocarbon, you can use it to predict other properties of that compound. E.g., if you're told that a certain hydrocarbon has a low boiling point, you can predict that it will have low viscosity, be easy to ignite, and come from a fraction that is collected towards the top of the fractionating column.

Pollutants

1 Acid rain is formed when certain gases dissolve in rainwater to form a dilute acid. **Grade 4-6**

a) Which of the following gases contributes to acid rain? Tick **one** box.

☐ **A** carbon dioxide

☐ **B** methane

☐ **C** sulfur dioxide

☐ **D** carbon monoxide

[1]

b) Give **two** possible negative effects of acid rain.

....

....

[2]

[Total 3 marks]

2 Combustion of fuels, such as petrol, in cars is a major contributor to air pollution. **Grade 6-7**

a) Explain how cars produce nitrogen oxides.

....

....

[2]

b) Fuel combustion can produce soot. What impact can soot have on human health?

....

[1]

c) State which toxic gas is produced by incomplete fuel combustion and explain why it is toxic.

....

....

....

[3]

d) Hydrogen gas can also be used as a fuel in cars. Give **two** advantages of
using hydrogen gas rather than fossil fuels as a means of powering vehicles.

....

....

....

[2]

[Total 8 marks]

Section 16 — Fuels and Earth Science

Cracking

1   Some hydrocarbons from crude oil undergo processing by the petrochemical industry. For instance, decane, $C_{10}H_{22}$, can undergo cracking as shown in the following equation:

$$C_{10}H_{22} \rightarrow C_8H_{18} + C_2H_4$$

Grade 6-7

a) C_2H_4 is an unsaturated hydrocarbon. To which homologous series does it belong? Tick **one** box.

☐ **A** alkanes ☐ **B** alkenes ☐ **C** alcohols ☐ **D** carboxylic acids

[1]

b) Explain why a petrochemical company may need to crack hydrocarbons.

....

....

[2]

c) Cracking can form a variety of products.
Write an alternative balanced equation for the cracking of decane.

....

[1]

[Total 4 marks]

2   The hydrocarbon fractions produced by the fractional distillation of crude oil are used in many industrial processes. **Figure 1** shows the approximate percentage of each fraction produced by an oil refinery and the demand for each fraction.

Grade 6-7

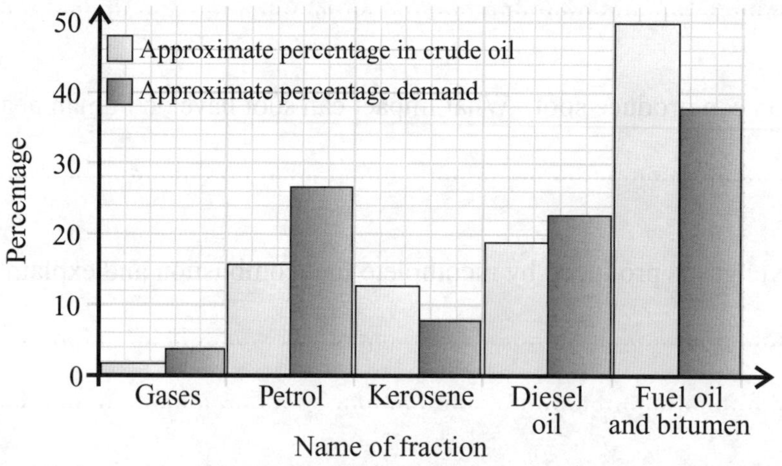

Figure 1

a) The demand for diesel oil is greater than the supply. Using **Figure 1**, name **two** other fractions whose demand is greater than their supply.

....

[2]

b) Suggest what could be done to help match the supply of diesel oil to the demand.

....

....

[1]

[Total 3 marks]

Target AO3

3   A group of students conducted an experiment to measure the volume of gas produced when they crack a long-chain hydrocarbon. The students' set-up is shown in **Figure 2**.

Figure 2

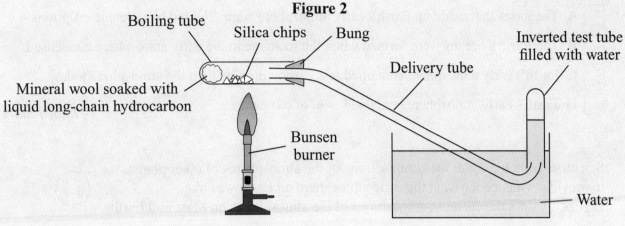

a)   The bung is used to ensure that any gas produced by the reaction goes into the delivery tube. Explain why the bung is also a necessary safety precaution when using a Bunsen burner to heat the boiling tube.

....

....
[2]

b)   One of the students had a lot more gas in their test tube than the others at the end of the experiment. Suggest an error that the student could have made that would cause this to occur.

....

....
[1]

c)   The students want to improve the accuracy of their results. Suggest **one** part of the set-up that could be changed in order to produce more accurate results.

....
[1]

d)   During the experiment, some water was sucked back into the delivery tube. Suggest why it is important to remove the apparatus from the water when this happens.

....
[1]

e)   Suggest why it would not be possible to carry out this experiment in a laboratory without a catalyst.

....

....
[1]

[Total 6 marks]

Exam Tip

In the exam, you might be asked about experiments and reactions that you've never seen before. Firstly — don't panic. Secondly — think about the information you've been given and if you can link it to your existing knowledge in some way.

      Section 16 — Fuels and Earth Science

The Atmosphere

1 Which of these statements about Earths's early atmosphere is **correct**? Tick **one** box.   *Grade 4-6*

☐ **A** The gases that made up Earth's early atmosphere were released by volcanic eruptions.

☐ **B** The Earth's oceans were formed when the methane in the early atmosphere condensed.

☐ **C** Earth's early atmosphere contained less carbon dioxide than the atmosphere today.

☐ **D** Earth's early atmosphere contained a lot of oxygen.

[Total 1 mark]

2 Scientists have looked at the compositions of the atmospheres of other planets to provide evidence for what the early atmosphere on Earth was like. *Grade 6-7*
Figure 1 shows the current compositions of the atmospheres on Mars and Earth.

	Percentage composition (%)					
	H_2O	Ne	CO_2	N_2	O_2	Ar
Mars	0.030	trace	95	2.7	0.13	1.6
Earth	0–4.0	0.0018	0.036	78	21	0.93

Figure 1

a) i) Scientists believe Earth's early atmosphere was similar to the atmosphere on Mars.
Using **Figure 1**, suggest which gas made up the majority of Earth's early atmosphere.

....

[1]

ii) Explain **two** ways in which this gas was removed from Earth's atmosphere as it evolved.

....

....

[2]

b) i) Explain how oxygen built up in Earth's atmosphere and suggest
why there is hardly any oxygen present in the atmosphere of Mars.

....

....

....

[2]

ii) Describe the chemical test for oxygen.

....

[1]

[Total 6 marks]

The Greenhouse Effect and Climate Change

Warm-Up

Identify the statements below that describe things that a family can do to reduce their carbon dioxide emissions. Tick **two** boxes.

Leaving lights on all day	☐	Using a tumble drier	☐
Walking to school	☐	Turning central heating down	☐
Leaving appliances on standby	☐	Using air conditioning	☐

1   The Earth's atmosphere contains greenhouse gases which contribute to the greenhouse effect.   *(Grade 4-6)*

a) Name **two** greenhouse gases.

    ....
                                                                                                                        [2]

b) Give **two** examples of types of human activity which are leading to an **increase** in the concentration of greenhouse gases in the atmosphere.

    ....

    ....
                                                                                                                        [2]
                                                                                                            [Total 4 marks]

2   The Earth absorbs some electromagnetic radiation from the sun. It then radiates some of the radiation it absorbs as infrared (IR) radiation. IR radiation contributes to the greenhouse effect by interacting with greenhouse gases.   *(Grade 6-7)*

a) Which of the following statements is **true**? Tick **one** box.

    ☐ **A** Greenhouse gases absorb all of the IR radiation that is radiated by Earth.

    ☐ **B** The greenhouse effect is caused by the absorption and reflection of IR radiation by greenhouse gases.

    ☐ **C** In general, the higher the concentration of greenhouse gases in the Earth's atmosphere, the colder the Earth becomes.

    ☐ **D** Greenhouse gases make up a large percentage of Earth's current atmosphere.
                                                                                                                        [1]

b) Elvis says he thinks that any amount of any greenhouse gases in the Earth's atmosphere is dangerous, as it could cause global warming. Is Elvis correct? Explain your answer.

    ....

    ....
                                                                                                                        [1]
                                                                                                            [Total 2 marks]

Section 16 — Fuels and Earth Science

3 Scientists believe that the increased burning of fossil fuels has contributed to global warming and this has caused glaciers to melt, resulting in rising sea levels.

Figure 1 shows CO_2 emissions by fossil fuels in the UK and Crown dependencies and the changes in sea levels between 1993 and 2013.

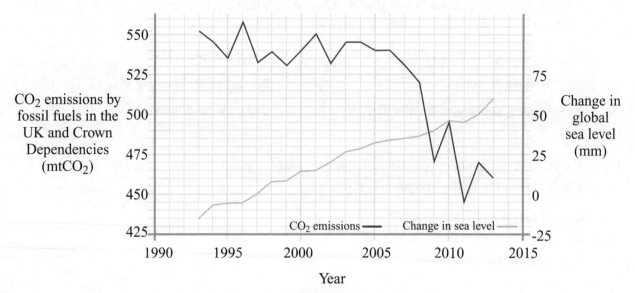

Figure 1

a)* Look at **Figure 1**. Explain whether the data shown on this graph supports a link between human activity and climate change. Discuss any problems associated with using this data to draw conclusions about the affect of carbon dioxide emissions on global sea levels.

....

....

....

....

....

....

....

....

[6]

b) Many governments are trying to decrease their country's CO_2 emissions.
Give **two** ways that the government in the UK is trying to reduce carbon dioxide emissions.

....

....

[2]

[Total 8 marks]

Exam Tip

If you're given some data about climate change to analyse, you need to think very carefully about what the data does and doesn't show, without making any assumptions. For example, if you're given some data that only relates to one country, you can't assume that the same pattern will be true for the whole world. You'd need more data to be certain.

Target AO3

4 Scientists in Antarctica use ice cores to measure how the Earth's atmosphere and temperature have changed over time.

a) Antarctic ice contains bubbles of gas that were trapped at different points depending on when the ice first froze. Suggest how these bubbles can be used to work out how the Earth's atmosphere has changed.

....

....

[1]

b) **Figure 2** shows the carbon dioxide concentration from one Antarctic ice core, as well as the global temperature anomaly for the same period. The global temperature anomaly is the temperature difference from the average temperature for the 20th century.

Figure 2

Year	CO_2 concentration (ppm)	Global temperature anomaly (°C)
1960	319	+ 0.1
1970	324	+ 0.1
1980	340	+ 0.3
1990	355	+ 0.5
2000	374	+ 0.6

A scientist states that there is a link between carbon dioxide concentration and global temperature. Is their conclusion supported by the data in **Figure 2**? Explain your answer.

....

....

....

[2]

c) Suggest how increasing carbon dioxide levels might affect the scientists' ability to collect new ice cores in the future.

....

....

....

[2]

d) Scientists are able to collect large ice cores from deep inside ice sheets. These cores can be up to 3 km long, and can contain ice from hundreds of thousands of years ago. Collecting these cores takes a long time. Suggest **one** other limitation to collecting large ice cores.

....

....

[1]

[Total 6 marks]

Distance, Displacement, Speed and Velocity

Write each word below in the table on the right to show whether it is a scalar or vector quantity.

acceleration   time   temperature

mass   weight   force

Scalar	Vector

1 Which of the following correctly defines a vector? *Grade 4-6*

☐ **A** Vector quantities only have magnitude.

☐ **B** Vector quantities show direction but not magnitude.

☐ **C** Vector quantities have both magnitude and direction.

☐ **D** Vector quantities are a push or pull on an object.

[Total 1 mark]

2 The speed of sound varies depending upon the substance it is travelling through. State the speed of sound in air. *Grade 4-6*

....

[Total 1 mark]

3 **Figure 1** shows the path taken by a football kicked by a child. When it is kicked at point A, the ball moves horizontally to the right until it hits a vertical wall at Point B. The ball then bounces back horizontally to the left and comes to rest at Point C. *Grade 4-6*

Figure 1

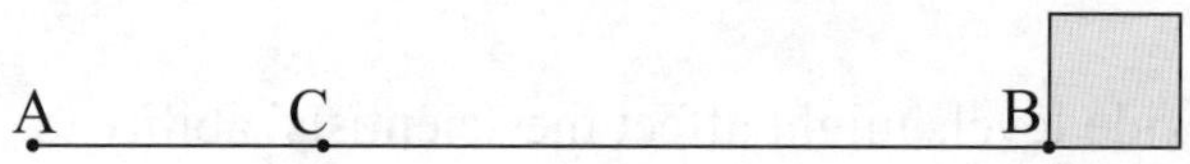

A   C   B   Scale 1 cm = 1 m

a) Determine the distance that the ball has moved through from A to B.

Distance = ... m

[1]

b) Determine the total distance that the ball has moved through from A to C.

Distance = ... m

[1]

c) Draw a vector arrow on **Figure 1** to show the displacement of the ball.

[1]

d) Determine the magnitude of the displacement of the ball after it has come to rest.

Magnitude of displacement = ... m

[1]

[Total 4 marks]

4 A student went for a run. She ran for exactly 22 minutes at an average speed of 4.0 m/s. *Grade 4-6*

a) State the equation that links distance travelled, average speed and time.

....

[1]

b) Calculate the distance that the student ran in km. Give your answer to two significant figures.

Distance = ... km

[4]

[Total 5 marks]

5 A journalist is deciding whether to walk, cycle or take a bus to get to work. There are two routes he could take. The shorter route is along a 3.5 km path that only pedestrians and cyclists are allowed to use. The bus takes a longer route along a road. *Grade 6-7*

a) Estimate how long it would take the journalist to walk the pedestrian route.

Time taken = ... s

[4]

b) Estimate how much time would be saved if the journalist were to cycle this route instead.

Time saved = ... s

[4]

c) Travelling to work by bus takes 15 minutes.
The total distance covered during this time is 7.2 km.
Calculate the average speed of the bus in m/s.

Speed = ... m/s

[3]

[Total 11 marks]

Section 17 — Motion and Forces

Acceleration

Warm-Up

Draw one line from each scenario on the left to the typical acceleration for that object.

A sprinter starting a race	10 m/s²
A falling object	2 × 10⁵ m/s²
A bullet shot from a gun	1.5 m/s²

1   Describe the motion of an object that has a negative acceleration.

....

[Total 1 mark]

2   A dog sets off from rest and reaches a speed of 3.2 m/s in 8.0 s.

a) Calculate the dog's average acceleration.

Acceleration = ... m/s²

[3]

b) The dog keeps running with this acceleration for a further 6.0 s. Calculate the dog's final speed.

Speed = ... m/s

[3]

[Total 6 marks]

3   A pebble is dropped from a height level with the end of a diving board above a lake. The velocity of the pebble immediately before it hits the surface of the water is 12 m/s.

Calculate the height of the diving board.

Height = ... m

[Total 3 marks]

4 A boat is travelling at a constant velocity of 5.0 m/s. It then starts to accelerate with a constant acceleration of 0.25 m/s^2 for a distance of 1.2 km.

a) Calculate the final velocity of the boat.

Velocity = ... m/s

[3]

b) Calculate the time it takes for the boat to travel this 1.2 km.

Time = ... s

[3]

[Total 6 marks]

5 A train travelling at 30 m/s slows down to 18 m/s over a distance of 360 m. Calculate the average deceleration of the train over this distance.

Deceleration = ... m/s^2

[Total 3 marks]

6 A cyclist is travelling along a main road. The cyclist stops at a red light. When the light changes to green, the cyclist accelerates with a uniform acceleration up to a speed of 21 km/hr. Estimate the cyclist's acceleration in m/s^2.

Acceleration = ... m/s^2

[Total 3 marks]

Exam Tip

Watch out for questions on acceleration — if you aren't given an equation in the question, you'll have to decide which acceleration equation you need to use. Making a list of the information you have can help, and look out for key words — 'uniform', 'constant', 'increasing' or 'decreasing' might give you a clue as to which equation to use.

Section 17 — Motion and Forces

Distance/Time Graphs

1 A boat is being rowed along a straight canal. Some students time how long after setting off the boat passes marker posts spaced 100 metres apart. **Figure 1** shows their results.

Figure 1

Distance (m)	0	100	200	300	400	500
Time (s)	0	85	165	250	335	420

Figure 2

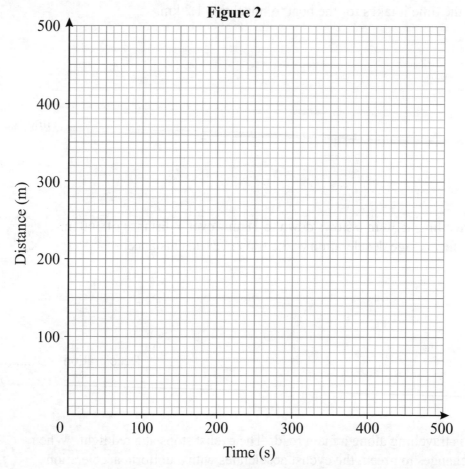

a) Draw the distance/time graph for the results in **Figure 1** on the axes shown in **Figure 2**.

[3]

b) Using **Figure 2**, determine how far the boat travelled in 300 s.

Distance = ... m

[1]

c) Determine the time taken for the boat to travel 250 m, using **Figure 2**.

Time = ... s

[1]

d) The students take the timings using a stopwatch. Suggest **one** way the students can make their measurements are as accurate as possible.

....

....

[1]

[Total 6 marks]

2 **Figure 3** shows the distance/time graph for a cyclist's bike ride.

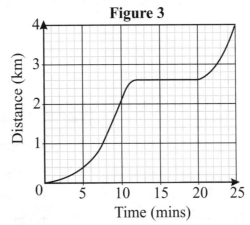

Figure 3

a) Determine how long the cyclist rode for before stopping for a rest.

....

[1]

b) Describe the cyclist's motion in the first five minutes of her journey.

....

[1]

[Total 2 marks]

3 **Figure 4** shows the distance/time graph for a car's journey.

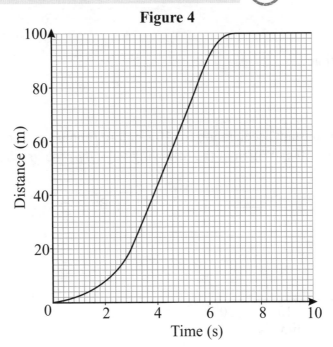

Figure 4

a) Use **Figure 4** to find the speed of the car 5 s into its journey.

Speed = ... m/s

[3]

b) Use **Figure 4** to find the speed of the car 2 s into its journey.

Speed = ... m/s

[3]

[Total 6 marks]

Section 17 — Motion and Forces

Velocity/Time Graphs

Use two of the phrases from the list below to correctly label the velocity/time graph.

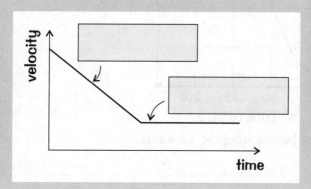

decreasing deceleration

steady speed

decreasing acceleration

constant acceleration

constant deceleration

---

1 Velocity/time graphs can be used to show the motion of an object.

Which quantity is represented by the area under a velocity/time graph?

☐ **A** speed

☐ **B** acceleration

☐ **C** distance

☐ **D** deceleration

[Total 1 mark]

---

2 A bear runs with a constant acceleration for 10 s before running at a constant velocity of 8 m/s for a further 10 s. Which of the following velocity/time graphs shows this?

☐ **A**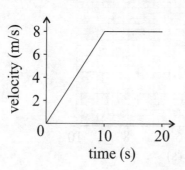

☐ **B**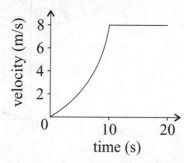

☐ **C**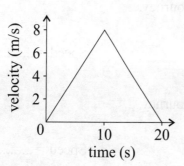

☐ **D**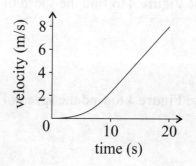

[Total 1 mark]

Section 17 — Motion and Forces

3 **Figure 1** shows an incomplete velocity/time graph for a rollercoaster ride.

Figure 1

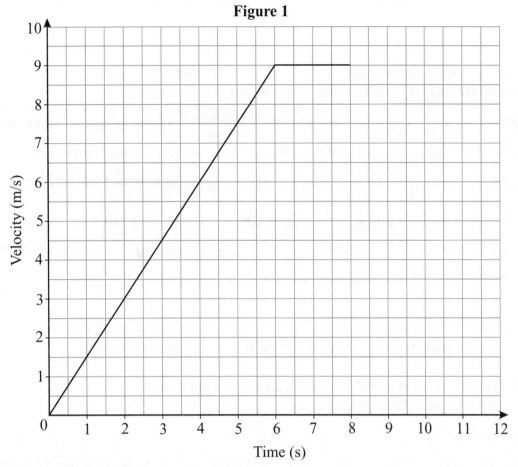

a) After 8 seconds, the rollercoaster decelerates at an increasing rate.
It comes to rest 4 seconds after it begins decelerating.
Complete the velocity/time graph in **Figure 1** to show this.

[2]

b) Calculate the acceleration of the rollercoaster during the first 6 seconds of the ride.

Acceleration = ... m/s^2
[2]

c) Calculate the distance travelled by the rollercoaster between 0 and 8 s.

Distance = ... m
[3]

d) Estimate the distance travelled by the rollercoaster between 8 and 12 seconds,
to the nearest metre.

Distance = ... m
[3]

[Total 10 marks]

Section 17 — Motion and Forces

Newton's First and Second Laws

Use the words and phrases below to correctly fill in the gaps in the passage.
You don't have to use all of them, but each one can only be used once.

Newton's .... Law of motion says that an object will remain stationary or

moving at .... if there is .... resultant force acting on it.

If there is .... resultant force acting on the object, it will ....

a constant velocity	accelerate	a zero	First
a non-zero	Second	remain stationary	an increasing speed

1 A rocket moves at a constant speed in space. In order to change its speed, it turns
on its thrusters, accelerates to the desired speed and then turns them off again.

Grade 4-6

a) The mass of the rocket is 110 000 kg and it accelerates at 5.0 m/s^2.
What is the force provided by the thrusters?

☐ **A** 550 000 N

☐ **B** 55 000 N

☐ **C** 22 000 N

☐ **D** 220 000 N

[1]

b) State why the rocket continues moving at a constant speed after turning off its thrusters.

....

....

[1]

[Total 2 marks]

2 A vase is knocked from a shelf. As the vase begins to fall, the resultant force acting
on it is 38 N. Acceleration due to gravity is 10 m/s^2. Calculate the mass of the vase.

Grade 4-6

Mass = ... kg

[Total 3 marks]

3 A sailboat has a mass of 60 kg and is accelerating at 0.4 m/s². The wind acting on the sail provides a force of 44 N. The drag from the water acts in the opposite direction.

Calculate the force of the drag acting on the boat. Show your working.

Force = ... N

[Total 4 marks]

4 A car is travelling at 14 m/s when it hits a wall. It experiences a large, constant deceleration and quickly comes to a stop.

a) Explain why very large decelerations can be dangerous.

....

....

[2]

b) Estimate the size of the resultant force acting on the car during the collision.

Force = ... N

[5]

[Total 7 marks]

5 **Figure 1** shows a 7520 kg lorry. The driver spots a hazard ahead and applies the brakes. The lorry decelerates uniformly and comes to a stop 50 m after the brakes are applied. Estimate the braking force needed to stop the lorry.

Figure 1

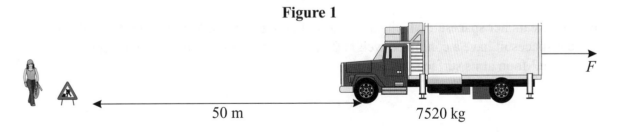

50 m   7520 kg

Force = ... N

[Total 5 marks]

Exam Tip

Watch out for questions talking about constant or uniform acceleration over a distance. They can be tricky with lots of steps. In the exam, use the equation from the equation sheet that links velocity, acceleration and distance to find the acceleration (or deceleration) of an object. Then stick it into Newton's 2nd Law to find the resultant force on the object.

Section 17 — Motion and Forces

Weight and Circular Motion

Warm-Up

State whether each of the following statements are true or false.

1) The acceleration of an object in free fall on Earth is 10 m/s². _____

2) The weight of an object is the same everywhere. _____

3) The mass of an object is the same everywhere. _____

4) The weight of an object on the moon is smaller than on Earth. _____

1 An astronaut weighs herself on Earth and on the Moon. *Grade 4-6*

a) State what is meant by weight.

....

....
[1]

b) On Earth, the astronaut has a mass of 65 kg. Calculate her weight on Earth.
Use the equation:

$$\text{weight} = \text{mass of object} \times \text{gravitational field strength}$$

Weight = ... N
[2]

c) She wears her spacesuit which has a mass of 80 kg. On the Moon, the astronaut and
the spacesuit have a combined weight 232 N. Calculate the gravitational field strength
of the Moon at its surface.

Gravitational field strength = ... Unit ....
[3]

[Total 6 marks]

2 Does a satellite orbiting the Earth at 3.07 x 10³ m/s have a constant velocity? *Grade 6-7*
Explain your answer.

....

....

....

[Total 2 marks]

3 A student is doing an experiment to determine the gravitational field strength on Earth.

To do this, the student intends to measure the weight of a set of iron standard masses.
Each standard mass is labelled with its mass, which is used as the value of mass in the experiment.

a) One of the standard masses is heavily rusted.
   Suggest why this mass shouldn't be used in the experiment.

   ....

   ....
   [1]

b) To measure the weight of a mass, the mass is placed on
   a small plastic tray that is hung from a newton meter,
   as shown in **Figure 1**. The force displayed on the
   newton meter is then recorded as the weight of the mass.

   Figure 1

   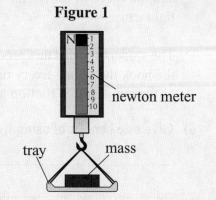

   newton meter

   i) State the type of error that is introduced
      to the results by using this method.

      ....
      [1]

   tray   mass

   ii) Explain how this error is caused.

      ....

      ....
      [1]

c) i) The student carries out the experiment, and records their results in **Figure 2**.
      Plot the student's results on the grid shown in **Figure 3**, and draw a line of best fit.

   Figure 2

Mass (kg)	Weight (N)
0.2	2.2
0.3	3.2
0.4	4.2
0.5	5.0
0.6	6.4
0.7	7.2
0.8	8.2

   Figure 3

   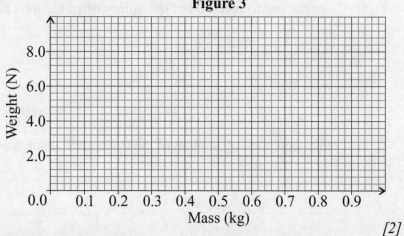
   [2]

   ii) Calculate a value for the Earth's gravitational field strength using the graph in **Figure 3**.

   Gravitational field strength = ... N/kg
   [3]

   [Total 8 marks]

Investigating Motion

1 A student uses the apparatus in **Figure 1** to investigate the effect of changing the mass of a trolley on its acceleration. The trolley is on a ramp to compensate for friction. *(Grade 6-7)*

The student records the mass of the trolley and the weight of the hook. The hook has a weight of 1.5 N.

Figure 1

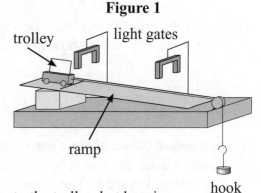

When the hook is allowed to fall, the trolley accelerates. The student then records the time it takes the trolley to travel between the two light gates and the speed of the trolley as it passes through each light gate.

The student repeats this process, each time adding a mass to the trolley, but keeping the hook the same. Every time she adds a mass to the trolley, she changes the height of the ramp so that friction between the ramp and the trolley can be ignored.

a) Give **one** benefit of using light gates to take measurements.

....

....

[1]

b) Describe how the student uses her measurements to determine the acceleration of the trolley.

....

....

[1]

c) i) Calculate the acceleration of the trolley when the total mass of the system is 3 kg.

Acceleration = ... m/s^2

[3]

ii) Predict how the acceleration of the trolley will change as the mass of the trolley is increased.

....

....

[1]

d) The student wants to calculate the uncertainty of one of her mean results.
Describe how she can do this.

....

....

[2]

[Total 8 marks]

Section 17 — Motion and Forces

Inertia and Newton's Third Law

Which of the following is Newton's Third Law? Tick **one** box.

A non-zero resultant force is needed to cause a change in speed or direction. ☐

A resultant force is inversely proportional to the mass of an object. ☐

When two objects interact, they exert equal and opposite forces on each other. ☐

A resultant force of zero leads to an equilibrium situation. ☐

1 All objects have an inertial mass. (Grade 6-7)

a) State the meaning of the term inertial mass.

....

[1]

Three identical shopping trolleys, A, B and C, are filled with different items and so that each trolley has a different mass. Each trolley is pushed with an equal force from the same starting point, and its velocity is recorded immediately afterwards. **Figure 1** shows the results.

Figure 1

Trolley	A	B	C
Velocity (m/s)	1.5	0.7	2.2

b) State which trolley has the highest inertial mass. Explain your answer.

....

....

[2]

[Total 3 marks]

2 Two students each stand at rest on a skateboard by a wall. They both push against the wall with a force of 24 N. You can assume there is no friction between the skateboards and the ground. (Grade 6-7)

a) Explain in terms of forces why the students would move away from the wall.

....

....

[2]

b) Student A and his skateboard have a combined mass of 80 kg. Student B and his skateboard have a combined mass of 40 kg. What is the difference in their accelerations?

☐ **A** 0.3 m/s^2 ☐ **B** 0.6 m/s^2

☐ **C** 1.6 m/s^2 ☐ **D** 3.3 m/s^2

[1]

[Total 3 marks]

☹ ☐   😐 ☐   🙂 ☐

Momentum

1 A motorbike is travelling at 25 m/s and has a mass of 220 kg. **Grade 4-6**

a) State the equation that links momentum, mass and velocity.

....

[1]

b) Calculate the momentum of the motorbike.

Momentum = ... kg m/s

[2]

[Total 3 marks]

2 A car is moving east with a velocity of 15 m/s and momentum 46 000 kg m/s. **Grade 4-6**

Calculate the mass of the car.

Mass = ... kg

[Total 3 marks]

3 **Figure 1** and **Figure 2** show a Newton's cradle. **Grade 6-7**
All of the balls on the cradle have the same mass.

Figure 1   **Figure 2**

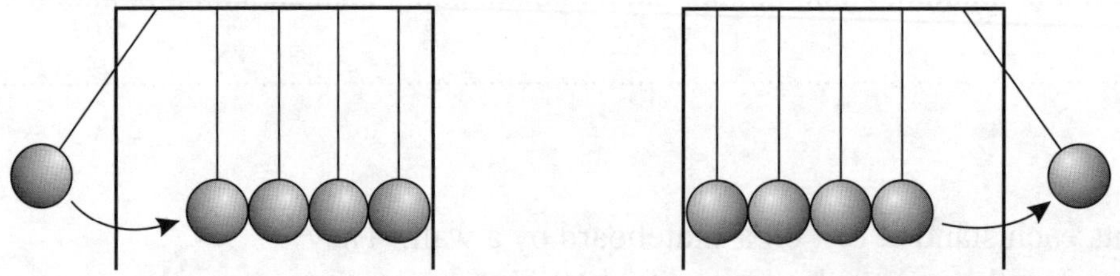

When a ball is lifted and allowed to hit the others as shown in **Figure 1**, it causes the last ball in the line to move outwards, as shown in **Figure 2**. The balls in between appear to remain stationary. Using conservation of momentum, explain this behaviour.

....

....

....

....

....

....

[Total 4 marks]

4 A ball moves with an initial velocity of 3 m/s. It comes to rest after 4 seconds due to a constant resistive force of 0.15 N. Calculate the mass of the ball.

Mass = ... kg

[Total 3 marks]

5 **Figure 3** shows two American football players running towards each other. They collide and cling together in a tackle. Calculate the velocity that they move together with once they have collided.

Figure 3

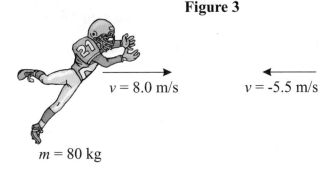

$v = 8.0$ m/s $v = -5.5$ m/s

$m = 80$ kg $m = 100$ kg

Velocity = ... m/s

[Total 4 marks]

6 **Figure 4** shows balls 1 and 2 before and after a collision.

Ball 1 initially travels with a velocity of u m/s. Ball 2 is stationary and has a mass of 0.2 kg. Ball 1 collides with ball 2 and this collision lasts for 0.1 s. Afterwards, both balls move in the direction of ball 1's initial velocity. Each ball has a different final velocity.

Figure 4

Before   After

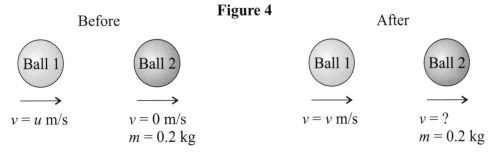

$v = u$ m/s $v = 0$ m/s $v = v$ m/s $v = ?$
                          $m = 0.2$ kg $m = 0.2$ kg

During the collision, a force of –6 N is exerted on ball 1 by ball 2.
Calculate the velocity of ball 2 after the collision.

Velocity = ... m/s

[Total 5 marks]

Section 17 — Motion and Forces

Stopping Distances and Reaction Times

1 The thinking distance for a driver in a car travelling at 40 mph is 12 m. The braking distance is 24 m.

Grade 4-6

a) State what is meant by thinking distance.

....

....
[1]

b) Calculate the car's stopping distance when it is travelling at 40 mph.

Stopping Distance = ... m
[1]

[Total 2 marks]

2 Different people have different reaction times.

Grade 4-6

a) What is the typical reaction time for a person?

☐ **A** 1.3 – 1.8 s   ☐ **B** 0.4 – 0.9 s   ☐ **C** 0.1 – 0.2 s   ☐ **D** 2.0 – 3.0 s
[1]

b) Give **three** factors that could affect a person's reaction time.

....

....
[3]

[Total 4 marks]

3 A car is travelling down a road, and the driver has to brake suddenly.

Grade 4-6

a) Describe what is meant by braking distance.

....

....
[1]

b) There are lots of leaves on the road, and the road surface is wet.
Explain what effect this will have on the car's braking distance.

....

....

....

....
[2]

[Total 3 marks]

4 The ruler drop test can be used to investigate people's reaction times. (Grade 6-7)

a) Describe **one** other method that can be used to test people's reaction times.

....

[1]

b) Describe the steps involved when using the ruler drop experiment to investigate reaction times.

....

....

....

....

....

....

....

....

[6]

[Total 7 marks]

5* A group of friends are driving home from a concert late at night. It is raining heavily and they are listening to loud music on the radio. (Grade 6-7)

Describe the factors that could affect the car's stopping distance and safety of the journey. Explain the effect each factor could have.

....

....

....

....

....

....

....

....

....

....

....

[Total 6 marks]

Energy Stores

Warm-Up

Match each of the following energy stores to the object which mainly has energy in that store.

Kinetic energy store	A nucleus about to undergo a nuclear reaction
Magnetic energy store	A stretched rubber band
Electrostatic energy store	A hot potato
Chemical energy store	A person on top of a mountain
Elastic potential energy store	A toy car rolling along the ground
Nuclear energy store	Two magnets attracted to each other
Thermal energy store	Petrol in a car
Gravitational potential energy store	Two electric charges repelling each other

1   A 0.1 kg toy contains a compressed spring. When the spring
     is released, the toy flies 0.5 m upwards from ground level.

Calculate the change in energy stored in the toy's gravitational potential energy store when it reaches its highest point. The gravitational field strength of Earth is 10 N/kg. Use the equation:

$$\text{change in gravitational potential energy} = \text{mass} \times \text{gravitational field strength} \times \text{change in vertical height}$$

Energy = ... J

[Total 2 marks]

2   A 0.50 kg rock is dropped from a cliff edge.
     It falls 42 m before entering the sea.

a)   State the equation that links the energy in an object's kinetic energy store, its mass and its speed.

....

[1]

b)   Calculate the speed of the rock when it hits the water.
     You can assume there is no air resistance and that all of the energy transferred from the
     rock's gravitational potential energy store is transferred to its kinetic energy store.
     Gravitational field strength = 10 N/kg.

Speed = ... m/s

[5]

[Total 6 marks]

Transferring Energy

Warm-Up

A ball is rolling along the ground. It slows down and eventually stops.
Fill in the blanks in the energy transfer diagram using the words given below.

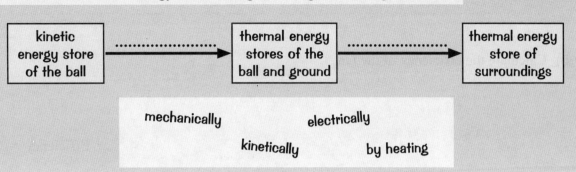

mechanically   electrically

kinetically   by heating

1 Energy can be transferred between different energy stores. **Grade 6-7**

a) State the principle of conservation of energy.

....

....

[1]

b) A kettle of cold water is plugged into the mains and brought to the boil.
Describe how is energy transferred from the mains to the kettle.

....

[1]

c) Describe the main energy transfer for a bike freewheeling down a hill.
You should refer to the energy stores that the energy is transferred between in your answer.

....

....

....

[3]

d) Describe the energy transfers for a golf club hitting a ball.
You should refer to the energy stores that the energy is transferred between in your answer.

....

....

....

....

....

[4]

[Total 9 marks]

Section 18 — Conservation of Energy

Efficiency

1 An electric fan transfers 7250 J of energy. 2030 J of this is wasted energy.

a) Suggest **one** way in which energy is wasted by the fan.

....

[1]

b) Calculate the efficiency of the fan.

Efficiency = ...

[3]

[Total 4 marks]

2 A student investigates the efficiency of a scale model of an electricity generating wind turbine using the equipment in **Figure 1**. He changes the number of sails on the turbine and calculates the energy transferred by the turbine's generator. The air blower is supplied with 30 kJ of energy and has an efficiency of 0.6.

Figure 1

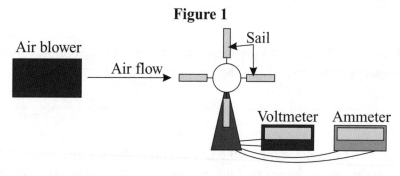

a) When using two sails, the efficiency of the turbine was 12%.
Calculate the useful energy transferred out from the turbine.

Energy transferred = ... J

[4]

b) Describe **two** ways the student could increase the efficiency of the turbine.

1. ....

2. ....

[2]

[Total 6 marks]

Exam Tip

Some of the energy input to a device is always dissipated or wasted. If you're asked to suggest ways to improve the efficiency of a device, think about how energy is wasted and then what could be done to reduce that waste.

Target AO3

3　A student is investigating whether the efficiency of a kettle varies with the volume of water in the kettle.

The kettle automatically switches off when the water in the kettle reaches its boiling point. The student carries out the following method:
1.　Fill the kettle with 500 ml of 20 °C water.
2.　Calculate the mass of the water, and calculate the energy that should be required to raise the temperature of the water from 20 °C to 100 °C (the useful energy transferred).
3.　Turn on the kettle, and allow it to boil the water and automatically switch off.
4.　Measure and record the energy supplied to the kettle whilst it was on using a joulemeter.
5.　Allow the kettle to cool, and then repeat steps 1-4 for different volumes of water.

a)　Suggest **one** way the student could improve the experiment.

....

....

[1]

b)　At one point during the experiment, the student forgets to allow the kettle to cool before carrying out a measurement for a new volume of water.　Explain how this will affect their results.

....

....

....

[2]

The student records the useful energy transferred by the kettle for each volume of water and the total energy supplied to the kettle in **Figure 2**.

Figure 2

Volume of water (cm³)	660	1000	1330	1660	2000
Total energy supplied (MJ)	0.212	0.302	0.388	0.474	0.547
Useful energy transferred (MJ)	0.168	0.252	0.336	0.420	0.504

c)　Before the experiment, the student predicted that the kettle would be more efficient for smaller volumes of water.　Explain whether the results are consistent with this prediction.

....

....

....

....

....

[4]

[Total 7 marks]

Exam Tip

For experiments with a detailed method, take the time to read through the individual steps before you tackle the question. You might also find it helpful to underline key information and data so that you can find it more easily later on.

Section 18 — Conservation of Energy

Reducing Unwanted Energy Transfers

1 A woman is cycling in a race. Before the race, she puts oil on the bike chain.

Explain why putting the oil on the bike chain increases the efficiency of the woman's cycling.

....

....

[Total 2 marks]

2 A builder is trying to minimise the rate at which a house cools. Grade 4-6

a) The builder can build the walls of the house using bricks A-D. Based on the information in the table below, which type of brick should she use?

		Thermal conductivity	Brick width
☐	**A**	High	10 cm
☐	**B**	High	15 cm
☐	**C**	Low	10 cm
☐	**D**	Low	15 cm

[1]

b) Give **one** other way the builder could reduce the rate at which the house cools.

....

[1]

c) **Figure 1** shows the energy transfer diagram for the builder's electric drill.
It shows the energy transferred when it is used for 30 seconds.

Figure 1

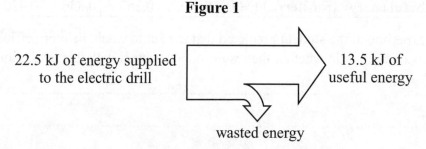

22.5 kJ of energy supplied to the electric drill

13.5 kJ of useful energy

wasted energy

Calculate how much energy is wasted during this time.

Wasted energy = ... kJ

[1]

[Total 3 marks]

Energy Resources

Warm-Up

Write the energy resources below in the correct column
to show whether they are renewable or non-renewable.

bio-fuel   hydro-electricity

        coal

solar

        wind   nuclear fuel

tidal

                gas

        oil

Renewable	Non-renewable

1 Describe the difference between renewable and non-renewable energy resources. *(Grade 4-6)*

....

....

[Total 2 marks]

2 Most cars, like the one in **Figure 1**, run on petrol or
diesel, which are both derived from fossil fuels. *(Grade 4-6)*

Figure 1

a) Name the **three** fossil fuels.

....

[1]

b) Give **one** other everyday use for fossil fuels.

....

[1]

c) Some modern cars are made to run on bio-fuels. State what is meant by bio-fuels.

....

....

[1]

d) Suggest **one** reason why car manufacturers are developing cars that run on alternative fuels to
petrol and diesel.

....

....

[1]

[Total 4 marks]

Section 18 — Conservation of Energy

3 A university is considering ways to reduce their energy bills. They are considering building either a single wind turbine nearby, or installing solar panels on top of their buildings. *(Grade 6-7)*

a) Suggest **two** reasons why students living near the turbine may prefer the use of solar power.

1. ....

2. ....

[2]

b) Suggest **one** reason why the university may choose a wind turbine over solar panels.

....

[1]

[Total 3 marks]

4 An energy provider is looking to replace their old fossil fuel power plant.
They are eligible for a government grant, so the initial building costs are negligible. *(Grade 7-9)*

a) The energy provider is interested in building a power plant that uses renewable energy resources. They have narrowed their choice to either a hydro-electric power plant or a tidal barrage. Compare generating electricity using these two energy resources, commenting on their reliability and their impact on the environment.

....

....

....

....

....

....

....

....

[5]

b)* An alternative is replacing the old power plant with a new power plant that is run on fossil fuels. Discuss the advantages and disadvantages of using fossil fuels to generate electricity.

....

....

....

....

....

....

....

[6]

[Total 11 marks]

Trends in Energy Resource Use

1 The bar chart in **Figure 1** below shows the electricity generated from renewable and non-renewable energy sources in a small country over 20 years.

Figure 1

= non-renewable sources

= renewable sources

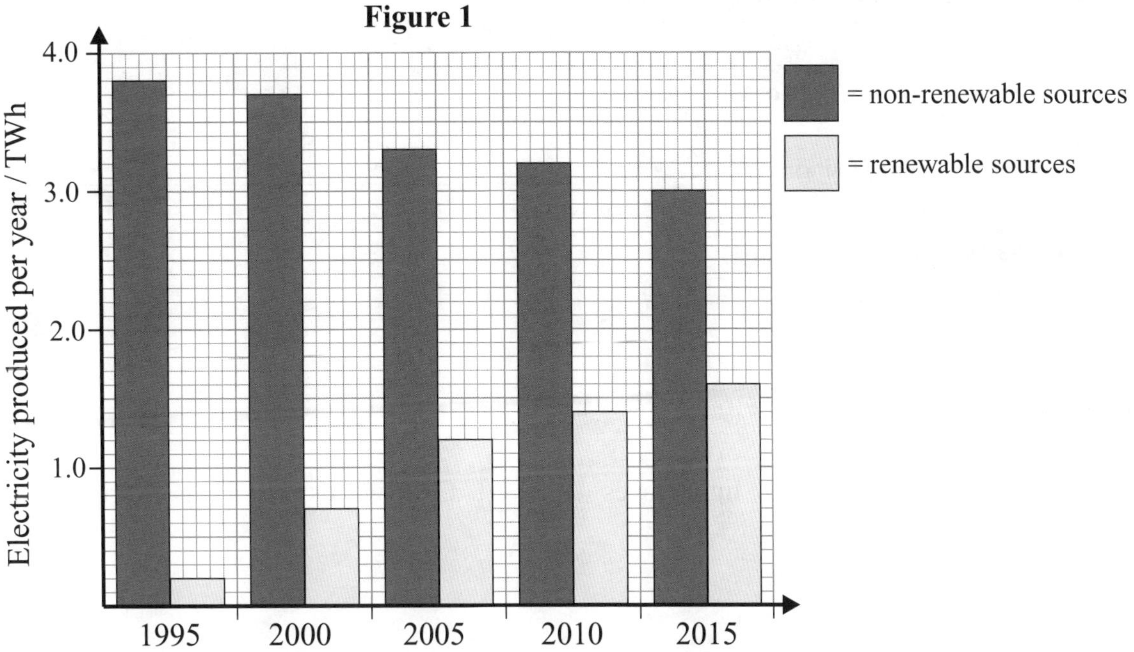

a) Determine how much electricity the country produced from renewable sources in 2005.

.... TWh
[1]

b) i) Calculate how much **more** electricity the country produced per year in 2015 than in 1995.

.... TWh
[2]

ii) Suggest **one** reason why the country needed to produce more electricity.

....
[1]

c) Describe the trends in use of energy resources shown by the graph.
Suggest reasons for these trends. You should refer to information from **Figure 1** in your answer.

....

....

....

....

....

....

....
[4]
[Total 8 marks]

Section 18 — Conservation of Energy

Wave Basics

Warm-Up

Add the labels below to the diagram of the wave.

amplitude   crest

rest position

wavelength   trough

distance (m)

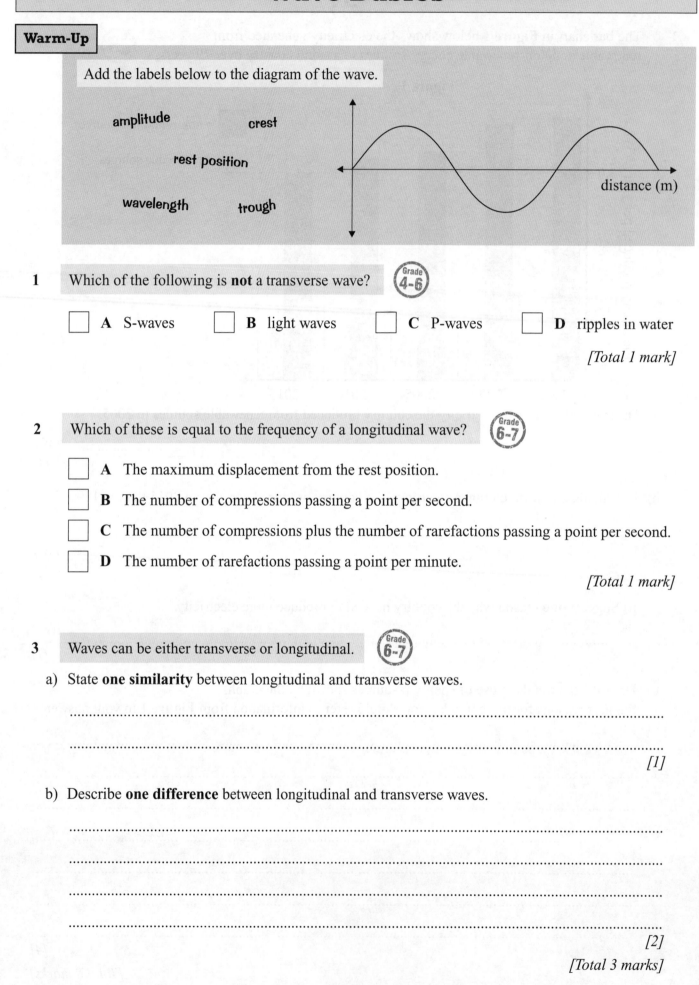

1 Which of the following is **not** a transverse wave?   Grade 4-6

☐ **A** S-waves   ☐ **B** light waves   ☐ **C** P-waves   ☐ **D** ripples in water

[Total 1 mark]

2 Which of these is equal to the frequency of a longitudinal wave?   Grade 6-7

☐ **A** The maximum displacement from the rest position.

☐ **B** The number of compressions passing a point per second.

☐ **C** The number of compressions plus the number of rarefactions passing a point per second.

☐ **D** The number of rarefactions passing a point per minute.

[Total 1 mark]

3 Waves can be either transverse or longitudinal.   Grade 6-7

a) State **one similarity** between longitudinal and transverse waves.

....

....

[1]

b) Describe **one difference** between longitudinal and transverse waves.

....

....

....

....

[2]

[Total 3 marks]

4 A child throws a stone into a pond. The stone creates ripples when it hits the water, which spread across the pond.

a) The ripples pass a leaf floating on the pond.
Explain why the ripples do not carry the leaf to the edge of the pond.

....

....

[1]

b) The ripples have a wavelength of 1.4 cm and a frequency of 15 Hz. Calculate their speed.
Use the equation:

wave speed = frequency × wavelength

Speed = ... m/s

[2]

c) The ripples have a period of 0.25 s. Explain what is meant by the period of a wave.

....

[1]

[Total 4 marks]

5 A violinist is practising in a village hall. Her teacher sits at the back of the hall to listen. As she plays, the vibrating violin string produces a sound wave.

a) i) State the equation that links wave speed, distance and time.

....

[1]

ii) The violinist's teacher sits 17 m away from her. The sound waves travel at a speed of 340 m/s. Calculate the time taken for the teacher to hear the sound produced by the violin when the student begins playing.

Time = ... s

[2]

b) The violinist then plays a note with a frequency of 220 Hz.
The violinist plays this note for 5.0 seconds.
Calculate how many complete sound waves are produced by the vibrating string in this time.

.... waves

[2]

[Total 5 marks]

Exam Tip

Be careful with units when you're working with waves. You need to remember to convert everything into the right units before you do any calculations, or your answers will come out either too big or too small, and you won't get full marks.

Section 19 — Waves and the Electromagnetic Spectrum

PRACTICAL

Measuring Waves

1 The wave speed in a solid can be found by hitting a metal rod with a hammer, shown in **Figure 1**. The sound waves produced when the rod is struck are recorded by the microphone and displayed by a computer.

Figure 1

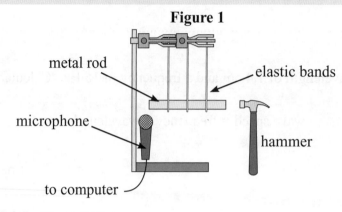

metal rod

elastic bands

microphone

hammer

to computer

A 20 cm metal rod is hit by the hammer. The peak frequency produced was 8500 Hz. Calculate the speed of the wave produced in the rod.

Speed = ... m/s

[Total 4 marks]

2 A student uses the equipment shown in **Figure 2** to investigate water waves in a ripple tank.

Figure 2

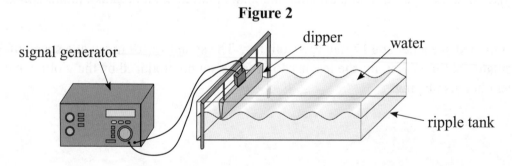

signal generator

dipper

water

ripple tank

a) The student wants to measure the frequency of the ripples. She floats a cork in the ripple tank, and counts how many times it bobs up in 30 seconds. The student repeats her experiment five times. She does not adjust the signal generator between repeats.

State **two** other factors that should remain the same between repeats.

....

....

[2]

Figure 3 shows the student's results. She recorded one of the results incorrectly.

Figure 3

trial	1	2	3	4	5
number of bobs in 30 seconds	12	11	21	11	14

b) i) Calculate the average number of times the cork bobbed up in 30 seconds, ignoring the anomalous result.

Average number of bobs = ...

[3]

ii) Using your answer to part i), calculate the average frequency of the ripples.

Frequency = ... Hz

[2]

c) The student then decides to adjust her experiment to investigate the speed of the ripples. She sets the signal generator to 12 Hz. She then places a piece of paper underneath the ripple tank and uses a strobe light set to the same frequency as the signal generator so the waves appear to not move.

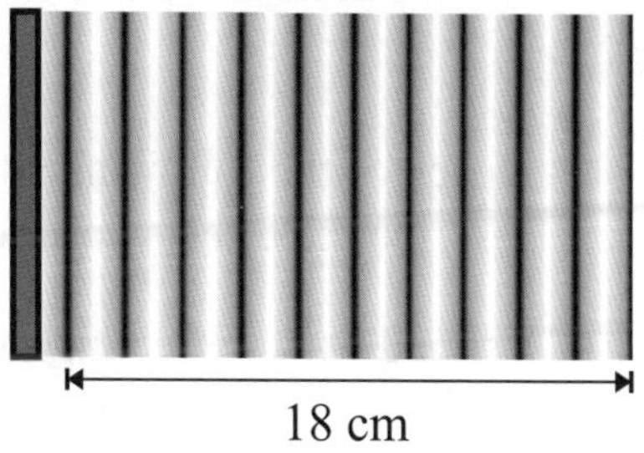

Figure 4 shows the wave pattern produced on the paper.

Figure 4

18 cm

i) Write down the equation that links wave speed, frequency and wavelength.

....

[1]

ii) Calculate the speed of the water ripples.
Give your answer to an appropriate number of significant figures.

Speed = ... m/s

[3]

[Total 11 marks]

3* Describe a method to measure the speed of sound waves in air. (Grade 7-9)

....

....

....

....

....

....

....

....

....

....

....

[Total 6 marks]

Section 19 — Waves and the Electromagnetic Spectrum

Wave Behaviour at Boundaries

At the boundary with a new material, a wave can be reflected, absorbed or transmitted.
Draw a line to match each option to the description which best matches it.

wave is reflected   it passes through the material

wave is absorbed   it bounces back off the material

wave is transmitted   it transfers all its energy to the material

1   In each of the following situations, a wave encounters a boundary between two materials.
Describe the effects you would expect to see for the following wave behaviours.

a)   A sound wave reflecting off a hard, flat surface.

....

[1]

b)   A ray of visible light being absorbed by a black object.

....

[1]

[Total 2 marks]

2   **Figure 1** shows a ray of light travelling from air into
a clear, rectangular block of an unknown material.

Figure 1

Air   Block of clear material

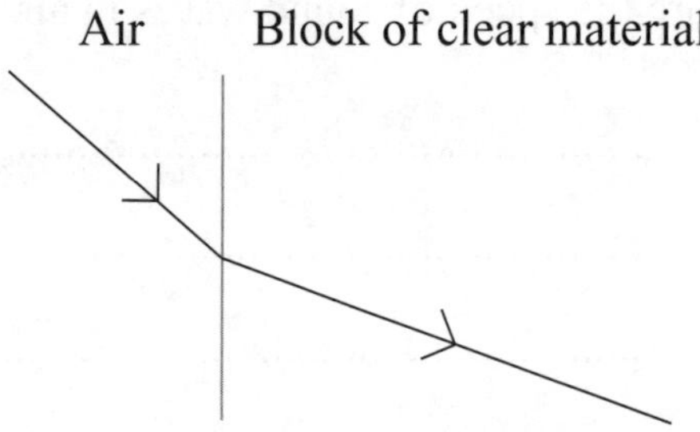

a)   What is the angle of incidence for the light ray entering the block?
Use a protractor to accurately measure the angle.

Angle of incidence = ... °
[1]

b)   State and explain **one** conclusion you can make about the material of the block, compared to air.

....

....

[2]

[Total 3 marks]

Investigating Refraction

1   A student is investigating refraction through different materials. The student uses a
    ray box to shine a ray of light into blocks of materials at a fixed angle of incidence,
    I. He traces the path of the ray entering and leaving the block on a sheet of paper.

a) Explain why a ray box was used for this experiment.

   ....

   ....

   [1]

Figure 1

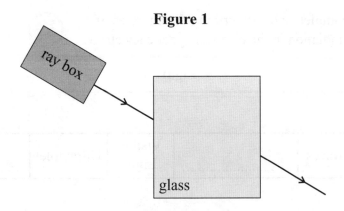

b) **Figure 1** shows the student's investigation for light refracted through a glass block.
   Complete the diagram by drawing the light ray as it passes through the glass block.

   [1]

c) The student measures the angle of refraction, *R*, of the light ray as it enters the block.
   Figure 2 shows the results for a range of materials. Complete **Figure 2** by measuring
   the angle of refraction for the glass block shown in **Figure 1**.

Figure 2

Material	*I*	*R*
Cooking Oil	30°	20°
Water	30°	22°
Plastic	30°	20°
Glass	30°	....

   [1]

d) State and explain which of the materials shown in **Figure 2** changes the speed of the light ray
   the least.

   ....

   ....

   ....

   [3]

   [Total 6 marks]

Section 19 — Waves and the Electromagnetic Spectrum

Electromagnetic Waves

For each sentence, circle whether it is true or false.

All electromagnetic waves are transverse.   True / False

All electromagnetic waves travel at the same speed in a vacuum.   True / False

Human eyes can detect a large part of the electromagnetic spectrum.   True / False

1   **Figure 1** is an incomplete table describing the energies of
different types of radiation in the electromagnetic spectrum.

Figure 1

Low Energy						High Energy
Radio Waves	Microwaves	....	Visible Light	Ultraviolet	....	Gamma Rays

a) Complete **Figure 1** by filling in the missing types of electromagnetic radiation.

[2]

b) Draw an arrow beneath **Figure 1** that points from the type of electromagnetic radiation with the
shortest wavelength towards the type with the longest wavelength.

[1]

c) The visible light section of the electromagnetic spectrum can be split further into the bands of
wavelengths that make up each colour. Complete the list in **Figure 2**, which lists the colours of
visible light in terms of decreasing wavelength.

Figure 2

Red, Orange, ... , ... , ... , ... , Violet

[2]

d) Electromagnetic waves can be generated by changes within atoms.
State which part of the atom can generate gamma rays.

....

[1]

[Total 7 marks]

2   Some types of electromagnetic wave can be harmful to people.

a) Describe how the potential danger an electromagnetic wave
poses to a person varies with its frequency.

....

[1]

b) Draw lines to match the types of electromagnetic radiation on the left to their potential side effects on the right.

Infrared	internal heating of cells
Microwaves	skin burns
X-rays	cell mutation and cancer

[1]

c) Another type of harmful electromagnetic radiation is ultraviolet radiation. Give **two** damaging effects of ultraviolet light.

1. ....

2. ....

[2]

[Total 4 marks]

3 X-rays are used in hospitals to diagnose broken bones. (Grade 6-7)

The X-rays are generated by accelerating electrons to high speeds then firing them at a metal plate. When the electrons hit the plate, X-rays are produced.

Staff who work with X-ray machines wear badges that monitor the levels of radiation they have been exposed to, shown in **Figure 3**. These badges contain a photographic film which undergoes a chemical change when exposed to X-rays.

Figure 3

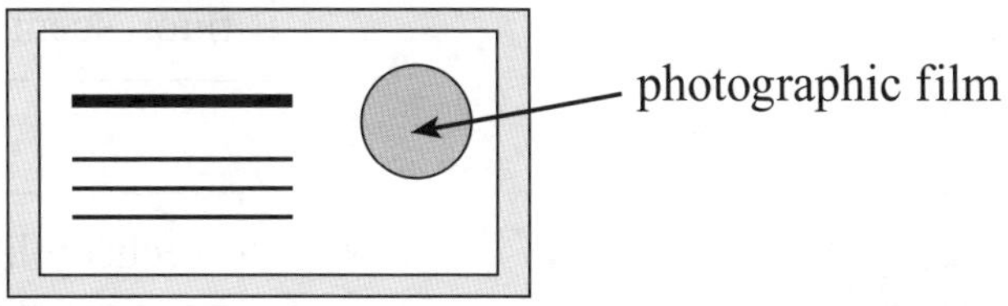

photographic film

a) i) Energy is transferred when the X-rays cause the chemical reaction in the badge. State the source and observer for this energy transfer.

....

[1]

ii) Describe the energy transfers involved in this process, from source to observer.

....

....

[2]

b) Give **one** other example of electromagnetic waves transferring energy from a source to an observer.

....

....

[1]

[Total 4 marks]

Section 19 — Waves and the Electromagnetic Spectrum

Uses of EM Waves

Tick the appropriate boxes to sort the radio wave facts from the fiction.

	True	False
Long-wave radio waves can be transmitted across long distances.	☐	☐
Long-wave radio waves bend and follow the curve of the Earth's surface.	☐	☐
Short-wave radio waves can only be used over short distances.	☐	☐
Wireless headsets use short-wave radio waves to transfer information.	☐	☐

1   Electromagnetic waves have a variety of different uses.   Grade 4-6

a) Draw lines to match each type of electromagnetic radiation on the left to its use on the right.

Ultraviolet		photography
Visible light		satellite communications
Infrared		fluorescent lights
Radio waves		security lights

[2]

b) Give **two** examples of infrared waves being used to transfer information.

1. ....

2. ....

[2]

c) A camper has bought a device that filters and sterilises water so he can drink it.
The device uses electromagnetic radiation to sterilise the water.
What is the most likely type of radiation that the device would use?

☐ **A** gamma rays   ☐ **B** ultraviolet   ☐ **C** infrared   ☐ **D** microwaves

[1]

[Total 5 marks]

2 A man uses a security pen to mark his belongings. The security pen contains fluorescent ink which cannot be seen in visible light. *(Grade 4-6)*

a) Which of the following is true for fluorescent ink?

☐ **A** Fluorescent ink emits radio waves after it absorbs ultraviolet light.

☐ **B** Fluorescent ink emits ultraviolet light after it absorbs visible light.

☐ **C** Fluorescent ink emits visible light after it absorbs ultraviolet light.

☐ **D** Fluorescent ink emits ultraviolet light after it absorbs radio waves.

[1]

b) Explain how the security ink can be used to find the man's property if it is stolen.

....

....

....

[2]

c) Give **one** other example of where fluorescence is used in security.

....

[1]

[Total 4 marks]

3 **Figure 1** shows an X-ray image of a skull. *(Grade 6-7)*

Figure 1

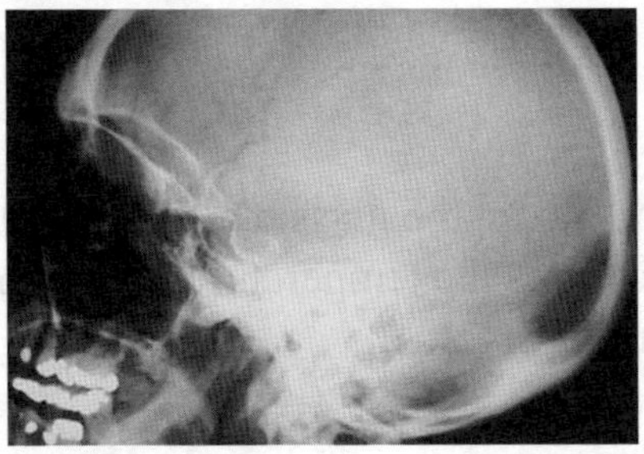

a) Explain how X-rays are used to form images like **Figure 1**.

....

....

....

....

[3]

b) Give **one** other non-medical use of X-rays.

....

[1]

[Total 4 marks]

Section 19 — Waves and the Electromagnetic Spectrum

210

4 A police helicopter has an infrared camera attached to its base.

Grade 6-7

a) Describe how an infrared camera works.

....

....

....

[2]

b) Explain the advantages of using an infrared camera rather than a normal camera when searching for criminals at night.

....

....

....

....

[3]

[Total 5 marks]

5 A student uses a microwave oven to cook a jacket potato on a glass plate.

Grade 6-7

a) Describe how microwaves cook the potato in the microwave oven.

....

....

....

[3]

b) The student cooks the potato on the glass plate for 10 minutes. She removes them from the microwave oven and measures the temperature of the potato and the edge of the glass plate. Her results are shown in **Figure 2**.

Figure 2

Object	Temperature / °C
Potato	78
Glass plate	30

Explain why there is a temperature difference between the potato and the edge of the glass plate.

....

....

....

[2]

[Total 5 marks]

Section 19 — Waves and the Electromagnetic Spectrum

6   Walkie-talkies use radio waves to communicate between each other. When a person speaks into the microphone, it creates an electric current. When the walkie-talkie receives a message, the microphone becomes a loudspeaker and converts electrical current into sound waves.

a) Briefly describe the steps involved for the creation, transmission and reception of a radio wave between a pair of walkie-talkies. You do not need to describe how microphones or loudspeakers work.

....

....

....

....

....

....

....

....

[6]

b)* A family from northern England are on holiday in France. Explain why they are unable to listen to their local FM radio station from back home, but are still able to listen to the same long-wave radio broadcasts as they do at home.

....

....

....

....

....

....

....

....

....

....

[6]

[Total 12 marks]

Exam Tip

In the exams, you may be asked to explain why a given electromagnetic wave is suited to a particular use. So make sure you understand the properties of the different electromagnetic wave types, and know some of their most common uses.

Section 19 — Waves and the Electromagnetic Spectrum

Section 20 — Radioactivity

The Model of the Atom

Which of the following best describes the typical size of an atom?

☐ 1 mm ☐ 1×10^{-5} m ☐ 1×10^{-10} m ☐ 1×10^{-20} m

1 Rutherford came up with a new model of the atom as a result of his scattering experiment. **Grade 4-6**

a) Name and describe the model that this model replaced.

....

....

[2]

b) State **one** property of Rutherford's model of the atom. Describe the observation from Rutherford's scattering experiment that provided evidence for this property.

Property: ....

Observation: ....

....

[2]

[Total 4 marks]

2 **Figure 1** is an incomplete table showing the relative charges of the subatomic particles in an atom. **Grade 4-6**

Figure 1

Particle	Proton	Neutron	Electron
Relative charge	....	....	−1

a) Complete **Figure 1**.

[2]

b) Describe how these subatomic particles are arranged in the atom.

....

....

[2]

c) An iron atom has 26 protons. State the number of electrons in an iron atom and use this to explain the overall charge of the atom.

....

....

....

[2]

[Total 6 marks]

☹ ☐ ☺ ☐ ☺ ☐

Electron Energy Levels

Choose from the labels on the left to fill in the blanks on the right.
You do not need to use all of the words.

other electrons   varying

fixed   the nucleus

loops   shells

In Bohr's atomic model, electrons orbit

.... at .... distances

called energy levels or ....

1   Niels Bohr suggested that electrons can move between energy levels. (Grade 4-6)

a) Describe how an inner electron can move between energy levels.

....

....

....

[2]

b) State the name of the type of particle created when an atom loses or gains outer electrons.

....

[1]

c) State the relative charge on the particle if it is created by an atom losing an outer electron.

....

[1]

[Total 4 marks]

2   A scientist is investigating the radiation emitted from a hydrogen discharge lamp. Inside the lamp, electrons in hydrogen atoms are constantly being excited to higher energy levels and then falling to lower levels. He finds that excited electrons falling back to the first energy level release ultraviolet radiation (frequency $\sim 3 \times 10^{15}$ Hz). Excited electrons falling back to the second energy level release visible light (frequency $\sim 5 \times 10^{14}$ Hz). (Grade 7-9)

Explain why electrons falling to the first energy level of hydrogen release electromagnetic radiation with a higher frequency than those falling to the second energy level.

....

....

....

....

....

....

[Total 4 marks]

Section 20 — Radioactivity

Isotopes and Nuclear Radiation

The standard notation used to represent atoms is shown. Use the words below to correctly fill in the labels. You don't have to use every phrase, but each phrase can only be used once.

electron number

neutron number

mass number

element symbol

charge   atomic number

1   **Figure 1** shows a smoke detector. Smoke detectors contain radioactive isotopes. These isotopes are unstable and undergo radioactive decay to become more stable. They do this by emitting nuclear radiation.

Figure 1

a) State what is meant by isotopes of an element.

....

....

[2]

b) Some nuclear radiation is ionising.
State **three** types of ionising radiation emitted by radioactive decay.

....

....

[3]

c) The unstable isotope in the smoke detector releases a particle made up of two protons and two neutrons from its nucleus.

i) State the name of this type of decay.

....

[1]

ii) State and explain the range in air of the released particle.

....

....

[2]

[Total 8 marks]

2 A student carries out an experiment to investigate two different radioactive sources. Her experiment is shown in **Figure 2**. She changes the material between the source and the Geiger-Muller tube and measures the count rate. **Figure 3** shows her results.

Figure 2

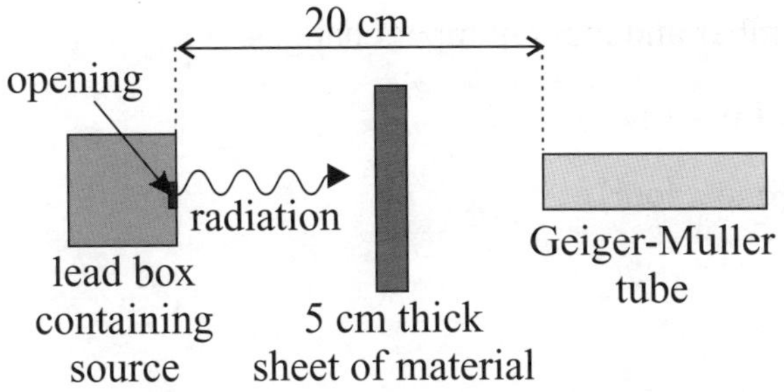

20 cm

opening

radiation

lead box containing source

5 cm thick sheet of material

Geiger-Muller tube

Figure 3

| Material | Count rate (counts per minute) | |
	Source A	Source B
No material	854	1203
Paper	847	1200
Aluminium	6	1199
Lead	5	280

a) Deduce the type of radiation source A emits.

....

[1]

b) State what kind of radiation source B emits. Explain your answer.

....

....

....

[3]

[Total 4 marks]

3 One isotope of sodium is $^{23}_{11}$Na.

a) Write down the nucleon number of this isotope.

....

[1]

b) Calculate the number of neutrons in the sodium nucleus.

Number of neutrons = ...

[1]

c) Which of the following is another isotope of sodium?

☐ **A** $^{11}_{23}$Na   ☐ **B** $^{11}_{24}$Na   ☐ **C** $^{23}_{12}$Na   ☐ **D** $^{24}_{11}$Na

[1]

d) An isotope of neon is $^{23}_{10}$Ne. State whether or not the charge on the neon isotope's nucleus is different to the charge on the nucleus of the sodium isotope. Explain your answer.

....

....

....

[2]

[Total 5 marks]

Nuclear Equations

An isotope emits an alpha particle. Circle the correct options in the sentences below to describe how the isotope's atomic number and mass number changes.

The atomic number (increases / decreases) by (one / two).

The mass number (increases / decreases) by (one / four).

1 An electron is emitted from a nucleus.

a) State the effect this has on the charge of the nucleus.

....

[1]

b) After emitting the electron, the atom is excited. The atom releases its excess energy in the form of a gamma ray. Describe what, if any, effect this has on the charge and mass of the nucleus.

....

[1]

[Total 2 marks]

2 A student writes down the following nuclear decay equation: $^{234}_{90}\text{Th} \longrightarrow\ ^{234}_{91}\text{Pa} + ^{0}_{0}\gamma$ **Grade 7-9**

a) Explain why this equation must be incorrect.

....

[1]

b) The student has missed out a particle from this decay equation.
Write down this particle as it would appear in a decay equation.

....

[1]

c) Radium (Ra) has atomic number 88. The isotope radium-226 undergoes alpha decay to form radon (Rn). Write a nuclear equation to show this decay.

....

[3]

d) The radon isotope then undergoes alpha decay to form an isotope of polonium (Po), which undergoes alpha decay to form an isotope of lead (Pb).
Calculate the number of neutrons in the nucleus of this lead isotope.

Number of neutrons = ...

[3]

[Total 8 marks]

Half-life

1 Each time an unstable nuclei in a sample decays, a 'count' is registered by a
radiation detector. **Figure 1** shows how the count-rate of a radioactive sample
changes over time, after background radiation has been taken into account.

Grade 4-6

a) State what is meant by half-life. Your answer
should refer to the number of undecayed nuclei.

....

....
[1]

b) Determine, using **Figure 1**, the half-life of
the sample.

Half-life = ... s
[1]

Figure 1

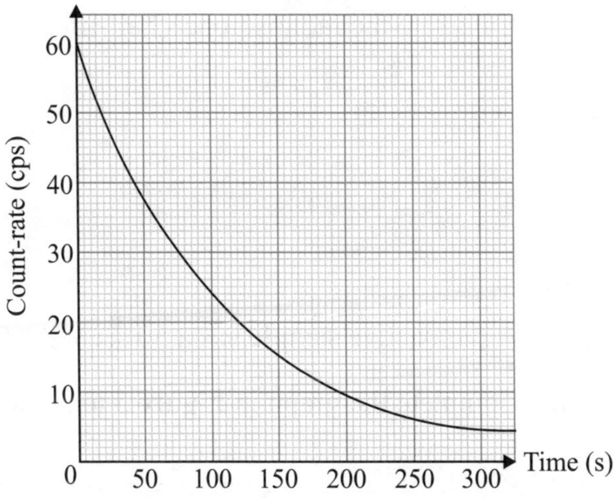

c) Initially, the sample contains approximately 800 undecayed nuclei.
Predict how many of these nuclei will have decayed after two half-lives.

Number of decayed nuclei = ...
[2]

d) After two half-lives, what is the ratio of the number of undecayed nuclei left to the initial number
of undecayed nuclei?

☐ **A** 1:2   ☐ **B** 2:1   ☐ **C** 1:4   ☐ **D** 4:1
[1]

[Total 5 marks]

2 **Figure 2** shows data about two radioactive sources. *Grade 6-7*

Figure 2

	Isotope 1	Isotope 2	Isotope 3
Number of undecayed nuclei	20 000	20 000	20 000
Half-life	4 minutes	72 years	5 years

a) State the isotope that is the most unstable.

....
[1]

b) Explain which isotope will have the highest activity initially.

....

....
[2]

[Total 3 marks]

Section 20 — Radioactivity

3 The activity of a radioisotope is 8800 Bq. Six hours later, the activity has fallen to 1100 Bq. **(Grade 6-7)**

a) Calculate how many half-lives have passed during the six hours.

Number of half-lives = ...

[3]

b) Calculate the radioisotope's half-life.

Half-life = ... hour(s)

[1]

[Total 4 marks]

4 A radioactive sample has a 50 second half-life. The initial activity of the sample is 120 Bq. **(Grade 7-9)**

a) Complete the graph in **Figure 3** to show how the activity will change in the first 150 seconds.

Figure 3

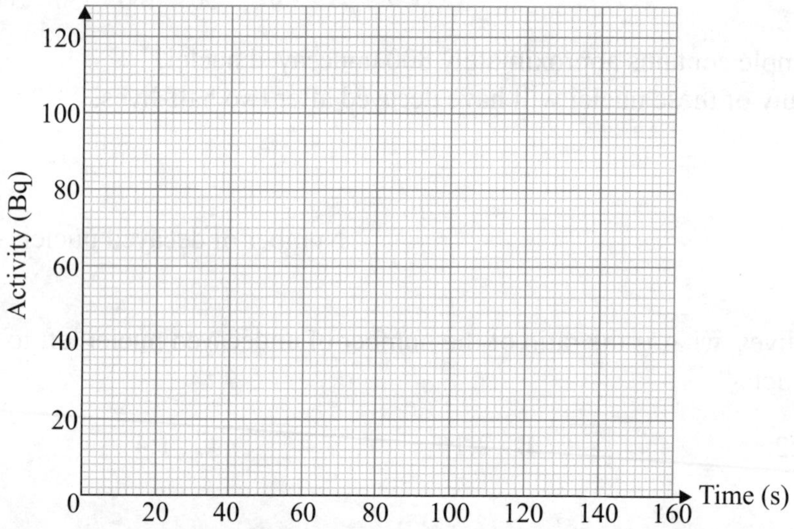

[Graph with y-axis labelled "Activity (Bq)" from 0 to 120, and x-axis labelled "Time (s)" from 0 to 160]

[2]

b) Predict, using your graph in **Figure 3**, the activity of the sample after 40 seconds.

Activity = ... Bq

[1]

c) Estimate the activity after 200 s. Give your answer to one significant figure.
Explain why this estimate is less likely to be correct than your prediction in part b).

....

....

....

[4]

[Total 7 marks]

Exam Tip

Half-life and activity are really important things to get your head around — they're a key thing to mention when talking about any radioactive substance. Remember that every activity-time graph showing radioactive decay has the same shape — radioactive decay is a random process, but by looking at lots of nuclei you can make fairly accurate estimates.

Section 20 — Radioactivity

Background Radiation and Contamination

1   Name **two** sources of background radiation.   Grade 4-6

1. ....

2. ....

[Total 2 marks]

2   A scientist is reviewing the safety procedures to be used in her lab. She is concerned about **contamination** and **irradiation**.   Grade 6-7

a)   Explain the difference between contamination and irradiation.

....

....

....

....

[2]

b)   The scientist is using a low activity radioactive sample. Give **one** example of how she can protect herself from irradiation and **one** example of how she can protect herself from contamination.

Irradiation: ....

Contamination: ....

[2]

[Total 4 marks]

3*   Radium-226 is an alpha source that was used in clocks until the 1960s to make the hands and numbers glow. Discuss whether a clockmaker should be more concerned about irradiation or contamination when repairing old clocks that contain radium.   Grade 7-9

....

....

....

....

....

....

....

....

....

....

[Total 6 marks]

Target AO3

4   A scientist is carrying out an experiment to find the half-life of a radioactive substance. Before bringing the radioactive substance into the laboratory, the scientist needs to measure the background radiation count-rate in the laboratory.

a) A student was doing an experiment using a radioactive source in the same laboratory. The scientist waited for the student to finish their experiment and fully clear away their equipment before measuring the background radiation. Explain how this will improve the accuracy of the scientist's measurements.

....

....

[1]

b) To measure the background radiation, the scientist measures the total counts detected by a Geiger-Muller tube and counter over 5 minutes. She repeats this measurement twice more, and records her results in **Figure 1**. Use the data in **Figure 1** to calculate the mean count-rate due to background radiation, in counts per second (cps).

Figure 1

Trial	Total counts in 5 mins
1	598
2	641
3	624

mean count-rate = ... cps

[3]

c) The scientist records the count-rate from the radioactive substance every 5 minutes using the equipment in **Figure 2**.

Figure 2

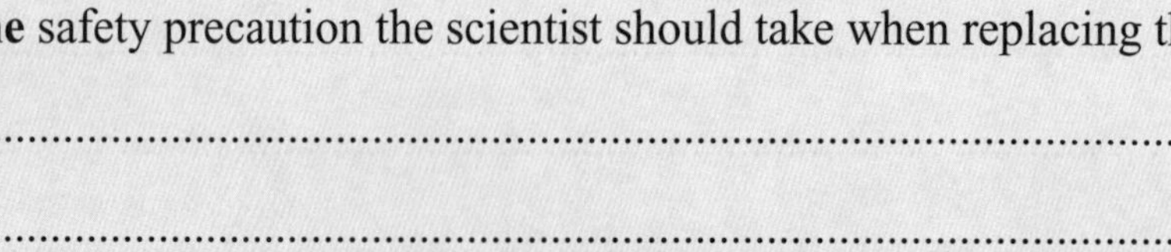

radioactive substance   Geiger-Muller tube   detector

0.50 m

Halfway through the experiment, the Geiger-Muller tube was knocked off the bench, and needed to be put back into place.

i) Suggest **one** safety precaution the scientist should take when replacing the Geiger-Muller tube.

....

....

[1]

ii) When the scientist replaces the Geiger-Muller tube, she places it 30 cm away from the source. Explain how this will affect the validity of the scientist's results.

....

....

....

[2]

[Total 7 marks]

Energy Transfers and Systems

1 Which of the following is correct for a closed system? *Grade* (4-6)

☐ **A** Energy into the system is always larger than energy out of the system.

☐ **B** Energy out of the system is always larger than energy into the system.

☐ **C** The net change of energy in a closed system is always zero.

☐ **D** Closed systems can only be changed by heating.

[Total 1 mark]

2 A filament bulb is connected to a battery, shown in **Figure 1**. You can assume that the wires connecting them have zero resistance. Complete the diagram in **Figure 2** to show the energy transfers that occur when the bulb in connected to thc battery. *Grade* (4-6)

Figure 1

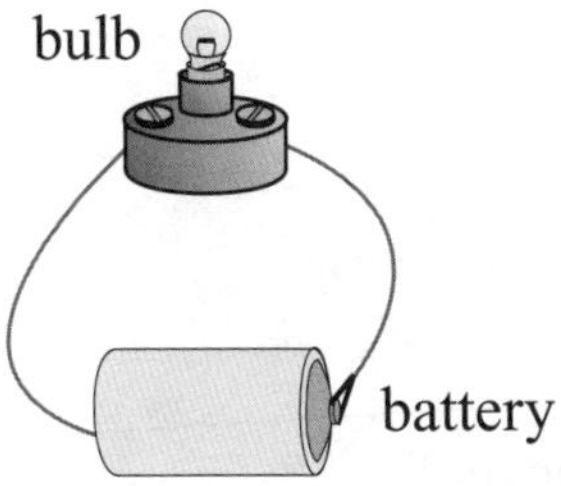

bulb

battery

Figure 2

┌──────────────────────────────────┐
│ chemical energy store of battery │
└──────────────────────────────────┘
                 ↓

[Total 3 marks]

3 An 80.0 g apple is a one-object system. The apple is hanging from a branch. *Grade* (6-7)

a) i) The apple falls from the branch. It reaches a speed of 7.00 m/s just before it hits the ground. Calculate the energy in the apple's kinetic energy store just before it hits the ground.

Energy = ... J

[3]

ii) State what causes the energy transfer within this system.

....

[1]

b) Assuming that there was no air resistance, calculate the height the apple fell from. (Gravitational field strength = 10 N/kg.)

Height = ... m

[4]

[Total 7 marks]

Work Done and Power

Warm-Up

Complete the sentences below using the words or phrases from the box.
You can only use each option once and you do not need to use every option.

As a rubber ball falls, it experiences a .... due to ....·

.... is done on the ball and .... is transferred from the ball's

.... energy store to its .... energy store.

| force | work | chemical potential | | kinetic | gravity |
| elastic potential | energy | | gravitational potential | heating |

---

1 Which of these is the definition of power? **Grade 4-6**

☐ **A** Power is the total work done by an object.

☐ **B** Power is the rate of energy transfer.

☐ **C** Power is the total energy transferred to an object.

☐ **D** Power is the minimum work done to an object to cause it to move.

[Total 1 mark]

---

2 A student is investigating the work done by different washing machines during a standard washing cycle. **Figure 1** shows the manufacturer's data about three machines. **Grade 6-7**

Figure 1

Machine	Power	Time needed
A	600 W	125 minutes
B	400 W	160 minutes
C	....	125 minutes

a) Calculate the work done by machine A during its standard washing cycle.
Give your answer in kJ.

Work done = ... kJ

[4]

b) Machine C's standard cycle lasts for 125 minutes. It does 3 930 000 J of work in that time.
Complete the table in **Figure 1** by calculating the power of machine C.

[2]

[Total 6 marks]

3 A woman pushes a 20 kg wheelbarrow 15 m along a flat path using a horizontal force of 50 N. *Grade 6-7*

a) i) State the equation that links work done, force applied and distance moved in the direction of the force.

....
[1]

ii) Calculate the work done by the woman.

Work done = ... J
[2]

b) Work has to be done against the frictional forces acting on the wheel of the wheelbarrow. Explain the effect this has on the temperature of the wheel.

....

....

....
[2]

[Total 5 marks]

4 A mechanic replaces a worn out engine of a car with a new, more efficient one. The old engine had a useful output power of 52 kW and an efficiency of 25%. The new engine has an efficiency of 30%. *Grade 7-9*

a) Calculate the useful output power of the new engine. You can assume that the input power of both engines is the same.

Output power = ... W
[5]

b) Explain the effect replacing the engine will have on the time taken for the car to accelerate from rest to 20 m/s.

....

....

....

....

....
[3]

[Total 8 marks]

Section 21 — Forces and Energy

Target AO3

5   A student wants to measure the useful power output of a motor.   (Grade 7-9)

The student has the following equipment she can use in an experiment:
- a motor, attached to an axle
- a power supply and basic circuitry
- a length of string
- a clamp and clamp stand
- a metre ruler
- a stopwatch
- a 1 kg mass

a)* Describe an experiment that the student could perform to determine
the useful power output of the motor, using the equipment listed.
You should include explanation of how the student can ensure the results are valid.

....

....

....

....

....

....

....

....

....

....

....

[6]

b) **Figure 2** shows the display of the stopwatch when the
student takes a time measurement during her experiment.
The time recorded was 18.5 s.

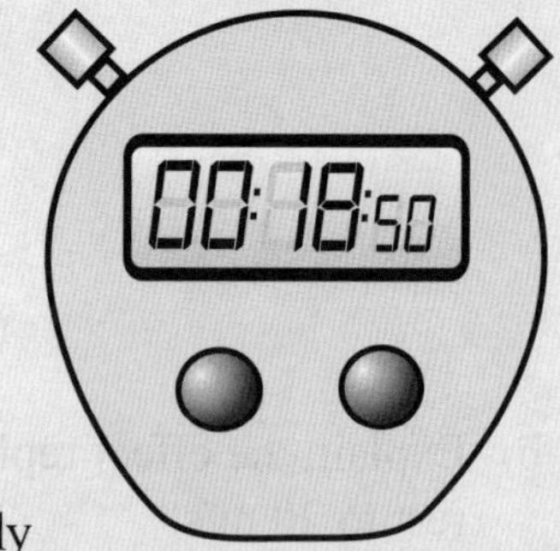

i) State the smallest increment of time the stopwatch can measure.

....
[1]

ii) Suggest why any errors in the student's time measurements are likely
to be larger than the smallest increment of time that can be measured by the stopwatch.

....

....

[2]

[Total 9 marks]

Figure 2

00:18:50

Exam Tip

Question 5a) is an example of a question which tests how well you can <u>write</u> (as well as your scientific knowledge).
These questions tend to be worth more marks than the other exam questions, so it's worth learning how to answer them
properly. Try to plan how you'll structure your answer first before you start, so you make sure you cover all the key points.

Forces

1   Forces are caused by interactions between objects.

    a) Forces can be split into contact and non-contact forces.

        i) Describe what is meant by a 'contact force'.

        ....

        ....
        [1]

        ii) Give **two** examples of a contact force.

          1. ....

          2. ....
        [2]

    b) Give **one** example of a non-contact force.

        ....
        [1]

        [Total 4 marks]

2   **Figure 1** shows four runners who are running in windy weather.
Which runner is experiencing the largest horizontal resultant force?

Figure 1

    A ☐   **B** ☐   **C** ☐   **D** ☐

    [Total 1 mark]

3   **Figure 2** shows a toy car. The weight of the car is 20 N. As it accelerates, it experiences
a driving force of 30 N. There is a 5 N resistive force acting against the motion of
the car. Add arrows to **Figure 2** to create a free body force diagram for the car.

Figure 2

    [Total 2 marks]

4   **Figure 3** shows an incomplete diagram of the forces acting on a
     ladder leaning against a wall. There is no friction between the ladder
     and the wall but there is friction between the ladder and the ground.

Figure 3

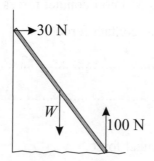

a) Complete **Figure 3** by drawing the missing frictional force.

                                                                    [2]

b) Using **Figure 3**, determine the weight of the ladder, W.

                                        Weight = ... N
                                                                    [1]
                                                         [Total 3 marks]

5   **Figure 4** shows a pair of identical magnets. There is a force of repulsion between them.

Figure 4

Magnet A   Magnet B

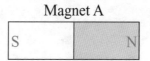   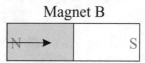

a) The arrow in **Figure 4** shows the force exerted on magnet B by magnet A. Complete the diagram
    in **Figure 4** by drawing another arrow representing the force that magnet B exerts on magnet A.
                                                                    [2]

b) Explain what is causing the force between the two magnets.

    ....

    ....
                                                                    [1]

c) Magnet B is replaced by a much stronger magnet.
    The strength of magnet A and the orientation of the magnets remains the same.
    Describe how you would redraw the arrows on the diagram to show this new force interaction.

    ....

    ....
                                                                    [2]
                                                         [Total 5 marks]

Exam Tip

Make sure you get your head around the difference between an interaction pair and a free body force diagram.
Free body force diagrams show the forces acting on a single object, whereas interaction pairs act on different objects.

Forces and Vector Diagrams

Find the sizes of the horizontal and vertical components of the force shown on the right. Each side of a square represents 1 N.

Horizontal component = ... N

Vertical component = ... N

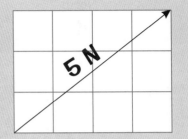

1   **Figure 1** shows a girl on a swing. Her weight of 500 N acts vertically downwards and a tension force of 250 N acts on the ropes at an angle of 30° to the horizontal.

Figure 1

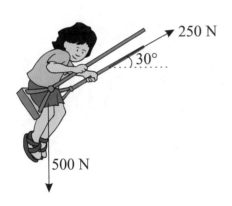

Figure 2

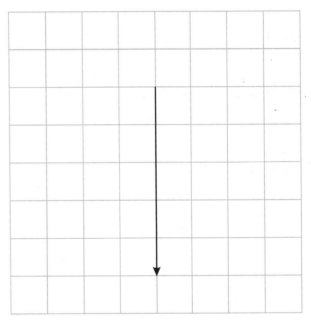

a) **Figure 2** shows an incomplete scale drawing for the forces acting on the girl.
Only the girl's weight has been drawn so far. Calculate the scale used in the drawing.

.... cm = ... N

[1]

b) Complete the scale drawing in **Figure 2** to find the magnitude of the resultant force acting on the girl.

Magnitude = ... N

[2]

[Total 3 marks]

Section 21 — Forces and Energy

2 One of the events at a school sports day is a three-way tug of war. Three teams each pull on a rope, all three of which are attached to a metal ring. **Figure 3** shows the forces exerted on the ring. It is not drawn to scale.

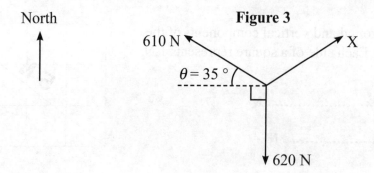

The ring is in equilibrium and does not move. Use the grid in **Figure 4** to create a scale drawing to determine the magnitude and direction as a bearing of force X.

Figure 4

Magnitude of force X = ... N

Direction = ... °

[Total 5 marks]

Current and Circuits

Warm-Up

Fill in the blanks in these sentences with the words below.
You don't have to use every word, but each word can only be used once.

.... is the rate of flow of electric charge (electrons) around a circuit.

A current will flow around a circuit if the circuit is .... and there is a

source of ....

The current flowing through a component .... when the potential difference

across it increases or when the resistance of the component ....

coulomb	energy	current	increases
potential difference	decreases	closed	

1 **Figure 1** shows a circuit symbol.

Figure 1

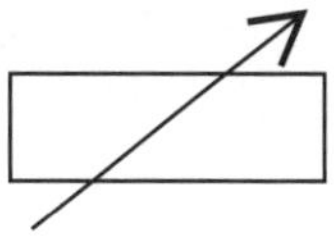

The circuit symbol shown is a

☐ **A** resistor.

☐ **B** variable resistor.

☐ **C** thermistor.

☐ **D** fuse.

[Total 1 mark]

2 A current of 3.5 A flows through a simple circuit containing a battery and a resistor.

a) Calculate how much charge passes through the light bulb in 120 seconds.

Charge = ... C

[3]

b) Calculate how long it will take for 770 C to pass through the light bulb.

Time = ... s

[3]

[Total 6 marks]

Potential Difference and Resistance

Warm-Up

For each statement, circle whether it is true or false.

Potential difference is the energy transferred per coulomb of charge.	True / False
One volt is one ampere per coulomb.	True / False
Potential difference is also known as voltage.	True / False

1 A kettle needs 276 000 J of energy to be electrically transferred to it in order to bring water to the boil. It is connected to the mains supply which has a voltage of 230 V.

a) Calculate the amount of charge that passes through the kettle to bring the water to the boil.

Charge = ... C

[3]

b) A toaster is connected to the same mains supply. When a slice of bread is toasted, the charge that passes through the toaster is 1000 C.

Calculate the energy transferred to toast the slice of bread. Give your answer in kJ.

Energy transferred = ... kJ

[2]

[Total 5 marks]

2 When a potential difference of 18 V is applied across a resistor, a current of 3 A flows through it.

a) Calculate the resistance of the resistor. State the units of your answer.

Resistance = ... Units ....

[4]

b) Over time, the current through the resistor begins to decrease. Explain why this happens.

....

....

....

....

....

[4]

[Total 8 marks]

Investigating Components

1 Voltmeters and ammeters are used to investigate circuits. (Grade 4-6)

a) A voltmeter should always be connected

☐ **A** in series with the component.

☐ **B** in series with the source of potential difference.

☐ **C** in parallel with a resistor.

☐ **D** in parallel with the component.

[1]

b) **Figure 1** shows a circuit. Draw an ammeter in an appropriate place on the diagram to measure the current flowing through the bulb.

Figure 1

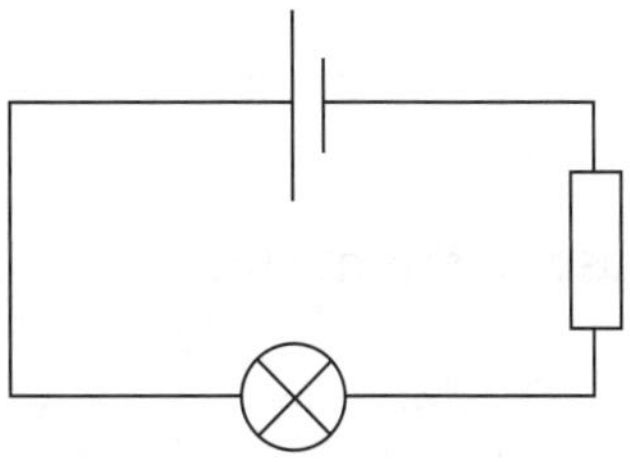

[1]

[Total 2 marks]

PRACTICAL

2* A student is investigating the resistance of a diode. He sets up the circuit shown in **Figure 2**. (Grade 7-9)

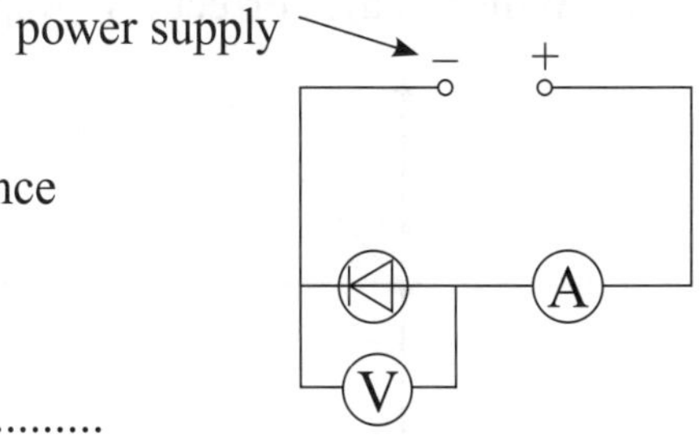

Describe how he could use this circuit to investigate the resistance of the diode. Include a discussion of the steps he should take to make sure his results are accurate and repeatable.

variable d.c. power supply **Figure 2**

....

....

....

....

....

....

....

....

....

....

[Total 6 marks]

Section 22 — Electricity and Circuits

Circuit Devices

Draw lines to match each circuit symbol to the name of the component that it's representing.

thermistor

LDR

diode

1 The resistance of a thermistor changes depending on its surroundings.

a) State what happens to the resistance of a thermistor as the surrounding temperature increases.

....
[1]

b) Give **one** example of a device that uses a thermistor.

....
[1]
[Total 2 marks]

2 Filament bulbs are a common circuit component.

a) Which is the correct *I-V* graph for a filament bulb?

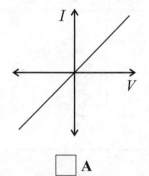 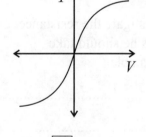 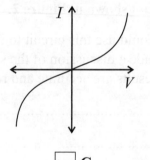 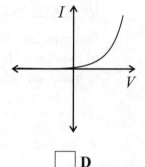

   ☐ **A**   ☐ **B**   ☐ **C**   ☐ **D**

[1]

b) Explain why the *I-V* graph for a filament bulb has this shape.

....

....

....
[2]
[Total 3 marks]

Series and Parallel Circuits

1 **Figure 1** shows a number of circuits. Tick the box below the diagram that shows all the components connected in series.

Figure 1

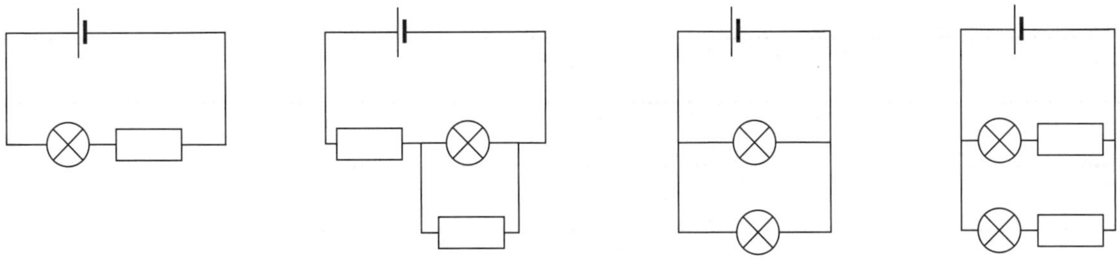

☐ **A**   ☐ **B**   ☐ **C**   ☐ **D**

[Total 1 mark]

2 Draw a circuit diagram consisting of a cell and two LDRs connected in parallel.

[Total 2 marks]

3 In the circuit in **Figure 2**, the reading on the ammeter is 75 mA.

a) Calculate the total resistance of the two resistors.

Figure 2

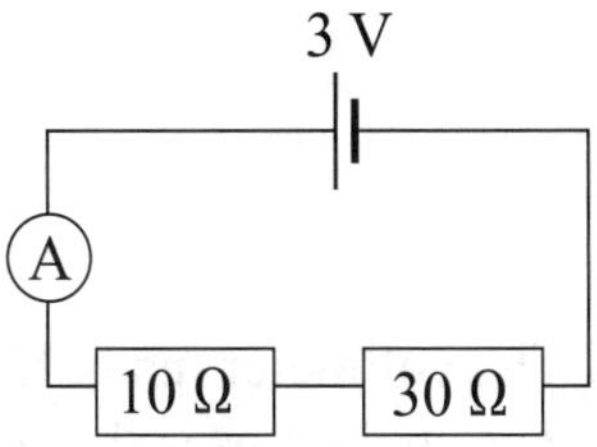

3 V

A

10 Ω   30 Ω

Resistance = ... Ω
[1]

b) Calculate the potential difference across the 30 Ω resistor.

Potential Difference = ... V
[3]

[Total 4 marks]

4* Explain why adding resistors in series with each other increases the total resistance of the resistors, whilst adding resistors in parallel with each other decreases the total resistance of the resistors.

....

....

....

....

....

....

....

....

....

....

....

....

[Total 6 marks]

PRACTICAL

5 A student is investigating series and parallel circuits, using bulbs which are labelled as having the same resistance. She sets up the circuit shown in **Figure 3**.

Figure 3

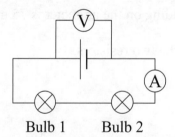

Bulb 1   Bulb 2

The voltmeter reads 12 V and the ammeter reads 0.25 A.
The student uses these values to calculate the resistance of each bulb.

a) Calculate the resistance of each bulb, assuming that the bulbs do have the same resistance.

Resistance = ... Ω

[3]

Section 22 — Electricity and Circuits

b) The student then adds a third bulb to the circuit, as shown in **Figure 4**.

Figure 4

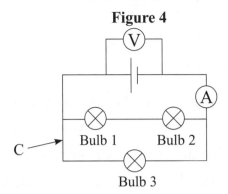

i) Assuming that bulb 3 is identical to bulbs 1 and 2, find the new current through the ammeter.

Current = ... A

[2]

ii) The student observes that bulb 3 is brighter than bulbs 1 and 2. Explain why.

....

....

[2]

c) The student then adds a resistor to the circuit in **Figure 4**, at the point marked C.

i) Describe the effect of this on the current through the ammeter.

....

[1]

ii) State how this affects the brightness of the three bulbs.

....

....

[2]

d) When the student's teacher marks her experiment, he says she should have measured the potential difference across and the current through each bulb throughout the experiment. Give **two** reasons why.

....

....

....

[2]

[Total 12 marks]

Exam Tip

Although we talk about series and parallel circuits as separate things, real circuits are often a mix — you might get a question where some components are connected in series with each other, but where there's more than one branch to the circuit. Don't panic, just remember that the rules of parallel circuits apply when you're looking at the different branches, and the rules of series circuits apply when you're looking at the components connected along one branch.

Energy in Circuits

1   Which of the following describes the energy transferred
to an electric heater connected to the mains?   *(Grade 4-6)*

    ☐   **A**   Energy is transferred electrically to the kinetic energy store of the heater.

    ☐   **B**   Energy is transferred by heating to the electrostatic energy store of the heater.

    ☐   **C**   Energy is transferred by heating to the gravitational potential energy store of the heater.

    ☐   **D**   Energy is transferred electrically to the thermal energy store of the heater.

[Total 1 mark]

2   A hairdryer contains of a motor which
turns a fan and a heating element.   *(Grade 6-7)*

a) State **one** part of the hairdryer where the heating effect of a current is **useful**.

....

[1]

b) State **one** part of the hairdryer where the heating effect of a current is **not useful**.

....

[1]

c) The hairdryer becomes less efficient the longer it is left on for. Explain why.

....

....

....

[3]

[Total 5 marks]

3   A kettle is filled with a litre of water from the cold tap.   *(Grade 6-7)*

a) It takes 355 000 J of energy to bring a litre of water to the boil. The kettle is attached to the
mains, at 230 V, and the current through the kettle is 12 A. Calculate how long it should take
the kettle to boil, to the nearest second.

Time = ... s

[3]

b) State **one** assumption that you made in order to answer part a).

....

....

[1]

[Total 4 marks]

☹ ☐   😐 ☐   🙂 ☐

Power in Circuits

1 A child is playing with a toy car. The car is powered by a battery and has two speed settings — fast and slow.

 Grade 6-7

a) The child sets the speed to slow and drives the car for 20 seconds. The power of the car at this speed is 50 W. Calculate the energy transferred by the car.

Energy transferred = ... J

[3]

b) The child now sets the speed to fast. The power of the car at this speed is 75 W.
Explain why the battery runs down more quickly when the car is set at a higher speed.

....

....

[2]

[Total 5 marks]

2 Fans use a motor to turn a set of blades. Grade 6-7

a) A 75 W ceiling fan in an office is powered by the mains supply at 230 V.
Calculate the current supplied to the fan.

Current = ... A

[3]

b) A smaller fan on someone's desk runs from a computer's USB port.
It has a power of 2.5 W, and draws a current of 0.50 A. Calculate its resistance.

Resistance = ... Ω

[3]

The ceiling fan from part a) breaks and the company investigate replacing it with a standing fan.
They look at three models, A-C, summarised in **Figure 1**.

Figure 1

Model	Power rating / W	Customer reviews
A	50	very noisy
B	40	breaks frequently, a bit small
C	45	quiet and reliable

c) i) Give the model that transfers energy at the fastest rate. ....

[1]

ii) Explain why your answer to part c) i) may not be the most efficient fan for cooling the office.

....

....

[2]

[Total 9 marks]

Section 22 — Electricity and Circuits

Electricity in the Home

In the table below, put a tick next to each statement to show whether it applies to direct current or alternating current.

	Direct current	Alternating current
Describes the current supplied by a battery		
Produced by a voltage that constantly changes direction		
Describes the current supplied by the UK mains		
Produced by a voltage with a constant direction		

1   Most houses in the UK are connected to the mains supply.   (Grade 4-6)

a) State the potential difference and frequency of the UK mains electricity supply.

....

[1]

b) A kettle is plugged into the mains with a three-core cable containing a live wire, a neutral wire and an earth wire.

i) State the colours of the live, neutral, and earth wires.

Live: ....

Neutral: ....

Earth: ....

[2]

ii) Complete the table in **Figure 1** to show the sizes of the potential differences between the wires that make up the three-core cable.

Figure 1

Wires	Potential difference / V
Live wire and neutral wire	....
Neutral wire and earth wire	....
Earth wire and live wire	....

[3]

[Total 6 marks]

2 A radio develops a fault such that the live wire is in electrical contact with the neutral wire. *(Grade 6-7)*

Explain whether you think the radio will work while this fault remains.

....

....

....

....

[Total 3 marks]

3 The cable that connects an iron to the mains supply has become worn with use. There is no insulation covering part of the live wire. The iron is plugged in, but switched off. *(Grade 6-7)*

a) State **two** purposes of the insulation that covers the live wire.

....

....

....

[2]

b) A man switches on the iron and touches the exposed live wire. He receives an electric shock. Explain why he receives an electric shock. You should refer to the electrical potential of the man in your answer.

....

....

....

....

[3]

c) The socket is switched off and the iron is unplugged.
Explain whether there is still a danger of the man receiving an electric shock from the plug socket.

....

....

....

....

[3]

[Total 8 marks]

Exam Tip

The voltage-time graph for an alternating current has a similar shape to the wave shown on p.200. The frequency of an alternating current is how many cycles it completes per second, where one cycle is, for example, from one crest to the next crest (or from one trough to the next trough). It's measured in Hz, just like wave frequency.

Section 22 — Electricity and Circuits

Fuses and Earthing

1 **Figure 1** shows an old-fashioned household fuse box.

Figure 1

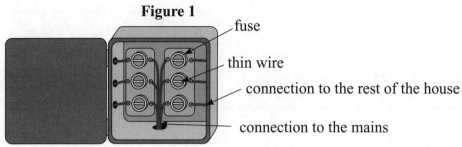

fuse

thin wire

connection to the rest of the house

connection to the mains

a) Explain why houses have fuse boxes.

....

[1]

b) In old-fashioned fuse boxes like this, home-owners sometimes replaced old fuses with pennies.
Explain why replacing fuses with pennies like this was dangerous.

....

....

[1]

c) Most modern houses uses circuit breakers, rather than fuse boxes.
Give **one** advantage and **one** disadvantage of using circuit breakers instead of fuses.

Advantage: ....

Disadvantage: ....

[2]

[Total 4 marks]

2 Many electrical devices include an Earth wire.

a) Explain how the earth wire and fuse work when a fault develops with a metal appliance.

....

....

....

....

[3]

b) The fuse in an electric heater is rated at 13 A. The fuse in a clock radio is rated at 3 A.
Suggest why these devices need fuses with different ratings.

....

....

....

[2]

[Total 6 marks]

Magnets and Magnetic Fields

For each statement, circle whether it is true (T) or false (F).

A magnetic field is a region where other magnets experience a force.   T / F

Field lines show the direction a force would act on a south pole at that point in the field.   T / F

The further away from a magnet you get, the weaker the field is.   T / F

1   All magnets produce magnetic fields.   (Grade 4-6)

a) Which of the following statements is correct for magnets?

☐ **A**   Like poles attract each other.

☐ **B**   Magnetic fields are weakest at the poles of a magnet.

☐ **C**   Unlike poles attract each other.

☐ **D**   Magnetic field lines go from the south pole to the north pole.   *[1]*

b) **Figure 1** shows a bar magnet. Draw the magnetic field lines onto the diagram in **Figure 1**.

Figure 1

| N   S |

[3]

Two bar magnets are placed near to each other, as shown in **Figure 2**.

Figure 2

| N | | S |

c) i) A uniform magnetic field is created between them. Explain what is meant by a uniform field.

....

....   *[1]*

ii) Draw the uniform field between the two poles shown in **Figure 2**.

[2]

[Total 7 marks]

2 A student places two magnetic objects near to each other on a flat, frictionless surface. **Figure 3** shows their magnetic fields. The student then releases the objects at the same time.

Grade 6-7

Figure 3

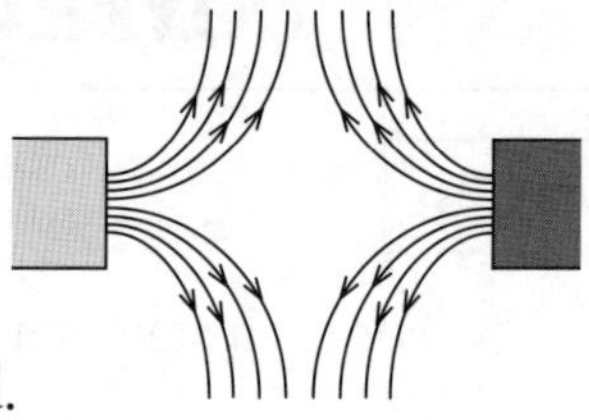

State and explain the behaviour of the two objects once they are released.

....

....

....

[Total 3 marks]

3 A student wants to investigate the magnetic field of a horseshoe magnet, shown in **Figure 4**.

Grade 6-7

Figure 4

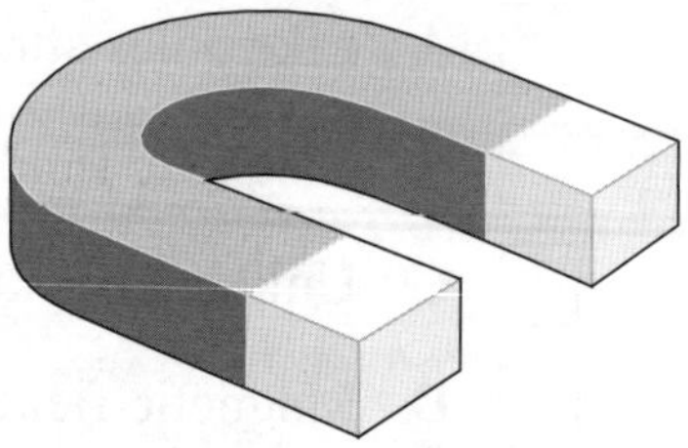

a) Describe how a compass could be used to determine the magnetic field pattern of the magnet.

....

....

....

....

....

....

....

....

....

....

....

....

[4]

b) State and explain what would happen to the compass if you were to move it far away from any magnets.

....

....

....

[2]

[Total 6 marks]

Exam Tip

Iron filings can also be used to see the shape of a magnetic field — but remember, they won't show you its direction.

Section 23 — Magnetic Fields

Permanent and Induced Magnets

1 Magnets can be permanent or induced. (Grade 4-6)

a) Describe the difference between a permanent magnet and an induced magnet.

....

....

....

[2]

b) Name **two** magnetic materials.

1. ....

2. ....

[2]

c) State **one** everyday use of magnets.

....

[1]

[Total 5 marks]

2 A block of cobalt is held in place near to a bar magnet, as shown in **Figure 1**. (Grade 6-7)

Figure 1

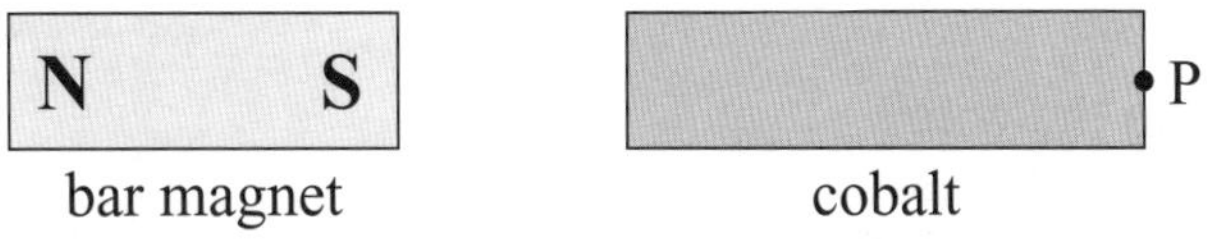

| N | S |

bar magnet   cobalt   •P

a) A steel paperclip is placed against the block of cobalt at point P, shown on **Figure 1**.
The paperclip sticks to the block of cobalt. Explain why this happens.

....

....

....

....

....

....

[3]

b) The bar magnet is removed. Explain what happens to the paperclip.

....

....

....

[2]

[Total 5 marks]

Section 23 — Magnetic Fields

Electromagnetism and the Motor Effect

The diagram shows a left hand being used for Fleming's left hand rule.
Using **three** of the labels below, label the thumb and fingers in the diagram.

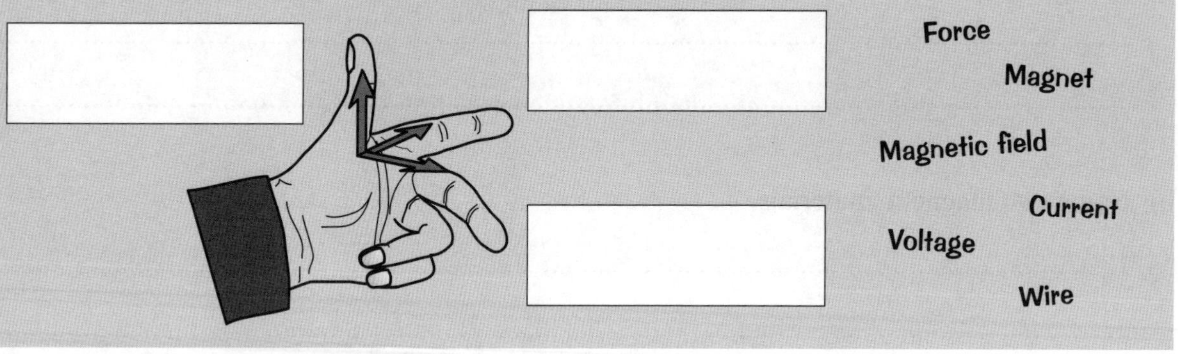

Force

Magnet

Magnetic field

Current

Voltage

Wire

1   A wire is placed between two magnets, as shown in **Figure 1**.
    A current is flowing through the wire, in the direction shown.

    Grade 4-6

Figure 1

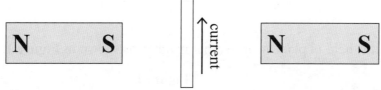

N   S   N   S

current

a) What will happen to the wire?

    ☐   **A**   It will move to the left.

    ☐   **B**   It will move away from you, into the paper.

    ☐   **C**   It will move towards you, out of the paper.

    ☐   **D**   It will remain stationary.

    [1]

b) This effect is called the motor effect. Explain the cause of the motor effect.

    ....

    ....

    [2]

c) State **three** factors which determine the magnitude of the force acting on the wire.

    1. ....

    2. ....

    3. ....

    [3]

    [Total 6 marks]

2 **Figure 2** shows a wire which has a current flowing through it. The arrow shows the direction of the current.

Figure 2

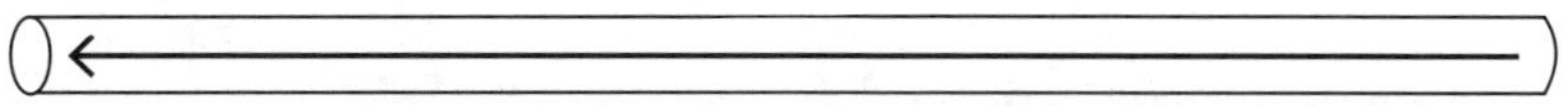

a) The flow of charge creates a magnetic field around the wire.
Draw field lines on **Figure 2** showing the direction of the magnetic field created.

[2]

b) The direction of the current is reversed. State the effect this will have on the magnetic field.

....

....

[1]

c) Give **one** way to increase the strength of the magnetic field produced by the wire.

....

[1]

[Total 4 marks]

3 A 0.75 m section of wire, carrying a current of 0.4 A, is placed into a magnetic field, shown in **Figure 3**. When the wire is perpendicular to the field, it experiences a force of 1.2 N.

Figure 3

wire

| S | • | N |

Calculate the magnetic flux density of the field. Give the correct unit in your answer.

Magnetic flux density = ...

Unit = ...

[Total 4 marks]

Exam Tip

Don't get confused between which hand you're using for a situation. Use your right hand for finding the magnetic field produced by a current-carrying conductor and your left hand for the force acting on a wire in a magnetic field.

Section 23 — Magnetic Fields

Solenoids and Electromagnetic Induction

For each statement, circle whether it is true (T) or false (F).

A single loop of current-carrying wire produces a magnetic field.	**T / F**
A solenoid is an example of a transformer.	**T / F**
An electromagnet can be turned on and off.	**T / F**
The magnetic field is weakest inside a solenoid.	**T / F**

1 This question is about statements 1 and 2, shown below. *Grade 4-6*

Statement 1: A potential difference is induced when an electrical conductor moves relative to a magnetic field.

Statement 2: A potential difference is induced when there is a change in the magnetic field around an electrical conductor.

Which of the following is correct?

☐ **A** Only statement 1 is true.

☐ **B** Only statement 2 is true.

☐ **C** Both statements 1 and 2 are true.

☐ **D** Neither statement 1 nor 2 is true.

[Total 1 mark]

2 Solenoids are an example of an electromagnet. *Grade 4-6*

a) State what is meant by an electromagnet.

....

....

[1]

b) i) Describe the magnetic field inside the centre of a solenoid.

....

....

[2]

ii) Describe the magnetic field of a solenoid outside of the solenoid.

....

....

[2]

[Total 5 marks]

3 A student sets up a simple circuit to measure the current generated when he moves a magnet in and out of a coil. The set-up of his apparatus is shown in **Figure 1**.

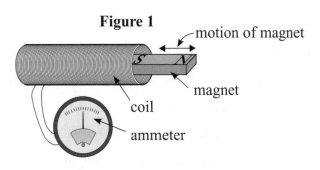

Figure 1

a) State and explain whether the set-up in **Figure 1** generates alternating or direct current.

....

....

....

....

[3]

b) State **three** ways to increase the potential difference induced by the set-up in **Figure 1**.

1. ....

2. ....

3. ....

[3]

[Total 6 marks]

4 A current-carrying solenoid has a magnetic field outside it similar to a bar magnet.

a) State how iron can be used to increase the magnetic field of the solenoid.

....

[1]

b) The north pole of a magnet is brought near to the current-carrying solenoid as shown in **Figure 2**. State whether the north pole is **attracted** or **repelled** by the solenoid. Explain your answer.

Figure 2

N

....

....

....

[3]

[Total 4 marks]

Section 23 — Magnetic Fields

Transformers

For each option, circle the word that correctly completes each sentence.

Transformers consist of two coils of wire, wrapped around a(n) (plastic / iron) core.

Transformers can change the size of (alternating / direct) potential differences.

(Step-up / Step-down) transformers decrease the output potential difference.

(Step-up / Step-down) transformers decrease the output current.

1   A transformer is 100% efficient. The current through the primary coil is 20.0 A and the potential difference across it is 30.0 V. The potential difference across the secondary coil is 40.0 V. Calculate the current through the secondary coil.

Current = ... A

[Total 3 marks]

2*   Transformers use electromagnetic induction to increase or decrease the potential difference that is supplied to them.

Explain how a step-up transformer uses electromagnetic induction to increase its output potential difference. Your answer should refer to the number of turns on each coil of the transformer.

....

....

....

....

....

....

....

....

....

....

[Total 6 marks]

3   **Figure 1** shows a basic model of how the national grid uses step-up and step-down transformers to vary the potential difference and current of the electricity it transmits. The national grid often transmits electricity at 400 000 V.

Figure 1

generator   transformer A   power lines   transformer B   consumer

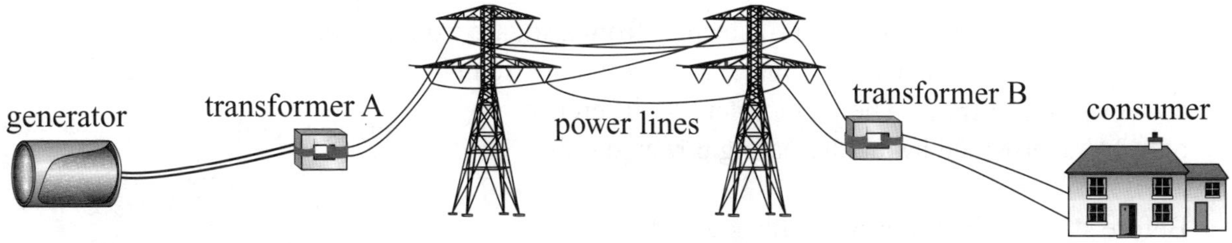

a) State what type of transformer the transformer's labelled A and B are.

Transformer A: ....

Transformer B: ....

[2]

b) The current generated in the secondary coil of any transformer creates its own magnetic field. Describe the direction of this magnetic field in relation to the magnetic field that caused it.

....

....

[1]

c)* Explain the advantages of using transformers and high-voltage cables to transfer large amounts of energy every second via the national grid. You should use equations to justify your answer.

....

....

....

....

....

....

....

....

....

....

[6]

[Total 9 marks]

Exam Tip

The equation you need for question one will be given to you in the exam — you just have to choose the correct equation from the list. To work out which one to use, it might help to make a list of all the values you've been given.

Target AO3

4   A student is doing an investigation into the properties of a transformer. They want to determine how the output potential difference, V_o, is related to the ratio of the number of turns on the secondary coil, N_s, to the number of turns on the primary coil, N_p.

The student constructs a basic transformer from a square iron core and two lengths of insulated wire. They then connect each coil to a circuit, as shown in **Figure 2**. The input potential difference, V_i, of 1.2 V is provided by an alternating power supply.

Figure 2

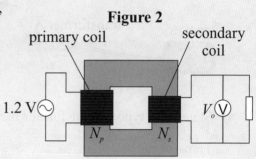

Before starting the experiment, the student notices that the insulation on the secondary coil has been worn through, and so she replaces the wire with an undamaged one.

a) Give **two** reasons why it is important that the wire is replaced.

....

....

....

[2]

The student carries out her experiment, and plots her results on a graph of V_o against the ratio $\frac{N_s}{N_p}$, as shown in **Figure 3**.

b) Calculate the gradient of the graph in **Figure 3**.

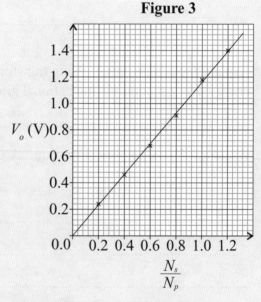

Figure 3

gradient = ... V

[2]

c) State and explain whether the results in **Figure 3** agree with the relationship $\frac{V_o}{V_i} = \frac{N_s}{N_p}$.

....

....

....

....

....

[3]

[Total 7 marks]

Exam Tip

When working out the gradient of a line, start off by drawing a right-angled triangle with your line as the longest side. Your triangle should cover more than half the length of the line. Next, write down the coordinates of the points on your line that are also the corners of the triangle. You can then use these coordinates to work out the gradient of the line.

Density

1   A 0.5 m³ block of tungsten has a mass of 10 000 kg.

   a) i) Write down the equation that links density, mass and volume.

   ....
                                                                                                    [1]

       ii) Calculate the density of tungsten.

                                                                        Density = ... kg/m³
                                                                                                    [2]

   b) Calculate the mass of a 0.02 m³ sample cut from the tungsten block.

                                                                        Mass = ... kg
                                                                                                    [2]
                                                                                        [Total 5 marks]

2   The titanium bar shown in **Figure 1** has a mass of 90.0 kg.

                              Figure 1

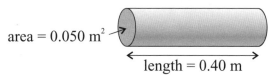

   area = 0.050 m²

   length = 0.40 m

   Calculate the density of titanium.

                                                                        Density = ... kg/m³
                                                                                        [Total 3 marks]

3   A student uses the apparatus in **Figure 2** to calculate the volumes
     of different rings to determine what materials they are made from.

                              Figure 2

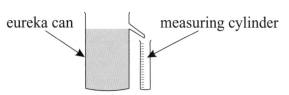

     eureka can   measuring cylinder

The can is filled up to the spout so that when a ring is placed in the can, the displaced water flows into the measuring cylinder. **Figure 3** shows an incomplete table of the student's results.

Figure 3

Ring	Mass (g)	Water displaced (ml)	Material
A	5.7	0.30	....
B	2.7	0.60	....
C	3.0	0.30	....

One ring is made from gold, one is made from silver and the other is made from titanium.
Complete **Figure 3** using the following information:

Density of gold = 19 g/cm³   Density of silver = 10 g/cm³   Density of titanium = 4.5 g/cm³

[Total 5 marks]

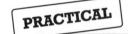

4   **Figure 4** shows a density bottle. When full, the density
bottle holds a set volume of liquid that is accurately known.

Describe how the student could use a density bottle and a mass
balance to calculate the density of a small, irregularly-shaped object.

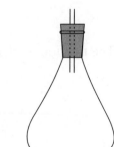

Figure 4

....

....

....

....

....

....

....

....

....

....

....

[Total 6 marks]

Exam Tip

You may be asked about experiments you've never seen before in an exam, but don't panic. To get full marks, take your time to read all the information carefully and work out what's going on before attempting any questions.

Section 24 — Matter

Kinetic Theory and States of Matter

The images below show the particles in a substance when it is in three different states of matter. Label each image to show whether the substance is a solid, a liquid or a gas.

....

1   Draw a line to match the change of state on the left to its description on the right.   *Grade 4-6*

| condensation | | gas to liquid |

| sublimation | | liquid to gas |

| evaporation | | solid to gas |

[Total 1 mark]

2   The density of different states of matter varies.   *Grade 4-6*

a) Which of the following statements is true about the different states of matter?

☐   **A** A liquid is usually less dense than a gas.

☐   **B** A liquid is usually more dense than a solid.

☐   **C** A solid is usually more dense than a gas.

☐   **D** A solid is usually less dense than a gas.

[1]

b) A student notices that ice cubes float when he puts them into a glass of water. This is because ice is less dense than liquid water. Explain what this suggests about the arrangement of the water molecules in each state.

....

....

....

....

[2]

[Total 3 marks]

3 A student leaves a sealed glass flask with 200 ml of purified water in it on a windowsill on a hot day. He checks the flask every hour and observes that the volume of liquid water decreases throughout the day.

Grade 4-6

a) Suggest why the volume of liquid water has decreased during the day.

....

[1]

b) Explain what happens to the total mass of the bottle and its contents during the day.

....

....

....

[2]

[Total 3 marks]

4 A student does an experiment to investigate methanol as it changes state. **Figure 1** shows their equipment. When the water bath is turned on, the water inside it begins to heat up.

Grade 6-7

Figure 1

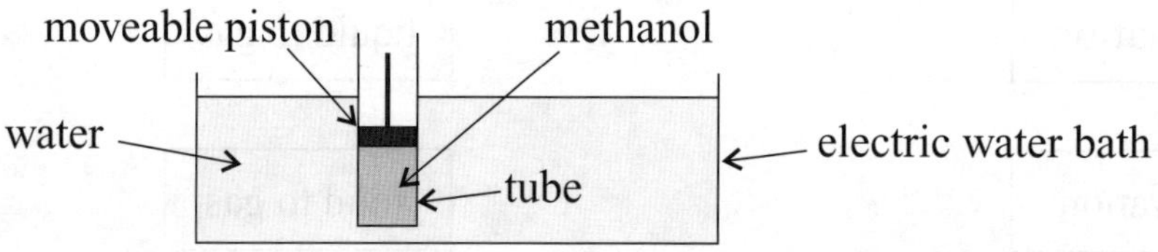

moveable piston   methanol

water →   ← electric water bath

← tube

As the water is heated, the piston begins to move upwards. After a short time, the tube containing the methanol begins to fill with gas. Explain this behaviour in terms of the energy transfers and the particles that make up the methanol.

....

....

....

....

....

....

....

....

[Total 5 marks]

Exam Tip

Remember that all changes of state are physical changes, not chemical changes. Chemical changes result in a new substance being created. During a change of state, the particles in a substance move and either get closer together or further apart. The particles themselves don't change, so a change of state has to be a physical change.

Section 24 — Matter

Specific Heat Capacity

Which of the following is the correct definition of specific heat capacity? Tick **one** box.

The energy transferred when an object is burnt. ☐

The maximum amount of energy an object can store before it melts. ☐

The energy needed to raise 1 kg of a substance by 10 °C. ☐

The energy needed to raise 1 kg of a substance by 1 °C. ☐

1 A student is measuring the specific heat capacity of different liquids. (Grade 6-7) **PRACTICAL**

For each liquid, she connects an immersion heater in a circuit with an ammeter, a voltmeter and a power supply. She also uses a thermometer, mass balance and stopwatch. She puts the immersion heater in the liquid and measures the potential difference across and current through the immersion heater as it heats.

a) i) The student measures the temperature of each liquid before and after it is heated.
Give **two** other values that the student would need to measure
to find the specific heat capacity of a given liquid.

1. ....

2. ....

[2]

ii) Explain how the student would calculate the specific heat capacity from her measurements.
Use equations from the equation sheet on page 323.

....

....

....

....

[3]

b) Each sample was heated to raise its temperature by 10 °C. The student then recorded her results, shown in **Figure 1**. Complete **Figure 1** to show the specific heat capacity of liquid C.

Figure 1

Liquid	Mass (kg)	Energy supplied (kJ)	Specific heat capacity (J/kg °C)
A	0.30	12.6	4200
B	0.30	6.6	2200
C	0.30	6.0	....

[3]
[Total 8 marks]

Target AO3

2 A student is testing three materials, A, B and C, to find their specific heat capacities. (Grade 7-9)

He heats a 100 g block of each material using an electric heater. The heater is connected to a joulemeter, which measures the amount of energy transferred to the block.
The student measures the temperature of each block for every 250 J of energy transferred.
Each block of material is wrapped in a layer of silicone foam while it is heated.

a) The student says, "Putting foam around the blocks while they are heated will improve the accuracy of my results." State and explain whether the student is correct.

....

....

....

[2]

A graph of the student's results for the three materials is shown in **Figure 2**.

Figure 2

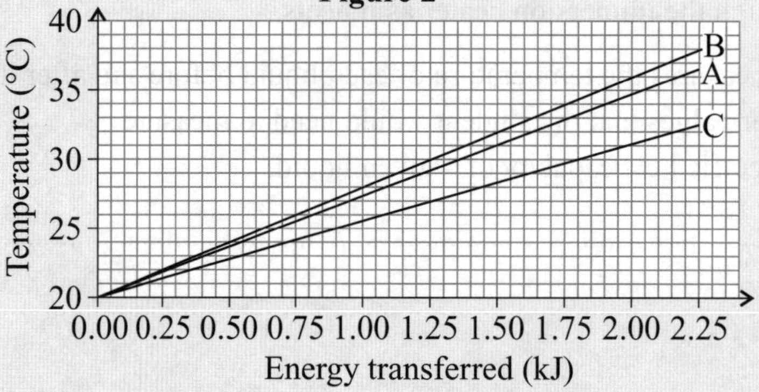

A graph with x-axis "Energy transferred (kJ)" from 0.00 to 2.25 and y-axis "Temperature (°C)" from 20 to 40, showing three lines labelled B, A and C.

b) Using the graph, explain which material has the greatest specific heat capacity.

....

....

....

....

....

[3]

c) Explain how the student can determine whether his results are valid.

....

....

....

[2]

[Total 7 marks]

Exam Tip

You may be asked to analyse the effect that using a particular piece of equipment, or method of measurement, will have on the quality of the experiment. It might help to think through how you've seen it used in other experiments.

Specific Latent Heat

1   **Figure 1** shows the mass and specific latent heat of vaporisation (SLH) of substances A-D. Which substance requires the most amount of energy to completely boil it?

Figure 1

		Mass (kg)	SLH (J/kg)
☐	**A**	1	1.5
☐	**B**	1	1.0
☐	**C**	2	1.5
☐	**D**	3	2.0

[Total 1 mark]

2   A student uses a freezer to freeze 0.50 kg of brine.

a) Define the term 'specific latent heat'.

....

.... *[1]*

b) Explain the difference between specific heat capacity and specific latent heat.

....

.... *[1]*

Figure 2 shows the temperature-time graph for brine as it was cooled.

Figure 2

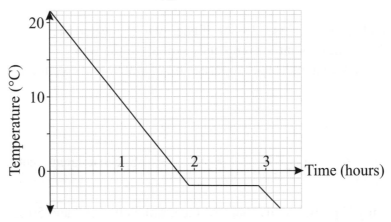

c) State the freezing point of brine.

Freezing point = ... °C

[1]

[Total 3 marks]

PRACTICAL

3   A student investigates the specific latent heat of water. They place 500 g of ice into an insulated beaker and use an immersion heater to heat the ice. They record the temperature of the water every 10 seconds. Their results are shown in **Figure 3**.

Figure 3

Time (s)	Temperature (°C)
0	0
10	0
20	0
30	0
40	0
50	0
60	7
70	21

Time (s)	Temperature (°C)
80	36
90	50
100	64
110	79
120	92
130	100
140	100
150	100

Figure 4

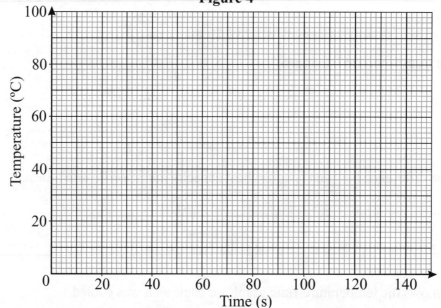

a)   Draw the temperature-time graph for the student's results on **Figure 4**.

[2]

b)   The immersion heater transfers 1.13 MJ of energy to the water once it has reached its boiling point to completely boil all of the water.
Calculate the specific latent heat of vaporisation of water. Give your answer in MJ/kg.

Specific latent heat = ... MJ/kg

[3]

c)   Explain, in terms of particles, the shape of the graph between 0 and 50 seconds.

....

....

....

[3]

[Total 8 marks]

Particle Motion in Gases

1 Describe, in terms of particles, what is meant by the term absolute zero. (Grade 4-6)

....

....

....

[Total 1 mark]

2 Two sealed containers, A and B, contain the same quantity of gas at the same temperature. The volume of container A is twice the volume of container B. (Grade 6-7)

Explain, in terms of particles, why the pressure of the gas in container A is lower than the pressure of the gas in container B.

....

....

....

....

[Total 2 marks]

3 A gas is held in a sealed container with a fixed volume. The initial temperature of the gas is 295 K. (Grade 6-7)

a) Give the initial temperature of the gas in degrees Celsius.

.... °C

[1]

b) The container is heated over a Bunsen burner.
Describe and explain how this affects the pressure of the gas inside the container.

....

....

....

[3]

[Total 4 marks]

Section 24 — Matter

4   **Figure 1** shows four sealed containers. Each contains the same mass of a gas. In which container is the pressure of the gas the highest?

Figure 1

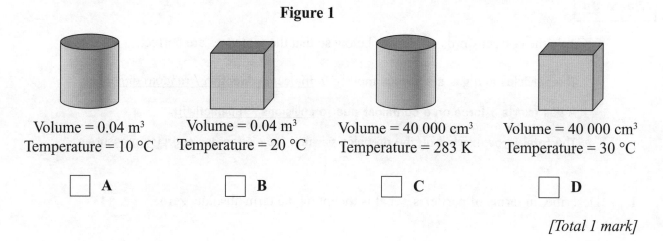

Volume = 0.04 m³
Temperature = 10 °C

☐ A

Volume = 0.04 m³
Temperature = 20 °C

☐ B

Volume = 40 000 cm³
Temperature = 283 K

☐ C

Volume = 40 000 cm³
Temperature = 30 °C

☐ D

[Total 1 mark]

5   A student investigates how varying the volume of a container full of a fixed mass of gas at a constant temperature affects the pressure of the gas. **Figure 2** is an incomplete table of his results.

Figure 2

Volume (m³)	Pressure (kPa)
8.0×10^{-4}	50
4.0×10^{-4}	100
2.5×10^{-4}	160
1.6×10^{-4}	....

Figure 3

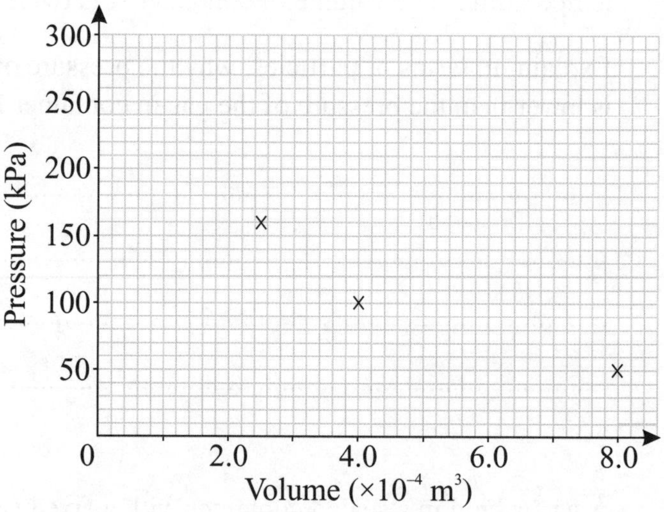

a) Complete **Figure 2** by calculating the missing pressure measurement.

[3]

b) Using information from **Figure 2**, complete the graph in **Figure 3** by plotting the missing data and drawing a line of best fit.

[2]

[Total 5 marks]

Exam Tip

Remember, one degree on the Kelvin scale is the same size as one degree on the Celsius scale, but 0 K is much, much colder than 0 °C. A temperature in Kelvin will always have a higher value than the same temperature in Celsius.

Forces and Elasticity

1   A child is playing with a toy that contains a spring.   **Grade 4-6**

a) Give the minimum number of forces that need to be applied to the spring in order to stretch it.

....
[1]

b) When the spring is compressed, it distorts elastically.
Explain the difference between elastic and inelastic distortion.

....

....

....
[2]

c) i) State the equation that links the force exerted on a spring, its spring constant and its extension.

....
[1]

ii) A 20 N force stretches the spring by 8 cm. Calculate the spring constant of the spring.

Spring constant = ... N/m
[2]

d) State **one** assumption you made to answer part c) ii).

....
[1]
[Total 7 marks]

2   **Figure 1** shows a piece of elastic being stretched between two pieces of wood. The spring constant of the elastic is 50 N/m and the unstretched length of the elastic is 3.1 cm.   **Grade 6-7**

Figure 1

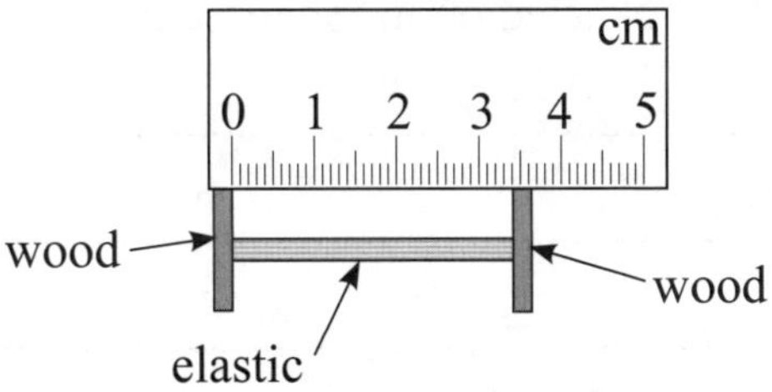

Given that the limit of proportionality hasn't been exceeded,
how much energy is stored in the stretched elastic?

☐ **A** 2.89×10^{-2} J   ☐ **B** 289 J   ☐ **C** 2.25 J   ☐ **D** 2.25×10^{-4} J

[Total 1 mark]

PRACTICAL

3   A student investigated the relationship between the extension of a spring and the forces acting on it. He hung different weights from the bottom of the spring and measured its extension with a ruler, as shown in **Figure 2**.

Figure 2

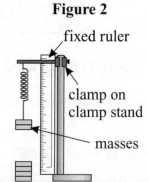

a) **Figure 3** shows the results that the student obtained in his investigation. Draw the force-extension graph for the student's results on the axes in **Figure 4**.

Figure 3

Force (N)	Extension (cm)
0.0	0.0
1.0	4.4
2.0	7.5
3.0	12.3
4.0	16.0
5.0	22.2
6.0	32.0

Figure 4

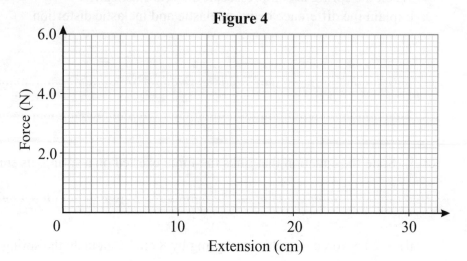

[3]

b) Using the graph you have drawn, calculate the spring constant of the spring being tested.

Spring constant = ... N/m

[2]

c) The student realised he had stretched the spring past its limit of proportionality. Explain how you can tell this from the graph.

....

....

[2]

d) The student removed the masses from the spring. Whilst he unloaded the spring, he measured its extension for each force again. He found that, when unloading the spring, the extension of the spring was 20.1 cm when a force of 4.0 N acted on it. Suggest and explain a reason for this.

....

....

....

[2]

[Total 9 marks]

Exam Tip

It's easy to get caught out by problems like question 2. Remember, for the equations for stretching (or compressing), you need to use the amount the length of an object has changed by, not its total length after it's been stretched.

Biology Mixed Questions

1   Aerobic respiration transfers energy from glucose.   **Grade 4-6**

   a)   i)   Name the subcellular structures where aerobic respiration takes place.

      ....

           [1]

     ii) Complete the word equation for aerobic respiration.

        glucose + ... $\rightarrow$ .... + water

           [2]

  Glucose is obtained through the diet.

   b)   Once it has passed through the digestive system, glucose is transported around the body in the blood.   Name the liquid component of blood.

      ....

           [1]

   c)   Some of the excess glucose from the diet is converted into glycogen and stored in the liver. Explain what happens to this glycogen if the blood glucose concentration falls below normal.

      ....

      ....

           [2]

          [Total 6 marks]

2   Alcohol is metabolised in the liver using alcohol dehydrogenase enzymes.   **Grade 4-6**

   a)   One of the functions of the liver is to break down excess amino acids. Which of the following molecules is made up of amino acids?

      ☐   **A**   a carbohydrate

      ☐   **B**   a protein

      ☐   **C**   a lipid

      ☐   **D**   glycerol

           [1]

   b)   Which **one** of the following sentences about enzymes is **true**?

      ☐   **A**   Enzymes speed up chemical reactions in living organisms.

      ☐   **B**   Enzymes are used up in chemical reactions.

      ☐   **C**   Enzymes are products of digestion.

      ☐   **D**   Enzymes are the building blocks of all living organisms.

           [1]

c) A scientist was investigating the effect of temperature on the rate of activity of alcohol dehydrogenase. **Figure 1** shows a graph of his results.

Figure 1

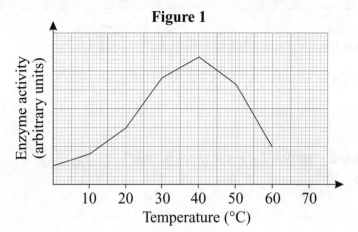

i) What is the optimum temperature for the enzyme? ....

[1]

ii) Suggest and explain the effect a temperature of 70 °C would have on the activity of the enzyme.

....

....

....

[3]

[Total 6 marks]

3 The menstrual cycle is controlled by hormones. **Figure 2** shows the change in the levels of these hormones during one menstrual cycle. It also shows the change in the lining of the uterus.

Grade 6-7

Figure 2

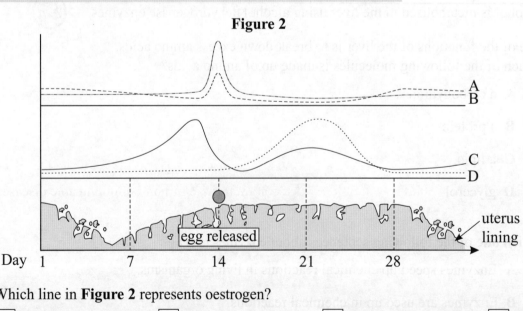

a) i) Which line in **Figure 2** represents oestrogen?

☐ A   ☐ B   ☐ C   ☐ D

[1]

ii) Which line in **Figure 2** represents luteinising hormone (LH)?

☐ A   ☐ B   ☐ C   ☐ D

[1]

b) Describe how a hormone travels from a gland to its target organ in the body.

....

....

[2]

c) Describe how a high progesterone level affects the secretion of hormones from the pituitary gland.

....

....

[2]

d) Name **two** hormones involved in maintaining the uterus lining.

1. ....

2. ....

[2]

e) State **two** effects of FSH during the menstrual cycle of a woman.

1. ....

2. ....

[2]

[Total 10 marks]

4   Crops can be genetically modified so that they produce substances that they wouldn't normally. An example of this is Golden Rice. Read the information about Golden Rice below.

Grade 6-7

> Golden Rice is a variety of rice that has been genetically modified to produce beta-carotene. Beta-carotene is used in the body to produce vitamin A.
>
> Vitamin A deficiency is a major health problem in some developing countries because many people struggle to get enough beta-carotene and vitamin A in their diet. Golden Rice could be used in these countries to help tackle vitamin A deficiency.
>
> Golden Rice was genetically engineered using a rice plant, a gene from a maize plant and a gene from a soil bacterium.

a) Explain whether vitamin A deficiency is a communicable or non-communicable disease.

....

....

[1]

b) Explain why the genome of Golden Rice will be different to the genome of normal rice.

....

....

[1]

c) Describe the process that may have been used to produce Golden Rice.

....

....

....

....

....

....

....

....

[4]

d) Fertilisers can be added to the soil to help Golden Rice grow.
   Explain how fertilisers can help a plant to make proteins.

....

....

....

[2]

[Total 8 marks]

5　Limiting factors affect the rate of photosynthesis.

a) A student was investigating the effect of limiting factors on the rate of photosynthesis
   by green algae. The student set up two boiling tubes like the one in **Figure 3**.
   She also set up a third tube that did not contain any algae.
   The colour of the indicator solution changes as follows:

Figure 3

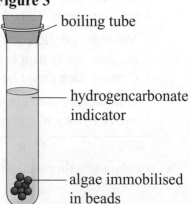

- At atmospheric CO_2 concentration, the indicator is red.
- At low CO_2 concentrations, the indicator is purple.
- At high CO_2 concentrations, the indicator is yellow.

The student covered one of the boiling tubes containing
algae with foil. No light was able to reach the algae in
this tube. All three tubes were left for several hours at a
controlled temperature with a constant light source.
The colour of the indicator solution was then recorded.
The results are shown in **Figure 4**.

Figure 4

	Algae?	Foil?	Indicator colour at start	Indicator colour at end
Tube 1	yes	yes	red	yellow
Tube 2	yes	no	red	purple
Tube 3	no	no	red	red

i) Name the waste product of photosynthesis.

....

[1]

ii) Name the limiting factor of photosynthesis that is being investigated in this experiment.

....

[1]

iii) Explain the results seen in Tube **1** and Tube **2**.

....

....

....

....

....

....

[4]

iv) Give **two** variables that needed to be controlled in this experiment.

1. ....

2. ....

[2]

b) A scientist investigating the effect of limiting factors on photosynthesis sketched the graph shown in **Figure 5**.

Figure 5

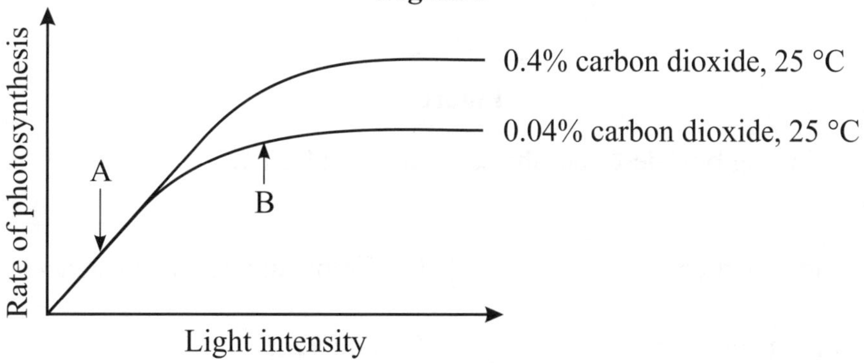

0.4% carbon dioxide, 25 °C

0.04% carbon dioxide, 25 °C

Rate of photosynthesis

Light intensity

i) Name the limiting factor at point **A**. Explain your answer.

....

....

[2]

ii) Name the limiting factor at point **B**.

....

[1]

[Total 11 marks]

Chemistry Mixed Questions

1 Calcium, Ca, and sulfuric acid, H_2SO_4, react together in a chemical reaction. **Grade 4-6**

a) Write a word equation for this reaction.

....
[2]

b) What is the chemical formula of the salt formed by this reaction?

....
[1]

c) Predict whether the salt formed will be soluble or insoluble.

....
[2]

d) The reaction of sulfuric acid with calcium is less violent than its reaction with sodium.
What does this tell you about the position of sodium, relative to calcium, in the reactivity series?

....
[1]

[Total 6 marks]

2 Chlorine is a Group 7 element that exists as molecules of Cl_2. **Grade 4-6**

a) Complete **Figure 1** to give a dot-and-cross diagram that shows the bonding in Cl_2.
You only need to show the outer electron shells.

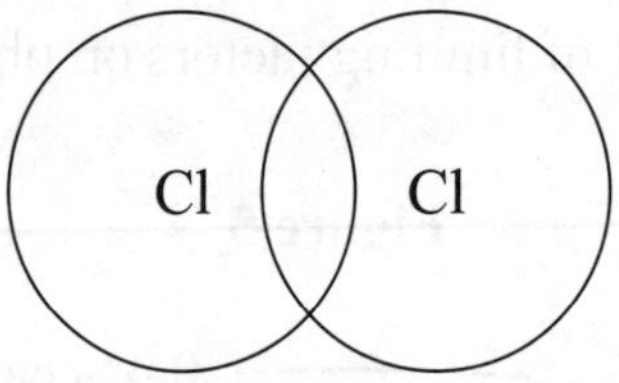

Cl   Cl

Figure 1
[2]

b) Which of the following **best** describes the structure of chlorine?
Tick **one** box.

☐ **A** Giant ionic lattice   ☐ **C** Simple molecular substance

☐ **B** Giant covalent structure   ☐ **D** Fullerene
[1]

c) Describe a test you could carry out for chlorine. Include any observations you would expect.

....

....
[2]

d) Chlorine has a melting point of −102 °C and a boiling point of −34 °C.
Predict what state chlorine would be in at −50 °C.

....
[1]

[Total 6 marks]

3 Ellie is using paper chromatography experiment to analyse the components in a sample.
Figure 2 shows the chromatogram produced by the experiment.

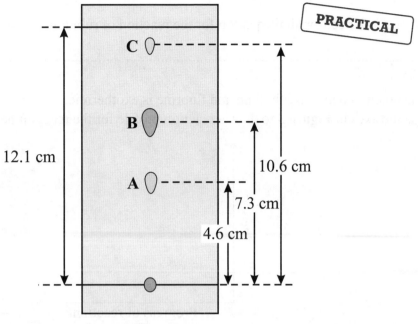

Figure 2

a) Identify the **stationary phase** in Ellie's experiment.

....
[1]

b) Use **Figure 2** to calculate the R_f values for spots **A**, **B**, and **C**.

$$R_f = \frac{\text{distance travelled by solute}}{\text{distance travelled by solvent}}$$

R_f of **A** = ...

R_f of **B** = ...

R_f of **C** = ...
[3]

c) From **Figure 2**, how can you tell that Ellie's sample contains
a substance that is insoluble in the mobile phase?

....
[1]

d) Use **Figure 2** to identify the **minimum** number of components in Ellie's sample. Tick **one** box.

☐ **A** 1 ☐ **B** 2 ☐ **C** 3 ☐ **D** 4
[1]

e) Ellie concludes that her sample is a mixture. Explain what is meant by the term 'mixture'.

....

....
[1]

f) The mixture contains some liquid components with similar boiling points.
Name a technique that Ellie could use to separate the different components in the mixture.

....
[1]

[Total 8 marks]

Mixed Questions

4   Rubidium is an element from Group 1 of the periodic table.
    Fluorine is an element from Group 7. Rubidium metal, Rb,
    and fluorine gas, F_2, react violently to produce a single product.

a) Write a balanced symbol equation for the reaction of rubidium metal and fluorine gas.

    ....

    [2]

b) The reaction between rubidium and fluorine is exothermic.
    Use the axes in **Figure 3** to draw a reaction profile for the reaction between rubidium and fluorine.

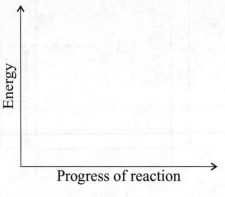

Figure 3

    [2]

    [Total 4 marks]

5   A student reacts chlorine water reacts with potassium
    iodide solution according to the following reaction.

$$Cl_{2\,(aq)} + 2KI_{(aq)} \rightarrow 2KCl_{(aq)} + I_{2\,(aq)}$$

a) Chlorine water is corrosive.
    State **one** safety precaution that the student should take when carrying out the reaction.

    ....

    [1]

b) Find the relative formula mass of potassium iodide, KI. $A_r(K) = 39$, $A_r(I) = 127$.

    ....

    [1]

c) Describe what the student would observe when he
    added chlorine water to potassium iodide solution.

    ....

    [1]

d) Explain why this reaction takes place.
    Give your answer in terms of the reactivity of the elements involved.

    ....

    ....

    [2]

e) Write a balanced ionic equation for the reaction between chlorine and potassium iodide.

    ....

    [2]

    [Total 7 marks]

Mixed Questions

6 Some elements have several different isotopes. Look at **Figure 4**.
It shows the percentage of the atoms of some elements that exist as each of their isotopes.

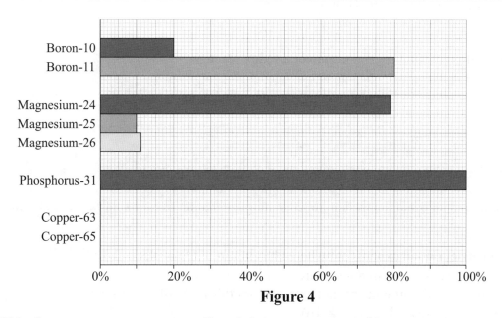

Figure 4

a) 69% of copper atoms are copper-63 and the rest are copper-65.
Complete **Figure 4** by adding bars for the two isotopes of copper.

[2]

b) Explain why the relative atomic mass of phosphorus is a whole number,
while the relative atomic masses of boron, magnesium and copper are not.

....

....

....

....

....

....

[3]

c) Use **Figure 4** to calculate the relative atomic mass of magnesium.
Give your answer to three significant figures.

relative atomic mass = ...

[4]

[Total 9 marks]

7 A student has a sample of sodium sulfate, Na_2SO_4, with a mass of 34.08 g.
How many oxygen atoms are in the sample, to 4 significant figures?

(relative atomic masses: Na = 23, S = 32, O = 16)

☐ **A** 1.442×10^{23} atoms ☐ **C** 1.015×10^{24} atoms

☐ **B** 5.779×10^{23} atoms ☐ **D** 1.442×10^{24} atoms

[Total 1 mark]

Mixed Questions

272

8 Aluminium can be obtained by electrolysis of the ore bauxite, Al_2O_3.

The overall equation for this reaction is:

$$2Al_2O_{3\,(l)} \rightarrow 4Al_{(l)} + 3O_{2\,(g)}$$

a) Explain why this reaction is an example of a redox reaction.

....

....
[1]

b) Write a half equation to show the reaction that occurs at the cathode.

....
[2]

c) A scientist carries out an experiment where aluminium oxide is electrolysed.
The scientist starts off with 40.8 g of pure aluminium oxide.
Predict the mass of aluminium she can extract from this mass of electrolyte.
(relative atomic masses: Al = 27, O = 16)

mass = ... g
[4]

d) Iron can be extracted from its ores by heating with carbon.
Explain why this method is **not** suitable for the extraction of aluminium from its ore.

....

....

....
[2]

e) In the UK, some metals are widely recycled. Give **two** advantages of recycling metals.

....

....
[2]
[Total 11 marks]

9 A scientist wants to produce a batch of aluminium sulfate for an experiment.
She plans to do this by reacting aluminium with an excess of sulfuric acid.
A chemical supplier offers three options to provide the quantity of aluminium she needs.

Which of these options will allow the scientist to complete her reaction in the **shortest** time?

☐ **A** 1 aluminium cube with side length 8 cm.

☐ **B** 8 aluminium cubes, each with side length 4 cm.

☐ **C** 64 aluminium cubes, each with side length 2 cm.

☐ **D** They will all take the same length of time.

[Total 1 mark]

Mixed Questions

10 Many different chemical substances are carbon based. (Grade 7-9)

a) Put the carbon based substances butane, diamond and poly(propene) in order of melting point, from **highest** to **lowest**. Explain your answer.

Order: ....

Explanation: ....

....

....

....

[5]

b) Which of the substances from c) i) would be most suitable for using in drill bits? Explain your answer with reference to the bonding in your chosen material.

....

....

....

[3]

[Total 8 marks]

11 A hydrogen-oxygen fuel cell is a type of electrical cell. Hydrogen-oxygen fuel cells can be used to power cars. (Grade 7-9)

a) Hydrogen is the fuel used in the hydrogen-oxygen fuel cell. Suggest **two** advantages associated with using hydrogen as a fuel for cars instead of petrol.

....

....

[2]

b) The reaction that occurs in a hydrogen-oxygen fuel cell is: $2H_2 + O_2 \rightarrow 2H_2O$

Figure 5 shows the energy of the bonds involved in this reaction.

Bond	Bond Energy (kJ mol^{-1})
O=O	498
H–H	436
O–H	463

Figure 5

Calculate the energy change for the reaction which takes place in the hydrogen-oxygen fuel cell.

energy change = ... kJ mol^{-1}

[3]

[Total 5 marks]

Mixed Questions

Physics Mixed Questions

1 A ray of light in a vacuum travels 1 foot in around 1 nanosecond. **(Grade 4-6)**

a) A foot is a measure of distance. State the SI unit for measuring distance.

....
[1]

b) One nanosecond is equal to

☐ **A** 1×10^9 seconds.   ☐ **C** 1×10^{-6} seconds.

☐ **B** 1×10^{-9} seconds.   ☐ **D** 1×10^{-6} seconds.

[1]

c) Distance and time are both scalar quantities. State what is meant by a scalar quantity.

....

....
[1]

[Total 3 marks]

2 A child pulls a toy along the ground. There is friction between the toy's wheels and the ground. The forces acting on the toy are shown in **Figure 1**. **(Grade 4-6)**

Figure 1

a) Which of the following shows the correct way to find the resultant force acting on the toy from a scale drawing of the forces acting on it? The dashed lines represent the forces acting on the toy, and the solid line represents the resultant force.

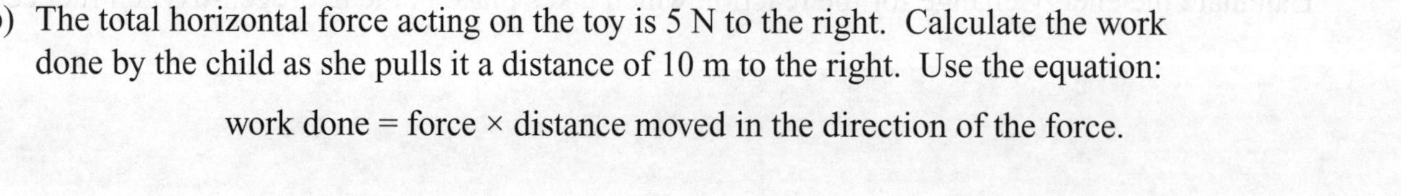

☐ **A**   ☐ **B**   ☐ **C**   ☐ **D**
[1]

b) The total horizontal force acting on the toy is 5 N to the right. Calculate the work done by the child as she pulls it a distance of 10 m to the right. Use the equation:

work done = force × distance moved in the direction of the force.

Work done = ... J
[2]

[Total 3 marks]

3 A girl is walking her dog. She decides to record the distance she had travelled during the walk every 5 minutes. *Grade 4-6*

a) She uses the information she collected to draw a distance/time graph for her walk. What does the gradient of a distance/time graph represent?

☐ **A** speed

☐ **B** acceleration

☐ **C** distance

☐ **D** deceleration

[1]

b) After exactly 5 minutes, she has walked a distance of 420 m. Calculate the average speed at which she walked. Use the equation:

average speed = distance travelled ÷ time.

Give the unit in your answer.

Average speed = ... Unit: ....

[3]

c) Whilst walking, the girl throws a ball for her dog to chase. Each time she throws the ball, she transfers energy to the ball's kinetic energy store. Which method correctly describes how energy is transferred to the ball?

☐ **A** electrically   ☐ **C** by heating

☐ **B** mechanically   ☐ **D** by radiation

[1]

[Total 5 marks]

4 X-rays and gamma rays are types of electromagnetic waves. *Grade 4-6*

a) Electromagnetic waves are transverse. Give **one** example of a longitudinal wave.

....

[1]

b) State **one** use of each of the following electromagnetic waves.

X-ray: ....

Gamma rays: ....

[2]

c) The equation shows a nucleus emitting a gamma ray. Determine the values of A and B.

$$^{99}_{43}\text{Tc} \rightarrow \, ^{A}_{43}\text{Tc} + \, ^{B}_{0}\gamma$$

A = ...   B = ...

[2]

[Total 5 marks]

Mixed Questions

5 Radiation is around us all the time. **(Grade 6-7)**

a) Radioactivity can be measured in different ways.
Suggest **one** method that could be used to measure the radioactivity of a source.

....

[1]

b) Draw a line from each type of radiation on the left to its correct description on the right.

alpha particle		an electromagnetic wave

beta-minus particle		a helium nucleus

gamma ray		an electron emitted from the nucleus

[1]

c) Beta decay can also occur through the emission of a beta-plus particle.
Which of the following statements is **incorrect** for beta-plus decay?

☐ **A** A neutron becomes a proton in the nucleus.

☐ **B** A positron is emitted from the nucleus.

☐ **C** A proton becomes a neutron in the nucleus.

☐ **D** The mass number of the nucleus remains the same.

[1]

d) i) The term 'activity' can be used when describing a radioactive source.
State what is meant by activity and give the unit it is measured in.

....

[2]

ii) On the axes in **Figure 2**, sketch how the
activity of a radioactive source varies over time.

Figure 2

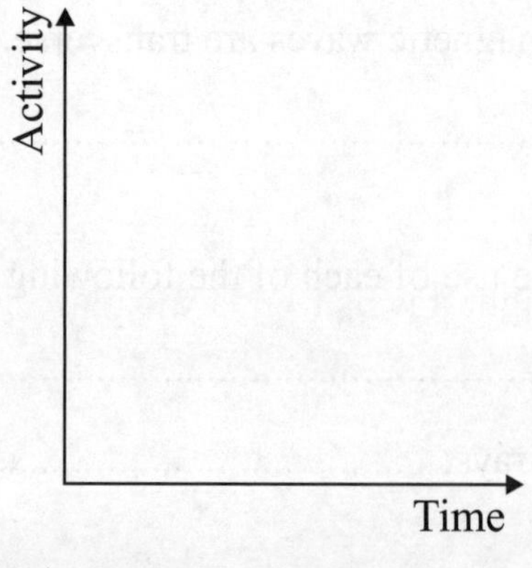

Activity ↑

Time →

[2]

e) The term 'half-life' can also be used when describing a source of radiation.
State what is meant by half-life. You should refer to activity in your answer.

....

....

[1]

[Total 8 marks]

6 A battery powered winch is used to raise a 40.0 kg crate vertically off the ground.

a) Complete **Figure 3** to show the main energy transfers that occur as the crate is lifted.

Figure 3

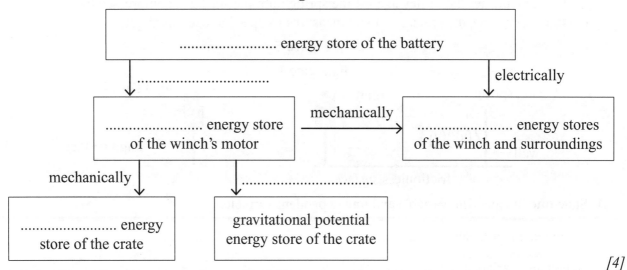

.... energy store of the battery

....

electrically

.... energy store of the winch's motor

mechanically

.... energy stores of the winch and surroundings

mechanically

....

.... energy store of the crate

gravitational potential energy store of the crate

[4]

b) The crate is raised 1.1 m vertically off the ground.
Calculate the energy transferred to the crate's gravitational potential energy store.

Energy transferred = ... J

[4]

[Total 8 marks]

7 Electromagnetic waves are able to travel through a vacuum.

a) i) An infrared wave is travelling through a vacuum. It has a wavelength of 1×10^{-6} m and a frequency of 3×10^{14} Hz. Calculate its speed. Give your answer in standard form.

Speed = ... m/s

[4]

ii) Determine the speed at which radio waves travel in a vacuum.

....

[1]

b) Visible light is another type of electromagnetic wave.
Visible light travels from a vacuum into a glass block, as shown
in **Figure 4**. Explain what happens to the wave as it enters
and leaves the glass block. In your answer, you should refer to the
direction in which the wave is travelling, and its speed.

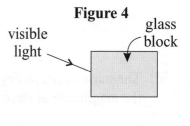

Figure 4

visible light

glass block

....

....

....

....

[4]

[Total 9 marks]

Mixed Questions

8 A student is investigating how the deceleration of a 0.50 kg trolley varies based on the surface it is travelling on. Her set-up is shown in **Figure 5**.

The student uses a spring attached to the wall to provide the driving force for the trolley. She pushes the trolley against the spring until the spring is compressed by 0.040 m each time, then releases it and measures its speed at each light gate.

Figure 5

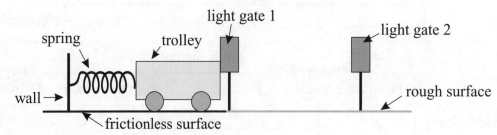

a) State **one** independent variable and **one** dependent variable.

Independent variable: ....

Dependent variable: ....

[2]

b) The table in **Figure 6** shows her results.
Complete the table in **Figure 6** by calculating the magnitude of the acceleration for each repeat.

Figure 6

Repeat	Speed at light gate 1 (m/s)	Speed at light gate 2 (m/s)	Time taken to travel between light gates 1 and 2 (s)	Acceleration (m/s²)
1	1.22	0.76	2.00	
2	1.16	0.62	2.25	
3	1.19	0.75	2.00	

[3]

Light gate 1 records the trolley's speed just after it leaves the spring. You can assume that no friction acts upon the trolley between it leaving the spring and it passing through light gate 1.

c) Using the information in the table, calculate the energy in the spring's elastic potential energy store when it is compressed. Give your answer to 2 significant figures.

Energy = ... J

[4]

d) The mass of the trolley is 300 g. Use information in the table to calculate the magnitude of the frictional force acting on the trolley.

Force = ... N

[4]

[Total 12 marks]

9 A student is designing a basic electronic toy. He wants the toy to be able to light up and spin around. He creates a basic circuit of a battery connected to a motor. In parallel to the motor, he connects two filament bulbs and a fixed resistor. The two bulbs and the resistor are all in series with each other. The bulbs and the motor can be switched on and off separately.

a) Draw the circuit diagram for the circuit created by the student.

[5]

b) The student notices that if the circuit is left on for a long period of time, the resistor and the motor both get hot. Explain the causes of this and suggest **one** way of reducing this heating.

....

....

....

....

....

....

....

[4]

c) The student turns on only the motor. The potential difference across the motor is 6.0 V and a current of 70 mA flows through the motor. After 10 minutes, the student switches off the motor and measures the temperature of the coil of wire inside the motor. He finds that it has increased by 25 °C since it was first turned on.

3.0 g of wire makes up the coil inside the motor.
The material it is made from has a specific heat capacity of 400 J/kg °C.

Calculate the amount of energy that is usefully transferred by the motor in 10 minutes.
You can assume that all energy not transferred to thermal energy stores is usefully transferred.
Give your answer to 2 significant figures.

Energy transferred usefully = ... J

[5]

[Total 14 marks]

Mixed Questions

Answers

Section 1 — Key Concepts in Biology

Pages 2-3 — Cells

Warm-up
plant/animal, plant/animal, simple, single

1 a)

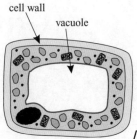

[1 mark]

b) Chloroplast — where photosynthesis occurs *[1 mark]*.
Cell wall — supports and strengthens the cell *[1 mark]*.

2 a) W – flagellum *[1 mark]*
X – cell wall *[1 mark]*
Y – plasmid DNA *[1 mark]*

b) It controls the cell's activities and replication *[1 mark]*.

3 a) i) nucleus *[1 mark]*
ii) chromosomal DNA / plasmid DNA *[1 mark]*

b) ribosome *[1 mark]*

c) cell membrane *[1 mark]*

4 Figure 4 is more likely to be a muscle cell since it contains more mitochondria than the cell in Figure 3 *[1 mark]*. Muscle cells need a lot of energy in order to contract *[1 mark]* so they will need lots of mitochondria as these are the site of respiration *[1 mark]*, the process which transfers energy to the cell *[1 mark]*.

Page 4 — Specialised Cells

1 a) 56 ÷ 2 = **28** *[1 mark]*
Egg cells are haploid, which means that there are half the number of chromosomes in the nucleus as in a normal body cell. So all you have to do is divide the number of chromosomes in a body cell by 2.

b) The acrosome contains enzymes *[1 mark]* that digest through the membrane of the egg cell *[1 mark]*.

c) i) It changes its structure to prevent any other sperm cells from getting in *[1 mark]*. This makes sure the offspring ends up with the right amount of DNA *[1 mark]*.

ii) The cytoplasm contains lots of nutrients to nourish the developing embryo *[1 mark]*.

2 a) ciliated epithelial cell *[1 mark]*

b) The cilia on the ciliated epithelial cells beat backwards and forwards *[1 mark]* and move the egg cell along the inner surface of the fallopian tubes towards the uterus *[1 mark]*.

You might not have met ciliated epithelial cells in this context before, but you should still be able to answer the question. Just think about what you know about the function of the cells (i.e. that they are specialised to move substances) and apply this knowledge to the context in the question.

Page 5 — Microscopy

1 a) i) × 4 *[1 mark]*
Remember, you should always start with the lowest-powered objective lens — this makes it easier to get your specimen into view.

ii) They bring the sample into focus by moving the stage/objective lenses up and down *[1 mark]*.

iii) She should select the × 40 or × 10 objective lens *[1 mark]* and use the adjustment knobs to bring the sample back into focus *[1 mark]*.

b) Any two from: e.g. she should use a sharp pencil. / She should draw outlines of the main features. / She should not colour or shade her drawing. / She should label her drawing with straight, uncrossing lines. / She should include the magnification used and a scale. / Her drawing should take up at least half of the space available. / She should keep the parts in proportion.
[2 marks — 1 for each correct answer.]

c) The image viewed with an electron microscope would be clearer and more detailed than the image viewed with the light microscope *[1 mark]*. This is because electron microscopes have a higher magnification *[1 mark]* and a higher resolution than light microscopes *[1 mark]*.

Pages 6-7 — More Microscopy

Warm-up

1

	÷ 1000 will convert to:	× 1000 will convert to:	in standard form will be:
mm	m	μm	× 10⁻³ m
μm	**mm**	**nm**	× 10⁻⁶ m
nm	**μm**	**pm**	× 10⁻⁹ m
pm	**nm**		× 10⁻¹² m

2 Total magnification
= **eyepiece lens** magnification × **objective lens** magnification
It doesn't matter which way round you write eyepiece lens and objective lens in the formula.

$$\text{magnification} = \frac{\text{image size}}{\text{real size}}$$

1 a) i) Total magnification
= eyepiece lens magnification × objective lens magnification
Total magnification = 10 × 100 = × **1000** *[1 mark]*

ii) 25 μm *[1 mark]*
The height of the cells is about 2 and a half times the length of the scale bar.

b) A *[1 mark]*

2 a) length of cell A in image = 24 mm
magnification = image size ÷ real size
= 24 ÷ 0.012 = × **2000**
[2 marks for correct answer, otherwise 1 mark for length of cell = 24 mm]

b) image size = magnification × real size
400 × 0.012 = **4.8 mm** *[2 marks for correct answer, otherwise 1 mark for 400 × 0.012]*

3 a) real size = image size ÷ magnification
real size = 10 mm ÷ 1000 = 0.01 mm
0.01 mm x 1000 = **10 μm** *[3 marks for correct answer, otherwise 1 mark for 10 ÷ 1000, 1 mark for 0.01 × 1000]*

b) $4 × 10^{-5}$ = 0.00004 mm
0.00004 mm × 1000 = 0.04 μm
0.04 μm × 1000 = **40 nm** *[3 marks for correct answer, otherwise 1 mark for 0.00004 × 1000, 1 mark for 0.04 × 1000]*

Pages 8-9 — Enzymes

1 a) A catalyst increases the rate of a reaction *[1 mark]*.

b) active site *[1 mark]*

c) It means usually only one type of substrate will fit into the active site of a specific enzyme *[1 mark]*.

2 a) A *[1 mark]*

b) After a certain point, all of the active sites on the enzymes are full *[1 mark]* and increasing substrate concentration does not result in more substrate molecules entering the active sites of enzymes, so the rate of the reaction is not affected *[1 mark]*.

3 At 38 °C enzyme A will be most active as this is its optimum temperature *[1 mark]*. At 60 °C, enzyme A is denatured and will not be active *[1 mark]* because the shape of the active site has changed *[1 mark]*.

4 a) i)

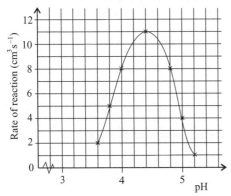

[1 mark for all points correctly plotted,
1 mark for a smooth curve of best fit]

ii) optimum pH = 4.4 *[1 mark]*

b) The enzyme activity decreases *[1 mark]* because the pH affects the bonds in the enzyme, causing the active site to change shape *[1 mark]* and denaturing the enzyme *[1 mark]*.

Page 10 — More on Enzymes

1 a) pH 6 as this was the pH at which the iodine solution stopped turning blue-black first *[1 mark]*, meaning the starch had been broken down the fastest *[1 mark]*.

b) E.g. the amylase was denatured by the high pH, so the starch was not broken down *[1 mark]*.

c) i) By putting the test tubes in a water bath *[1 mark]*.

ii) Any two from: e.g. the concentration of starch solution / the concentration of amylase / the volume of starch and amylase solution added to the iodine / the volume of iodine solution in the wells *[1 mark for each correct answer.]*

d) E.g. test the solutions more frequently (e.g. every 10 seconds) *[1 mark]*.

Page 11 — Enzymes in Breakdown and Synthesis

1 a) A: carbohydrase *[1 mark]*
B: protein *[1 mark]*
C: amino acids *[1 mark]*

b) Organisms need to be able to break down large molecules into smaller components so that they can be absorbed into the bloodstream and into cells *[1 mark]* to be used for growth and other life processes *[1 mark]*.

2 Orlistat prevents lipase from working so lipids are not broken down *[1 mark]* into fatty acids and glycerol *[1 mark]*. This means lipids are not absorbed into the blood and instead pass through the digestive system and into the faeces *[1 mark]*.

Pages 12-13 — Diffusion, Osmosis and Active Transport

Warm-up

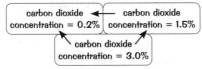

1 a) Diffusion is the net movement *[1 mark]* of particles from an area of higher concentration to an area of lower concentration *[1 mark]*.

b) A *[1 mark]*

Proteins are too large to diffuse through a cell membrane.

2 a) C *[1 mark]*

*Remember, osmosis involves the movement of **water** molecules (so the answer isn't option B or D) across a partially permeable membrane (so the answer isn't option A).*

b) Osmosis is the net movement of water molecules *[1 mark]* across a partially permeable membrane *[1 mark]* from a region of higher water concentration to a region of lower water concentration *[1 mark]*.

3 a) ——————————————▶ *[1 mark]*

b) ——————————————▶ *[1 mark]*

c) ◀—————————————— *[1 mark]*

For this question you need to work out the relative concentration of the molecules on each side of the membrane and read the question carefully to see what process is involved in their movement.

4 a) The epithelial cells have a higher concentration of amino acids than the gut *[1 mark]*, so amino acids have to be moved up their concentration gradient into the epithelial cells *[1 mark]* before they can pass into the bloodstream *[1 mark]*.

b) The structures labelled A are mitochondria *[1 mark]*. These are the site of respiration reactions, which transfer the energy needed for active transport *[1 mark]*.

Pages 14-15 — Investigating Osmosis

1 a) % change in mass
= ((final mass − initial mass) ÷ initial mass) × 100
= ((9.3 − 10) ÷ 10) × 100 = −0.07 × 100 = −7% *[1 mark]*

b) The water concentration was lower inside the potato chips than in the solution in the beaker *[1 mark]*, so the potato chips gained mass as water was drawn into them by osmosis *[1 mark]*.

c)

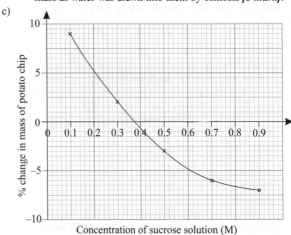

[1 mark for correctly plotting the data, 1 mark for labelling the axes correctly, 1 mark for choosing a sensible scale, 1 mark for drawing a smooth curve of best fit. Allow plotting mark even if value calculated incorrectly in part a).]

d) Find the sucrose concentration where the curve of best fit crosses the x-axis / where there is no change in mass of the potato chip *[1 mark]*.

2 a) Any two from: e.g. the volume of sucrose solution the student puts in the Visking tubing. / The volume of sucrose solution the student puts in the beaker. / The temperature the beaker is kept at. / The size of the Visking tubing bag *[2 marks]*.

b) It will stay the same *[1 mark]*. The water concentration of the solution in the tubing is the same as the water concentration of the solution in the beaker, so there will be no net movement of water molecules *[1 mark]*.

c) E.g. at first, the level of the solution in the beaker will gradually increase *[1 mark]*. The water concentration of the solution in the tubing is greater than the water concentration of the solution in the beaker, so there will be a net movement of water molecules out of the tubing *[1 mark]*. Later, the level of the solution in the beaker will stop changing *[1 mark]*. The water concentration of the solutions in the tubing and the beaker will have become the same, so there will be no net movement of water molecules *[1 mark]*.

Section 2 — Cells and Control

Page 16 — Mitosis

1 a) Prophase — the chromosomes condense *[1 mark]* and the membrane around the nucleus breaks down *[1 mark]*. Telophase — membranes form around each new set of chromosomes *[1 mark]*, forming the nuclei of the two new cells *[1 mark]*.

b) A *[1 mark]*

The cells are diploid because they contain two copies of each chromosome (just like the original cell). They each contain exactly the same sets of chromosomes as each other, meaning they are genetically identical.

c) So the organism can grow. / So the organism can reproduce asexually. *[1 mark]*

2 a) A cell's DNA is duplicated *[1 mark]*, so that there will be one copy of the DNA for each new cell produced by mitosis *[1 mark]*.
   b) i) anaphase *[1 mark]*
      ii) Spindle fibres pull the chromosomes apart *[1 mark]* and then the chromatids are pulled to opposite ends of the cell *[1 mark]*.
   c) The cytoplasm and cell membrane divide to form two separate cells *[1 mark]*.

Pages 17-18 — Cell Division and Growth

1 a) D *[1 mark]*
Cell division in a plant usually just happens in the meristems, which are found in the tips of roots and shoots.
   b) cell elongation *[1 mark]*
2 a) To produce specialised cells *[1 mark]*.
Cell differentiation has the same purpose whatever the age of the animal — it has the same purpose in plants too.
   b) Any two from: e.g. all growth in animals happens by cell division/animals don't grow by cell elongation, but growth in plants occurs by cell division and cell elongation. / Animals tend to grow while they're young, and then they reach full growth and stop growing, while plants often grow continuously. / In most animals, cell differentiation is lost at an early stage but plants continue to differentiate to develop new parts throughout their lives. *[2 marks — 1 mark for each correct answer.]*
3 a) A change in one of the genes that controls cell division *[1 mark]* causes cell to divide uncontrollably *[1 mark]*. This creates an abnormal mass of cells (a tumour) *[1 mark]*.
   b) When the tumour invades and destroys surrounding tissue *[1 mark]*.
4 a) i) It's the 25th percentile *[1 mark]*. It shows the mass that 25% of children will have reached at a certain age *[1 mark]*.
      ii) E.g. the child's weight was around the 50th percentile until it was 6 months of age *[1 mark]* but by 10 months it had increased to the 98th percentile *[1 mark]*. A doctor may be concerned because the child's weight has increased by more than two percentile lines in this time *[1 mark]*.
   b) E.g. length/height *[1 mark]*, head circumference *[1 mark]*
5 a) Amount of growth between 0 and 60 weeks =
      mass at 60 weeks – mass at birth = 120 – 20 = 100 kg
      rate of growth = 100 kg ÷ 60 weeks = **1.7 kg week⁻¹**
      [2 marks for correct final answer, otherwise 1 mark for 100 ÷ 60]
A rate is how much something changes over time. The animal's age in weeks is a measure of time in this question.
   b) There would be no cell differentiation happening at the point marked X on the graph *[1 mark]*. This is because (for most animals) cell differentiation is lost at an early stage in life *[1 mark]*.
Remember, this is not true for plants — they continue to develop by cell differentiation throughout their life.

Page 19 — Stem Cells

Warm-Up
differentiate, specialised, early human embryos, growing, any cell type
1 a) C *[1 mark]*
Stem cells are cells which have not yet differentiated to become specialised cells. Gametes are cells needed for sexual reproduction (e.g. egg and sperm cells).
   b) i) E.g. embryonic stem cells have the potential to produce any type of cell at all *[1 mark]*, whereas adult stem cells are less versatile *[1 mark]*.
      ii) E.g. some people think it's wrong to destroy a potential human life *[1 mark]*.
   c) meristem tissue *[1 mark]*
For this question it's no good writing 'the tips of roots' or 'the tips of shoots' — you've been asked to name the tissue that produces stem cells, not give its location within a plant.

2 Any two from: e.g. there may be a risk of tumour development *[1 mark]* if the rate at which the new insulin-secreting cells divide inside the patient can't be controlled *[1 mark]*. / There may be a risk of disease transmission from the donor to the recipient *[1 mark]* if viruses are present within the embryonic stem cells used to develop the new insulin-secreting cells *[1 mark]*. / There may be a risk of rejection/an immune response being triggered *[1 mark]* as the insulin-secreting cells have not been grown using the patient's own stem cells *[1 mark]*.

Pages 20-21 — The Nervous System

Warm-up
receptors, sensory, motor, effectors
1 a) i)

[1 mark]
Impulses travel along the axon, away from the cell body.
      ii) Part X is the myelin sheath *[1 mark]*. It speeds up the electrical/nervous impulse along the neurone *[1 mark]*.
      iii) Any two from: e.g. sensory neurones have one long dendron, whereas motor neurones have many short dendrites *[1 mark]*. / Sensory neurones have a cell body located in the middle of the neurone, whereas motor neurones have a cell body at one end *[1 mark]*. / Sensory neurones have a short axon, whereas motor neurones have a long axon *[1 mark]*.
   b) The motor neurones don't work properly, so impulses don't get passed on from the CNS *[1 mark]* to the muscles involved in swallowing *[1 mark]*.
   c) 58 cm = 0.58 m
      0.58 ÷ 110 = 0.00527... s × 1000 = **5.27 ms**
      [3 marks for the correct answer, otherwise 1 mark for 0.58 and 1 mark for 0.58 ÷ 110]
2 a) E.g. it will reduce the effect of random errors on their results *[1 mark]*.
   b) uncertainty = range ÷ 2 = (25 – 15) ÷ 2 = 10 ÷ 2
      = **± 5 mm** *[2 marks for correct answer, otherwise 1 mark for correct working.]*
   c) E.g. move the toothpicks together at smaller intervals (e.g. 1 mm) around the point where the person can only feel one toothpick *[1 mark]*.
   d) Repeat the experiment on the forearm more times to see if it still doesn't fit in with the rest of the results *[1 mark]*.
   e) The students have only tested three parts of the body / they haven't tested all parts of the body *[1 mark]*, so they can only conclude that the palm is the most sensitive out of the parts tested *[1 mark]*.

Page 22 — Synapses and Reflexes

1 a) C *[1 mark]*
Reflexes don't involve conscious parts of the brain — they're automatic and very fast (because you don't waste time thinking about the response).
   b) i) relay neurone *[1 mark]*
      ii) spinal cord *[1 mark]*, (an unconscious part of) the brain *[1 mark]*
      iii) Sensory neurone *[1 mark]*. It's function is to carry nervous impulses from receptors to the central nervous system *[1 mark]*.
      iv) To reduce the chance of the hand being injured by the flame. / To quickly move the hand away from the flame. *[1 mark]*
2 By preventing the release of neurotransmitters, opioids prevent information being transmitted across synapses *[1 mark]* between sensory neurones and (relay) neurones in the spinal cord *[1 mark]*. This means the information about the stimulus doesn't reach the brain, so no pain is felt *[1 mark]*.

Section 3 — Genetics

Page 23 — Sexual Reproduction and Meiosis

1 a) D *[1 mark]*
 b) D *[1 mark]*
 c) zygote *[1 mark]*
2 a)

[2 marks for the correct answer, otherwise 1 mark for two X-shaped chromosomes]

A cell duplicates its DNA before meiosis, which is why the chromosomes are X-shaped in Figure 1.

 b) Haploid gametes are needed so that when two gametes fuse at fertilisation *[1 mark]*, the resulting cell/zygote ends up with the full/diploid number of chromosomes *[1 mark]*.

Pages 24-25 — DNA

1 a) A *[1 mark]*
 b) A section of DNA that codes for a particular protein *[1 mark]*.
 c) It is stored as chromosomes *[1 mark]*, which are long, coiled-up molecules of DNA *[1 mark]*.
2 a) X = T/thymine *[1 mark]*, Y = G/guanine *[1 mark]*
 b) A double helix is a double stranded spiral *[1 mark]*.
 c) It is made up of lots of repeating units (nucleotides) *[1 mark]*.
3 a) salt *[1 mark]*, detergent *[1 mark]*
 b) Add ice-cold alcohol to the boiling tube *[1 mark]*. This will make the DNA come out of solution (and form a precipitate) as DNA is not soluble in cold alcohol *[1 mark]*.
4 a) hydrogen bonds *[1 mark]*

You're told in the question that it's the bonds between bases on opposite DNA strands that break and you should know that the pairs of bases on opposite strands are held together by hydrogen bonds.

 b) Any two from: e.g. as the temperature increases, the percentage of denatured DNA in this sample increases. / The DNA in this sample only starts to denature above 62 °C. / All the DNA has denatured by 90 °C. / DNA denaturation in this sample is fastest between about 70 and 80 °C. *[1 mark for each correct answer, up to a maximum of 2 marks]*
 c) % of DNA denatured at 70 °C = 25%
 25% of 8.14×10^4 = ($8.14 \times 10^4 \div 100$) × 25 = 20350
 = 2.04×10^4 base pairs *[2 marks for correct answer, or 1 mark for correctly calculating 25% of 8.14×10^4]*

Pages 26-27 — Genetic Diagrams

Warm-Up
genotype — The combination of alleles an organism has.
phenotype — The characteristics an organism has.
allele — A version of a gene.
heterozygous — Having two different alleles for a particular gene.
homozygous — Having two alleles the same for a particular gene.

1 No. The tall allele/T is dominant over the dwarf allele/t, so its presence will determine what characteristic is displayed in the phenotype *[1 mark]*. A tall plant could have the alleles TT or Tt *[1 mark]*.
2 a) E.g.

	N	N
n	Nn	Nn
n	Nn	Nn

[1 mark]

If you're given letters for the dominant and recessive alleles in the question, make sure you use them.

b) E.g.

	N	n
N	NN	Nn
n	Nn	nn

[1 mark for a genetic diagram showing the correct genotypes of the parents and the offspring]
ratio of polled calves : horned calves = 3 : 1 *[1 mark]*

You could have drawn a different type of genetic diagram and still got the marks here. Also, don't let the fact that there's one bull and multiple cows throw you — each separate cross between the bull and a cow produces a likely ratio of 3 : 1 polled calves: horned calves, so the overall ratio will still be 3 : 1.

3 a) BB *[1 mark]*, Bb *[1 mark]*
 b) i) E.g.

	B	b
b	Bb	bb
b	Bb	bb

[1 mark for a genetic diagram showing the correct genotypes of the parents and the offspring]
probability of offspring being a tabby: 50% / 0.5 / 1 in 2 *[1 mark]*
 ii) 6 × 0.5 = **3**
 [1 mark for 3. Allow 1 mark if incorrect answer to part b) i) is used correctly here.]
4 Breed the short-haired hamster with a long-haired hamster *[1 mark]*. If any of the offspring have long hair, then the short-haired hamster must have the genotype Hh *[1 mark]*. If all the offspring have short hair, then the short-haired hamster could have the genotype HH or Hh *[1 mark]*. Further crosses would need to be done to confirm the genotype *[1 mark]*.

Page 28 — More Genetic Diagrams

1 a)

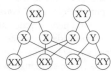

[1 mark]
 b) 50 : 50 *[1 mark]*
2 a) i) hh *[1 mark]*
 ii) hh *[1 mark]*, Hh *[1 mark]*
 b)

	H	h
H	HH	Hh
h	Hh	hh

[1 mark]
probability of having a child who does not have the disorder: 75% *[1 mark]*

Pages 29-30 — Variation

1 a) Phenotype is the characteristics an organism displays *[1 mark]*.
 b) C *[1 mark]*.

Mutations that have no effect on phenotype are most common, followed by mutations that only slightly affect the phenotype. It's very rare for a single mutation to have a big effect on an organism's phenotype, but it does happen.

2 a) sexual reproduction *[1 mark]*
 b) B *[1 mark]*

It's an acquired characteristic — a characteristic that an organism acquires (develops) during their lifetime.

 c) Figure 1 shows that this species of plant grows to different heights in different environments *[1 mark]*, which suggests that variation in height in this species is partly down to the environment *[1 mark]*. Figure 1 also shows that plants of this species grow to similar heights in the same environment *[1 mark]*, which suggests variation in height in this species is also partly genetic *[1 mark]*.

3 a) $(0.42 + 0.41 + 0.48) \div 3 = 0.44$
$(0.43 + 0.40 + 0.52) \div 3 = 0.45$
$0.45 - 0.44 = 0.01$ *[3 marks for the correct answer or 1 mark for 0.44 and 1 mark for 0.45]*

b) Any three from: e.g. population 3 has the highest level of genetic variation in both years *[1 mark]*. / Genetic variation in populations changes over time *[1 mark]*. / Genetic variation in populations 1 and 3 increased over the ten-year period *[1 mark]*. / Genetic variation in population 2 decreased over the ten-year period *[1 mark]*.

c) Lower because sexual reproduction increases genetic variation in a species *[1 mark]*. Without sexual reproduction, no new combinations of alleles would be produced in the offspring *[1 mark]*.

Page 31 — The Human Genome Project

1 a) To find every gene in the human genome *[1 mark]*.

b) E.g. knowledge of genetic variations that affect how we respond to a disease/treatment could help scientists to develop drugs that are tailored to these variations *[1 mark]*. / Knowing how a disease affects us on a molecular level should make it possible to design more effective treatments with fewer side-effects *[1 mark]*.

c) E.g. scientists are now able to identify the genes/alleles suspected of causing an inherited disorder much more quickly than they could do in the past *[1 mark]*. Once an allele that causes an inherited disorder has been identified, people can be tested for it./It may be possible to develop better treatments or even (eventually) a cure for the disease *[1 mark]*.

2 a) E.g. if testing identifies that a person has a genetic variant that increases their risk of developing late onset Alzheimer's *[1 mark]*, they may be able to make diet/lifestyle changes that could reduce their risk of developing the disease *[1 mark]*.

b) E.g. it could cause increased stress for a person if they are identified as having a high risk genetic variant (and they may still never go on to develop Alzheimer's) *[1 mark]*. / A person with a high risk genetic variant may face discrimination from insurers *[1 mark]*.

Section 4 — Natural Selection and Genetic Modification

Pages 32-34 — Natural Selection and Evidence for Evolution

Warm-up
beneficial, predation/competition, competition/predation, adapted to, offspring

1 a) B *[1 mark]*
b) through mutation *[1 mark]*

2 a) They reproduce very rapidly *[1 mark]*.
b) A mutation in the bacterium's DNA may give it resistance to the antibiotic *[1 mark]*.
c) i) exposure to the antibiotic *[1 mark]*
ii) Bacteria with the antibiotic resistance allele are more likely to survive than bacteria without the allele *[1 mark]* and so they reproduce many more times *[1 mark]*. This leads to the allele for antibiotic resistance being passed on to lots of offspring and so it becomes more common in the population *[1 mark]*.

3 a) They are more likely to survive if they are exposed to warfarin *[1 mark]*. This means that they are more likely to pass their alleles on to the next generation *[1 mark]*.

b) There was no warfarin resistance in the population at the time the warfarin was first introduced *[1 mark]*. After the introduction of warfarin, the percentage of the rats with warfarin resistance increased over time *[1 mark]*. This suggests that random mutations occurred that caused some rats to be resistant to warfarin *[1 mark]*. After the introduction of warfarin, the resistance allele then became more common in the population over time through natural selection *[1 mark]*.

4* How to grade your answer:
Level 0: There is no relevant information. *[0 marks]*
Level 1: There is some information about evolution by natural selection. The points made are basic and not linked together. *[1-2 marks]*
Level 2: There is some explanation about how evolution by natural selection may lead to a change in the beak size of the finches. Some of the points made are linked together. *[3-4 marks]*
Level 3: There is a clear and detailed explanation of how evolution by natural selection may lead to a change in the beak size of the finches. The points made are well-linked and the answer has a clear and logical structure. *[5-6 marks]*

Here are some points your answer may include:
After the storm, there will be fewer larger seeds available on the island. Birds with larger beaks will be less able to get food and seed size will become a selection pressure.
Small seeds will still be available, so birds with smaller beaks will be better adapted to their environment than the birds with larger beaks. This makes birds with smaller beaks more likely to survive and reproduce than birds with larger beaks.
In turn, this means that the alleles responsible for small beaks are more likely to be passed on to the next generation than the alleles for larger beaks. The alleles for smaller beaks will become more common in the population over time and eventually, all the finches in the population will have smaller beaks.

5 a) How to grade your answer:
Level 0: There is no relevant information. *[No marks]*
Level 1: There is a brief description of a method that could be used to carry out the investigation. Very little detail is included and some steps may be in the wrong order. *[1 to 2 marks]*
Level 2: There is a good description of a method that could be used to carry out the investigation. Some detail is missing, but all of the steps are in a sensible order. *[3 to 4 marks]*
Level 3: There is a clear and detailed description of a method that could be used to carry out the investigation. All of the steps are in a sensible order. *[5 to 6 marks]*

Here are some points your answer may include:
Use a sterile pipette to measure out equal volumes of sterile nutrient broth solution into four sterile glass bottles.
Use another sterile pipette to add equal volumes of ampicillin solution to two of the glass bottles.
Use another sterile pipette to transfer some of strain A to one bottle with ampicillin in it and one bottle without ampicillin.
Use another sterile pipette to transfer some of strain B to one bottle with ampicillin and one bottle without ampicillin.
Set up a control experiment without bacteria / just broth solution and the antibiotic.
Put lids on all of the bottles. Store them all at the same temperature for a few days.
Observe each bottle to see if the nutrient broth solution has gone cloudy.

b) E.g. if strain B is resistant to ampicillin, it may cause bacterial infections that are difficult to treat if it is released into the general population, so it must be disposed of properly. / The bacteria used may pose a health risk to humans if not disposed of properly. / If the antibiotic used is not disposed of properly it may be released into the environment, where other bacteria may develop resistance to it *[1 mark]*.

Pages 35-37 — Fossil Evidence for Human Evolution

Warm-up

The timeline should have 'Ardi' at 4.4 million years ago, 'Lucy' at 3.2 million years ago and 'Turkana boy' at 1.6 million years ago.

1 a) D *[1 mark]*

b) Any two from: e.g. Turkana Boy had longer legs than Ardi or Lucy. / Turkana Boy had shorter arms than Ardi and Lucy. / Turkana Boy had a larger brain size than Ardi and Lucy. / The structure of Turkana Boy's legs were more suitable to walking upright than those of Ardi or Lucy.
[2 marks — 1 mark for each correct answer.]

2 a) i) C, A, B *[1 mark]*
Remember that the oldest rock layers will be deeper, so any tools or fossils found in these layers will be older than ones found in the layers above.

ii) E.g. by studying the structural features of the tools *[1 mark]*. Using carbon-14 dating to date any carbon-containing material found with the tools *[1 mark]*.

b) Stone tools became more complex in shape over time *[1 mark]*, suggesting that the brain was getting larger and allowing human ancestors to create more complex tools *[1 mark]*.

3 a) i) Specimen 1
ii) Specimen 3
iii) Specimen 2
[2 marks for all 3 answers to i)-iii) correct, or 1 mark for 1-2 answers correct.]

You should know the general trend in evolution of brain size in human ancestors — the more recent the species, the larger its brain is likely to be. So if you compare the brain sizes with the species on the timeline, you can see that Homo species have the largest, Australopithecus species are next on the scale and Ardipithecus species have the smallest brains.

b) E.g. they were shorter because they had shorter legs *[1 mark]*

4 a) i) an opposable/ape-like big toe *[1 mark]*

ii) E.g. an ape-like big toe is needed for climbing trees/grasping branches *[1 mark]* and humans don't spend much time climbing trees/don't climb trees as much as chimpanzees *[1 mark]*.

b) The two fossils show that human ancestors had a foot structure that was intermediate between that of a human and a chimpanzee *[1 mark]*.

c) E.g. fossil B would have shorter arms/longer legs than a chimpanzee. / Fossil B would have a leg bone structure that allowed it to walk upright like a human, unlike a chimpanzee. *[1 mark]*

Page 38 — Classification

1 a) plants, animals, fungi, prokaryotes and protists *[1 mark]*
b) D *[1 mark]*

Remember, a species is the smallest group in the five kingdom classification system. Genus is the next smallest group.

2 a) plants, animals and protists *[1 mark]*.
b) Archaea *[1 mark]*, Bacteria *[1 mark]*

3 a) The DNA sequences for the same gene in different organisms can be compared *[1 mark]*. The more similar the DNA base sequences are to each other, the more closely related the organisms are *[1 mark]*.

b) Genetic analysis led to the discovery that members of the prokaryote kingdom were not as closely related as previously thought *[1 mark]*, so it was suggested that the organisms in it were split into the two domains of Archaea and Bacteria *[1 mark]*.

Page 39 — Selective Breeding

1 a) Any two from: e.g. to breed animals with higher meat/milk yields. / To breed crops with greater disease resistance. / To breed plants with bigger fruit.
[2 marks — 1 mark for each correct answer.]

b) E.g. breeding animals to have a preference for alcohol *[1 mark]*.

2 a) Select only those cows with a high milk yield for further breeding with males *[1 mark]*. Select the best offspring and breed them with each other *[1 mark]*. Continue to breed the most desirable offspring over several generations, so that the milk yield gets bigger and bigger *[1 mark]*.

b) The selective breeding of the cows has reduced the gene pool for his herd *[1 mark]*. A smaller gene pool means that it's more likely that individuals will inherit harmful genetic defects, such as Weaver Syndrome *[1 mark]*.

c) There's less genetic variation in the new herd, because they have been selectively bred *[1 mark]*. This means that there's less chance of there being any alleles in the herd that would give the cows resistance to bovine tuberculosis *[1 mark]*. The cattle are closely related, so if one individual gets the disease, the others are also likely to succumb to it *[1 mark]*.

Pages 40-41 — Genetic Engineering

Warm-up

restriction enzyme — cuts DNA open
plasmid — a type of vector
ligase — sticks DNA ends together
GM organism — an organism with DNA from a different species
vector — transfers DNA into a cell

1 a) i) A restriction enzyme would be used to cut the gene out of the organism's genome *[1 mark]*.

ii) The vector is cut using the same restriction enzyme that was used to isolate the desired gene *[1 mark]*. The ligase enzyme is used to join the vector DNA and the desired gene together (at their sticky ends) *[1 mark]*. The resulting recombinant DNA/vector containing the desired gene is then inserted into the bacterial cell *[1 mark]*.

b) B *[1 mark]*

c) E.g. bacteria can be grown in large numbers *[1 mark]* so the desired protein can be produced in large quantities *[1 mark]*.

2 a) E.g. herbicide resistance / additional nutrients / improved drought resistance *[1 mark]*.

b) Any two from: e.g. some people worry that if transplanted genes escape into the environment, they may be picked up by other plants, resulting in superweeds. / Some people worry that GM crops could have a negative impact on food chains/human health.
[1 mark for each correct answer. Maximum of 2 marks.]

3 How to grade your answer:

Level 0: There is no relevant information. *[0 marks]*

Level 1: There is some information about the advantages of the scientist's findings or concerns about genetic engineering. The points made are basic and not linked together. *[1-2 marks]*

Level 2: There is some discussion about the potential advantages of the scientist's findings, as well as concerns about genetic engineering. Some of the points made are linked together. *[3-4 marks]*

Level 3: There is a clear and detailed discussion about the potential advantages of the scientist's findings, as well as concerns about genetic engineering. The points made are well-linked and the answer has a clear and logical structure. *[5-6 marks]*

Here are some points your answer may include:

Advantages:

The hens may be genetically engineered to produce proteins used in drugs/to treat human diseases in their eggs.

These proteins might include insulin for diabetes or antibodies used in therapy for arthritis/cancer/MS.

The hens may be genetically engineered to produce proteins for medical research in their eggs.

They may be genetically engineered to produce eggs with extra nutrients for human consumption.

Concerns:

There may be unforeseen consequences of inserting human DNA into the hens' DNA. For example, some hens may suffer from health problems later in life as a result of being genetically engineered. Many embryos may not survive the genetic engineering process.

There may be an impact on food chains as a result of genetically engineering the hens.

There may be adverse consequences for human health if the eggs are used for human consumption.

Section 5 — Health, Disease & the Development of Medicines

Pages 42-43 — Health and Disease

Warm-up

Chalara ash dieback — fungus, Tuberculosis — bacterium,
Malaria — protist, Cholera — bacterium

1 a) Health is a state of complete physical, mental and social well-being *[1 mark]*, and not merely the absence of disease or infirmity *[1 mark]*.

b) A communicable disease can be transmitted between individuals (by a pathogen), whereas a non-communicable disease can not *[1 mark]*.

2 a) E.g. it is spread through the air when infected individuals cough *[1 mark]*.

b) E.g. coughing/lung damage *[1 mark]*.

c) E.g. infected individuals should avoid crowded public spaces *[1 mark]*. / Good hygiene should be practiced by the infected person *[1 mark]*. / The infected person should sleep alone *[1 mark]*. / The infected person's home should be well-ventilated *[1 mark]*.

3 a) E.g. leaf loss *[1 mark]* and bark lesions *[1 mark]*.

b) E.g. carried by the wind / by import of diseased trees from affected areas in Europe *[1 mark]*.

c) E.g. young, infected trees could be removed and new species replanted in their place *[1 mark]*. / The import of ash trees could be restricted to prevent any further infected trees entering the country *[1 mark]*.

4 How to grade your answer:

Level 0: There is no relevant information. *[0 marks]*

Level 1: There is some explanation about how mosquito nets could help to protect people against malaria. The points made are basic and not linked together. *[1 to 2 marks]*

Level 2: There is some explanation about why people in high altitude areas should learn how to use mosquito nets. Some of the points made are linked together. *[3 to 4 marks]*

Level 3: There is a clear and detailed explanation about why people in high altitude areas should learn how to use mosquito nets. The points made are well-linked and the answer has a clear and logical structure. *[5 to 6 marks]*

Here are some points your answer may include:
Mosquitoes are animal vectors for *Plasmodium*. / Mosquitoes transmit *Plasmodium* between people when they bite them. Mosquito nets prevent mosquitoes from biting humans at night. Climate change may mean that *Plasmodium* is able to mature at higher altitudes than was previously possible. This means that *Plasmodium* may become more common at higher altitudes. Therefore people at higher altitudes will be more at risk of developing malaria in the future. By learning how to use mosquito nets, people living at higher altitudes will be able to reduce this risk of developing malaria in the future.

Page 44 — STIs

1 a) a bacterium *[1 mark]*

b) By sexual contact *[1 mark]*.

c) i) E.g. screening may identify individuals infected with *Chlamydia [1 mark]*. This means they can be treated, so that they can no longer pass it on to others *[1 mark]*.

ii) E.g. using a condom during sex *[1 mark]*.

2 a) HIV kills white blood cells, which are an important part of the immune response *[1 mark]*. This means that the person is more vulnerable to infection by other pathogens *[1 mark]*.

b) HIV is spread via bodily fluids *[1 mark]*. By sharing needles there's a risk of injecting infected bodily fluids/blood from the previous user of the needle *[1 mark]*.

HIV isn't just spread through sexual contact, although that's a common means of transmission.

Page 45 — Fighting Disease

1 a) E.g. skin / mucus / cilia *[1 mark]*.

b) D *[1 mark]*

c) Hydrochloric acid *[1 mark]*

2 a) The immune response to a specific pathogen *[1 mark]*.

b) B-lymphocytes detect antigens on a pathogen in the blood *[1 mark]*. The B-lymphocytes produce specific antibodies *[1 mark]*, which lock on to the pathogen and destroy it *[1 mark]*. The antibodies are then produced rapidly and flow throughout the body to find all similar pathogens *[1 mark]*.

3 Cells that line the airways in the lungs have cilia *[1 mark]*, which sweep mucus containing any trapped pathogens out of the lungs *[1 mark]*. If the cilia don't work properly then pathogens will remain in the lungs and will be more likely to cause infections *[1 mark]*.

Page 46 — Memory Lymphocytes and Immunisation

1 a) A *[1 mark]*

b) At the time of the second exposure the body has some memory lymphocytes that will recognise the pathogen's antigens *[1 mark]* and trigger more antibodies to be made *[1 mark]*. This means antibodies are produced much more quickly following the second exposure (so the curve is steeper) *[1 mark]*.

2 a) To kill/inactivate the virus *[1 mark]*.

b) Their body would respond to the vaccine by producing antibodies and memory lymphocytes *[1 mark]*. Because of this, if the virus enters their body again, their immune system will recognise the foreign antigens and respond more quickly *[1 mark]*, meaning they will be more likely to eradicate the virus before it causes polio *[1 mark]*.

Page 47 — Antibiotics and Other Medicines

1 a) i) D *[1 mark]*

In preclinical trials, animals are used to test the drug on a whole body or multiple body systems, so the animal needs to be alive. You wouldn't want to test on humans at this stage, just in case the drug proves to be dangerous.

ii) E.g. toxicity / efficacy / dosage *[1 mark]*

b) In case the drug has any harmful effects *[1 mark]*.

c) i) To ensure that any effect of the drug is due to the drug itself and not because the patient is expecting to feel better *[1 mark]*.

A placebo is a substance that's like the drug being tested but doesn't do anything.

ii) So that neither the patients nor the doctors are able to subconsciously influence the results of the trials *[1 mark]*.

In a double-blind trial neither the patient nor the doctor knows whether the patient is receiving the drug or a placebo.

2 a) Antibiotics kill/prevent the growth of bacterial cells *[1 mark]*, but they do not harm human cells *[1 mark]*.

b) Viruses can only reproduce inside their host's cells *[1 mark]*. This means that it is very hard to develop drugs which target the virus but not the cells of the host *[1 mark]*.

Pages 48-49 — Non-Communicable Diseases

1 a) It is a factor associated with an increased likelihood of getting a disease *[1 mark]*.
   b) When alcohol is broken down in the liver, toxic products are released *[1 mark]*. Too many of these toxic products can cause permanent liver damage/liver disease *[1 mark]*.
   c) E.g. cardiovascular disease *[1 mark]*
2 How to grade your answer:
   Level 0: There is no relevant information. *[No marks]*
   Level 1: There is a brief explanation of the lifestyle factors likely to be tackled and the economical reasons behind the campaign. The points made are basic and not linked together. *[1 to 2 marks]*
   Level 2: There is some explanation of the lifestyle factors likely to be tackled and the economical reasons behind the campaign. Some of the points made are linked together. *[3 to 4 marks]*
   Level 3: There is a clear and detailed explanation of the lifestyle factors likely to be tackled and the economical reasons behind the campaign. The points made are well-linked and the answer has a clear and logical structure. *[5 to 6 marks]*

Here are some points your answer may include:
The campaign is likely to encourage children to eat healthily and exercise. If children eat healthily and exercise then they are less likely to become overweight or obese. Healthy children are then less likely to grow up to become overweight or obese. Obesity is a risk factor for many other non-communicable diseases, so healthy children are also less likely to suffer from other non-communicable diseases, such as type 2 diabetes, later in life. This means that there will be less pressure on the resources of local hospitals and the National Health Service as a whole to treat people with obesity and related health issues. This also means that more people in society will be able to work and contribute to the UK's economy. Since fewer resources are being spent on helping people with obesity and obesity-related health issues and there are more people contributing to the economy, this means that the scheme should be beneficial for society as a whole.

3 a) The number of people with diabetes increased between 2012 and 2018 *[1 mark]*.
   b) In support of the student's statement: e.g. both the rate of obesity and the rate of diabetes increase overall between 2012 and 2018. / It is generally accepted that obesity is a risk factor for Type 2 diabetes.
   Against the student's statement: e.g. a correlation between the number of people with diabetes and the prevalence of obesity doesn't show that diabetes is caused by obesity — there may be another factor that affects both. / Figure 1 shows that the percentage of people with obesity fell between 2015 and 2016, while the number of people with diabetes increased in the same year, which contradicts the student's statement. / The student is only comparing data for seven years — it may be that the trend is not present over a longer period of time.
   [4 marks — 1 mark for each point. Maximum of 3 marks if answer does not include points both in support of the statement and against it.]

Page 50 — Measures of Obesity

1 a) waist-to-hip ratio = waist circumference ÷ hips circumference = 91 ÷ 84 = **1.1** *[1 mark]*
   b) i) 170 cm = 1.70 m
      BMI = mass (kg) ÷ height (m)^2 = 73.5 ÷ 1.70^2
      25.4 kg m^{-2} [3 marks for correct answer, otherwise 1 mark for 1.70 m and 1 mark for BMI = mass (kg) ÷ height (m)^2]
   ii) E.g. she has dropped a lot of weight in a short amount of time / if she loses much more weight she may become underweight *[1 mark]*.
2 a) Patient C because she has a high BMI and her waist-to-hip ratio indicates she is obese *[1 mark]*. Being obese is a risk factor for cardiovascular disease *[1 mark]*.
   b) Her body mass may be high in relation to her height because she has a lot of muscle (rather than fat) *[1 mark]*. This would mean she has a high BMI but is not likely to be at risk of developing obesity-related disorders *[1 mark]*.

Page 51 — Treatments for Cardiovascular Disease

Warm-up
heart, blood pressure, arteries, strokes
1 a) Any two from: e.g. cut down on foods high in saturated fat / eat a healthy, balanced diet *[1 mark]* / quit smoking *[1 mark]* / exercise regularly *[1 mark]* / lose weight if necessary *[1 mark]*.
   b) i) A stent could be inserted into the artery *[1 mark]* to keep the artery open and maintain blood flow to the heart *[1 mark]*.
   ii) Any two from: e.g. there is a risk of infection *[1 mark]*, there is a risk of bleeding *[1 mark]* / there is a risk of developing blood clots *[1 mark]* / there is a risk that the artery might narrow again *[1 mark]*.
   c) Any two from: e.g. statins *[1 mark]*, these reduce his blood cholesterol levels *[1 mark]*. / Anticoagulants *[1 mark]*, these make blood clots less likely *[1 mark]*. / Antihypertensives *[1 mark]*, these reduce blood pressure *[1 mark]*.

Section 6 — Plant Structures and Their Functions

Pages 52-53 — Photosynthesis

Warm-up
algae, light, glucose, chloroplasts
1 a) carbon dioxide + water ⟶ glucose + oxygen *[1 mark]*
   b) A *[1 mark]*
2 a) E.g. building the plant's biomass *[1 mark]*.
   b) Energy stored in the biomass of photosynthetic organisms is transferred along food chains *[1 mark]* as animals eat these organisms and each other *[1 mark]*. That means that many organisms rely on photosynthesis as a source of energy/biomass *[1 mark]*.
3 a) oxygen *[1 mark]*
   b) 1.2 ÷ 2 = 0.6 cm^3 h^{-1} *[1 mark]*
   c) i) As the distance from the lamp increases, the rate of gas production decreases *[1 mark]*. This is because the intensity of the light reaching the plant decreases as the test tube is placed further away *[1 mark]*, and light intensity is a limiting factor for photosynthesis *[1 mark]*.
   ii) E.g. by repeating the experiment with more distances from the light source / at greater distances from the light source *[1 mark]*.
   d) E.g. different lamps may produce different intensities of light *[1 mark]*, so using the same lamp helps to ensure that the distance between the lamp and the test tube is the only thing affecting the light intensity *[1 mark]*.

Page 54 — Limiting Factors in Photosynthesis

1 a) the inverse square law *[1 mark]*
   b) The light intensity reaching the plant would be four times greater *[1 mark]*.
   The inverse square law is light intensity ∝ 1/d^2. This means that as the square of the distance decreases, light intensity increases proportionally — in other words, if you halve the distance, the light intensity will be four times greater.
   c) As carbon dioxide concentration increases, the rate of photosynthesis also increases *[1 mark]*, until carbon dioxide is no longer the limiting factor and the rate stays the same *[1 mark]*.
2 a) The rate of photosynthesis increases between points A and B *[1 mark]*. This is because increasing the temperature (up to the optimum) increases the rate at which the enzymes involved in photosynthesis work *[1 mark]*.
   b) Increasing the temperature after point B causes the rate of photosynthesis to fall *[1 mark]*. This is because the temperatures are too high for the enzymes involved in photosynthesis to work *[1 mark]*. At point C, no photosynthesis is occurring because all the enzymes are denatured *[1 mark]*.

Page 55 — Transport in Plants

Warm-up

A. living cells, B. dead cells, C. end wall with pores,
D. lignin, E. phloem tube, F. xylem tube

1 a) i)   E.g. sucrose *[1 mark]*
   ii) E.g. water *[1 mark]*, mineral ions *[1 mark]*
  b)   A *[1 mark]*

Transport via the phloem is called translocation (not transpiration) and it requires energy to happen. It transports substances all over the plant, from the roots to the leaves and in the opposite direction.

2 a)   *Pythium* destroys root hair cells and therefore decreases the surface area available for the absorption of water from the soil *[1 mark]*. This will mean that less water will be available to be drawn up from the roots by the transpiration stream *[1 mark]*.
  b)   If the root hair cells are destroyed, a plant will have difficulty absorbing mineral ions from the soil *[1 mark]*. The disruption to the transpiration stream will also reduce the plant's ability to transport mineral ions from the roots to where they're needed in the plant *[1 mark]*.

Pages 56-57 — Stomata and Transpiration

1 a)   To allow gas exchange/the movement of carbon dioxide and oxygen into and out of a plant *[1 mark]*.
  b)   guard cells *[1 mark]*
  c)   Water vapour diffuses out of leaves through the stomata *[1 mark]*. When the stomata are open, water is able to diffuse out of the leaves and more water is pulled up the plant by transpiration *[1 mark]*. When the stomata are closed, less water is able to diffuse out of the leaves and so less water is pulled up the plant by transpiration *[1 mark]*

2 a)   To stop the loss of water by evaporation *[1 mark]*.
  b)

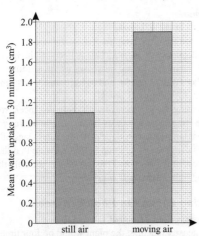

[1 mark for correctly drawn bars, 1 mark for correctly labelled axes / drawn to a sensible scale.]

  c)   The greater the air flow around the plant, the greater the transpiration rate *[1 mark]*.
  d)   E.g. increasing air flow carries more water vapour away from the plant/reduces the concentration of water vapour outside the leaves *[1 mark]*. This increases the rate of diffusion of water from the leaf cells to the air *[1 mark]*.
  e)   rate of transpiration = mean volume of water uptake ÷ time
30 minutes ÷ 60 = 0.5 hours
$1.9 ÷ 0.5 = 3.8$ cm^3 hour^{-1} *[2 marks for the correct answer, otherwise 1 mark for 1.9 ÷ 0.5]*

Section 7 — Animal Coordination, Control and Homeostasis

Page 58 — Hormones

1 a)   C *[1 mark]*
  b)   C *[1 mark]*
  c)   A — pituitary *[1 mark]*, B — thyroid *[1 mark]*, C — adrenal *[1 mark]*, D — pancreas *[1 mark]*, E — ovary *[1 mark]*
  d)   Any two from: e.g. the endocrine system uses hormones rather than electrical/nervous impulses *[1 mark]*. / In the endocrine system messages travel via the blood rather than via neurones *[1 mark]*. / The effects of the endocrine system are slower *[1 mark]*. / The effects of the endocrine system are longer lasting *[1 mark]*.

2 a)   bones *[1 mark]*
  b)   Testes produce testosterone *[1 mark]* so having the testes removed will mean there's less testosterone acting on the bones, therefore increasing the risk of bones becoming brittle *[1 mark]*.

Page 59 — Adrenaline and Thyroxine

Warm-up

Clockwise from top left: **increase in** level of hormone detected, release of hormone **inhibited**, **normal** level of hormone, release of hormone **stimulated**, **decrease in** level of hormone detected.

1 a)   adrenal glands *[1 mark]*
  b)   E.g. it increases heart rate / blood pressure / blood flow to the muscles / the blood glucose level *[1 mark]*.
  c)   fight or flight *[1 mark]*

2 a)   E.g. it regulates metabolic rate *[1 mark]*.
  b)   When the blood thyroxine level becomes higher than normal, release of TRH/thyrotropin releasing hormone is inhibited *[1 mark]*. This reduces the production of TSH/thyroid stimulating hormone *[1 mark]*, meaning the thyroid gland is not stimulated to produce thyroxine, so the blood thyroxine level falls *[1 mark]*.

Page 60 — The Menstrual Cycle

1 a)   ovary *[1 mark]*
  b)   FSH/follicle-stimulating hormone *[1 mark]*
  c)   It causes it to thicken and grow *[1 mark]*.

2 a)   A *[1 mark]*

Oestrogen and progesterone are involved in the growth and maintenance of the uterus lining, so menstruation (the breakdown of the uterus lining) occurs during time period A when the levels of these two hormones are low.

  b)   E.g.

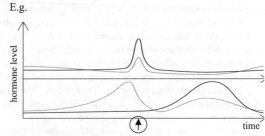

[1 mark for arrow drawn in line with the LH peak or its rapid descent]

Remember, the rapid increase in LH is what stimulates ovulation.

  c)   FSH/follicle-stimulating hormone *[1 mark]*
  d)   After ovulation, the remains of the follicle develop into a corpus luteum *[1 mark]*, which secretes progesterone *[1 mark]*. Progesterone maintains the uterus lining *[1 mark]*.

Pages 61-62 — Controlling Fertility

1 a)   E.g. (male/female) condom / diaphragm *[1 mark]*.
  b)   They prevent sperm from meeting an egg *[1 mark]*.
  c)   E.g. some barrier methods (condoms) can protect against sexually transmitted infections/STIs, unlike hormonal methods *[1 mark]*. Barrier methods don't have unpleasant side-effects, such as headaches/mood changes/acne, like hormonal methods can *[1 mark]*.

2 a) If the woman doesn't ovulate regularly, then there is less chance that an egg will be present to be fertilised by a sperm after sexual intercourse *[1 mark]*.

b) Clomifene therapy causes more FSH and LH *[1 mark]* to be produced by the body, which stimulate egg maturation and ovulation *[1 mark]*, increasing a woman's chances of becoming pregnant after intercourse *[1 mark]*.

c) i) *in vitro* fertilisation/IVF *[1 mark]*

   ii) To stimulate egg production/allow multiple eggs to be collected *[1 mark]*.

3 a) A high level of oestrogen inhibits FSH production *[1 mark]*, which causes egg production and development to stop *[1 mark]*.

b) E.g. hormonal methods are generally more effective at preventing pregnancy than barrier methods when used correctly *[1 mark]*. Hormonal methods mean the couple don't have to think about contraception each time they have intercourse, unlike with barrier methods *[1 mark]*.

4 a) i) Progesterone inhibits the release of FSH *[1 mark]* and LH *[1 mark]*, which stimulate egg maturation and ovulation *[1 mark]*.

   ii) E.g. it stimulates the production of thick cervical mucus *[1 mark]*, which prevents sperm from entering the uterus and reaching an egg *[1 mark]*.

b) So they are protected against sexually transmitted infections/STIs *[1 mark]*.

c) E.g. she doesn't need to remember to take a pill (at the same time) every day *[1 mark]*.

Page 63 — Homeostasis — Control of Blood Glucose

1 a) It means maintaining a constant internal environment *[1 mark]*.

b) pancreas *[1 mark]*

2 a) The blood glucose concentration starts increasing as glucose from the drink is absorbed into the blood *[1 mark]*. The pancreas detects a high blood glucose concentration and secretes insulin *[1 mark]*. Insulin causes the blood glucose concentration to fall back to normal *[1 mark]*.

b) i) glucagon *[1 mark]*

   ii) It increases the concentration of glucose in the blood *[1 mark]* because it causes glycogen stores in the liver and muscles *[1 mark]* to be converted into glucose, which is released into the blood *[1 mark]*.

Page 64 — Diabetes

1 a) i) So he can calculate the patient's BMI *[1 mark]*, as obesity/ a BMI above 30 is associated with an increased risk of developing type 2 diabetes *[1 mark]*.

   ii) Her waist circumference and hip circumference *[1 mark]*. These measurements will allow him to calculate the patient's waist-to-hip ratio *[1 mark]*, as a high waist-to-hip ratio/ abdominal obesity is associated with an increased risk of developing type 2 diabetes *[1 mark]*.

b) Any two from: e.g. eat a healthy diet / get regular exercise / lose weight (if necessary) / take medication/insulin injections *[2 marks]*

c) The pancreas doesn't produce enough insulin *[1 mark]*. A person becomes resistant to insulin *[1 mark]*.

2 a) i) The pancreas of a person with type 1 diabetes produces little or no insulin *[1 mark]*, so a pancreas transplant would provide the person with a permanent new source of insulin *[1 mark]*.

   ii) E.g. a pancreas transplant is a serious operation, which carries the risk of complications *[1 mark]*. / There aren't enough donor pancreases available *[1 mark]*. / Drugs need to be taken afterwards to suppress the immune system *[1 mark]*.

You're not expected to know the answer to this question, you're just expected to make a sensible suggestion.

b) E.g. regular insulin injections/insulin therapy *[1 mark]*.

Section 8 — Exchange and Transport in Animals

Page 65 — Exchange of Materials

Warm-up

Surface area: (8 mm × **8** mm) × 2 + (8 mm × **25** mm) × 4 = **928** mm²

Volume: **8** mm × **8** mm × **25** mm = **1600** mm³

1 a) Any two from: e.g. oxygen / mineral ions / water / dissolved food molecules. *[2 marks — 1 mark for each correct answer]*

b) E.g. carbon dioxide *[1 mark]*, urea *[1 mark]*

2 a) X = (3 × 3) × 6 = **54 cm²** *[1 mark]*

   Y = 3 × 3 × 3 = **27 cm³** *[1 mark]*

   Z = 150 ÷ 125 = **1.2** *[1 mark]*

b) 5 × 5 × 5, because it has the smallest surface area to volume ratio *[1 mark]*.

As this cube had the smallest surface area in relation to its volume, it would take the acid longest to diffuse throughout this cube and change its colour.

Page 66 — Specialised Exchange Surfaces — the Alveoli

1 Sticklebacks are multicellular *[1 mark]* so they can't simply exchange all the substances they need across the outer surface of their body *[1 mark]*. They need specialised exchange surfaces for efficient diffusion of substances into and out of their body *[1 mark]* and a mass transport system to carry substances around their body *[1 mark]*.

2 a) A — carbon dioxide *[1 mark]*, B — oxygen *[1 mark]*

b) Blood flowing past the alveolus has a lower concentration of oxygen than in the alveolus *[1 mark]* and a higher concentration of carbon dioxide than in the alveolus *[1 mark]*. This means there's a high concentration gradient for both gases so the rate of diffusion is high *[1 mark]*.

c) Any two from: e.g. they have a moist lining *[1 mark]* to allow gases to dissolve *[1 mark]*. / The walls of the alveoli are very thin *[1 mark]* to minimise the distance that the gases must diffuse across *[1 mark]*. / There are many alveoli in the lungs *[1 mark]* to maximise the total surface area over which gas exchange takes place *[1 mark]*.

Page 67 — Circulatory System — Blood

1 a) B *[1 mark]*

b) white blood cells / lymphocytes *[1 mark]*

c) It is a liquid *[1 mark]* that transports many different substances in the blood *[1 mark]*.

2 a) plasma *[1 mark]*

b) Red blood cells carry oxygen around the body *[1 mark]*. A biconcave shape increases the surface area to allow a greater absorption of oxygen *[1 mark]*.

c) Platelets are involved in helping blood to clot at a wound *[1 mark]*. Therefore, a low level of platelets may lead to excessive bleeding/bruising / an inability to form blood clots *[1 mark]*.

Pages 68-69 — Circulatory System — Blood Vessels

Warm-up

A — artery, B — vein, C — capillary

1 a) i) veins *[1 mark]*

   ii) To ensure that blood keeps flowing in the right direction *[1 mark]*.

b) capillaries *[1 mark]*

2 a) Arteries have a thicker layer of smooth muscle compared to veins *[1 mark]*. Arteries transport blood away from the heart *[1 mark]* so the blood is at a greater pressure than the blood carried in veins *[1 mark]*. The thicker layer of muscle in arteries makes them stronger to withstand this pressure *[1 mark]*.

b) Being narrow allows capillaries to squeeze into the gaps between cells *[1 mark]* so they can exchange substances with every cell *[1 mark]*.

3 a) E.g. the graph shows that as an increasing amount of mass was added and then removed from the ring of artery, the percentage change in the ring's length remained at 0 *[1 mark]*, so the ring returned to its original length each time the mass was removed *[1 mark]*. As the amount of mass added and then removed from the ring of vein increased, the percentage change in the ring's length increased *[1 mark]*, so the ring did not return to its original length once the mass was removed and the greater the mass, the further it was from its original length *[1 mark]*.

b) Any sensible precaution, e.g. wear safety goggles / wear gloves / disinfect the workstation after the experiment / wash hands after the experiment *[1 mark]*.

Pages 70-71 — Circulatory System — Heart
Warm-up
Deoxygenated, vena cava, right ventricle, artery, lungs, valve

1 a) X: aorta *[1 mark]*, Y: pulmonary vein *[1 mark]*, Z: left atrium *[1 mark]*

b)

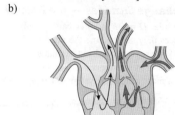

[1 mark for arrow(s) showing blood flow from the vena cava, through the right atrium and ventricle, then up through the pulmonary artery.]

2 The wall of the left ventricle is thicker than the wall of the right ventricle *[1 mark]*. This is because the left ventricle needs to be stronger than the right ventricle *[1 mark]* because it pumps blood around the whole body, whereas the right ventricle only pumps blood to the lungs *[1 mark]*.

3 a) The volume of blood pumped by one ventricle each time it contracts *[1 mark]*.

b) cardiac output = heart rate × stroke volume
$57 \times 84 = $ **4788 cm³ min⁻¹** *[2 marks for correct answer, otherwise 1 mark for 57 × 84.]*

c) heart rate = cardiac output ÷ stroke volume
$4095 \div 65 = $ **63 bpm** *[2 marks for correct answer, otherwise 1 mark for 4095 ÷ 65.]*

d) The ventricles of a larger heart are likely to have a greater volume than those in a smaller heart *[1 mark]*. This means that a person with a larger heart is likely to have a greater stroke volume than a person with a smaller heart *[1 mark]*. A greater stroke volume is likely to mean a greater cardiac output *[1 mark]*.

e) The increase in heart rate will lead to an increased cardiac output *[1 mark]*.

Pages 72-73 — Respiration
1 a) A *[1 mark]*

b) They result in the transfer of energy from glucose/food *[1 mark]*, which is used for important metabolic processes *[1 mark]*.

c) i) E.g. glucose *[1 mark]*
ii) oxygen *[1 mark]*
iii) carbon dioxide *[1 mark]* and water *[1 mark]*

d) Aerobic respiration is more efficient / transfers more energy compared to anaerobic respiration *[1 mark]*. / Unlike anaerobic respiration, aerobic doesn't produce lactic acid, which can be painful *[1 mark]*.

e) E.g. during vigorous exercise *[1 mark]*.

f) In plants the products of anaerobic respiration are ethanol *[1 mark]* and carbon dioxide *[1 mark]*, whereas in animals the only product is lactic acid *[1 mark]*.

2 a) The percentage of oxygen in exhaled air is less than in inhaled air because oxygen has been used by the body in aerobic respiration *[1 mark]*.

b) There will be a greater percentage of carbon dioxide in exhaled air than in inhaled air *[1 mark]* because carbon dioxide is produced in the body by aerobic respiration *[1 mark]*.

Remember that carbon dioxide (a waste product of respiration) diffuses from the blood to the air in the alveoli in the lungs, which is then breathed out.

3 a) Oxygen consumption increased rapidly at first then more slowly *[1 mark]*, until around 8 minutes when it levelled off *[1 mark]*.

b) In the final two minutes of exercise, the man's oxygen consumption remained constant *[1 mark]*. This suggests that his muscles were respiring anaerobically to supply the extra energy needed for his muscles to continue to work harder, as this process doesn't require oxygen *[1 mark]*.

Pages 74-75 — Investigating Respiration
1 a) E.g. the snail must have enough oxygen for two hours / the snail must not dry out *[1 mark]*.

b) The glass beads are acting as a control *[1 mark]* to show that any change in the carbon dioxide concentration of Beaker A is due to the snail and not some other factor *[1 mark]*.

c) The percentage of carbon dioxide in the air has increased over the two hours because the snail releases carbon dioxide as it respires *[1 mark]*.

d) It would have decreased *[1 mark]* because the snail would have used up oxygen as it respired *[1 mark]*.

2 a) Any two from, e.g. the mass of the peas or glass beads in the flask / the size of the flask / the type of peas / the temperature outside of the flasks / the temperature of the peas at the start of the experiment *[2 marks]*.

b) E.g. she could repeat her experiment and calculate a mean temperature increase for each flask *[1 mark]*.

c) The boiled peas will not germinate, so flask 2 is included to show that the increase in temperature in flask 1 is due to the peas germinating *[1 mark]*. Flask 3 is included to show that the temperature change is due to the presence of the peas and no other factor *[1 mark]*.

The temperature in flask 3 should remain constant — if it changed, this would suggest there was an error in the experiment.

d) E.g. she could include another flask that contained disinfected boiled peas. / She could disinfect the peas (and the glass beads) with an antiseptic before starting the experiment *[1 mark]*.

If there was no temperature change in a flask containing disinfected boiled peas, the student could conclude that the temperature increase in the flask of boiled peas in her first experiment was due to the presence of microorganisms.

Section 9 — Ecosystems and Material Cycles

Pages 76-77 — Ecosystems & Interactions Between Organisms
Warm-up:

Abiotic	Biotic
pollutants	prey species
temperature	predators
light intensity	competition
water	

1 a) B *[1 mark]*

b) A community of organisms and the abiotic conditions in which they live *[1 mark]*.

2 a) E.g. the number of birds in the grassland may decrease *[1 mark]*, as the new predator would compete with the birds over the insects *[1 mark]*.

b) E.g. it may decrease *[1 mark]*. With fewer birds to eat the insects, insect numbers may increase *[1 mark]*. More insects would eat more grass, reducing grass plant numbers *[1 mark]*.

3 a) Parasitism *[1 mark]* because the cuckoo benefits from the relationship but the host does not *[1 mark]*.

b) B *[1 mark]*

The information given in the question describes benefits for both the ants and the trees. This is what makes it a mutualistic relationship.

4 a) E.g. it may have increased *[1 mark]* because prickly acacia grow best when there is plenty of water *[1 mark]*.
 b) E.g. the prickly acacia may become distributed over a wider area *[1 mark]*, as they may spread into areas that were previously too cold for them *[1 mark]*.
 c) E.g. the prickly acacia may compete with the grasses for resources (such as light, water, space and nutrients) *[1 mark]* causing their populations to decrease *[1 mark]*.

Pages 78-80 — Investigating Ecosystems

1 a) i) To avoid any bias in the sampling *[1 mark]*.
  ii) E.g. divide the field into a grid and place the quadrats at coordinates selected using a random number generator *[1 mark]*.
 b) 13 buttercups *[1 mark]*
Remember that the mode is the most frequently occurring number.
 c) 15.5 buttercups *[1 mark]*
To answer this question, simply put the numbers of buttercups in each quadrat in order from the smallest to the largest, like this: 12, 13, 13, 13, 15, 16, 16, 23, 23, 26. The median number is halfway along this list — so it lies halfway between 15 and 16.
 d) 15 + 13 + 16 + 23 + 26 + 23 + 13 + 12 + 16 + 13 = 170
  170 ÷ 10 = 17 buttercups per 0.5 m² *[1 mark]*
 e) 17 × 2 = 34 per m²
  34 × 1750 = 59 500 buttercups *[2 marks for the correct answer, otherwise 1 mark for multiplying answer to part d) by 2.]*
2 a) Zone B and Zone C *[1 mark]*
 b) long grass *[1 mark]*
 c) Zone A is closest to the pond where the soil has more moisture *[1 mark]*. Zone A also has the highest light intensity *[1 mark]*.
 d) Zone B *[1 mark]* because only short grass grows here *[1 mark]*.
 e) E.g. the light level may be too low *[1 mark]*. / They are unable to compete with the trees for resources, e.g. water *[1 mark]*.
3 a) E.g. the ground might be slippery / there might be large waves from the sea / the tide might come in *[1 mark]*.
Any sensible suggestion of a hazard you might find at a beach would get you the mark for this question.
 b) Advantage: e.g. you can cover a larger distance in the same amount of time / it takes less time to collect data from along the transect *[1 mark]*.
  Disadvantage: e.g. the results might not be as accurate / some species might get missed *[1 mark]*.
 c) The percentage cover of bladderwrack increases between 2 m and 18 m from the low tide point / the further the distance from the low tide point, the higher the percentage cover of bladderwrack, up to 18 m *[1 mark]*. The percentage cover then falls between 18 m and 20 m *[1 mark]*.
 d) E.g. they could measure the salt concentration of the water around the bladderwrack at each interval *[1 mark]*.

Page 81 — Human Impacts on Biodiversity

1 Any two from: e.g. they may have out-competed native species for resources/food/shelter *[1 mark]*. / They may have brought new diseases to New Zealand, which infected/killed large numbers of native species *[1 mark]*. / They may have fed/preyed on native species *[1 mark]*.
2 a) How to grade your answer:
  Level 0: There is no relevant information. *[0 marks]*
  Level 1: There is some information about how the application of fertilisers on farmland may reduce the biodiversity of nearby water sources. The points made are basic and not linked together. *[1-2 marks]*
  Level 2: There is some explanation of how the application of fertilisers on farmland may reduce the biodiversity of nearby water sources. Some of the points made are linked together. *[3-4 marks]*
  Level 3: There is a clear and detailed explanation of how the application of fertilisers on farmland may reduce the biodiversity of nearby water sources. The points made are well-linked and the answer has a clear and logical structure. *[5-6 marks]*

Here are some points your answer may include:
Many fertilisers contain nitrates. If too much fertiliser is applied to the fields, it will run off the fields when it rains into nearby water sources, leading to eutrophication. This is where excess nitrates in the water cause algae to grow fast and block out light. This means that less light reaches plants, which then can't photosynthesise and so die. The microorganisms that feed on dead plants increase in number and use up the oxygen in the water. This means that there is not enough oxygen available for other organisms, e.g. fish, which then also die. The death of all of these organisms reduces biodiversity.
 b) E.g. the food given to the fish/the waste produced by the fish leaks out into the surrounding water and increases the nutrient content of the water *[1 mark]*. This leads to eutrophication in the same way fertilisers in the water do *[1 mark]*.
 c) Any two from: e.g. other species may swim into the nets and become trapped and die, reducing the number of species and therefore biodiversity in the water *[1 mark]*. / Farmed fish may escape into the wild and cause the death of indigenous species, leading to a reduction in biodiversity *[1 mark]*. /
  The fish farms may acts as a breeding ground for parasites which could get out and infect and kill wild populations of fish, reducing biodiversity *[1 mark]*.

Page 82 — Conservation and Biodiversity

1 a) If one species goes extinct then the food chain that it is a part of will be disrupted *[1 mark]*. Protecting one species, will help to protect the species that feed on it *[1 mark]*. / Efforts to protect one species may involve the protection of the habitat of that species *[1 mark]*, in which case, other species within that habitat will also be protected *[1 mark]*.
 b) E.g. the species may attract ecotourism which brings money to a country. / The protection of the species may lead to the creation of jobs *[1 mark]*.
Make sure you read the question carefully here — whatever you write down must be relevant to helping the economy of the country in some way.
2 How to grade your answer:
  Level 0: There is no relevant information. *[0 marks]*
  Level 1: There is some information about the possible benefits of reforestation for biodiversity or local farmers or Ethiopian society. The points made are basic and not linked together. *[1-2 marks]*
  Level 2: There is some discussion of the possible benefits of reforestation for at least two of biodiversity, local farmers and Ethiopian society. Some of the points made are linked together. *[3-4 marks]*
  Level 3: There is a clear and detailed discussion of the possible benefits of reforestation for biodiversity, local farmers and Ethiopian society. The points made are well-linked and the answer has a clear and logical structure. *[5-6 marks]*
Here are some points your answer may include:
By reforesting the land, the soil will be less exposed to the rain and Sun, so there will be less soil erosion and drought.
This will help to increase soil quality and make it easier for farmers to grow crops on the land. This in turn will mean that there will be more food available for the rest of the Ethiopian population. Increased forest cover is also likely to increase the biodiversity of the area, as many more species will be able to survive in the forested areas. Increased biodiversity may bring more money to Ethiopia through ecotourism, which will help to benefit Ethiopian society. Ecotourism and the reforestation programmes themselves will create new jobs, so more people will have an income. Reforestation may also help to protect species that are important to Ethiopia's cultural heritage, or plants that could be beneficial as medicines.

Page 83 — The Carbon Cycle

1 a) i) photosynthesis *[1 mark]*
    ii) Process A / photosynthesis converts carbon dioxide from the air into carbon compounds in plants, making carbon available for use in the ecosystem *[1 mark]*.
  b) burning/combustion *[1 mark]*
  c) Carbon dioxide is returned back to the atmosphere *[1 mark]* when the microorganisms involved in decay respire *[1 mark]*.
  d) Biotic: e.g. animals / plants / microorganisms *[1 mark]*
     Abiotic: e.g. fossil fuels / air *[1 mark]*

Page 84 — The Water Cycle

Warm-up
evaporate, water vapour, cools, precipitation

1 a) B *[1 mark]*
  b) The concentration of salt in sea water is too high *[1 mark]*.
2 E.g. by boiling sea water in a vessel *[1 mark]* so that the water evaporates to form steam and leaves the salt behind *[1 mark]*. The steam then enters a pipe connected to the vessel, where it condenses *[1 mark]* back into pure water, which can be collected for drinking *[1 mark]*. /
Sea water may be fed into a vessel with a partially permeable membrane at a high pressure *[1 mark]*. The high pressure will cause the water molecules to move in the reverse direction to osmosis/from a higher salt concentration to a lower salt concentration *[1 mark]*. The water is forced through the membrane, leaving the salt behind *[1 mark]* and allowing pure water to be collected for drinking *[1 mark]*.

Pages 85-86 — The Nitrogen Cycle

1 a) E.g. to make proteins *[1 mark]*
  b) B *[1 mark]*
2 a) i) C *[1 mark]*
    ii) D *[1 mark]* and E *[1 mark]*
    iii) A *[1 mark]* and B *[1 mark]*
  b) D *[1 mark]*
  c) Decomposers break down proteins in dead plants and animals/ urea *[1 mark]* and turn it into ammonia *[1 mark]*.
3 a) There are lots of nitrogen-containing compounds in the soil in the new plot *[1 mark]* because the pea plants/legumes that were previously grown in the plot contained nitrogen-fixing bacteria in their root nodules *[1 mark]*. This means that the cabbages were able to obtain more nitrogen in the new plot and no longer showed any nitrogen deficiency symptoms *[1 mark]*.
  b) To add nitrogen-containing compounds back into the soil which the vegetable plants need for growth *[1 mark]*.
  c) Wet soils will mean that denitrifying bacteria are more active, and so more nitrates in the soil will be turned back into nitrogen gas *[1 mark]*, which plants can't use directly *[1 mark]*. This means less nitrogen will be available to the cabbages and they may start to show deficiency symptoms again *[1 mark]*.

Section 10 — Key Concepts in Chemistry

Pages 87-88 — Chemical Equations

1 C *[1 mark]*
2 $CaCO_3(s) + 2HNO_3(aq) \rightarrow Ca(NO_3)_2(aq) + H_2O(l) + CO_2(g)$
   [1 mark for correct left-hand side, 1 mark for correct right-hand side.]
3 $4Na + O_2 \rightarrow 2Na_2O$
   [2 marks for all formulas correct and a correctly-balanced equation, otherwise 1 mark for correct formulas in an unbalanced equation.]
For any question that involves balancing an equation, you should also get the mark if you gave matching multiples of the correct numbers.
4 a) That the substance is dissolved in water / aqueous *[1 mark]*.
  b) $2Al_{(s)} + 3H_2SO_{4\,(aq)} \rightarrow Al_2(SO_4)_{3\,(aq)} + 3H_{2\,(g)}$ *[1 mark]*
5 a) $4NH_3 + 5O_2 \rightarrow 4NO + 6H_2O$ *[1 mark]*
  b) There are 7 oxygen atoms on the left hand side of the equation and only 6 on the right hand side *[1 mark]*.

6 a) A solid precipitate of AgCl is formed *[1 mark]*.
  b) $Ag^+_{(aq)} + Cl^-_{(aq)} \rightarrow AgCl_{(s)}$
     [1 mark for left side correct, 1 mark for right side correct.]
7 $S + 6HNO_3 \rightarrow H_2SO_4 + 6NO_2 + 2H_2O$ *[1 mark]*
8 $Zn_{(s)} + Sn^{2+}_{(aq)} \rightarrow Zn^{2+}_{(aq)} + Sn_{(s)}$
   [1 mark for left side correct, 1 mark for right side correct.]
Remember — the overall charge on an ionic compound is zero (it's neutral). So, since the sulfate ion, SO_4^{2-}, has a charge of −2, the tin ion in $SnSO_4$ must have a charge of +2. (The same applies to the zinc ion in $ZnSO_4$.)

Page 89 — Hazards and Risk

1 a) B *[1 mark]*
  b) E.g. wear safety goggles / wear a lab coat / wear gloves / use the reagent in low concentrations *[1 mark]*.
2 The label shows that the chemical is an environmental hazard *[1 mark]*. The technician needs to dispose of chemicals like this carefully as if they get into water supplies/the environment, they can damage organisms *[1 mark]*.
3 How to grade your answer:
   Level 0: Nothing written worthy of credit *[No marks]*.
   Level 1: Some hazards or safety precautions are given, but there is little detail and key information is missing. The points made are basic and not linked together *[1–2 marks]*.
   Level 2: Some of the hazards associated with the experiment have been identified. Some explanation of the relevant safety precautions needed is given, but some detail is missing. Some of the points made are linked together *[3–4 marks]*.
   Level 3: A clear and detailed description of all of the hazards associated with the experiment is given. The safety precautions needed to reduce the risks are described fully. The points made are well-linked and the answer has a clear and logical structure *[5–6 marks]*.
Here are some points your answer may include:
Harmful chemicals can cause irritation/blistering of the skin.
Corrosive chemicals destroy materials, including skin/eyes.
The gas produced by the experiment may be harmful/toxic.
The student should wear safety goggles, a lab coat and gloves when handling the chemicals.
The student should carry out the reaction in a fume hood to avoid releasing the gas into the air.
The student should use small quantities of the harmful and corrosive chemicals where possible.
The student should use the harmful and corrosive chemicals in low concentrations.

Page 90 — The History of the Atom

Warm-up
Plum pudding model — A positively charged 'ball' with negatively charged electrons in it.
Bohr's model — Electrons in fixed orbits surrounding a small, positively charged nucleus.
Rutherford's nuclear model — A small, positively charged nucleus surrounded by a 'cloud' of negative electrons.

1 A *[1 mark]*
2 a) During the gold foil experiment, most of the particles did pass straight through the foil *[1 mark]* as most of the atom is 'empty' space *[1 mark]*. However, a small number of particles were deflected backwards *[1 mark]* because they hit the nucleus *[1 mark]*.
  b) Niels Bohr *[1 mark]*.

Page 91 — The Atom

1 a) nucleus *[1 mark]*
   b) electron *[1 mark]*
   c) Neutrons and protons *[1 mark]*.
   d) Protons have a relative charge of +1 *[1 mark]* and electrons have a relative charge of −1 *[1 mark]*. Because there is an equal number of protons and electrons in an atom, the positive charges on the protons cancel out the negative charges on the electrons *[1 mark]*.
   Neutrons have a relative charge of zero, which means that they don't affect the overall charge of the atom (so you don't need to mention them here).
   e) C *[1 mark]*
2 a) mass number = 39 *[1 mark]*
   b) atomic number = 19 *[1 mark]*
   c) protons = 19 *[1 mark]*
   neutrons = mass number − atomic number
   = 39 − 19 = **20** *[1 mark]*
   electrons = 19 *[1 mark]*

Pages 92-93 — Isotopes and Relative Atomic Mass

1 a)

Isotope	No. of Protons	No. of Neutrons	No. of Electrons
^{32}S	16	16	16
^{33}S	16	17	16
^{34}S	16	18	16
^{36}S	16	20	16

[3 marks for all rows correct, otherwise 2 marks for 3 rows correct, and 1 mark for 1 or 2 rows correct.]

   b) X and Z are isotopes *[1 mark]*. They have the same atomic number / same number of protons *[1 mark]* but different mass numbers / number of neutrons *[1 mark]*.
2 a) 29 − 14 = **15** *[1 mark]*
   b) relative atomic mass = (28 × 92.2) + (29 × 4.70) + (30 × 3.10) ÷ 100 = (2581.6 + 136.3 + 93) ÷ 100
   = 2810.9 ÷ 100 = **28.1**
   [2 marks for correct answer, otherwise 1 mark for correctly substituting in values for abundances and atomic masses.]
   If you're dealing with isotopic abundances which are given to you as percentages, they will always add up to 100.
3 a) Isotopes are atoms of the same element that have the same number of protons but a different number of neutrons *[1 mark]*.
   b) Br-79: Number of neutrons = 79 − 35 = **44**
   Br-81: Number of neutrons = 81 − 35 = **46**
   [1 mark for both correct]
   c) relative atomic mass = (79 × 12.67) + (81 × 12.32) ÷ (12.67 + 12.32) = (1000.93 + 997.92) ÷ 24.99
   = 1998.85 ÷ 24.99 = 79.98... = **80**
   [2 marks for a correct answer given to 2 significant figures, otherwise 1 mark for correctly substituting in values for abundances and atomic masses.]
4 a) The relative atomic mass of an element is the average mass of one atom of the element *[1 mark]*, compared to 1/12th of the mass of one atom of carbon-12 *[1 mark]*.
   b) Relative atomic mass is an average of the mass numbers of all the different isotopes of an element, taking into account the abundance of each one *[1 mark]*.
5 % isotopic abundance of Ga-71 = 100 − 60.1 = 39.9
   relative atomic mass = (69 × 60.1) + (71 × 39.9) ÷ 100
   = (4146.9 + 2832.9) ÷ 100 = **69.8**
   [3 marks for correct answer, otherwise 1 mark for working out % abundance of Ga-71, 1 mark for correctly substituting in values for abundances and atomic masses.]

Page 94 — The Periodic Table

1 a) By atomic number *[1 mark]*.
   b) B *[1 mark]*
2 a) Mendeleev left some gaps in order to keep elements with similar properties in the same group *[1 mark]*.
   b) i) Any value between 2.4 and 7.2 g/cm³ *[1 mark]*.
   ii) $EkCl_4$ *[1 mark]*
   iii) Very slow *[1 mark]*.

Page 95 — Electronic Configurations

1 C *[1 mark]*
The electronic structure of neon is 2.8, so has 8 electrons in its outer shell.
2 a) 2.8.6 *[1 mark]*
   b)
   [1 mark]
3 a) The group number tells you how many electrons are in the outer shell, so magnesium has 2 outer shell electrons *[1 mark]*. The period number tells you how many electron shells the atom has in total, so magnesium has three shells *[1 mark]*. All the shells apart from the outer shell will be filled (the first holds 2 electrons and the second holds 8) *[1 mark]*.
   b) 2.8.2 *[1 mark]*

Page 96 — Ions

Warm-up
A^+ — A metal from Group 1. D^- — A non-metal from Group 7.
X^{2+} — A metal from Group 2. Z^{2-} — A non-metal from Group 6.
1 a) The atom gains one or more electrons *[1 mark]*.
   b) i) +2 *[1 mark]*
   ii) Number of electrons = 12 − 2 = **10** *[1 mark]*
2 a) C *[1 mark]*
   b) protons = 8 *[1 mark]*, electrons = 8 − (−2) = 10 *[1 mark]*, neutrons = 16 − 8 = 8 *[1 mark]*
The number of protons is equal to the atomic number. The number of electrons is equal to the atomic number minus the charge (and since oxygen is in Group 6 of the periodic table, its ions will have a charge of −2). The number of neutrons is equal to the mass number minus the atomic number.

Page 97 — Ionic Bonding

1 a) calcium chloride *[1 mark]*
Ionic compounds are made up of a metal bonded to a non-metal. All the other options only contain non-metals, so they can't be ionic.
   b)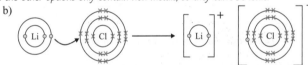
   [1 mark for arrow showing electron transfer from Li to Cl, 1 mark for adding seven crosses and one dot to outer shell of the chloride ion, 1 mark for correct charges on both ions.]
   c) electrostatic attraction / electrostatic force *[1 mark]*
   d) E.g. the particles in the compound are oppositely charged ions / have opposite charges / the bond is formed by electrons being transferred from one atom to another *[1 mark]*.
2
   [1 mark for correct electronic structure of fluoride ions, 1 mark for correct electronic structure of calcium ion, 1 mark for correct charge on calcium ion, 1 mark for correct charge on fluoride ions.]

Pages 98-99 — Ionic Compounds

Warm-up
In an ionic compound, the particles are held together by **strong** forces of attraction. These forces act **in all directions** which results in the particles bonding together to form **giant lattices**.
1 a) D *[1 mark]*
   b) giant ionic lattice *[1 mark]*
2 a) Sodium chloride contains positive sodium ions (Na^+) *[1 mark]* and negative chloride ions (Cl^-) *[1 mark]* that are arranged in a regular lattice/giant ionic lattice *[1 mark]*. The oppositely charged ions are held together by electrostatic forces acting in all directions *[1 mark]*.
   b) To melt sodium chloride, you have to overcome the very strong electrostatic forces/ionic bonds between the ions *[1 mark]*, which requires lots of energy *[1 mark]*.

294

3 a)   E.g.

*[1 mark for K+ ions,
1 mark for Br– ions,
1 mark for correct structure,
with alternating ion]*

*You'd also get the marks if you labelled all the white circles as Br⁻ and all
of the grey circles as K⁺.*

   b)   Advantage: e.g. the diagram shows the 3D arrangement of
         the ions / it suggests the structure is extended / it shows the
         regular (repeating) pattern of the ions *[1 mark]*.
         Disadvantage: e.g. the diagram doesn't correctly represent
         the sizes of ions / it shows gaps between the ions *[1 mark]*.
   c)   soluble *[1 mark]*
4   Boiling point: lithium chloride has strong ionic bonds/strong
       electrostatic forces of attraction between the ions *[1 mark]*.
       In order to boil it, these bonds need to be broken, which takes a
       lot of energy *[1 mark]*.
       Electrical conductivity of solid: the ions are in fixed positions
       in the lattice *[1 mark]* and so are not able to move and carry a
       charge through the solid *[1 mark]*.
       Electrical conductivity of solution: in solution, the ions are
       free to move *[1 mark]*, so they can carry a charge *[1 mark]*.

Pages 100-101 — Covalent Bonding

1 a)   The bonds between the atoms in a molecule are strong *[1 mark]*,
         but the forces between the molecules are weak *[1 mark]*.
   b)   The forces between the molecules / the intermolecular forces
         [1 mark]
2   A silicon atom has four outer shell electrons, so it needs
       another four to have a full outer shell *[1 mark]*.
       So a silicon atom will form four covalent bonds *[1 mark]*.

3 a)

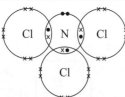

         *[1 mark for correctly showing three chlorine-nitrogen bonds
         as shared pairs of electrons, 1 mark for showing one extra
         electron pair on the nitrogen atom, 1 mark for showing three
         extra electron pairs on each chlorine atom.]*
   b)   Nitrogen trichloride won't conduct electricity because it doesn't
         contain any free electrons / ions / charged particles *[1 mark]*.
4   Hashim is wrong. Simple molecular substances have low
       melting and boiling points *[1 mark]*. To melt or boil a
       simple molecular substance, you only need to overcome the
       intermolecular forces which hold the molecules together
       [1 mark]. Intermolecular forces are weak, so they can be
       broken with a small amount of energy *[1 mark]*.
5 a)   Carbon needs four more electrons to get a full outer shell
         [1 mark], which it gains by forming four covalent bonds with
         hydrogen atoms *[1 mark]*. Hydrogen only needs one more
         electron to complete its outer shell *[1 mark]*, so each hydrogen
         atom forms one covalent bond to the carbon atom *[1 mark]*.
   b)   polymer *[1 mark]*
   c)   Poly(ethene) molecules are larger than methane molecules
         [1 mark]. As molecules get bigger, the strength of the
         intermolecular forces between them increases *[1 mark]*.
         So the forces between the molecules are stronger in poly(ethene)
         than they are in methane *[1 mark]* and more energy is needed to
         overcome them *[1 mark]*.

Page 102 — Giant Covalent Structures and Fullerenes

1 a) i)   graphite *[1 mark]*
      ii)   fullerene / buckminster fullerene *[1 mark]*
   b)   Both structures have delocalised / free electrons *[1 mark]*,
         which can move and carry a charge *[1 mark]*.
   c)   Graphite (figure 1) should have the higher melting point
         [1 mark]. It has a giant covalent structure, so to melt it you need
         to break the strong covalent bonds holding the atoms together
         [1 mark]. Fullerenes (figure 2) are molecular, so to melt them
         you only need to break the weak intermolecular forces holding
         the molecules together *[1 mark]*.
   d)   E.g. diamond: OR graphene:

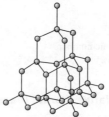   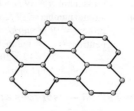

       [1 mark for correct name, 1 mark for correct structure]

Page 103 — Metallic Bonding

1 a)

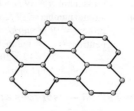

       *[1 mark for regular arrangement of metal ions,
       1 mark for delocalised electrons, 1 mark for labels]*
   b)   There is a strong electrostatic attraction *[1 mark]* between the
         delocalised electrons and the positive metal ions *[1 mark]*.
   c) i)   Metals generally have high boiling points, because the metallic
            bonds / electrostatic forces between the ions and the electrons
            are strong *[1 mark]* so a lot of energy is needed to break them
            [1 mark].
      ii)   Solid B is iodine, since elements that are non-metals tend to have
            lower melting points than metallic elements *[1 mark]*.
   d)   Metals contain delocalised electrons *[1 mark]*, which are free to
         move through the structure and carry a charge *[1 mark]*.
   e)   Metallic structures have layers of atoms *[1 mark]* that are able to
         slide over one another *[1 mark]*.

Page 104 — Conservation of Mass

1   The total mass of the contents of the flask would be
       3.0 + 15.8 = **18.8 g** *[1 mark]*. This is because, during a reaction,
       mass conserved / the total mass of the system doesn't change
       [1 mark].
2 a)   The total mass of the flask and its contents will decrease over
         the course of the reaction *[1 mark]* as one of the products is
         hydrogen gas, which is lost from the flask *[1 mark]*.
   b)   The total mass of the flask and its contents would stay the
         same over the course of the reaction *[1 mark]* as the reaction
         is happening in a closed system / any hydrogen gas evolved
         wouldn't be able to escape, so no reactants are lost *[1 mark]*.

Pages 105-106 — Relative Masses and Chemical Formulas

Warm-up
F_2 — 38 C_2H_6 — 30   CaO — 56   NaOH — 40
1   D *[1 mark]*
2   The largest number that goes into both 10 and 14 exactly is 2.
       B: 10 ÷ 2 = 5   H: 14 ÷ 2 = 7
       So the empirical formula of decaborane is B_5H_7 *[1 mark]*.
3 a) $H_2S_2O_6$ *[1 mark]*
   b)   The largest number that goes into all the numbers in the
         molecular formula exactly is 2.
         H: 2 ÷ 2 = 1   S: 2 ÷ 2 = 1   O: 6 ÷ 2 = 3
         So the empirical formula is HSO_3 *[1 mark]*

Answers

4　M_r of $Ba(NO_3)_2 = A_r$ of $Ba + (2 \times (A_r$ of $N + (3 \times A_r$ of $O)))$
　　$= 137 + (2 \times (14 + (3 \times 16))) = 137 + (2 \times (14 + 48))$
　　$= 137 + (2 \times 62) = 137 + 124 = \textbf{261}$
　　[2 marks for correct answer, otherwise 1 mark for writing a
　　expression that could be used to calculate the M_r of $Ba(NO_3)_2$.]

5　Emmy is incorrect, e.g. because she not has divided the numbers
　　in the molecular formula by the largest number that will go into
　　both exactly / she has divided both numbers in the formula by 4,
　　but she could have divided by 8 / $8 \div 8 = 1$ and $16 \div 8 = 2$, so the
　　empirical formula is CH_2 *[1 mark]*.

6　M_r of $X_2O_3 = (2 \times A_r$ of $X) + (3 \times A_r$ of $O)$
　　So $160 = (2 \times A_r$ of $X) + (3 \times 16)$
　　$160 = (2 \times A_r$ of $X) + 48$
　　$2 \times A_r$ of $X = 160 - 48 = 112$
　　so A_r of $X = 112 \div 2 = \textbf{56}$
　　[3 marks for the correct answer, otherwise 1 mark for a correct
　　equation for finding the M_r of X_2O_3 and 1 mark for correctly
　　substituting in the M_r of X_2O_3 and A_r of O.]

7　Relative mass of empirical formula is
　　$(2 \times A_r$ of $C) + (A_r$ of $H) + (A_r$ of $F) = (2 \times 12) + 1 + 19$
　　$= 24 + 1 + 19 = 44$
　　M_r of $Q \div M_r$ of empirical formula $= 132 \div 44 = 3$
　　So to get the molecular formula, multiply the numbers of atoms
　　in the empirical formula by 3:
　　molecular formula $= \textbf{C}_6\textbf{H}_3\textbf{F}_3$
　　[3 marks for correct answer, otherwise 1 mark for finding the
　　relative mass of the empirical formula and 1 mark for dividing
　　the relative mass of the molecular formula by the relative mass
　　of the empirical formula.]

Pages 107-109 — Moles and Concentration

1　D *[1 mark]*

2　A *[1 mark]*

3　$M_r(C_9H_8O_4) = (12 \times 9) + (1 \times 8) + (16 \times 4) = 180$
　　mass $=$ moles $\times M_r = 12.4 \times 180 = \textbf{2232 g}$
　　[2 marks for the correct answer, otherwise
　　1 mark for calculating the M_r of $C_9H_8O_4$.]

4　no. molecules $=$ moles $\times$ Avogadro's constant
　　　　　　　$= 7 \times (6.02 \times 10^{23}) = 4.214 \times 10^{24}$
　　In 1 molecule of ammonia, there are 4 atoms, so in
　　4.214×10^{24} molecules of ammonia, there must be
　　$4.214 \times 10^{24} \times 4 = 1.6856 \times 10^{25} = \textbf{1.69} \times \textbf{10}^{25}$ **atoms**
　　[2 marks for correct answer, otherwise 1 mark for correctly
　　working out number of ammonia molecules]

5　220 cm$^3 = (220 \div 1000)$ dm$^3 = 0.220$ dm^3
　　mass $=$ concentration $\times$ volume $= 75.0 \times 0.220$
　　$= \textbf{16.5 g}$ *[1 mark]*

6 a)　400 cm$^3 = (400 \div 1000)$ dm$^3 = 0.4$ dm^3
　　Concentration $=$ mass $\div$ volume
　　$= 56 \div 0.4 = \textbf{140 g dm}^{-3}$ *[1 mark]*

 b)　300 cm$^3 = (300 \div 1000)$ dm$^3 = 0.300$ dm^3
　　Mass $=$ concentration $\times$ volume $= 140 \times 0.300 = \textbf{42 g}$ *[1 mark]*

If your answer to a) was incorrect, award 1 mark for correct working in b).

7 a)　600 cm$^3 = (600 \div 1000)$ dm$^3 = 0.6$ dm^3
　　mass of NaOH $= 52 \times 0.6 = 31.2$ g
　　moles of NaOH $=$ mass $\div M_r = 31.2 \div 40.0 = \textbf{0.78 mol}$
　　[2 marks for correct answer, otherwise 1 mark for working out
　　the mass of NaOH]

 b) i)　Volume $=$ mass $\div$ concentration $= 36.0 \div 80.0 = 0.450$ dm^3
　　0.450 dm$^3 = (0.450 \times 1000)$ cm$^3 = \textbf{450 cm}^3$
　　[2 marks for correct answer, otherwise 1 mark for calculating
　　volume in dm^3]

　　ii)　Double the volume of water / add an extra 450 cm^3 of water to
　　　　the solution *[1 mark]*.

8 a)　$(1.204 \times 10^{25}) \div (6.02 \times 10^{23}) = \textbf{20 moles}$ *[1 mark]*

 b)　A_r of element $= (9.3 \times 10^{-23}) \times (6.02 \times 10^{23}) = 56$ (2 s.f.)
　　So the element is **iron**.
　　[2 marks for correct answer, otherwise 1 mark for working out
　　the relative atomic mass of the element].

9 a)　$M_r =$ mass $\div$ moles $= 343 \div 3.5 = \textbf{98}$ *[1 mark]*

 b)　65% of $98 = (98 \div 100) \times 65 = 63.7$
　　Moles of O in 63.7 g $= 63.7 \div 16 = 3.98... = \textbf{4 moles}$
　　[2 marks for correct answer, otherwise 1 mark for working out
　　the mass of oxygen.]

---

 c)　Mass of 1 mole of S $= 32$ g
　　Mass of 4 moles of O $= 16 \times 4 = 64$ g
　　Mass of H in 1 mole of acid $= 98 - 64 - 32 = 2$ g *[1 mark]*
　　Moles of H in 2 g $= 2 \div 1 = 2$
　　Ratio of S : O : H $= 1 : 4 : 2$ *[1 mark]*
　　chemical formula $= \textbf{H}_2\textbf{SO}_4$
　　[3 marks for correct answer, otherwise 1 mark for working out
　　mass of S, O and H in acid and 1 mark for working out the
　　ratio between S, O and H in the acid.]

Page 110 — Calculating Empirical Formulas

1　moles $=$ mass $\div A_r$
　　moles Pb $= 2.07 \div 207 = 0.01$ moles
　　moles O $= 0.16 \div 16 = 0.01$ moles
　　ratio of Pb : O $= 0.01 : 0.01$
　　Dividing by the smallest number (0.01) gives a ratio of
　　Pb : O of $1 : 1$. The empirical formula is **PbO**.
　　[2 marks for correct answer, otherwise 1 mark for finding
　　moles of Pb and O.]

2　mass of Cu $= 53.66 - 10.8 = 42.86$
　　moles $=$ mass $\div A_r$
　　moles of Cu $= 42.86 \div 63.5 = 0.6749...$
　　moles of O $= 10.8 \div 16 = 0.675$
　　ratio of Cu : O $= 0.6749... : 0.675$
　　Dividing by the smallest number ($0.6749...$) gives a ratio
　　of Cu : O of $1 : 1$. The empirical formula is **CuO**.
　　[3 marks for correct answer, otherwise 1 mark for finding the
　　mass of Cu and 1 mark for finding the moles of Cu and O.]

3　In 100 g of the hydrocarbon:
　　83 g is C and $(100 - 83 =)$ 17 g is H.
　　moles $=$ mass $\div A_r$
　　moles of C $= 83 \div 12 = 6.916...$
　　moles of H $= 17 \div 1 = 17$
　　ratio of C : H $= 6.916... : 17$
　　Dividing by the smallest number ($6.916...$) gives a ratio of
　　C : H of $1 : 2.5$. The smallest whole number ratio is $2 : 5$, so the
　　empirical formula must be $\textbf{C}_2\textbf{H}_5$.
　　[3 marks for correct answer, otherwise 1 mark for finding
　　the mass of C and H in 100 g and 1 mark for finding the
　　moles of C and H.]

4 a)　E.g. a crucible *[1 mark]*.

 b)　mass of O $= 5.440 - 3.808 = 1.632$ g
　　moles $=$ mass $\div A_r$
　　moles of Fe $= 3.808 \div 56 = 0.068$
　　moles of O $= 1.632 \div 16 = 0.102$
　　ratio of Fe : O $= 0.068 : 0.102$.
　　Dividing by the smallest number (0.068) gives a ratio of
　　Fe : O of $1 : 1.5$. The smallest whole number ratio is $2 : 3$,
　　so the empirical formula must be $\textbf{Fe}_2\textbf{O}_3$.
　　[3 marks for correct answer, otherwise 1 mark for finding the
　　mass of O and 1 mark for finding the moles of Fe and O.]

Pages 111-112 — Limiting Reactants

Warm-up

1)　If the amount of limiting reactant in a reaction is decreased,
　　then the amount of product made will **decrease**.

2)　If the amount of limiting reactant in a reaction is increased,
　　then the amount of product made will **increase**.

3)　If the amount of an excess reactant is increased,
　　then the amount of product made will **not change**.

1 a)　magnesium *[1 mark]*

 b)　The hydrochloric acid is the limiting reactant *[1 mark]* as there
　　is magnesium metal left over when the reaction has finished,
　　showing that it's in excess *[1 mark]*.

2　$M_r(C_2H_4) = (12 \times 2) + (1 \times 4) = 28$
　　moles $=$ mass $\div M_r = 53 \div 28 = 1.8...$ moles
　　From the reaction equation, 1 mole of C_2H_4 produces
　　1 mole of CH_3CH_2OH, so $1.89...$ moles of C_2H_4 will
　　produce $1.89...$ moles of CH_3CH_2OH.
　　$M_r(CH_3CH_2OH) = 12 + (1 \times 3) + 12 + (1 \times 2) + 16 + 1 = 46$
　　mass $=$ moles $\times M_r = 1.89... \times 46 = \textbf{87 g}$
　　[2 marks for correct answer, otherwise 1 mark for
　　working out moles of C_2H_4.]

3 a) $M_r(O_2) = 16 \times 2 = 32$
moles = mass ÷ M_r = 128 ÷ 32 = 4
From the reaction equation, 7 moles of O_2 produce
6 moles of H_2O, so 4 moles of O_2 will produce
$((4 \div 7) \times 6) = 3.42...$ moles of H_2O.
$M_r(H_2O) = (1 \times 2) + 16 = 18$
mass = moles × M_r = 3.42... × 18 = **61.7 g**
[3 marks for correct answer, otherwise 1 mark for working out moles of O_2 and 1 mark for multiplying the moles of O_2 by the M_r of H_2O.]

b) $M_r(CO_2) = 12 + (16 \times 2) = 44$
4.4 tonnes = 4.4 × 1 000 000 = 4 400 000 g
moles = mass ÷ M_r = 4 400 000 ÷ 44 = 100 000
For every 4 moles of CO_2 produced, 2 moles of ethane are burnt.
So if 100 000 moles of CO_2 are produced,
((100 000 ÷ 4) × 2 =) 50 000 moles of ethane are burnt.
$M_r(C_2H_6) = (12 \times 2) + (1 \times 6) = 30$
mass = moles × M_r = 50 000 × 30 = 1 500 000 g
1 500 000 g = 1 500 000 ÷ 1 000 000 = **1.5 tonnes**
[3 marks for correct answer, otherwise 1 mark for finding moles of CO_2, 1 mark for finding mass of C_2H_6 in g.]

4 a) $M_r((NH_2)_2CO) = 2 \times (14 + (1 \times 2)) + 12 + 16 = 60$
120.6 tonnes = 120.6 × 1 000 000 = 120 600 000 g
moles = mass ÷ M_r = 120 600 000 ÷ 60 = 2 010 000
From the reaction equation, 1 mole of $(NH_2)_2CO$ is made from 1 mole of CO_2, so making 2 010 000 moles of $(NH_2)_2CO$ will require 2 010 000 moles of CO_2.
$M_r(CO_2) = 12 + (16 \times 2) = 44$
mass = moles × M_r = 2 010 000 × 44 = 88 440 000 g
88 440 000 g = 88 440 000 ÷ 1 000 000 = **88.44 tonnes**
[3 marks for correct answer, otherwise 1 mark for finding moles of $(NH_2)_2CO$, 1 mark for finding mass of CO_2 in g.]

b) $M_r(NH_3) = 14 + (1 \times 3) = 17$
59.5 tonnes = 59.5 × 1 000 000 = 59 500 000 g
moles = mass ÷ M_r = 59 500 000 ÷ 17 = 3 500 000
From the reaction equation, 2 moles of NH_3 make 1 mole of $(NH_2)_2CO$, so 3 500 000 moles of NH_3 will make (3 500 000 ÷ 2 =) 1 750 000 moles of $(NH_2)_2CO$.
From a), $M_r((NH_2)_2CO) = 60$
mass = moles × M_r = 1 750 000 × 60 = 105 000 000 g
105 000 000 = 105 000 000 ÷ 1 000 000 = 105 tonnes
difference between masses of $(NH_2)_2CO$ = 120.6 – 105 = **15.6 tonnes**
[4 marks for correct answer, otherwise 1 mark for finding moles of (NH_3), 1 mark for finding mass of $(NH_2)_2CO$ in g, 1 mark for finding mass of $(NH_2)_2CO$ in tonnes.]

Page 113 — Balancing Equations Using Masses

1 a)   280 – 200 = **80 g** *[1 mark]*

b)   E.g. moles = mass ÷ M_r
moles of X = 200 ÷ 40 = 5 moles
moles of O_2 = 80 ÷ (2 × 16) = 2.5 moles
Since X is a metal, its formula must be just be X.
From the question, you know the reaction produced 5 moles of X oxide, so the ratio of X : O_2 : X oxide is 5 : 2.5 : 5.
Dividing all of these by 2.5 gives a ratio of 2 : 1 : 2.
$2X + O_2 \rightarrow 2(X \text{ oxide})$
Since X oxide is the only product, and there are two atoms of both X and O on the left-hand side of the equation, the formula of X oxide must be XO.
So, balanced equation = $2X + O_2 \rightarrow 2XO$
[4 marks for correct answer, otherwise 1 mark for calculating the moles of X and the moles of O_2 gas, 1 mark for working out the simplest ratio of X : O : X oxide, 1 mark for stating the formula of X oxide.]

You could have done some of the working for this question differently, so don't worry if you've approached it in another way. If your answer is right you'll get full marks anyway. If your answer is wrong, you should get marks for your working, as long as the method you've used is sensible.

2   E.g. moles = mass ÷ M_r
moles of Na = 1.0 ÷ 23 = 0.043
moles of Cl_2 = 1.0 ÷ 71 = 0.014
Ratio of Na : Cl_2 = (0.043 ÷ 0.014) : (0.014 ÷ 0.014) = 3.1 : 1
Ratio of Na to Cl_2 in balanced equation = 2:1
Sodium is in excess, so chlorine is the limiting reactant.
[1 mark for calculating the moles of Na present, 1 mark for calculating the moles of Cl_2 present, 1 mark for stating that chlorine is the limiting reactant.]

Don't worry if you've done the working for this question a bit differently too — as long as your method and answer are correct, you'll get all the marks.

3   E.g. mass of metal halide produced = 3.57 + 15.24 = 18.81 g
moles = mass ÷ M_r
moles of Sn = 3.57 ÷ 119 = 0.03 moles
moles of I_2 = 15.24 ÷ 254 = 0.06 moles
moles of metal halide = 18.81 ÷ 627 = 0.03
The ratio of Sn : I_2 : metal halide is 0.03 : 0.06 : 0.03.
Dividing all of these by 0.03 gives a ratio of 1 : 2 : 1.
$Sn + 2I_2 \rightarrow$ metal halide
Since all of the reactants end up in the product, and there is one atom of Sn and four atoms of I on the left-hand side of the equation, the formula of the metal halide must be SnI_4.
So, the balanced equation is: $Sn + 2I_2 \rightarrow SnI_4$
[5 marks for correct answer, otherwise 1 mark for calculating the mass of metal halide made, 1 mark for calculating the number of moles of reactants and product, 1 mark for working out the simplest ratio of Sn : I_2 : metal halide, 1 mark for stating the formula of the metal halide.]

The same goes for this question if you've approached it a different way. The correct answer gets full marks anyway, but if your answer's wrong, you should get marks for correct working that uses a correct sensible method.

Section 11 — States of Matter and Mixtures

Page 114 — States of Matter

Warm-up
Particles in liquids are held in fixed positions by strong forces.

1 a)   solid *[1 mark]*
b)   liquid *[1 mark]*
2   When the substance is in the liquid state, the particles are constantly moving with a random motion *[1 mark]*. In the solid state the particles can only vibrate around fixed positions *[1 mark]*. When the substance is in the liquid state, the particles have more energy than when it is in the solid state *[1 mark]*.

Page 115 — Changes of State

1 a)   C *[1 mark]*.
b)   B and D *[1 mark]*. In these equations new products have been formed / the atoms in the reactants have been rearranged to form different chemicals *[1 mark]*.
2   The first change seen would be bromine freezing from a red-brown liquid to a red-brown solid *[1 mark]*.
The next change would be mercury freezing from a silvery metallic liquid to a silvery metallic solid *[1 mark]*.
Near the end of the experiment, the fluorine would condense from a pale yellow gas to a bright yellow liquid *[1 mark]*.
The rubidium would start out as a silvery-white metallic solid, and remain unchanged throughout *[1 mark]*.

Page 116 — Purity

1   The scientific definition of a pure substance is one that contains only one element or compound *[1 mark]*. Although it is labelled 'pure', Stanley's spring water is likely to contain traces of other compounds or elements as well as water molecules *[1 mark]*.
2   Sample A *[1 mark]*. The purer the substance, the smaller the range of the melting point / pure substances have sharp melting points, whereas impure substances melt over a range of temperatures *[1 mark]*.
3 a)   The pure compound will have a single, sharp melting point *[1 mark]* whereas the mixture will melt gradually over a range of temperatures *[1 mark]*.
b)   melting point apparatus / water bath and thermometer *[1 mark]*

Pages 117-120 — Separating Mixtures

1 a) i) A: fractionating column *[1 mark]*
   ii) B: condenser *[1 mark]*
  b) i) fractional distillation *[1 mark]*
   ii) A mixture of liquids *[1 mark]* with similar boiling points *[1 mark]*.
   iii) E.g. electric heater / water bath *[1 mark]*

You don't get the mark here for naming any heating device with an open flame (like a Bunsen burner).

2 How to grade your answer:
  Level 0: There is no relevant information. *[No marks]*
  Level 1: A method is described which would allow you to obtain a pure sample of only one of the components. The points made are basic and not linked together. *[1 to 2 marks]*
  Level 2: A method is described which would allow you to obtain pure samples of both components, but some details may be missing or incorrect. Some of the points made are linked together. *[3 to 4 marks]*
  Level 3: A method is described clearly and in full, which would allow you to obtain pure samples of both components. The points made are well-linked and the answer has a clear and logical structure. *[5 to 6 marks]*

  Here are some points your answer may include:
  Mix the powder with water. This will dissolve the potassium iodide, but not the barium sulfate.
  Filter the mixture through a filter paper in a funnel.
  The potassium iodide solution will pass through the paper and can be collected in a flask.
  The solid barium sulfate will be left in the filter paper.
  The solid barium sulfate can be washed with water to remove any traces of potassium iodide and then dried in a drying oven / desiccator / warm place.
  The remaining liquid part of the mixture will be a solution of potassium iodide.
  To obtain pure potassium iodide from this solution, you can use crystallisation.
  Gently heat the solution in an evaporation dish until some of the water has evaporated / until crystals start to form.
  Allow the solution to cool, then filter out the crystals.
  Dry the crystals by leaving them in a warm place / using a drying oven / using a desiccator.

3 a) Filtration *[1 mark]* would separate sodium chloride and ethanol, as the liquid ethanol would flow through the filter paper, leaving behind the solid sodium chloride *[1 mark]*. However, a mixture of sodium chloride and water is a solution, so both the water and dissolved sodium chloride would pass through the filter paper *[1 mark]*.
  b) E.g. simple distillation *[1 mark]*. Water and ethanol would both evaporate off and leave behind the solid sodium chloride *[1 mark]*.

4 The difference in the boiling points of cyclohexane and cyclopentane is quite large, so you could separate them using simple distillation *[1 mark]*. But the boiling points of cyclohexane and ethyl ethanoate are similar, so you would need to use fractional distillation to separate them *[1 mark]*.

5 a) No, it will not work as ethanol boils at 78 °C and water boils at 100 °C, so the liquids will both evaporate before 120 °C is reached *[1 mark]*.
  b) In step 1 of the method, the student should heat the mixture to a temperature between 78 and 100 °C *[1 mark]*. This will cause the ethanol in the mixture to evaporate, but not the water *[1 mark]*.
  c) Ethanol is a flammable solvent so the mixture could catch fire if there is a lot left in the solution *[1 mark]*.
  d) Gently heat the solution in an evaporating dish until some of the liquid has evaporated. When crystals start to form, remove the dish from the heat and leave to cool *[1 mark]*. Filter the crystals out of the solution and leave to dry in a warm place *[1 mark]*.

Pages 121-123 — Chromatography

1 a) ethanol *[1 mark]*
  b) The chromatogram suggests there are at least two components in the mixture *[1 mark]*, since the mixture has separated into two spots *[1 mark]*.
  c) Distance from baseline to spot B = 0.8 cm / 8 mm *[1 mark]*
   Distance from baseline to solvent front = 4.0 cm / 40 mm *[1 mark]*
   R_f = distance travelled by solute ÷ distance travelled by solvent
    = 0.8 ÷ 4.0 = **0.2**
   [1 mark for correctly dividing measured distance to spot B by measured distance to solvent front.]
  d) Olivia could re-run the experiment with spots of the pure chemicals alongside the mixture / analyse samples of each of the pure chemicals using paper chromatography, under the same conditions as the mixture *[1 mark]*. The R_f values of / distance travelled by each spot in the mixture will match the R_f values of / distance travelled by the pure sample of the chemical responsible for that spot *[1 mark]*.

2 a) i) e.g. simple distillation *[1 mark]*
   ii) If he uses a thermometer in his distillation set-up, Lamar will be able to find the boiling point of the solvent, which he may be able to use to identify it *[1 mark]*.
  b) Draw a line in pencil near the bottom of a piece of chromatography paper *[1 mark]*. Place a small spot of each ink on the line *[1 mark]*. Pour a shallow layer of water / solvent into a beaker and place the chromatography paper in the beaker *[1 mark]*. The water should be below the pencil line and the ink spots *[1 mark]*. Place a lid on the beaker and leave until the solvent has risen close to the top of the paper *[1 mark]*.
  c) E.g. the ink has a spot at the same height as dye B, so dye B could be in the ink *[1 mark]*. The ink has a spot at the same height as dyes C and E, so either (or both) of these dyes could be in the ink *[1 mark]*. The ink has no spot at the same height as dyes A and D, so these dyes are not in the ink *[1 mark]*. The ink has a spot with a height different to all of the dyes, so it must also contain at least one other dye *[1 mark]*.

3 a) There are at least five compounds in the ink *[1 mark]* because there are 5 spots on the chromatogram *[1 mark]*. There is at least one insoluble compound *[1 mark]*, because there is still a spot on the baseline *[1 mark]*.

The student can't know exactly how many compounds are in the ink, as some compounds may not be soluble in the solvent, and others may have similar R_f values so their spots will overlap.

  b) The student drew line A from the baseline to the top of the spot *[1 mark]*. They should have drawn the line to the centre of the spot *[1 mark]*. The student drew line B from the baseline to the top of the paper *[1 mark]*. They should have drawn line B from the baseline to the solvent front *[1 mark]*.

Page 124 — Water Treatment

Warm-up
Potable water is the same as drinking water — true.
Potable water can only be produced from fresh water found in rivers, streams and reservoirs — false.
Ordinary tap water can be used in chemical analysis — false.

1 a) E.g. ground water / surface water / waste water / lakes / rivers / reservoirs *[1 mark]*
  b) Distillation is expensive because it requires a lot of energy *[1 mark]* so it is not used in the UK as there are sufficient cheaper sources of water *[1 mark]*.
2 a) filtration *[1 mark]*
  b) Aluminium sulfate makes fine particles in the water clump together and settle at the bottom *[1 mark]*.
  c) Chlorine gas is bubbled through the water *[1 mark]* to kill harmful bacteria / microbes *[1 mark]*.

Answers

Section 12 — Chemical Changes

Pages 125-126 — Acids and Bases

Warm-up

The following sentences should be circled:

As H^+ concentration increases, pH decreases.

Alkalis turn Universal indicator blue/purple.

Acids have pHs of less than 7.

Alkalis are soluble bases.

1 a) beer *[1 mark]*
  b) pink *[1 mark]*
  c) B *[1 mark]*
2 A *[1 mark]*
3 a) acid + base → salt + water *[1 mark]*
  b) $H^+_{(aq)} + OH^-_{(aq)} \rightarrow H_2O_{(l)}$ *[1 mark]*

You still get the marks if you didn't include state symbols.

4 Solution C has the lowest concentration of hydroxide ions *[1 mark]*, because the higher the concentration of hydroxide ions in an alkaline solution, the higher its pH will be / the lower the concentration of hydroxide ions in an alkaline solution, the lower its pH will be *[1 mark]*.

5 a) E.g. pipette / measuring cylinder *[1 mark]*
  b) i) Red / orange / yellow *[1 mark]*. Since all the calcium hydroxide reacted, the acid must be in excess *[1 mark]*, so the solution is acidic *[1 mark]*.
    ii) Green *[1 mark]*. At this point all of the acid must have reacted with / been neutralised by the base *[1 mark]*, leaving a neutral solution *[1 mark]*.

Page 127 — Strong and Weak Acids

1 A *[1 mark]*
2 a) A weak acid doesn't fully ionise in solution / only a small proportion of molecules in a weak acid dissociate to release hydrogen ions *[1 mark]*.
  b) $HCOOH \rightleftharpoons HCOO^- + H^+$ *[1 mark for correct equation, 1 mark for arrow showing reversible reaction.]*
3 a) D *[1 mark]*
  b) 1 *[1 mark]*

An increase in the hydrogen ion concentration by a factor of 10 decreases the pH by 1. So an increase by a factor of 100 will reduce the pH by 2.

Page 128 — Reactions of Acids

1 D *[1 mark]*
2 From top to bottom: $Zn(NO_3)_2$ *[1 mark]*, $CaSO_4$ *[1 mark]*, Na_2SO_4 *[1 mark]*, KCl *[1 mark]*
3 a) The gas produced is carbon dioxide *[1 mark]*. If you bubble carbon dioxide through limewater *[1 mark]*, the limewater will turn cloudy *[1 mark]*.
  b) $ZnCO_3 + 2HCl \rightarrow ZnCl_2 + H_2O + CO_2$ *[2 marks for all formulas correct and a correctly-balanced equation, otherwise 1 mark for correct formulas in an unbalanced equation.]*
  c) zinc chloride *[1 mark]*

Pages 129-130 — Making Insoluble Salts

1 D *[1 mark]*
2 a) E.g. silver nitrate / $AgNO_3$ and sodium chloride / NaCl *[1 mark for any soluble silver salt, 1 mark for any soluble chloride salt.]*
  b) Jerry has poured too much solution into the funnel / the level of the solution goes above the filter paper *[1 mark]*. This means that some of the solid could pass down the sides of the filter paper and into the conical flask below, reducing the amount of solid that's extracted from the solution *[1 mark]*.
  c) Deionised water doesn't contain any other ions which might contaminate the pure salt *[1 mark]*.
3 a) C *[1 mark]*
  b) E.g. calcium chloride / $CaCl_2$ and sodium carbonate / Na_2CO_3 *[1 mark for any soluble calcium salt, 1 mark for any soluble carbonate.]*

4 a) $Fe(OH)_3$ *[1 mark]*
  b) i) E.g. to make sure that all of the precipitate is transferred from the beaker to the funnel / to make sure she doesn't lose any of the product *[1 mark]*.
    ii) E.g. scrape the product on to a clean piece of filter paper and dry in an oven / desiccator / warm place *[1 mark]*.
    iii) Fe^{3+}, NO_3^- and Na^+ / iron(III) ions, nitrate ions and sodium ions *[2 marks for all three correct, otherwise 1 mark for any two correct]*.

Pages 131-132 — Making Soluble Salts

Warm-up

The following pieces of equipment should be circled:

filter funnel, fume cupboard, desiccator, water bath, conical flask, safety glasses, filter paper

1 a) C *[1 mark]*
  b) $Mg(OH)_{2\,(s)} + H_2SO_{4\,(aq)} \rightarrow MgSO_{4\,(aq)} + 2H_2O_{(l)}$ *[3 marks for a correctly balanced equation with all formulas and state symbols correct, otherwise 1 mark for correct formulas in an unbalanced equation, and 1 mark for all state symbols correct.]*
2 a) It dissolves in water *[1 mark]*.
  b) $2KOH + H_2SO_4 \rightarrow K_2SO_4 + 2H_2O$ *[2 marks for all formulas correct and a correctly-balanced equation, otherwise 1 mark for correct formulas in an unbalanced equation.]*
  c) No, because the salt will be contaminated by the indicator *[1 mark]*.
3 a) $H_2SO_4 + CuO \rightarrow CuSO_4 + H_2O$ *[2 marks for all formulas correct and a correctly-balanced equation, otherwise 1 mark for correct formulas in an unbalanced equation.]*
  b) How to grade your answer:
  Level 0: There is no relevant information. *[No marks]*
  Level 1: There is a brief explanation of how to prepare the salt but no details are given. The points made are basic and not linked together. *[1 to 2 marks]*
  Level 2: There is some explanation of to prepare the salt, including necessary equipment and how to isolate the salt, but the method is missing key details. Some of the points made are linked together. *[3 to 4 marks]*
  Level 3: There is a clear and detailed explanation of how to produce and extract a pure sample of the salt. The points made are well-linked and the answer has a clear and logical structure. *[5 to 6 marks]*

Here are some points your answer may include:

Warm the sulfuric acid in a water bath.

Warm the acid in a fume cupboard to avoid releasing acid fumes into the room.

Add copper oxide to the acid.

When the reaction is complete and the copper oxide is in excess, the solid copper oxide will sink to the bottom.

Filter the reaction mixture to remove the excess copper oxide.

Heat the remaining solution gently (using a Bunsen burner) to evaporate off some of the water.

Leave the solution to cool and allow the salt to crystallise.

Filter off the solid salt and leave the crystals to dry.

Pages 133-135 — Electrolysis

1 a) The ions in solid potassium chloride are not free to move and so can't carry a charge *[1 mark]*, so the potassium chloride must be molten or dissolved so that the ions are free to move and carry a charge *[1 mark]*.
  b) cathode *[1 mark]*
2 a) B *[1 mark]*
  b) i) Bubbles of green gas would form *[1 mark]*.
    ii) Copper metal would coat the electrode *[1 mark]*.

3 a) Inert electrodes are electrodes that do not react with the electrolyte *[1 mark]*.

b) H^+, Cl^-, Na^+, OH^- *[2 marks for all four correct, otherwise 1 mark for any three correct.]*

c) i) $2Cl^- \rightarrow Cl_2 + 2e^-$
[2 marks for all formulas correct and a correctly-balanced equation, otherwise 1 mark for correct formulas in an unbalanced equation.]

ii) $2H^+ + 2e^- \rightarrow H_2$
[2 marks for all formulas correct and a correctly-balanced equation, otherwise 1 mark for correct formulas in an unbalanced equation.]

4 a) A liquid or solution *[1 mark]* that can conduct electricity *[1 mark]*.

b) PbI_2 *[1 mark]*

5 How to grade your answer:

Level 0: There is no relevant information. *[No marks]*

Level 1: The method is vague, and misses out important details. Predictions about products or observations of the electrolysis are unclear and incomplete. The points made are basic and not linked together. *[1 to 2 marks]*

Level 2: The method is clear, but misses out a few key details. Correct predictions of products and observations of the electrolysis are given but are missing some important details. Some of the points made are linked together. *[3 to 4 marks]*

Level 3: There is a clear and detailed method. The products of the electrolysis are correctly predicted and the observations are described in full. The points made are well-linked and the answer has a clear and logical structure. *[5 to 6 marks]*

Here are some points your answer may include:
Use two platinum/graphite electrodes.
Clean the electrodes using some emery paper.
Place the electrodes in a beaker filled with sodium chloride solution.
Connect the electrodes to a power supply using crocodile clips and wires.
Turn the power supply on and allow the electrolysis to occur.
Bubbles of (hydrogen) gas will be seen at the cathode.
Bubbles of green (chlorine) gas will be seen at the anode.

6 a) Sodium sulfate solution contains hydrogen ions (as well as sodium ions) *[1 mark]*. Sodium ions are more reactive than hydrogen ions *[1 mark]*, so hydrogen gas is discharged at the cathode *[1 mark]*.

b) oxygen *[1 mark]* and water *[1 mark]*

c) Electrolysis of e.g. molten sodium sulfate / sodium chloride *[1 mark]* with inert electrodes *[1 mark]*.

You get the first mark for any named sodium salt here, as long as you also remember to say that it must be molten.

7 a) The mass of cell A would be less than the mass of cell B after 1 hour *[1 mark]*. In both cells, at the cathode copper ions gain electrons to become copper atoms: $Cu^{2+} + 2e^- \rightarrow Cu$ *[1 mark]*. In cell A, at the anode, oxygen gas is formed: $4OH^- \rightarrow O_2 + 2H_2O + 4e^-$ *[1 mark]*. Mass is lost from cell A as oxygen gas escapes from the system *[1 mark]*. In cell B, at the anode, copper atoms lose electrons to become copper ions: $Cu \rightarrow Cu^{2+} + 2e^-$ *[1 mark]*. The copper ions stay in the cell, so the mass of cell B stays constant *[1 mark]*.

b) Similarity: any one from: e.g. both use copper sulfate solution as an electrolyte / both involve wires and a power supply *[1 mark]*. Difference: e.g. in the cell used to purify copper, the anode is an impure lump of copper / in the cell used to purify copper, a sludge of impurities will gather at the bottom (which will not be present in Cell B) *[1 mark]*.

8 Cathode: $2H^+ + 2e^- \rightarrow H_2$
Anode: $4OH^- \rightarrow O_2 + H_2O + 4e^-$
[For each half-equation: 2 marks for all formulas correct and a correctly-balanced equation, otherwise 1 mark for correct formulas in an unbalanced equation.]

Section 13 — Extracting Metals and Equilibria

Pages 136-137 — Reactivity Series and Reactivity of Metals

1 Oxidation can describe the addition of oxygen *[1 mark]*. When a metal is burnt in air, the metal gains oxygen to form a metal oxide / an oxygen-containing products *[1 mark]*.

2 a) sodium + water → sodium hydroxide + hydrogen *[1 mark]*

b) Iron is more resistant to oxidation than sodium / it loses (its outer) electrons and forms positive ions less easily *[1 mark]*.

You'd also get the mark here for saying that sodium is more easily oxidised than iron / loses its outer electrons and forms positive ions more easily.

3 a) i) $Ca_{(s)} + 2H_2O_{(l)} \rightarrow Ca(OH)_{2(aq)} + H_{2(g)}$
[1 mark for each correct product]

ii) Calcium is oxidised *[1 mark]* because it has gained oxygen *[1 mark]*.

iii) E.g. lithium / sodium / potassium *[1 mark]*. As it is higher in the reactivity series than calcium / loses electrons more easily than calcium / forms positive ions more easily *[1 mark]*.

b) potassium, sodium, zinc *[1 mark[*

4 A *[1 mark]*

5 a) magnesium, zinc, iron, copper *[1 mark]*

b) i) zinc oxide *[1 mark]*

ii) Metal X was sodium, because it reacted vigorously with cold water *[1 mark]*.

Page 138 — Displacement Reactions

1 Magnesium is oxidised / loses electrons to form magnesium ions *[1 mark]* and simultaneously iron ions are reduced / gain electrons to form iron metal *[1 mark]*.

2 a) Yes, because lead can displace silver from a salt solution / silver cannot displace lead from a salt solution *[1 mark]*.

b) $3Mg + 2AlCl_3 \rightarrow 2Al + 3MgCl_2$
[2 marks for all formulas correct and a correctly balanced equation, otherwise 1 mark for correct formulas in an unbalanced equation]

c) The solution would change colour from colourless to green *[1 mark]*. The piece of shiny grey nickel will be coated in dull grey lead *[1 mark]*.

Page 139 — Extracting Metals Using Carbon

1 a) A metal ore is a rock which contains enough metal to make it economically worthwhile extracting the metal from it *[1 mark]*.

b) Copper can be extracted from its ore by reduction with carbon *[1 mark]*.

c) tin / zinc *[1 mark]*

2 a) $2Fe_2O_3 + 3C \rightarrow 4Fe + 3CO_2$
[1 mark for correct equation, 1 mark for correct balancing]

b) The impurity is zinc *[1 mark]*. Zinc is lower than carbon in the reactivity series/less reactive than carbon *[1 mark]*, so the zinc oxide in the iron ore would also be reduced by carbon to zinc metal in the blast furnace *[1 mark]*.

Calcium is more reactive than carbon so the calcium in calcium oxide wouldn't be reduced to calcium metal in the blast furnace.

Page 140 — Other Methods of Extracting Metals

1 a) electrolysis *[1 mark]*

b) To lower the melting point of the electrolyte / ore *[1 mark]*.

c) E.g. to carry out electrolysis, you need large amounts of electricity, which is expensive *[1 mark]*. There are also costs associated with dissolving aluminium in cryolite *[1 mark]*.

2 a) Plants are grown in soil containing metal compounds, which they absorb (via their roots) *[1 mark]*. The plants can neither use nor dispose of the metals, so they accumulate in the leaves *[1 mark]*. The plants are harvested, dried and burned in a furnace *[1 mark]*. Metals can be extracted from the metal compounds in the ash using electrolysis or displacement reactions *[1 mark]*.

b) Advantage: e.g. less damaging to the environment than traditional methods *[1 mark]*.
Disadvantage: e.g. process is very slow *[1 mark]*.

c) E.g. bioleaching / bacterial methods *[1 mark]*.

Page 141 — Recycling

1 a) E.g. takes up space / pollutes surroundings / doesn't preserve materials *[1 mark]*.
  b) Any two from: e.g. often uses less energy / conserves the amount of raw materials in the Earth
  [1 mark for each correct answer].
  c) Any two from: e.g. recycling often uses less energy than extracting materials, so it costs less / recycling creates jobs
  [1 mark for each correct answer].
2 a) Material B. Only a small amount of energy is needed to recycle it whereas a lot of energy is needed to extract it *[1 mark]*. Material B also has limited availability, so in the long term it may run out if it is not recycled *[1 mark]*.
  b) Crude oil is a non-renewable resource so it is important to conserve it *[1 mark]*.

Pages 142-144 — Life Cycle Assessments

Warm-up

Recyclability of the product, Source of raw materials

1 a) A life cycle assessment looks at each stage of the life of a product to work out the potential environmental impact at each stage *[1 mark]*.
  b) Timber is the better choice. Timber comes from trees, which are renewable, so it is sustainable *[1 mark]*. Polypropene comes from crude oil, which is non-renewable, and so is not sustainable *[1 mark]*. Also, extracting timber from trees uses less energy than making polypropene, so extracting timber uses less fuel / creates less pollution *[1 mark]*.

You don't need to consider cost when thinking about sustainability, you just need to think about how using a material might affect the environment.

  c) Any two from: e.g. how much waste is produced by each process / how much pollution each process would produce / how long chairs made from each type of material would last / how much water each process uses / how easy each type of chair would be to dispose of sustainably at the end of their usable life *[1 mark for each correct answer]*.
2 a) Any two from: e.g. extracting iron from its ore uses a lot of energy / extracting iron from its ore creates pollution / mining iron ore can damage the environment that it is taken from
  [1 mark for each correct answer].
  b) E.g. landfill takes up limited space / generates pollution / prevents resources from being reused/recycled *[1 mark]*.
  c) E.g. by recycling it *[1 mark]*.
3 E.g. toy A has the highest CO_2 emissions, solvent use and energy consumption, so toy A would have the highest environmental impact *[1 mark]*. Toy B has the second lowest CO_2 emissions and the second lowest solvent use, but uses the second highest amount of energy, so it would have a medium impact / a higher impact than D, but a lower impact than A or C *[1 mark]*. Toy C has the second highest CO_2 emissions and solvent use, but the lowest energy consumption, so would have a medium impact / a lower impact than A, but a higher impact than B or D *[1 mark]*. Toy D has the lowest CO_2 emissions, the lowest solvent use and the second lowest energy consumption, so would have the lowest environmental impact *[1 mark]*.
4 a) E.g. glass bottles can be reused multiple times, but cans are usually only used once *[1 mark]*.
  b) E.g. it would be more positive as the raw material would be recycled cans rather than aluminium ore *[1 mark]*. Using recycled cans would save energy and would produce a lower amount of greenhouse gases than extracting aluminium from ore *[1 mark]*.

You could also mention that it would preserve the supply of valuable raw materials, or that it would eliminate the environmental problems associated with mining.

  c) The glass bottles have to be separated from the rest of the glass objects before they can be recycled *[1 mark]*, which could lead to more waste if some batches are contaminated *[1 mark]*.
  d) Any one from: e.g. how likely they are to be recycled / how easy it is to recycle them / the environmental costs of disposal if they are sent to landfill / their biodegradability *[1 mark]*

Page 145 — Dynamic Equilibrium

Warm-up

The Haber Process is **a reversible** reaction that forms **ammonia** from hydrogen and nitrogen. The nitrogen used in the process is extracted from **the air** and the hydrogen is extracted from **natural gas**.

The conditions used for the Haber Process are a temperature of **450 °C**, a pressure of **200 atm** and in the presence of an **iron** catalyst.

1 a) At dynamic equilibrium, the rates of the forward and the backward reaction are equal/the same *[1 mark]* and the relative concentrations of the reactants and products at equilibrium do not change *[1 mark]*.
  b) A closed system is a system where none of the reactants or products can escape *[1 mark]*.
  c) The concentration of the reactants should be increased *[1 mark]*.
2 a) That the reaction is reversible / can go both ways *[1 mark]*.
  b) The system has reached equilibrium *[1 mark]*. This mixture contains both blue copper(II) ions and the yellow copper compound, so the colours mix to form green *[1 mark]*.

Pages 146-148 — Le Chatelier's Principle

1 a) The system will try to counteract that change *[1 mark]*.
  b) The temperature *[1 mark]* and the concentration of the reactants / products *[1 mark]*.
2 a) The concentration of the products is greater than the concentration of the reactants *[1 mark]*.
  b) D *[1 mark]*
  c) Russell. Decreasing the pressure will move the position of equilibrium to the left / to the side with more moles of gas / favour the backward reaction *[1 mark]*. This will decrease the yield of methanol *[1 mark]*.
3 a) At higher temperatures there will be more ICl and less ICl_3 *[1 mark]*. This is because the reverse reaction is endothermic, so heating the mixture moves the equilibrium to the left *[1 mark]*.
  b) There would be more ICl_3 and less ICl *[1 mark]* because the increase in pressure causes the equilibrium position to move to the side with the fewest molecules of gas *[1 mark]*.
4 a) At higher temperature there's more product / (brown) NO_2 in the equilibrium mixture *[1 mark]*. This suggests that the equilibrium has moved to the right *[1 mark]*, so the forward reaction is endothermic *[1 mark]*.

From Le Chatelier's principle, you know that increasing the temperature will favour the endothermic reaction (since the equilibrium position will move to oppose the change). So the forward reaction must be endothermic, as there's more NO_2 in the equilibrium mixture at higher temperatures.

  b) The mixture would go a darker brown *[1 mark]*, as the decrease in pressure causes the equilibrium to move to the side with the most molecules of gas *[1 mark]*, meaning more NO_2 is formed *[1 mark]*.
5 a) At time A, some of the sulfur trioxide was removed from the reaction, lowering the concentration present *[1 mark]*. As the reaction continued, more sulfur trioxide was produced, increasing the concentration present in the reaction *[1 mark]*.
  b) The forward reaction must be exothermic *[1 mark]*, as the equilibrium shifts to favour the reverse reaction in order to lower the temperature of the reaction *[1 mark]*.
  c) At time B, the pressure of the system was increased *[1 mark]*. The graph shows the concentration of SO_3 increasing and the concentration of SO_2 decreasing after this point, so the equilibrium has shifted in the direction of the side with fewer gas molecules *[1 mark]*.
  d)

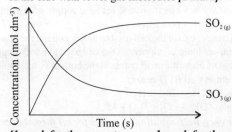

[1 mark for the correct curves, 1 mark for the correct labels]

At low pressure, the equilibrium will move towards the side of the reaction that has more molecules of gas (i.e. the products).

Section 14 — Groups in the Periodic Table

Page 149 — Group 1 — Alkali Metals

1 a)   B *[1 mark]*
  b)   The alkali metals all have one outer electron *[1 mark]*, so losing one electron gives them a +1 ion with a stable electronic structure/full outer shell *[1 mark]*.
2 a)   potassium hydroxide *[1 mark]*, hydrogen *[1 mark]*
  b)   Any two from: it would float around on the surface of the water / vigorous fizzing / it would decrease in size (as it melts and dissolves) / hydrogen gas produced by the reaction will ignite *[1 mark for each correct answer]*.
  c)   Rubidium is more reactive than potassium *[1 mark]* because the outer electron is further away from the nucleus / the atomic radius is larger *[1 mark]*. So, rubidium will react more violently with water than potassium / may explode when placed in water *[1 mark]*.

Pages 150-151 — Group 7 — Halogens

Warm-up
They are non-metals that exist as molecules of two atoms.
1 a)   damp blue litmus paper *[1 mark]*
  b)   chlorine *[1 mark]*
2 a) i) sodium bromide *[1 mark]*
   ii) potassium iodide *[1 mark]*
  b) $2Li + Cl_2 \rightarrow 2LiCl$
     [2 marks for all formulas correct and a correctly-balanced equation, otherwise 1 mark for correct formulas in an unbalanced equation.]
3 a) i) $H_2 + Cl_2 \rightarrow 2HCl$
     [2 marks for all formulas correct and a correctly-balanced equation, otherwise 1 mark for correct formulas in an unbalanced equation.]
   ii) red *[1 mark]* A hydrogen halide/hydrogen chloride forms an acidic solution when dissolved in water *[1 mark]*.
  b)   Fluorine *[1 mark]*. It is the only other halogen that is a gas at room temperature *[1 mark]*.
  c)   A red-brown *[1 mark]* liquid *[1 mark]*.
4 a)   The halogens have seven electrons in their outer shell *[1 mark]*. As you go further down the group additional shells are added / the outer electron is further away from the nucleus *[1 mark]*.
  b)   Both astatine and fluorine have 7 outer shell electrons so react in a similar way *[1 mark]*. So astatine will react with sodium to form sodium astatide *[1 mark]*. However, astatine will react more slowly than fluorine since reactivity decreases down the group *[1 mark]*.

Page 152 — Halogen Displacement Reactions

1 a)   chlorine water and sodium iodide solution:
     solution turns brown *[1 mark]*
     bromine water and sodium bromide solution:
     no reaction *[1 mark]*
  b)   Iodine is less reactive than bromine *[1 mark]*, so iodine cannot displace bromine from sodium bromide *[1 mark]*.
  c) i) $Cl_2 + 2NaBr \rightarrow Br_2 + 2NaCl$
     [1 mark for all reactants and products correct, 1 mark for equation being correctly balanced.]
   ii) During the reaction, the chlorine is reduced (it gains electrons) *[1 mark]* and the bromide ions are simultaneously oxidised (they lose electrons) *[1 mark]*.
  d)   Yes *[1 mark]*, as chlorine is more reactive than astatine *[1 mark]*.

Page 153 — Group 0 — Noble Gases

1   Argon has a full outer shell of electrons, giving it a stable electronic structure *[1 mark]*. It won't easily give up or gain electrons, making it inert *[1 mark]*. This means that it won't react with the metal filament in the light bulb *[1 mark]*.
2 a) i) A boiling point higher than −152 °C *[1 mark]*.
   ii) A density between 1.0 kg m⁻³ and 3.6 kg m⁻³ *[1 mark]*.
  b)   Higher, because the boiling points of the elements increase as you go down Group 0 *[1 mark]*.

Section 15 — Rates of Reaction and Energy Changes

Pages 154–156 — Reaction Rate Experiments

1 a)   Add the calcium carbonate to the hydrochloric acid in a conical flask and seal with a gas syringe *[1 mark]*. Immediately start the stopwatch and use the gas syringe to measure the volume of carbon dioxide produced *[1 mark]* at set time intervals until gas production stops *[1 mark]*.
  b)   E.g.

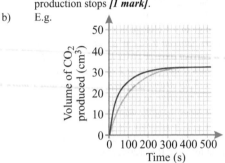

     [1 mark for your curve having a steeper gradient at the start. 1 mark for your curve finishing at the same volume of CO_2 as the original curve.]
  c)   B *[1 mark]*
2 a)   Remove the two solutions from the water bath and immediately mix the solutions in a conical flask *[1 mark]*. Place the flask over a black mark on a piece of paper *[1 mark]* and time how long it takes for the black mark to disappear through the sulfur precipitate *[1 mark]*.
  b) i) The reaction will have a lower rate *[1 mark]*.
   ii) E.g. the concentration of the acid/sodium thiosulfate / the volume of acid/sodium thiosulfate used / the depth of the acid/sodium thiosulfate *[1 mark for any sensible answer]*.
3 a)   The higher the concentration, the faster the rate of reaction *[1 mark]*. Reaction M has a curve of a steeper gradient / the reaction finishes sooner, which signifies a greater rate and so a higher concentration *[1 mark]*.
  b)

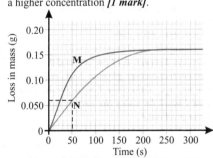

    change in y = 0.060   change in x = 50
    Gradient = change in y ÷ change in x
           = 0.060 ÷ 50 = **0.0012 g s⁻¹**
    [2 marks for correct answer, otherwise 1 mark for a correct equation to calculate the gradient.]

Pages 202-203 — Measuring Waves

1   Rod length = $\lambda \div 2$, so $\lambda = 2 \times 0.2 = 0.4$ m
     $v = f\lambda = 8500 \times 0.4 = $ **3400 m/s**
     [4 marks for correct answer, otherwise 1 mark for correct calculation of wavelength, 1 mark for correct equation, 1 mark for correct substitution]

2   a)   Any two from: e.g. the position of the dipper / the position of the cork when she starts timing / the depth of water in the tank / the equipment used.
     [2 marks — 1 mark for each correct answer]

   b)   i)   The result of the third trial is anomalous.
     $(12 + 11 + 11 + 14) \div 4 = $ **12**
     [3 marks for correct answer, otherwise 1 mark for identifying the anomalous result, 1 mark for correct method for calculating the average number of bobs]

     ii)   Frequency = number of bobs per second
     $12 \div 30 = $ **0.4 Hz**
     [2 marks for a correct answer, otherwise 1 mark for correct calculation.]

   c)   i)   wave speed = frequency × wavelength *[1 mark]*

     ii)   10 waves cover 0.18 m
     So 1 wavelength = $0.18 \div 10 = 0.018$ m
     $v = 12 \times 0.018 = 0.216 = $ **0.22 m/s (to 2 s.f.)**
     [3 marks for correct answer to correct number of significant figures, otherwise 1 mark for correct substitution, 1 mark for correct numerical value for wave speed.]

3   How to grade your answer:
     Level 0:   There is no relevant information. *[0 marks]*
     Level 1:   A simple method to find the speed of sound waves in air is partly outlined. The points made are basic and not linked together. *[1-2 marks]*
     Level 2:   A method to find the speed of sound in air is outlined in some detail. Some of the points made are linked together. *[3-4 marks]*
     Level 3:   A method to find the speed of sound waves in air is fully explained in detail. The points made are well-linked and the answer has a clear and logical structure. *[5-6 marks]*
     Here are some points your answer may include:
     Connect a signal generator to a speaker and set it to generate a sound of a specific frequency.
     Connect two microphones to an oscilloscope so that the waves detected at each microphone will be displayed as separate waveforms on the oscilloscope.
     Place the microphones next to each other in front of the speaker. At this point, the waveforms will be aligned with each other on the oscilloscope (i.e. peaks and troughs appear at the same point).
     Keeping both microphones directly in front of the speaker, slowly move one microphone away from the speaker, until the two wave-forms on the oscilloscope next become aligned.
     The microphones should now be located one wavelength of the sound apart.
     Measure this distance, λ, and note down the frequency of the sound generated, f.
     Use the formula $v = f\lambda$ to calculate the speed of sound, v.
     To get more accurate results the experiment can be repeated for different frequencies and a mean value calculated.

Page 204 — Wave Behaviour at Boundaries

Warm-up
wave is reflected — it bounces back off the material
wave is absorbed — it transfers all its energy to the material
wave is transmitted — it passes through the material

1   a)   E.g. an echo would be created *[1 mark]*
   b)   E.g. the black object would heat up *[1 mark]*
2   a)   40° *[1 mark]*
   b)   The material is (optically) denser than air *[1 mark]* because the refracted ray bends towards the normal *[1 mark]*.

Page 205 — Investigating Refraction

1   a)   E.g. A ray box creates a thin ray of light which is easy to trace
     [1 mark]
   b)

[1 mark for a correctly completed diagram]

   c)   10° *[1 mark]* (Allow between 9° and 11°)
   d)   Water *[1 mark]* as it has the largest angle of refraction *[1 mark]* which means it has bent the ray the least and so the change of speed of the ray is the smallest *[1 mark]*.

Pages 206-207 — Electromagnetic Waves

Warm-up
True, True, False
1   a)   From left to right: Infrared *[1 mark]*, X-rays. *[1 mark]*
   b)   Arrow must point to the left (i.e. from gamma rays to radio waves / from high energy to low energy) *[1 mark]*.
   c)   From left to right: yellow, green, blue, indigo
     [2 marks for all correct, 1 mark for 3 correct]
   d)   The nucleus *[1 mark]*
2   a)   As the frequency increases, so does the potential danger
     [1 mark].
   b)   Infrared — skin burns
     Microwaves — internal heating of cells
     X-rays — cell mutation and cancer
     [1 mark for all 3 correct]
   c)   Any two from: e.g. damage to surface cells of skin/skin cancer *[1 mark]* / damage to surface cells of eyes/eye conditions *[1 mark]*
3   a)   i)   Source: X-ray machine
     Observer: Photographic film/Radiation badge
     [1 mark for two sensible answers]
     ii)   Energy is transferred from the kinetic energy store of the electrons *[1 mark]* by radiation (the X-rays) to the chemical energy store of the photographic film *[1 mark]*.
   b)   E.g. infrared waves transferring energy from a heater's thermal energy store to the thermal energy store of a person *[1 mark]*.

Pages 208-211 — Uses of EM Waves

Warm-up
True, True, False, True.
1   a)   Ultraviolet — fluorescent lights
     Visible light — photography
     Infrared — security lights
     Radio waves — satellite communications
     [2 marks for all four correct, 1 mark for 3 correct]
   b)   Any two from: e.g. TV remotes / optical fibres / sending files between phones and laptops
     [2 marks — 1 mark for each correct answer]
   c)   B *[1 mark]*
2   a)   C *[1 mark]*
   b)   A UV light can be shone onto the stolen object which will cause the ink to glow/become visible *[1 mark]* and can be used to prove the object belongs to him *[1 mark]*.
   c)   E.g. marking bank notes *[1 mark]*
3   a)   X-rays are directed at the body part being imaged. A detector is placed behind the body. The X-rays are absorbed by bones *[1 mark]*, but transmitted by the rest of the body tissue/muscles *[1 mark]*. A negative image is formed with brighter areas where fewer X-rays get through, indicating the bones *[1 mark]*.
   b)   E.g. security scans at airports *[1 mark]*

Answers

4 a) It detects infrared radiation emitted by an object and converts this into an electrical signal which is displayed on a screen as an image *[1 mark]*. Different temperatures appear brighter/ as different colours, so you can build a thermal image of the surroundings *[1 mark]*.

b) When it is dark there is very little visible light for a normal camera to pick up so a hiding criminal could be hard to see *[1 mark]*. The criminal will be warmer than the surroundings and so will emit more infrared radiation *[1 mark]*. This will make them stand out from the surroundings if using an infrared camera *[1 mark]*.

5 a) The microwaves are absorbed by water molecules in the potato *[1 mark]*. This transfers energy to the water molecules, causing the water in the potato to heat up *[1 mark]*. The water molecules transfer the energy they have absorbed to the rest of the molecules in the potato (by conduction), cooking it *[1 mark]*.

b) The glass plate does not absorb any microwaves as it does not contain any water molecules *[1 mark]*. This means that it is only heated by (conduction from) the potato, so it doesn't get as hot as the potato *[1 mark]*.

6 a) An alternating current (a current made of oscillating charges) flows through walkie-talkie *[1 mark]*. Electrons in the walkie-talkie's aerial oscillate, producing radio waves *[1 mark]*. These radio waves travel through the air to the aerial of the second walkie-talkie, where they are absorbed *[1 mark]*. The energy carried by the radio waves is transferred to the electrons in the receiver aerial *[1 mark]*. This causes electrons in the aerial to oscillate *[1 mark]* which produces an alternating current in the second walkie-talkie *[1 mark]*.

b) How to grade your answer:

Level 0: There is no relevant information. *[0 marks]*

Level 1: There is a brief explanation of the differences between radio wave types used for broadcasting. The points made are basic and not linked together. *[1-2 marks]*

Level 2: There is some explanation of the differences between radio wave types used for broadcasting, including their different ranges and how this affects which broadcast can be heard. Some of the points made are linked together. *[3-4 marks]*

Level 3: There is a clear and detailed explanation of the differences between radio wave types used for broadcasting, including their different ranges and how this affects which broadcast can be heard. The points made are well-linked and the answer has a clear and logical structure. *[5-6 marks]*

Here are some points your answer may include:
FM radio is transmitted using very short wavelength radio waves. These radio waves can only be received while the receiver is in direct sight of the transmitter.
This is because these wavelengths are easily absorbed by obstacles, e.g. buildings, and cannot bend much around obstacles.
France is far away, so the signal cannot be received in France.
Long-wave radio waves can be transmitted over long distances. This is because long-wave radio waves bend around the curved surface of the Earth.
Long-wave radio waves can also bend around obstacles such as mountains.
Hence the signal can travel a long distance and be received in France.

Section 20 — Radioactivity

Page 212 — The Model of the Atom

Warm-up
1×10^{-10} m

1 a) The plum pudding model *[1 mark]*. This model describes an atom as a sphere of positive charge, with electrons spread throughout it *[1 mark]*.

b) E.g.:
Property: The atom is mostly made up of empty space / most of the atom's mass is concentrated at the centre in a tiny nucleus *[1 mark]*.
Observation: Most of the alpha particles they fired at the thin gold foil passed straight through *[1 mark]*.

2 a) Proton: (+)1 *[1 mark]*
Neutron: 0 *[1 mark]*

b) The protons and neutrons make up a central nucleus *[1 mark]* and the electrons orbit the nucleus *[1 mark]*.

c) 26 electrons *[1 mark]*. Protons and electrons have equal but opposite charges (and neutrons are neutral). As there are the same number of protons and neutrons in an atom, atoms are neutral *[1 mark]*.

Page 213 — Electron Energy Levels

Warm-up
In Bohr's atomic model, electrons orbit the nucleus at fixed distances called energy levels or shells.

1 a) An electron can move into a higher energy level / further from the nucleus, by absorbing electromagnetic radiation *[1 mark]*, and move into a lower energy level / closer to the nucleus, by emitting electromagnetic radiation *[1 mark]*.

b) Ion *[1 mark]*

c) +1 *[1 mark]*

2 As you get further away from a nucleus, the energy levels get closer together *[1 mark]*. So electrons falling to the first energy level have a greater change in energy than those falling to the second energy level *[1 mark]*. This means they release electromagnetic radiation with a higher energy *[1 mark]* and so a higher frequency is released when an electron falls to the first energy level *[1 mark]*.

Pages 214-215 — Isotopes and Nuclear Radiation

Warm-up
A — mass number, Z — atomic number, X — element symbol

1 a) Atoms with the same number of protons *[1 mark]* but different numbers of neutrons (in their nucleus) *[1 mark]*.

b) alpha, beta, gamma
[3 marks in total — 1 mark for each correct answer]

c) i) alpha *[1 mark]*
ii) E.g. a few centimetres *[1 mark]* because alpha particles are strongly ionising *[1 mark]*.

2 a) beta *[1 mark]*

b) Gamma *[1 mark]* because it is highly penetrating so it can travel through paper and aluminium *[1 mark]*. It can be absorbed by sheets of lead *[1 mark]*.

3 a) 23 *[1 mark]*
Remember that the nucleon number is another name for the mass number.

b) 23 − 11 = 12 neutrons *[1 mark]*
The number of neutrons is the difference between the mass number and the atomic number.

c) D *[1 mark]*
An isotope has the same number of protons (so the same atomic number), but a different number of neutrons (so a different mass number).

d) The atomic number of the neon isotope is lower, so there are fewer protons in the neon isotope's nucleus *[1 mark]*. So the charge on the neon isotope's nucleus is lower than the charge on the sodium isotope's nucleus *[1 mark]*.

Page 216 — Nuclear Equations

Warm-up
The atomic number decreases by two.
The mass number decreases by four.

1 a) It increases the positive charge on the nucleus / makes the nucleus 'more positive' *[1 mark]*.

b) No effect *[1 mark]*

2 a) The atomic numbers on each side are not equal *[1 mark]*.

b) $_{-1}^{0}e$ or $_{-1}^{0}\beta$ *[1 mark]*
The other particle must be a beta-minus particle, as this will balance the equation.

c) $^{226}_{88}\text{Ra} \longrightarrow {}^{222}_{86}\text{Rn} + {}^{4}_{2}\text{He}$

[3 marks in total — 1 mark for each correct nucleus or particle in standard notation]

You know that the mass number of the radium is 226 (that's what 'radium-226' means). You also know that an alpha particle is $^{4}_{2}\text{He}$, so you can find the mass and atomic numbers of radon by balancing the equation.

d) Rn-222 has 222 − 86 = 136 neutrons *[1 mark]*
2 alpha decays = 2 × 2 = 4 neutrons released *[1 mark]*
136 − 4 = **132** *[1 mark]*

Pages 217-218 — Half-life

1 a) E.g. the average time taken for the number of radioactive nuclei in an isotope to halve *[1 mark]*.

b) 75 s *[1 mark]*

You need to find the time it takes for the count rate to halve. For example, the initial count-rate is 60 cps. Half of this is 30 cps, which corresponds to 75 seconds on the time axis.

c) After 1 half-life, there will be 800 ÷ 2 = 400 undecayed nuclei remaining. After 2 half-lives, there will be
400 ÷ 2 = 200 undecayed nuclei remaining.
So 800 − 200 = **600** nuclei will have decayed.
[2 marks for correct answer, otherwise 1 mark for correctly calculating the number of decayed/undecayed nuclei after one half-life]

d) C *[1 mark]*

After 2 half-lives, there are 200 undecayed nuclei. The ratio is 200:800, which simplifies to 1:4. You don't even need the numbers to work out this ratio. For any radioactive isotope, after two half lives, the initial number of undecayed nuclei will have halved and then halved again. It will be one quarter of the original number, so the ratio is always 1:4.

2 a) Isotope 1 (it has the shortest half-life) *[1 mark]*.

b) Isotope 1 *[1 mark]*, because each isotope starts with the same number of nuclei, but isotope 1 has the shortest half-life, so more nuclei will decay per second *[1 mark]*.

For isotope 1, it takes 4 minutes for 10 000 nuclei to decay, but it takes 72 years for 10 000 nuclei of isotope 2 to decay and 5 years for 10 000 nuclei of isotope 3 to decay. The activity of isotope 1 quickly decreases, but it takes longer for isotope 2 and isotope 3's activity to decrease.

3 a) E.g.
After 1 half-life, the activity will be 8800 ÷ 2 = 4400 Bq.
After 2 half-lives, the activity will be 4400 ÷ 2 = 2200 Bq.
After 3 half-lives, the activity will be 2200 ÷ 2 = 1100 Bq.
So it will take **3 half-lives**.
[3 marks for correct answer, otherwise 1 mark for correct method, 1 mark for correct calculations]

b) 6 hours is the same as 3 half-lives
which means that 1 half-life is
6 hours ÷ 3 = **2 hours** *[1 mark]*.

4 a)

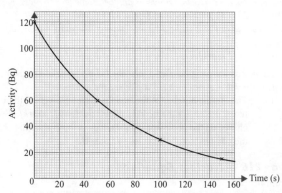

[1 mark for all points plotted correctly, 1 mark for smooth curve joining the points]

Start the graph at 120 Bq. After 50 s, this will have halved to 60 Bq. After another 50 s (i.e. 100 s altogether), it will have halved again, to 30 Bq. Plot these points, then join them up with a nice smooth curve.

b) 70 Bq (accept between 68 Bq and 72 Bq)
[1 mark for correct value from your graph]

c) From a), you know that the activity has dropped to 15 Bq in the first 150 s. 200 s is one more half-life after this.
After 200 s, 15 ÷ 2 = 7.5 = **8 Bq**
[2 marks — 1 mark for correct calculation of activity, 1 mark for correct activity to one significant figure]
E.g. radioactive decay is random *[1 mark]* and the effect of randomness on the results will be greater for lower activities *[1 mark]*.

Pages 219-220 — Background Radiation and Contamination

1 Any two from: e.g. rocks / space/cosmic rays / fallout from nuclear weapons
[2 marks — 1 mark for each correct answer]

2 a) Contamination is when unwanted radioactive particles get onto an object *[1 mark]*. Irradiation is when an object is exposed to radiation *[1 mark]*.

b) For irradiation: e.g. use shielding/stand behind barriers / work in a different room to the source / store the sample in a lead-lined box.
For contamination: e.g. wear gloves / handle the source with tongs / wear a protective suit or mask.
[2 marks in total — 1 mark for a correct measure for irradiation, 1 mark for a correct measure for contamination]

3 How to grade your answer:

Level 0: There is no relevant information. *[0 marks]*

Level 1: There is a brief explanation of the dangers of contamination or radiation. The points made are basic and not linked together. *[1-2 marks]*

Level 2: There is some explanation of the dangers and risks of contamination and radiation and a conclusion is given with some logical justification. Some of the points made are linked together. *[3-4 marks]*

Level 3: There is a clear and detailed explanation of the dangers and risks of contamination and radiation, used to justify the conclusion that the clockmaker should either be more concerned about contamination or irradiation. The points made are well-linked and the answer has a clear and logical structure. *[5-6 marks]*

Here are some points your answer may include:
Alpha particles are stopped by skin or thin paper.
Being irradiated won't make the clockmaker radioactive.
But irradiation may do some damage to his skin.
However, the radiation cannot penetrate his body and cause damage to his tissue or organs.
If the clockmaker's hands get contaminated with radium-226, he will be exposed to more alpha particles. Or he may accidentally ingest (eat) some.
Or if particles of the radium get into the air, he could breathe them in.
The radium will then decay whilst inside his body.
Alpha particles are strongly ionising.
This means that the alpha particles can do lots of damage to nearby tissue or organs.
So he should be more concerned about contamination.

4 a) E.g. the student's radioactive source could contribute to the count-rate recorded, but would not be present during the scientist's experiment, causing an overestimate in the background count-rate *[1 mark]*.

b) First, find the mean counts in 5 minutes.
Mean counts = (598 + 641 + 624) ÷ 3 *[1 mark]*
= 621 *[1 mark]*
To get count-rate in cps, divide by the number of seconds in 5 minutes.
mean count-rate = 621 ÷ (5 × 60) = **2.07 cps** *[1 mark]*

Alternatively, you could add the three counts together and divide by the number of seconds in fifteen minutes — i.e. combining the steps.

c) i) E.g. put the radioactive substance back into its storage case while replacing the Geiger-Muller tube / place a shielding barrier around the radioactive substance while replacing the Geiger-Muller tube *[1 mark]*.

ii) The scientist's results will be less valid, as changing the distance may change the count-rate detected / the distance between the substance and the Geiger-Muller tube was a control variable in the experiment *[1 mark]*, so the results won't be valid as a measure of only how the count-rate varies with time, and cannot be used to accurately calculate the half-life *[1 mark]*.

Section 21 — Forces and Energy

Page 221 — Energy Transfers and Systems

1   C *[1 mark]*

2   E.g.

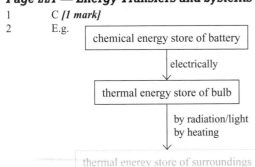

[1 mark for energy transferred electrically from battery, 1 mark for thermal energy store of bulb, 1 mark for energy transfer by radiation or heating from bulb]

3 a) i) $KE = \frac{1}{2}mv^2 = 0.5 \times 0.08 \times 7.00^2 = \textbf{1.96 J}$
    [3 marks for correct answer, otherwise 1 mark for correct equation, 1 mark for correct substitution]

   ii) Work done by gravitational force *[1 mark]*

  b) $\Delta GPE = mg\Delta h = 1.96$
    $\Delta h = 1.96 \div mg = 1.96 \div (0.08 \times 10) = \textbf{2.45 m}$
    [4 marks for correct answer, otherwise 1 mark for using correct equation, 1 mark for correct rearrangement, 1 mark for correctly substituting in all of the values]

Pages 222-224 — Work Done and Power

Warm-up

As a rubber ball falls, it experiences a <u>force</u> due to <u>gravity</u>. <u>Work</u> is done on the ball and <u>energy</u> is transferred from the ball's <u>gravitational potential</u> energy store to its <u>kinetic</u> energy store.

1   B *[1 mark]*

2 a) $t = 125 \times 60 = 7500$ seconds
    $P = E \div t$ so $E = Pt = 600 \times 7500 = 4\,500\,000 = \textbf{4500 kJ}$
    [4 marks for the correct answer, otherwise 1 mark for correct equation, 1 mark for the correct substitution, 1 mark for correct conversion to kJ]

  b)   Time taken $= 125 \times 60 = 7500$ seconds
    $P = E \div t = 3\,930\,000 \div 7500 = \textbf{524 W}$
    [2 marks for correct answer, otherwise 1 mark for correct substitution]

3 a) i)   Work done = force applied × distance moved in the direction of the force *[1 mark]*

   ii) $50 \times 15 = \textbf{750}$
    [2 marks for correct answer, otherwise 1 mark for correct substitution]

  b)   The temperature of the wheel increases *[1 mark]* because doing work causes some energy to be transferred to the thermal energy store of the wheel *[1 mark]*.

4 a)   Efficiency = useful energy transferred by the device ÷ total energy supplied to the device
    Power is the energy transferred per second, so in 1 s the old engine transfers 52 000 J usefully.
    Total energy supplied to the engine (in 1 second) = useful energy transferred by the engine ÷ efficiency
    $= 52\,000 \div 0.25 = 208\,000$ J

For the new engine:
Useful energy transferred by the engine (in 1 second)
= efficiency × total energy supplied to the engine
$= 0.30 \times 208\,000 = 62\,400$ J
So every second, the new engine outputs 62 400 J of energy. Power is energy per second, so the output power of the new engine is **62 400 W**.
[5 marks for correct answer, otherwise 1 mark for correct efficiency equation, 1 mark for finding total energy supplied to the engine, 1 mark for converting efficiency to a decimal, 1 mark for correctly substituting into the efficiency equation at any point]

You could also have put power = energy ÷ time straight into the efficiency equation to get efficiency = power output ÷ power input and then used this for your calculations.

  b)   It will decrease the time *[1 mark]* because more energy is being transferred to the kinetic energy store of the car per second *[1 mark]*. This decreases the time needed for enough energy to be in the car's kinetic energy store to cause it to travel at 20 m/s *[1 mark]*.

5 a)   How to grade your answer:
    Level 0: There is no relevant information. *[No marks]*
    Level 1: There are some relevant points, but the answer is unclear. There is some description of the experimental set-up, but the details are unclear. There are explanations of the measurements and calculations that should be made, but they may be incomplete. The points made are basic and not linked together. *[1 to 2 marks]*
    Level 2: There is a more detailed description of the experimental set-up, and there is some explanation of the measurements and calculations that should be made. There is also an explanation of how the student can ensure validity in the results, but it may be incomplete. Some of the points made are linked together. *[3-4 marks]*
    Level 3: There is a clear and detailed description of how the equipment listed should be set up and used to carry out an experiment safely. There are full explanations of the measurements and calculations that should be made to determine the useful output power of the motor. There is also a full explanation of how the student can ensure validity in the results. The points are well-linked and the answer has a clear and logical structure. *[5 to 6 marks]*

Here are some points your answer may include:
Securely attach the clamp stand to the edge of a bench/worktop.
Set up the motor so that it is connected to the circuit, and clamped to the clamp stand. Make sure there is at least a metre of clear space between the motor and the ground.
Attach one end of the string to the axle of the motor (so that it will wind around the axle when the motor spins).
Attach the other end of the string to the 1 kg mass securely, so it hangs from the string.
Set up the ruler to stand vertically, parallel to the string.
Attach a marker to the bottom of the mass so that the distance moved by the mass can be accurately measured.
Turn on the motor, and, using the stopwatch, record the time taken for the motor to lift the mass through a fixed vertical height, e.g. 60 cm, measured by the metre ruler.
Repeat this at least two more times, and calculate an average value of the time taken from the three results.
Use the height to calculate the change in gravitational potential energy of the mass, and so the useful energy transferred by the motor.
Calculate the useful power by dividing this value of energy by the average value of time taken.
Valid results are repeatable and reproducible and answer the original question. To ensure the results are valid, the student must make the experiment a fair test by identifying the control variables and keeping them constant. E.g. the same equipment should be used for all repeats, and the same person should operate the stopwatch each time.

Answers

314

b) i) 0.01 s *[1 mark]*.

   ii) The errors in the student's time measurements will mostly be caused by human error and her reaction time *[1 mark]*. Human reaction times are typically much larger than the smallest time measured by the stopwatch (0.2-0.6 s compared to 0.01 s) *[1 mark]*.

Pages 225-226 — Forces

1 a) i) E.g. a force that acts between objects that are touching *[1 mark]*.

   ii) Any two from: e.g. friction / normal contact force / air resistance *[2 marks — 1 mark for each correct answer]*

 b) E.g. gravitational force / magnetic force / electrostatic force *[1 mark]*

2 C *[1 mark]*

3

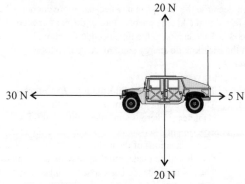

[1 mark for correct directions of forces, 1 mark for arrows drawn to scale]

4 a)

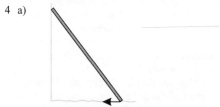

[1 mark for correct arrow length (same as 30 N arrow length), 1 mark for correct direction]

 b) 100 N *[1 mark]*

As the ladder isn't moving, there must be a resultant force of zero acting on it. This means that the weight of the ladder must equal the vertical force between the ladder and the ground.

5 a)

Magnet A   Magnet B

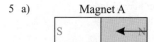 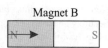

[1 mark for correct arrow length (same as the arrow on magnet B), 1 mark for correct direction]

 b) E.g. the magnetic fields of the two magnets interacting *[1 mark]*.

 c) Both arrows need to be longer (to indicate the stronger interaction) *[1 mark]*. The arrows need to be the same size as each other *[1 mark]*.

The repulsion forces between the magnets are an interaction pair — so they are always equal in size but act in the opposite direction to each other.

Pages 227-228 — Forces and Vector Diagrams

Warm-up

Horizontal component = 4 N

Vertical component = 3 N

1 a) 1 cm = 100 N *[1 mark]*

 b)

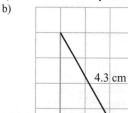

4.3 cm

1 cm = 100 N, so 4.3 cm = 4.3 × 100 = 430 N

Magnitude = **430 N** (accept between 420 N and 440 N)

[1 mark for correct construction of resultant force, 1 mark for correct magnitude]

2 E.g.

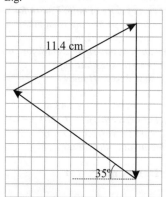

11.4 cm

35°

Scale for drawing above: 1 cm = 50 N

Length of 620 N force: 620 ÷ 50 = 12.4 cm

Length of 610 force: 610 ÷ 50 = 12.2 cm

Length of force X = 11.4 cm

11.4 × 50 = 570 N

Magnitude of force X = **570 N** (accept between 565 and 575)

Direction = **062 °** (accept between 61 and 63 °)

[1 mark for using a sensible scale, 1 mark for correctly drawing a closed shape, 1 mark for vector arrows the correct length and in the correct direction, 1 mark for correct magnitude of force X, 1 mark for direction of force as a bearing]

Section 22 — Electricity and Circuits

Page 229 — Current and Circuits

Warm-up

Current is the rate of flow of electric charge (electrons) around a circuit. A current will flow around a circuit if the circuit is closed and there is a source of potential difference. The current flowing through a component increases when the potential difference across it increases or when the resistance of the component decreases.

1 B *[1 mark]*

2 a) charge = current × time = 3.5 × 120 = **420 C**

 [3 marks for correct answer, otherwise 1 mark for using the correct equation, 1 mark for substituting in correct values]

 b) Rearrange charge = current × time for time:

 time = charge ÷ current = 770 ÷ 3.5 = **220 s**

 [3 marks for correct answer, otherwise 1 mark for rearranging charge equation for time, 1 mark for substituting in the correct values]

Page 230 — *Potential Difference and Resistance*

Warm-up

True, False, True

1 a) $E = Q \times V$, so
   $Q = E \div V = 276\,000 \div 230 = \mathbf{1200\ C}$
   [3 marks for correct answer, otherwise 1 mark for rearranging energy transferred equation for charge,
   1 mark for correctly substituting in the values]

   b) $E = Q \times V = 1000 \times 230 = 230\,000 = \mathbf{230\ kJ}$
   [2 marks for correct answer, otherwise 1 mark for correctly substituting in the values]

2 a) $V = IR$ so $R = V \div I$
   $R = 18 \div 3 = \mathbf{6\ \Omega}$
   [4 marks for correct answer, otherwise 1 mark for correctly rearranging the equation for resistance, 1 mark for substituting in the correct values, 1 mark for correct value, or 1 mark for correct unit]

   b) When current flows through the resistor, electrons collide with the ions in the lattice of the resistor *[1 mark]*. This transfers energy to the ions *[1 mark]* causing them to vibrate more and causing the resistor to heat up *[1 mark]*. The more the ions vibrate, the harder it is for the electrons to pass through the lattice, so the current decreases *[1 mark]*.

Page 231 — *Investigating Components*

1 a) D *[1 mark]*

   b)

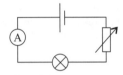

   [1 mark for an ammeter anywhere in series on the circuit]

2   How to grade your answer:
   Level 0:   There is no relevant information. *[0 marks]*
   Level 1:   There is a brief description of a method to investigate the resistance of the diode. The points made are basic and not linked together.
   [1-2 marks]
   Level 2:   There is a description of a method to investigate the resistance of the diode. There is some discussion of accuracy and repeatability. Some of the points made are linked together.
   [3-4 marks]
   Level 3:   There is a clear and detailed description of a method to investigate the resistance of the diode. The answer includes a full discussion of accuracy and repeatability. The points made are well-linked and the answer has a clear and logical structure.
   [5-6 marks]
   Here are some points your answer may include:
   The student should change the output potential difference of the power supply.
   For each setting of the power supply he should record the potential difference across the diode and the current through the circuit.
   To make his results more accurate and repeatable, he should take repeated readings of current and potential difference for each setting of the power supply, and calculate an average.
   He should allow the circuit to cool down between readings, as if the circuit starts to heat up it could interfere with the accuracy and repeatability of his results.
   He should plot the average potential difference and current values on a graph of current against potential difference, then draw a line of best fit.
   The resistance can be found for any potential difference by reading off the value of current from the line of best fit for that potential difference and then using the equation of resistance = potential difference ÷ current.

Page 232 — *Circuit Devices*

Warm-up

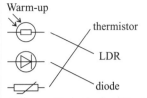

1 a) The resistance decreases *[1 mark]*.

   b) E.g. temperature detectors in thermostats/car engines *[1 mark]*.

2 a) B *[1 mark]*

   b) E.g. when the current increases, so does the temperature of the filament *[1 mark]*. This makes the resistance increase, so the graph is curved *[1 mark]*.

Pages 233-235 — *Series and Parallel Circuits*

1   A *[1 mark]*

2   E.g.

   [1 mark for using the correct symbols for an LDR and a cell, 1 mark for correctly drawing the LDRs in parallel]

3 a) $10 + 30 = \mathbf{40\ \Omega}$ *[1 mark]*

   b) $V = IR = 0.075 \times 30 = \mathbf{2.25\ V}$
   [3 marks for a correct answer, otherwise 1 mark for quoting the correct equation, 1 mark for substituting in the correct values]

4   How to grade your answer:
   Level 0:   There is no relevant information. *[0 marks]*
   Level 1:   There is a brief explanation about the effect of adding resistors in series or parallel. The points made are basic and not linked together.
   [1-2 marks]
   Level 2:   There is a comparison between adding resistors in series and parallel and an explanation of their effects. Some of the points made are linked together. *[3-4 marks]*
   Level 3:   A logical and detailed comparison is given, explaining why adding resistors in series increases the total resistance but adding them in parallel reduces it. The points made are well-linked and the answer has a clear and logical structure. *[5-6 marks]*
   Here are some points your answer may include:
   In series, resistors share the potential difference from the power source.
   The more resistors that are in series, the lower the potential difference across each one, and so the lower the current through each resistor (as $V = IR$).
   Current is the same all around a series circuit, so adding a resistor will decrease the current for the whole circuit.
   A decrease in total current means an increase in total resistance.
   In parallel, all resistors have the same potential difference as the source.
   Adding another resistor in parallel (forming another circuit loop) increases the current flowing in the circuit, as there are more paths for the current to flow through.
   An increase in total current means a decrease in total resistance (because $V = IR$).

5 a) Find the equivalent resistance of the circuit:
   potential difference = current × resistance so
   resistance = potential difference ÷ current = $12 \div 0.25 = 48\ \Omega$
   This is the resistance of both bulbs, so divide by 2: $48 \div 2 = \mathbf{24\ \Omega}$
   [3 marks for the correct answer, otherwise 1 mark for rearranging the equation for resistance, 1 mark for using this to correctly calculate the equivalent resistance of the circuit]

   b) i) First find the current through the circuit branch with bulb 3:
   potential difference = current × resistance, so
   current = potential difference ÷ resistance = $12 \div 24 = 0.5\ A$
   0.25 A is still flowing through the branch with bulbs 1 and 2.

Then find the current through ammeter by adding the currents flowing through each branch:

current = 0.25 + 0.5 = **0.75 A**

[2 marks for correct answer, otherwise 1 mark for calculating the current for the branch with bulb 3]

The current flowing through the branch with bulbs 1 and 2 on it doesn't change when bulb 3 is added, as the resistance of this branch and the potential difference across it don't change.

    ii) Because the potential difference across bulb 3 is the same as the source potential difference, but bulbs 1 and 2 share the source potential difference *[1 mark]*, so the current through bulb 3 is higher *[1 mark]*.

  c) i) The current through the ammeter decreases *[1 mark]*.

    ii) The brightness of bulbs 1 and 2 doesn't change *[1 mark]*. Bulb 3 gets dimmer *[1 mark]*.

  d) Because the bulbs may not have been identical *[1 mark]*. Because the bulbs may have got hotter as the experiment went on, which would increase their resistance *[1 mark]*.

Page 236 — Energy in Circuits

1   D *[1 mark]*

2 a) The heating element *[1 mark]*.

  b) In the wires / in the motor *[1 mark]*.

  c) The longer the hairdryer is on for, the more the motor/wires heat up *[1 mark]*. This increases the resistance of the wires/ motor *[1 mark]*, meaning less energy is transferred usefully *[1 mark]*.

3 a) $E = I \times V \times t$

so $t = \dfrac{E}{I \times V}$ = 355 000 ÷ (12 × 230) = 128.623...

    = **129 s (to the nearest second)**

[3 marks for correct answer, otherwise 1 mark for correctly rearranging the equation for time, 1 mark for calculating a value of 128.623...s]

  b) E.g. that the kettle was 100% efficient / that all the energy transferred to the kettle was used heating the water / that no energy was transferred to heating the wires/surroundings *[1 mark]*.

Page 237 — Power in Circuits

1 a) $E = P \times t = 50 \times 20 = $ **1000 J**

[3 marks for correct answer, otherwise 1 mark for using the correct equation, 1 mark for correctly substituting the values into the equation]

  b) The power of the car is higher *[1 mark]*. So more energy is transferred away from the chemical energy store of the battery per second *[1 mark]*.

2 a) $P = I \times V$

so $I = P \div V = 75 \div 230 = 0.3260...$ = **0.33 A (to 2 s.f.)**

[3 marks for the correct answer rounded to 1 or 2 significant figures, otherwise 1 mark for rearranging the equation for current, 1 mark for calculating a value of 0.3260... A]

  b) $P = I^2 \times R$ so $R = \dfrac{P}{I^2} = 2.5 \div 0.50^2 = $ **10 Ω**

[3 marks for correct answer, otherwise 1 mark for rearranging the equation for resistance, 1 mark for substituting in the correct values]

  c) i) model A *[1 mark]*

    ii) Because it is very noisy *[1 mark]* which means it may be transferring a lot of energy away as sound, making it less efficient *[1 mark]*.

Pages 238-239 — Electricity in the Home

Warm-up

describes the current supplied by a battery — direct current

produced by a voltage that constantly changes direction — alternating current

describes the current supplied by the UK mains — alternating current

produced by a voltage with a constant direction — direct current

1 a) 230 V, 50 Hz *[1 mark]*

  b) i) Live: brown
Neutral: blue
Earth: green and yellow
[2 marks for all three correct, otherwise 1 mark for two correct]

    ii)

Wires	Potential difference / V
Live wire and neutral wire	230
Neutral wire and earth wire	0
Earth wire and live wire	230

[1 mark for each correct row]

2   No, the radio won't work *[1 mark]*. A closed loop has been formed, where current from the live wire is carried away by the neutral wire *[1 mark]*, so no (or very little) current will flow through the radio *[1 mark]*.

3 a) To stop an electric current from flowing out of the live wire and potentially causing an electric shock (i.e. for safety) *[1 mark]*. To make it easy to identify the live wire *[1 mark]*.

  b) The man has an electric potential of 0 V *[1 mark]* and the wire has an electric potential (of 230 V) so a potential difference exists between them *[1 mark]*. This causes a current to flow through the man *[1 mark]*.

  c) Yes *[1 mark]*. Although there is no current flowing when it is switched off, there is still a potential difference in the live wire inside the socket *[1 mark]*. Touching it could cause a current to flow through you to the Earth *[1 mark]*.

Page 240 — Fuses and Earthing

1 a) To protect the wiring of the house and prevent fires in the event of a fault *[1 mark]*.

  b) Because pennies won't melt like a fuse wire in the event of a current surge, so the circuit won't be broken *[1 mark]*.

  c) Advantage: e.g. circuit breakers break the circuit more quickly than fuses / circuit breakers are easier to reset that fuses *[1 mark]*.
Disadvantage: e.g. circuit breakers are more expensive than fuses *[1 mark]*.

2 a) If the live wire comes loose and touches the metal, a large current will flow through the fuse, the live wire and the earth wire *[1 mark]*. This current melts the thin wire in the fuse *[1 mark]*, cutting off the electricity supply to the device *[1 mark]*.

  b) The fuse needs to be rated slightly higher than the normal operating current of the device *[1 mark]*, and the electric heater has a higher operating current than the clock radio *[1 mark]*.

Section 23 — Magnetic Fields

Pages 241-242 — Magnets and Magnetic Fields

Warm-up

T, F, T

1 a) C *[1 mark]*

  b)

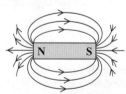

[1 mark for at least two lines between the north and south poles, 1 mark for at least three lines at each pole, 1 mark for at least one arrow in the correct direction with no arrows in the incorrect direction]

  c) i) E.g. a uniform field has the same strength everywhere / the field lines are parallel and equally spaced *[1 mark]*

    ii)

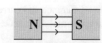

[1 mark for at least three straight, evenly spaced field lines, 1 mark for at least one arrow in the right direction with no arrows in the incorrect direction]

2   A force is acting on both magnets (due to their interacting magnetic fields) *[1 mark]*. This force is repulsive — the magnetic field lines of both objects are travelling away from each other *[1 mark]*. So the two objects move away from each other *[1 mark]*.

3 a) E.g. the needle of a compass points in the direction of the magnetic field it is in *[1 mark]*. Put the magnet on a sheet of paper and place a compass near to it. Mark where the north pole of the compass is pointing *[1 mark]*. Move the compass so its south pole is next to the mark, and again mark where the north pole of the compass is pointing. Repeat this until you've moved the compass around the entire magnet *[1 mark]*. Join up these marks to create a diagram of the magnetic field lines *[1 mark]*.

b) It would point north *[1 mark]* because it is aligning itself with the magnetic field of the Earth *[1 mark]*.

Page 243 — Permanent and Induced Magnets

1 a) E.g. a permanent magnet produces its own magnetic field at all times *[1 mark]*. An induced magnet only produces a magnetic field when it is close to another magnet *[1 mark]*.

b) Any two from: e.g. iron / steel / cobalt / nickel *[2 marks — 1 mark for each correct answer]*

c) E.g. cranes in scrapyards *[1 mark]* use induced electromagnets to pick up, move and put down scrap metal *[1 mark]*.

2 a) The block of cobalt becomes an induced magnet when it is placed in the magnetic field of the bar magnet *[1 mark]*. The magnetic field of the cobalt then makes the paperclip an induced magnet *[1 mark]*, which causes a force of attraction between the paperclip and the cobalt *[1 mark]*.

b) When the bar magnet is removed, the cobalt will quickly demagnetise *[1 mark]*, so the paperclip will become unstuck *[1 mark]*.

Pages 244-245 — Electromagnetism and the Motor Effect

Warm-up

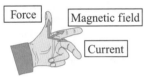

1 a) C *[1 mark]*

Use Fleming's left-hand rule here. Point your first finger in the direction of the field (i.e. from the north pole to the south pole of the magnets). Point your second finger in the direction of the current (shown in the diagram). Your thumb will then show the direction of motion of the wire.

b) The current in the wire creates its own magnetic field *[1 mark]* which interacts with the magnetic field between the poles of the magnets (which results in a force) *[1 mark]*.

c) E.g. the size of the current going through the wire / the strength of the magnetic field that the wire is in / the length of wire inside the magnetic field. *[3 marks — 1 mark for each correct answer]*

2 a)

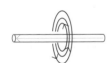

[1 mark for concentric circles around the wire, 1 mark for at least one arrow showing the direction of the field]

b) The direction of the field will also be reversed *[1 mark]*.

c) E.g. increase the current *[1 mark]*.

3 $F = BIl$ so $B = F \div Il$
$B = 1.2 \div (0.4 \times 0.75) = \mathbf{4}$
Unit = **T** or **N/Am**
[4 marks for correct answer, otherwise 1 mark for rearranging, 1 mark for correct substitution, 1 mark for correct numerical value, 1 mark for the correct unit]

Pages 246-247 — Solenoids and Electromagnetic Induction

Warm-up
T, F, T, F

1 C *[1 mark]*

2 a) E.g. a magnet which can be controlled (turned on and off) by an electric current *[1 mark]*.

b) i) E.g. the magnetic field is strong *[1 mark]* and almost uniform *[1 mark]*.

ii) E.g. the magnetic field is weak *[1 mark]* and is a similar shape to that of a bar magnet *[1 mark]*.

3 a) Alternating current *[1 mark]*. As he moves the magnet in, the changing magnetic field induces a potential difference, and so current, in the coil in one direction *[1 mark]*. As he moves it out again, it induces a potential difference, and so current, in the opposite direction *[1 mark]*.

b) Increase the speed that the magnet is moved / use a stronger magnet / have more turns per unit length on the coil. *[3 marks — 1 mark for each correct answer]*

4 a) By putting a block of iron in the centre of the solenoid *[1 mark]*.

b) Repelled *[1 mark]*, because the direction of the current means that the left-hand end of the solenoid acts as a north pole *[1 mark]*, and like poles repel *[1 mark]*.

Pages 248-250 — Transformers

Warm-up

Transformers consist of two coils of wire, wrapped around an <u>iron</u> core. Transformers can change the size of <u>alternating</u> potential differences. <u>Step-down</u> transformers decrease the output potential difference. <u>Step-up</u> transformers decrease the output current.

1 $V_p \times I_p = V_s \times I_s$ so $I_s = (V_p \times I_p) \div V_s$
$I_s = (30.0 \times 20.0) \div 40.0 = \mathbf{15\ A}$
[3 marks for correct answer, otherwise 1 mark for correct rearrangement, 1 mark for correct substitution]

2 How to grade your answer:

Level 0: There is no relevant information. *[No marks]*

Level 1: There is a brief description of how electromagnetic induction can induce a potential difference. The points made are basic and not linked together. *[1-2 marks]*

Level 2: There is a more detailed description of how electromagnetic induction in transformers can induce a potential difference. Some of the points made are linked together. *[3-4 marks]*

Level 3: There is a clear detailed description of how electromagnetic induction is used in transformers to induce a potential difference. There is an explanation as to how the increased number of turns leads to an increased output potential difference. The points made are well-linked and the answer has a clear and logical structure. *[5-6 marks]*

Here are some points your answer may include:
A step-up transformer has two coils wrapped around a metal (usually iron) core.
Iron is used because it is easy to magnetise.
When a current flows through a wire, it produces a magnetic field around the wire.
The direction of this magnetic field depends on the direction of the current, so when the current is alternating, the magnetic field produced also alternates.
So an alternating current flowing through the primary coil of the transformer creates an alternating magnetic field in the metal core of the transformer.
As the magnetic field in the metal core is alternating, the magnetic field across the secondary coil is always changing. This change in magnetic field causes a potential difference to be induced in the secondary coil.
In a step-up transformer, there are more turns on the secondary coil than there are on the primary coil.
This means that the potential difference induced in the secondary coil is larger than the potential difference across the primary coil.

3 a) Transformer A: step-up transformer *[1 mark]*
Transformer B: step-down transformer *[1 mark]*

b) In the opposite direction to the (changing) magnetic field that caused it *[1 mark]*.

c) How to grade your answer:

Level 0: There is no relevant information. *[No marks]*

Level 1: There is a brief description of an advantage of using transformers or high-voltage cables. The points made are basic and not linked together. *[1-2 marks]*

Level 2: There is a more detailed description of how transferring power at a high voltage results in a lower current and the advantages of this. Some of the points made are linked together. *[3-4 marks]*

Level 3: There is a clear detailed description of the advantages of using transformers and high-voltage cables, as well as correct equations being used to support the answer. The points made are well-linked and the answer has a clear and logical structure. *[5-6 marks]*

Here are some points your answer may include:
The national grid needs to transfer a lot of energy each second, so the power transmitted is very high.
Power is the rate of doing work/transferring energy.
$P = E \div t$
Power = current × potential difference / $P = IV$
So for a large output power you need either a large current or a large potential difference.
A high current causes energy to be wasted as it heats the cables.
Using a step-up transformer increases the potential difference of the output electricity.
So increasing the output p.d. reduces the output current.
This reduces the power lost / This makes the national grid more efficient.

4 a) E.g. if the exposed wire came into contact with the iron core, it could cause electricity to flow through the core, leading to inaccurate results *[1 mark]*.
The exposed wire could cause an electric shock *[1 mark]*.

b) E.g.

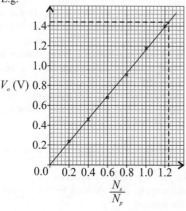

$$\text{gradient} = \frac{\text{change in } y}{\text{change in } x} = \frac{1.44 - 0}{1.24 - 0} \text{ [1 mark]}$$
$$= 1.1612...$$
$$= \textbf{1.2 V (to 2 s.f.)} \text{ [1 mark]}$$

c) The results do agree with this relationship. E.g. rearranging the relationship to $V_o = V_i \frac{N_s}{N_p}$ and comparing it to the equation of a straight line, it can be seen that a graph of V_o against $\frac{N_s}{N_p}$ should give a straight line through the origin, with a gradient equal to V_i *[1 mark]*. The graph in Figure 3 does pass through the origin *[1 mark]*, and it has a constant gradient which is equal to 1.2 V to 2 significant figures, which is equal to V_i, so it does agree with the relationship *[1 mark]*.

Section 24 — Matter

Pages 251-252 — Density

1 a) i) $\rho = m \div V$ *[1 mark]*
   ii) $\rho = 10\ 000 \div 0.5 = \textbf{20 000 kg/m}^3$
       [2 marks for correct answer, otherwise 1 mark for correct substitution]

b) The density is the same for the whole block, so $\rho = 20\ 000 \text{ kg/m}^3$
    $\rho = m \div V$ so $m = \rho \times V = 20\ 000 \times 0.02 = \textbf{400 kg}$
    [2 marks for correct answer, otherwise 1 mark for correct substitution]

2   volume = area × length = $0.050 \times 0.40 = 0.02 \text{ m}^3$
    $\rho = m \div V = 90.0 \div 0.02 = \textbf{4500 kg/m}^3$
    [3 marks for correct answer, otherwise 1 mark for calculating the volume of the bar, 1 mark for correct substitution into equation for density]

3   $\rho = m \div V$
    1 ml of water = 1 cm³
    A: $\rho = 5.7 \div 0.30 = 19 \text{ g/cm}^3$. So A is gold.
    B: $\rho = 2.7 \div 0.60 = 4.5 \text{ g/cm}^3$. So B is titanium.
    C: $\rho = 3.0 \div 0.30 = 10 \text{ g/cm}^3$. So C is silver.
    [5 marks for correct answer, otherwise 1 mark for stating 1 ml = 1 cm³, 1 mark for correct substitutions and 1 mark for each correct conclusion]

4   Measure the mass (m_1) of the object using the mass balance *[1 mark]*. Fill the bottle with a liquid of a known density. Measure the mass of the filled bottle (m_2) *[1 mark]*. Empty the bottle and place the object inside it. Fill it with the same liquid as before. Measure the mass of the bottle again (m_3) *[1 mark]*. Calculate the mass of the liquid displaced by the object ($m_2 - [m_3 - m_1]$) *[1 mark]* then use this to calculate the volume of the liquid displaced from $V = m \div \rho$, where ρ is the density of the liquid, (which equals the volume of the object) *[1 mark]*. Use this volume and the mass of the object to calculate its density using $\rho = m \div V$ *[1 mark]*.

Pages 253-254 — Kinetic Theory and States of Matter

Warm-up
From left to right: liquid, solid, gas

1   condensation — gas to liquid
    sublimation — solid to gas
    evaporation — liquid to gas
    [1 mark for all 3 correct]

2 a) C *[1 mark]*

b) There is a smaller mass (and so fewer particles) in a given volume of ice than of water *[1 mark]*. So the water molecules are further apart in ice than they are in liquid water *[1 mark]*.
Substances are usually more dense as a solid than as a liquid, but water is an exception to this.

3 a) It has evaporated/it has become water vapour *[1 mark]*.

b) The total mass stays the same *[1 mark]* because all of the particles are still in the flask/its a closed system *[1 mark]*.

4   As the water is heated, energy is transferred from its thermal energy store to the thermal energy store of the methanol *[1 mark]*. This means the methanol particles have more energy in their kinetic energy stores *[1 mark]*, so will move around more — causing the methanol to increase in volume and move the piston *[1 mark]*. As energy is continuously being transferred to them, some particles gain enough energy to overcome their attraction to each other *[1 mark]* and some of the methanol changes state into a gas *[1 mark]*.

Pages 255-256 — Specific Heat Capacity

Warm-up

The energy needed to raise 1 kg of a substance by 1 °C.

1 a) i) The time taken for the liquid to heat *[1 mark]*.
The mass of the liquid *[1 mark]*.

ii) Calculate the change in temperature by subtracting the temperature before from the temperature after *[1 mark]*. Calculate the change in thermal energy using energy transferred = current × potential difference × time *[1 mark]*. Calculate specific heat capacity by rearranging change in thermal energy = mass × specific heat capacity × change in temperature *[1 mark]*.

b) $\Delta Q = mc\Delta\theta$ so $c = \Delta Q \div m\Delta\theta$
$$= 6000 \div (0.3 \times 10)$$
Specific heat capacity = **2000 J/kg °C**
[3 marks for correct answer, otherwise 1 mark for rearranging, 1 mark for correct substitution]

2 a) Yes, he is correct. The foam will serve as insulation, which will reduce the transfer of energy away from the block while it is being heated *[1 mark]*. This means the student's energy measurements will more accurately reflect the amount of energy that is transferred to the block and causes an increase in temperature *[1 mark]*.

b) Material C has the highest specific heat capacity *[1 mark]*. E.g. The higher the specific heat capacity of a material, the more energy is required to increase the temperature of 1 kg of the material by 1 °C *[1 mark]*. Material C had the smallest increase in temperature when the same amount of energy was transferred to the same mass of each material, so it must have the highest specific heat capacity *[1 mark]*.

You could also have answered this question using the specific heat capacity equation. $\Delta Q = mc\Delta\theta$, so the gradient of the graph is equal to $\frac{1}{mc}$. Since m is the same for all of the materials, this means the line with the shallowest gradient shows the highest specific heat capacity.

c) Valid results are repeatable and reproducible. To confirm that his results are repeatable, the student should repeat the experiment with the same method, and check that he gets very similar results *[1 mark]*. To confirm his results are reproducible, he should repeat the experiment using different equipment and/ or a different experimental method, and check that he gets very similar results *[1 mark]*.

Pages 257-258 — Specific Latent Heat

1 D *[1 mark]*

2 a) The amount of energy required to change the state of one kilogram of a substance with no change in temperature *[1 mark]*.

b) E.g. specific heat capacity is the energy needed to cause a temperature rise without causing a change of state, but specific latent heat is the energy needed to cause a change of state, where the temperature remains constant *[1 mark]*.

c) −2 °C *[1 mark]*

3 a)

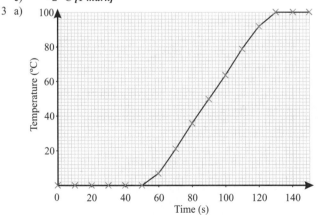

[1 mark for all points plotted correctly, 1 mark for a correctly drawn line connecting the points]

b) 500 g = 0.5 kg
$Q = m \times L$ so $L = Q \div m = 1.13 \div 0.5 = $ **2.26 MJ/kg**
[3 marks for correct answer, otherwise 1 mark for rearranging, 1 mark for correct substitution]

c) As the substance is heated, energy is transferred to the kinetic energy stores of its particles *[1 mark]*. As the substance melts (from 0-50 s), all of this energy is used to break the intermolecular bonds between the particles *[1 mark]* so there is no increase in the substance's temperature as it changes state *[1 mark]*.

Pages 259-260 — Particle Motion in Gases

Warm-up

The particles in a gas are always moving in <u>random directions</u>.
A gas exerts a force on a container due to <u>collisions</u>.
The total force exerted by the particles per unit area is the gas <u>pressure</u>.

1 Absolute zero is the temperature at which particles barely move / the temperature at which particles have the smallest amount of energy possible in their kinetic energy stores *[1 mark]*.

2 Container A holds the same number of particles, travelling at the same speed, as container B, but in a larger volume *[1 mark]*. This means the particles hit the walls of container A less often and so exert less pressure *[1 mark]*.

3 a) 295 − 273 = **22 °C** *[1 mark]*

b) The pressure of the gas increases *[1 mark]*. This is because increasing the temperature of the gas increases the speed of the gas particles *[1 mark]* so they collide with the walls of the container more often and with more force *[1 mark]*.

4 D *[1 mark]*
The volume of each container is the same (0.04 m³ = 40 000 cm³). Container D has the highest temperature (the temperature of container C is 283 − 273 = 10 °C). A fixed mass and volume of a gas has a higher pressure at a higher temperature.

5 a) $P_1V_1 = P_2V_2$ so $P_2 = P_1V_1 \div V_2$
Use the data from the first row of the table to find the missing pressure:
$P_2 = (50 \times 10^3) \times (8.0 \times 10^{-4}) \div (1.6 \times 10^{-4})$
$$= 250\,000 = \textbf{250 kPa}$$
[3 marks for correct answer, otherwise 1 mark for correctly rearranging the equation and 1 mark for correctly substituting in values.]

You could have used any row from the table to help you find the missing value — as long as you did the calculation correctly you'd get the marks.

b)

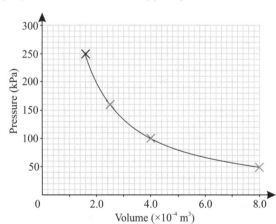

[1 mark for correctly plotted point, 1 mark for a curved line connecting them]

Pages 261-262 — Forces and Elasticity

1 a) Two *[1 mark]*
  b) An object that has been elastically distorted will go back to its original shape and length when the distorting forces are removed *[1 mark]*. An object that has been inelastically distorted won't *[1 mark]*.
  c) i) $F = kx$ *[1 mark]*
     ii) $k = F \div x = 20 \div 0.08 = 250$ **N/m**
        [2 marks for correct answer, otherwise 1 mark for correct substitution]
  d) That stretching the spring by 8 cm doesn't exceed its limit of proportionality *[1 mark]*.
2 D *[1 mark]*
3 a)

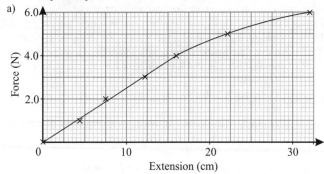

[1 mark for points plotted correctly, 1 mark for line of best fit showing linear relationship between 0 cm and at least 12 cm, 1 mark for curved line of best fit towards the end of the graph]

  b) $F = kx$
     so $k = F \div x$ = gradient of the linear section of the graph
     $k = 3.0 \div 0.12 = 25$ **N/m**
     [2 marks for correct answer between 24 and 26 N/m, otherwise 1 mark for correct calculation]
  c) The limit of proportionality is exceeded when the relationship between force and extension becomes non-linear *[1 mark]*. This is shown by the graph beginning to curve *[1 mark]*.
  d) When he was loading the spring he distorted the spring inelastically *[1 mark]* so when the force was removed, the spring didn't return to its original length *[1 mark]*.

You could also refer to the student exceeding the elastic limit of the spring, which would mean it was inelastically distorted.

Mixed Questions

Pages 263-267 — Biology Mixed Questions

1 a) i) mitochondria *[1 mark]*
     ii) oxygen *[1 mark]*, carbon dioxide *[1 mark]*
  b) plasma *[1 mark]*
  c) Glucagon is released into the blood *[1 mark]*, which converts glycogen back into glucose *[1 mark]*.
2 a) B *[1 mark]*
  b) A *[1 mark]*
  c) i) 40 °C *[1 mark]*
     ii) The enzyme will not work *[1 mark]* because the high temperature will change the shape of its active site/denature the enzyme *[1 mark]* and the substrate will no longer fit *[1 mark]*.
3 a) i) C *[1 mark]*
     ii) B *[1 mark]*
  b) The hormone is secreted directly into the blood *[1 mark]*. It is then carried in the blood to the target organ *[1 mark]*.
  c) It inhibits the secretion of both FSH *[1 mark]* and LH *[1 mark]*.
  d) oestrogen *[1 mark]*, progesterone *[1 mark]*
  e) It causes an egg to mature in one of the ovaries *[1 mark]*. It stimulates the ovaries to produce oestrogen *[1 mark]*.

4 a) A non-communicable disease because it is not transmitted between individuals/is not caused by a pathogen *[1 mark]*.
Remember, communicable diseases are caused by pathogens and can be spread between individuals. Vitamin A deficiency is caused by deficiencies in the diet, so it's non-communicable.
  b) It will contain genes not found in normal rice / DNA from a bacterium and a maize plant *[1 mark]*.
  c) E.g. the genes to be used from the maize plant and the soil bacterium were cut out using restriction enzymes *[1 mark]*. The same restriction enzymes were used to cut open the DNA of a vector *[1 mark]*. The genes extracted from the maize plant and the soil bacterium were then joined to the vector DNA using ligase enzymes *[1 mark]*. The recombinant DNA/vector containing the desired genes were then have been inserted into a rice plant to produce Golden Rice *[1 mark]*.
  d) Plants make proteins using nitrogen *[1 mark]* from nitrates/ nitrogen ions in the fertiliser *[1 mark]*.
5 a) i) oxygen *[1 mark]*
     ii) light intensity *[1 mark]*
The foil prevents any light from reaching the algae.
     iii) Tube 1 shows that in the dark, the algae are producing more carbon dioxide than they take in *[1 mark]*. The concentration of carbon dioxide is high because the cells are respiring, but not photosynthesising (as there's no light for photosynthesis to take place) *[1 mark]*. Tube 2 shows that in the light, the algae are taking up more carbon dioxide than they produce *[1 mark]*. The concentration of carbon dioxide has reduced because the cells are photosynthesising faster than they are respiring *[1 mark]*.
Plant cells respire all the time but they can only photosynthesise when it's light.
     iv) Any two from: e.g. the temperature of the boiling tubes / the volume of hydrogencarbonate indicator / the concentration of hydrogencarbonate indicator / the number of beads in each tube / the concentration of algal cells in each bead *[2 marks — 1 mark for each correct answer]*.
  b) i) Light intensity *[1 mark]* because the rate of photosynthesis is increasing as the light intensity increases *[1 mark]*.
     ii) carbon dioxide concentration *[1 mark]*

Pages 268-273 — Chemistry Mixed Questions

1 a) calcium + sulfuric acid → calcium sulfate + hydrogen
     [1 mark for correct left-hand side, 1 mark for correct right-hand side.]
  b) $CaSO_4$ *[1 mark]*
Calcium is in group 2, so it forms 2+ ions. Sulfate ions have a −2 charge (this is one you just need to remember). So, for a neutral compound, you need a ratio of $Ca^{2+} : SO_4^{2-}$ of 1 : 1.
  c) insoluble *[1 mark]*
All sulfates are soluble, except for lead, barium and calcium sulfate.
  d) Sodium is above calcium in the reactivity series *[1 mark]*.
2 a)

[1 mark for shared pair of electrons, 1 mark for six further electrons in the outer shell of each chlorine atom]

  b) C *[1 mark]*
  c) Hold a piece of damp blue litmus paper in the gas *[1 mark]*. It will be bleached white in the presence of chlorine *[1 mark]*.
  d) liquid *[1 mark]*
−50 °C is between the melting and boiling points of chlorine, so chlorine would be a liquid at this temperature.
3 a) a piece of (filter) paper *[1 mark]*
  b) R_f of **A** = 4.6 ÷ 12.1 = **0.38** *[1 mark]*
     R_f of **B** = 7.3 ÷ 12.1 = **0.60** *[1 mark]*
     R_f of **C** = 10.6 ÷ 12.1 = **0.876** *[1 mark]*
  c) There is a spot of substance on the baseline / there is a substance with an R_f value of 0 *[1 mark]*.
  d) D *[1 mark]*
  e) A mixture is a substance that contains different compounds or different elements that aren't all part of a single compound *[1 mark]*.
  f) E.g. fractional distillation *[1 mark]*

Answers

4 a) $2Rb + F_2 \rightarrow 2RbF$
[2 marks for all formulas correct and a correctly-balanced equation, otherwise 1 mark for correct formulas in an unbalanced equation]

b)

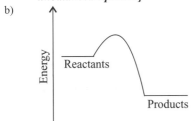

Progress of reaction
[1 mark for showing and labelling reactants and products, with products having less energy than reactants, 1 mark for a correctly-shaped curve joining reactants and products.]

5 a) E.g. wear safety goggles / wear a lab coat / wear gloves / use dilute concentrations of chlorine water *[1 mark]*.

b) M_r of KI = 39 + 127 = **166** *[1 mark]*

c) The solution would turn from colourless to brown *[1 mark]*.

d) Chlorine is more reactive than iodine *[1 mark]*, so it displaces iodine from the potassium iodide solution *[1 mark]*.

e) $Cl_2 + 2I^- \rightarrow 2Cl^- + I_2$
[1 mark for correct left-hand side, 1 mark for correct right-hand side]

6 a)

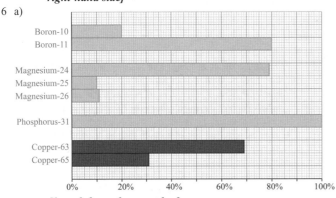

[1 mark for each correct bar]

b) The relative atomic mass of an element is the average of the mass numbers of all the atoms of that element *[1 mark]*. Phosphorus only has one isotope, so its relative atomic mass is equal to the mass number of its atoms (31) *[1 mark]*. Boron, magnesium and copper all have more than one isotope, which exist in different quantities, so the average of their mass numbers won't be a whole number *[1 mark]*.

c) % Mg-24 = 79%, % Mg-25 = 10%, % Mg-26 = 11%
So, relative atomic mass of Mg =
$[(24 \times 79) + (25 \times 10) + (26 \times 11)] \div 100$
= 2432 ÷ 100 = **24.32**
[4 marks for a correct answer, but deduct 1 mark if not correctly rounded to 3 s.f.. Otherwise 1 mark for correct % abundances of Mg isotopes and 1 mark for correctly substituting the atomic masses and abundances into an equation to work out relative atomic mass.]

7 B *[1 mark]*
M_r of Na_2SO_4 = (2 × 23) + 32 + (4 × 16) = 142
moles of Na_2SO_4 = 34.08 ÷ 142 = 0.24 moles
In one mole of Na_2SO_4 there are 4 moles of oxygen atoms. So, in 0.24 moles of Na_2SO_4 there are (0.24 × 4 =) 0.96 moles of oxygen atoms.
number of particles in one mole = 6.02 × 10²³, so,
number of atoms in 0.96 moles = 0.96 × 6.02 × 10²³ = 5.7792 × 10²³
= 5.779 × 10²³ atoms (to 4 s.f.)

8 a) Aluminium is reduced and oxygen is oxidised / aluminium gains electrons and oxygen loses electrons [1 mark].

b) $Al^{3+} + 3e^- \rightarrow Al$ [1 mark for correct reactants and products, 1 mark for correct electrons]

c) $M_r(Al_2O_3) = (2 \times 27) + (3 \times 16) = 102$
moles = mass ÷ M_r
moles of Al_2O_3 = 40.8 ÷ 102 = 0.400 moles
From the balanced equation, 2 moles of aluminium oxide produce 4 moles of aluminium.
So, 0.400 moles of aluminium oxide will produce $(0.400 \div 2) \times 4 = 0.800$ moles of aluminium.
$A_r(Al) = 27$, so mass of Al = 0.800 × 27 = **21.6 g**
[4 marks for correct answer, otherwise 1 mark for correctly calculating M_r of Al_2O_3, 1 mark for working out how many moles of Al_2O_3 are in 40.8 g and 1 mark for working out how many moles of Al are made.]

d) Heating with carbon will only reduce metals that are less reactive than carbon [1 mark]. Aluminium is more reactive than carbon, so heating with carbon will not extract aluminium metal from its ore [1 mark].

e) Any two from: e.g. Recycling reduces waste going to landfill. / Recycling generally requires less energy than extracting metals from their ores. / Recycling is generally cheaper than extracting metals from their ores. / Recycling reduces the need to mine ores, so it therefore reduces damage to the landscape cause by mining. / Recycling preserves natural resources, so it is more sustainable.
[1 mark for each valid advantage.]

9 C [1 mark]

10 a) Order: diamond, poly(propene), butane [1 mark].
Explanation: Diamond is a giant covalent substance, whilst poly(propene) and butane are molecular [1 mark]. Diamond has the highest melting point as you need to break the strong covalent bonds between the atoms to melt it [1 mark]. Poly(propene) molecules are larger than butane molecules, so poly(propene) has stronger intermolecular forces [1 mark], which require more energy to break [1 mark].

b) E.g. diamond would be the best choice [1 mark]. Diamond is strong and hard as it has a rigid structure, held together by strong covalent bonds [1 mark]. These properties make diamond a suitable material to use in drill bits, as it would be able to withstand the forces involved in drilling [1 mark].

11 a) Any two from: e.g. the only waste product made when hydrogen reacts with oxygen is water/burning hydrogen doesn't produce pollutants (e.g. carbon dioxide, carbon monoxide, sulfur dioxide) / hydrogen can be extracted from a renewable resource (water), but petrol is non-renewable/ hydrogen fuel can be extracted from the waste water made by the cell / fuel cells are more efficient than conventional engines *[1 mark for each correct answer]*.

b) Bonds broken:
(2 × H–H) + O=O = (2 × 436) + 498
= 872 + 498 = 1370 kJ mol⁻¹
Bonds formed:
4 × O–H = 4 × 463 = 1852 kJ mol⁻¹
Energy change = 1370 – 1852 = **–482 kJ mol⁻¹**
[3 marks for correct answer, otherwise 1 mark for correct energy value for bonds broken, 1 mark for correct energy value for bonds formed.]

Pages 274-279 — Physics Mixed Questions

1 a) metre *[1 mark]*

b) B *[1 mark]*

c) A quantity that has a magnitude/size, but not a direction *[1 mark]*.

2 a) B *[1 mark]*

b) work done = force × distance = 5 × 10 = **50 J**
[2 marks for correct answer, otherwise 1 mark for correct substitution]

3 a) A *[1 mark]*

b) average speed = distance travelled ÷ time
= 420 ÷ (5 × 60) = **1.4 m/s**
[3 marks for correct answer, otherwise 1 mark for correct substitution, 1 mark for correct numerical answer, 1 mark for correct unit]

c) B *[1 mark]*

4 a)   E.g. sound / P-waves *[1 mark]*

b)   X-ray: e.g. medical imaging/diagnosing broken bones / airport security scanners *[1 mark]*.

Gamma rays: e.g. sterilising food/medical equipment / tracers / radiotherapy/treating cancer *[1 mark]*.

c)   A = 99 *[1 mark]*

B = 0 *[1 mark]*

All electromagnetic waves travel at the same speed in a vacuum.

5 a)   E.g. photographic film / Geiger-Müller tube *[1 mark]*

b)   alpha particle — a helium nucleus

beta-minus particle — an electron emitted from the nucleus

gamma ray — an electromagnetic wave

[1 mark for all three correct]

c)   A *[1 mark]*

d) i)   E.g. the rate at which a radioactive source decays *[1 mark]*. Its unit is the becquerel/Bq *[1 mark]*.

ii)

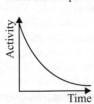

[1 mark for activity decreasing over time, 1 mark for correct shape of the graph]

e)   The time taken for the activity to halve *[1 mark]*.

6 a)

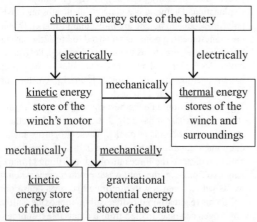

[4 marks for all correct, otherwise 3 marks for five correct, or 2 marks for three or four correct, or 1 mark for one or two correct]

b) $\Delta GPE = m \times g \times \Delta h = 40.0 \times 10 \times 1.1 = $ **440 J**

[4 marks for correct answer, otherwise 1 mark for correct equation, 1 mark for correct substitution, 1 mark for correctly recalling the value of g]

7 a) i) $v = f\lambda$

so $v = (3 \times 10^{14}) \times (1 \times 10^{-6}) = 300\,000\,000 = $ **3×10^8 m/s**

[4 marks for correct answer, otherwise 1 mark for correct equation, 1 mark for correct substitution, 1 mark for answer not in standard form]

ii) 3×10^8 m/s *[1 mark for answer matching the speed calculated in part a)]*

b)   As the wave enters the glass block, it refracts and bends towards the normal *[1 mark]* and slows down *[1 mark]*. As the wave leaves the glass block, it refracts again, this time bending away from the normal *[1 mark]* and speeding up *[1 mark]*.

8 a)   Independent variable: Roughness of surface *[1 mark]*.

Dependent variable: Deceleration / speed of trolley *[1 mark]*.

b)   Repeat 1 = 0.23 *[1 mark]* Repeat 2 = 0.24 *[1 mark]*

Repeat 3 = 0.22 *[1 mark]*

Use acceleration = change in velocity ÷ time.

c)   Assuming that all of the energy in the spring's elastic potential energy store is transferred to the trolley's kinetic energy store:

Mean speed at light gate 1 = (1.22 + 1.16 + 1.19) ÷ 3 = 1.19 m/s

Use this in the equation for calculating the energy in the kinetic energy store:

$KE = \frac{1}{2} \times m \times v^2 = 0.5 \times 0.50 \times 1.19^2 = 0.354...$ J

So energy in the spring's elastic potential energy store

= **0.35 J (to 2 s.f.)**

[4 marks for correct answer, otherwise 1 mark for equating energy in elastic potential and kinetic energy stores, 1 mark for correct substitution, 1 mark for correct numerical answer]

d)   Mean magnitude of acceleration = (0.23 + 0.24 + 0.22) ÷ 3

= 0.23 m/s²

Convert g to kg: 300 ÷ 1000 = 0.30

force = mass × acceleration = 0.30 × 0.23 = 0.069 N

So magnitude of frictional force = **0.069 N**

[4 marks for correct answer, otherwise 1 mark for calculating the mean acceleration, 1 mark for the correct conversion, 1 mark for substituting the values into the force equation]

9 a)   E.g.

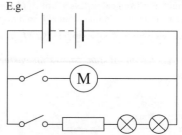

[1 mark for filament lamps and resistor in series with each other, 1 mark for motor in parallel with other components, 1 mark for correct placement of switches, 2 marks for all circuit symbols correctly drawn, otherwise 1 mark for 4 symbols correctly drawn]

b)   E.g. as current flows through both the resistor and the motor, the charges do work against resistance *[1 mark]*. This causes energy to be transferred electrically to the thermal energy stores of the resistor and the motor *[1 mark]*. The motor also does work against friction (as it is moving) which causes energy to be transferred mechanically to the thermal energy store of the motor *[1 mark]*. A way to reduce this heating would be to lubricate the moving parts inside the motor *[1 mark]*.

c) $E = V \times I \times t = 6.0 \times (70 \times 10^{-3}) \times (10 \times 60) = 252$ J

3 g = 3 ÷ 1000 = 0.003 kg

$\Delta Q = m \times c \times \Delta\theta = 0.003 \times 400 \times 25 = 30$ J

252 − 30 = 222 J = **220 J (to 2 s.f.)**

[5 marks for correct answer, otherwise 1 mark for correctly stating E = VIt, 1 mark for correctly substituting into this equation, 1 mark for correct substitution into $\Delta Q = mc\Delta\theta$, 1 mark for both energies correctly calculated]

Equations

Here are some equations you might find useful for the Physics sections — you'll be given these in the exams.

Section 17 — Motion and Forces

$v^2 - u^2 = 2 \times a \times x$	(final velocity)^2 – (initial velocity)^2 = 2 × acceleration × distance
$F = \dfrac{(mv - mu)}{t}$	force = change in momentum ÷ time

> Make sure you understand all the equations on this page, and you're happy using and rearranging them.

Section 22 — Electricity and Circuits

$E = I \times V \times t$	energy transferred = current × potential difference × time

Section 23 — Magnetic Fields

$F = B \times I \times l$	force on a conductor at right angles to a magnetic field carrying a current $=$ magnetic flux density × current × length
$V_p \times I_p = V_s \times I_s$	potential difference across primary coil × current in primary coil $=$ potential difference across secondary coil × current in secondary coil (for transformers with 100% efficiency)

Section 24 — Matter

$\Delta Q = m \times c \times \Delta\theta$	change in thermal energy = mass × specific heat capacity × change in temperature
$Q = m \times L$	thermal energy for a change of state = mass × specific latent heat
$E = \frac{1}{2} \times k \times x^2$	energy transferred in stretching = 0.5 × spring constant × (extension)^2

The Periodic Table

Key:

Relative atomic mass
1
H
Hydrogen
1

Atomic (proton) number →

Periods	Group 1	Group 2												Group 3	Group 4	Group 5	Group 6	Group 7	Group 0
1																			4 **He** Helium 2
2	7 **Li** Lithium 3	9 **Be** Beryllium 4												11 **B** Boron 5	12 **C** Carbon 6	14 **N** Nitrogen 7	16 **O** Oxygen 8	19 **F** Fluorine 9	20 **Ne** Neon 10
3	23 **Na** Sodium 11	24 **Mg** Magnesium 12												27 **Al** Aluminium 13	28 **Si** Silicon 14	31 **P** Phosphorus 15	32 **S** Sulfur 16	35.5 **Cl** Chlorine 17	40 **Ar** Argon 18
4	39 **K** Potassium 19	40 **Ca** Calcium 20	45 **Sc** Scandium 21	48 **Ti** Titanium 22	51 **V** Vanadium 23	52 **Cr** Chromium 24	55 **Mn** Manganese 25	56 **Fe** Iron 26	59 **Co** Cobalt 27	59 **Ni** Nickel 28	63.5 **Cu** Copper 29	65 **Zn** Zinc 30		70 **Ga** Gallium 31	73 **Ge** Germanium 32	75 **As** Arsenic 33	79 **Se** Selenium 34	80 **Br** Bromine 35	84 **Kr** Krypton 36
5	85 **Rb** Rubidium 37	88 **Sr** Strontium 38	89 **Y** Yttrium 39	91 **Zr** Zirconium 40	93 **Nb** Niobium 41	96 **Mo** Molybdenum 42	[98] **Tc** Technetium 43	101 **Ru** Ruthenium 44	103 **Rh** Rhodium 45	106 **Pd** Palladium 46	108 **Ag** Silver 47	112 **Cd** Cadmium 48		115 **In** Indium 49	119 **Sn** Tin 50	122 **Sb** Antimony 51	128 **Te** Tellurium 52	127 **I** Iodine 53	131 **Xe** Xenon 54
6	133 **Cs** Caesium 55	137 **Ba** Barium 56	139 **La** Lanthanum 57	178 **Hf** Hafnium 72	181 **Ta** Tantalum 73	184 **W** Tungsten 74	186 **Re** Rhenium 75	190 **Os** Osmium 76	192 **Ir** Iridium 77	195 **Pt** Platinum 78	197 **Au** Gold 79	201 **Hg** Mercury 80		204 **Tl** Thallium 81	207 **Pb** Lead 82	209 **Bi** Bismuth 83	[209] **Po** Polonium 84	[210] **At** Astatine 85	[222] **Rn** Radon 86
7	[223] **Fr** Francium 87	[226] **Ra** Radium 88	[227] **Ac** Actinium 89	[261] **Rf** Rutherfordium 104	[262] **Db** Dubnium 105	[266] **Sg** Seaborgium 106	[264] **Bh** Bohrium 107	[277] **Hs** Hassium 108	[268] **Mt** Meitnerium 109	[271] **Ds** Darmstadtium 110	[272] **Rg** Roentgenium 111								

The lanthanoids (atomic numbers 58-71) and the actinoids (atomic numbers 90-103) are not shown in this table.